Max Emanuel Kramer

Specification Languages for Preserving Consistency between Models of Different Languages

The Karlsruhe Series on Software Design and Quality
Volume 24

Chair Software Design and Quality
Faculty of Computer Science
Karlsruhe Institute of Technology

and

Software Engineering Division
Research Center for Information Technology (FZI), Karlsruhe

Editor: Prof. Dr. Ralf Reussner

Specification Languages for Preserving Consistency between Models of Different Languages

by
Max Emanuel Kramer

KIT Scientific Publishing

Dissertation, Karlsruher Institut für Technologie
KIT-Fakultät für Informatik

Tag der mündlichen Prüfung: 10. Februar 2017
Gutachter: Prof. Dr. Ralf H. Reussner
Prof. Dr. Colin Atkinson (Universität Mannheim)

Impressum

KIT Scientific Publishing

Karlsruher Institut für Technologie (KIT)
KIT Scientific Publishing
Straße am Forum 2
D-76131 Karlsruhe

www.ksp.kit.edu

Print on Demand 2019 – Gedruckt auf FSC-zertifiziertem Papier

ISSN 1867-0067
ISBN 978-3-7315-0784-0
DOI: 10.5445/KSP/1000081446

Abstract

In this thesis, we present three languages for the development of tools that keep different system representations consistent during software development.

When complex IT systems are developed, it is common practice to use several programming and modelling languages. System parts are designed and represented using different languages in order to support various design and development tasks. The overall structure of a system, for example, is often represented with an architectural description language. To specify the detailed behavior of individual system parts, a state-based modelling language or a general purpose programming language are, however, more appropriate. As these system parts and development tasks are related, these representations often also contain redundant information. Such partially redundant representations are usually not used in a static way but evolve during system development, which can lead to *inconsistencies* that yield faulty designs and implementations. Therefore, consistent system representations are crucial for the development of such systems.

There are various approaches to achieve consistent system representations by *avoiding* inconsistencies. It is possible, for example, to create a central, redundancy-free representation that encompasses all information so that all other representations can be projected from it[1]. Creating such a redundancy-free representation and editable projections is, however, not always feasible, especially if existing languages and editors have to be supported. Another possibility to evade inconsistencies is to only allow modifications for a piece of information at a unique source representation so that all other representations can only read this information. This makes

[1] C. Atkinson et al. "Orthographic Software Modeling: A Practical Approach to View-Based Development". In: *Evaluation of Novel Approaches to Software Engineering*. Vol. 69. Communications in Computer and Information Science. Berlin/Heidelberg: Springer, 2010, pp. 206–219.

it possible to always override such information in all read-only representations, but it also makes it necessary to completely isolate all editable regions of representations.

If inconsistent representations cannot be completely avoided during system development, developers or tools have to actively preserve consistency when representations are modified. Manual consistency preservation is, however, a time-consuming and error-prone task. Therefore, consistency preservation tools that semi-automatically update models during system development are developed in academia and industry. Such special software engineering tools can be developed with general purpose programming languages and with dedicated languages for consistency preservation.

In this thesis, we have identified four major challenges that are currently only insufficiently addressed by languages for developing consistency preservation tools. First, these languages do not combine specific consistency preservation support with the expressive power and flexibility of established general purpose programming languages. Therefore, developers are either restricted to designated use cases or have to repeatedly develop solutions to generic consistency preservation problems. Second, these languages *either* support solution- or problem-oriented programming paradigms, which forces developers to also provide preservation instructions for cases in which consistency declarations would be sufficient. Third, these languages do not abstract away from enough consistency preservation details, which requires developers to explicitly consider, for example, preservation directions, change types, or matching problems. Last, these languages yield preservation behavior that often appears to be detached from the specific use case when interpreters and compilers run or generate code that is not needed to realize a particular consistency specification.

To address these issues of current approaches, this thesis makes the following contributions: First, we present a collection and classification of consistency preservation challenges and discuss, for example, which challenges should not be addressed when consistency is specified but only when it is enforced. Second, we introduce an approach for preserving consistency according to abstract specifications and formalize it using set theory. This formalization is independent of how consistency enforcement is finally realized. With the presented approach, consistency is always preserved according to monitored edit operations in order to avoid well-known matching and diffing problems. Last, we contribute three new languages for the development of tools that follow this specification-driven approach and which we briefly explain in the following.

We present an imperative language that can be used to precisely define how models have to be updated in reaction to specific changes in order to preserve consistency in one direction. This reactions language provides solutions to common problems, such as identifying and retrieving changed or corresponding model elements. Furthermore, it achieves unlimited expressive power as it allows developers to fallback to a general purpose programming language. A second, bidirectional language for abstract mappings can be used for cases in which different edit operations do not need to be distinguished and preservation directions are not always relevant. With this mappings language, developers can declare conditions for model elements that should be considered consistent without bothering about details of checking and enforcing consistency. For this, the compiler automatically derives enforcement code from checks and bidirectionalizes conditions that are specified for one consistency preservation direction. This bidirectionalization is based on an extensible set of composable, operator-specific inverters that fulfill common round-trip requirements. As a result, developers can express common consistency requirements concisely and do not need to repeat code for different consistency preservation directions, change types, or properties of model elements. A third, normative language can be used to complete the previous ones with parameterized consistency invariants. This invariants language adopts collection operators and iterators from the Object Constraint Language (OCL). Furthermore, it relieves developers from writing code that searches for invariant-violating elements as queries that perform this task are automatically derived for invariant parameters. The three languages can be used in combination or individually. They give developers the possibility to specify consistency using different programming paradigms and language abstractions. We also present prototypical compilers and editors for the three consistency specification languages based on the multi-view modelling framework Vitruvius. With this framework, changes in textual and graphical editors are automatically monitored to trigger reactions, to enforce mappings, and to check invariants by executing the Java source code that is produced by our compilers.

For all languages presented in this thesis, we have evaluated theoretical completeness and correctness as well as practical applicability and benefits. We show that the languages completely cover the intended range of use and analyze their computational completeness. Furthermore, we discuss correctness for each language individually and for specific language features. The operator-specific inverters that we have developed to bidirectionalize mapping conditions, for example, always fulfill a new notion of *best-possible behaved round-trips*. It is based on the established notion of well-behaved transformations[2] and guarantees that common round-trip laws are fulfilled whenever this is possible. We demonstrate the practical applicability with case studies in which consistency was successfully preserved with tools that were written using the presented languages. Finally, we discuss potential benefits of the languages and compare, for example, consistency preservation tools that were realized in two case studies. Those tools that were developed using the reactions language have between 33% and 71% fewer source lines of code than functionally equivalent tools that were written in Java or the Java dialect Xtend.

2 J. N. Foster et al. "Combinators for Bidirectional Tree Transformations: A Linguistic Approach to the View-update Problem". In: *ACM Transactions on Programming Languages and Systems (TOPLAS)* 29.3 (May 2007).

Zusammenfassung

In dieser Dissertation stellen wir drei Sprachen für die Entwicklung von Werkzeugen vor, welche Systemrepräsentationen während der Softwareentwicklung konsistent halten.

Bei der Entwicklung komplexer informationstechnischer Systeme ist es üblich, mehrere Programmiersprachen und Modellierungssprachen zu nutzen. Dabei werden Teile des Systems mit unterschiedlichen Sprachen konstruiert und dargestellt, um verschiedene Entwurfs- und Entwicklungstätigkeiten zu unterstützen. Die übergreifende Struktur eines Systems wird beispielsweise oft mit Hilfe einer Architekturbeschreibungssprache dargestellt. Für die Spezifikation des detaillierten Verhaltens einzelner Systemteile ist hingegen eine zustandsbasierte Modellierungssprache oder eine Allzweckprogrammiersprache geeigneter. Da die Systemteile und Entwicklungstätigkeiten in Beziehung zueinander stehen, enthalten diese Repräsentationen oftmals auch redundante Informationen. Solche partiell redundanten Repräsentationen werden meist nicht statisch genutzt, sondern evolvieren während der Systementwicklung, was zu *Inkonsistenzen* und damit zu fehlerhaften Entwürfen und Implementierungen führen kann. Daher sind konsistente Systemrepräsentationen entscheidend für die Entwicklung solcher Systeme.

Es gibt verschiedene Ansätze, die konsistente Systemrepräsentationen dadurch erreichen, dass Inkonsistenzen *vermieden* werden. So ist es beispielsweise möglich, eine zentrale, redundanzfreie Repräsentation zu erstellen, welche alle Informationen enthält, um alle anderen Repräsentationen daraus projizieren zu können[3]. Es ist jedoch nicht immer praktikabel solch eine redundanzfreie Repräsentation und editierbare Projektionen zu erstellen,

[3] C. Atkinson u. a. "Orthographic Software Modeling: A Practical Approach to View-Based Development". In: *Evaluation of Novel Approaches to Software Engineering*. Bd. 69. Communications in Computer and Information Science. Berlin/Heidelberg: Springer, 2010, S. 206–219.

insbesondere wenn existierende Sprachen und Editoren unterstützt werden müssen. Eine weitere Möglichkeit zur Umgehung von Inkonsistenzen besteht darin Änderungen einzelner Informationen nur an einer eindeutigen Quellrepräsentation zuzulassen, sodass alle anderen Repräsentationen diese Information nur lesen können. Dadurch können solche Informationen in allen lesend zugreifenden Repräsentationen immer überschrieben werden, jedoch müssen dazu alle editierbaren Repräsentationsbereiche komplett voneinander getrennt werden.

Falls inkonsistente Repräsentationen während der Systementwicklung nicht völlig vermieden werden können, müssen Entwickler oder Werkzeuge aktiv die Konsistenz erhalten, wenn Repräsentationen modifiziert werden. Die manuelle Konsistenthaltung ist jedoch eine zeitaufwändige und fehleranfällige Tätigkeit. Daher werden in Forschungseinrichtungen und in der Industrie Konsistenthaltungswerkzeuge entwickelt, die teilautomatisiert Modelle während der Systementwicklung aktualisieren. Solche speziellen Software-Entwicklungswerkzeuge können mit Allzweckprogrammiersprachen und mit dedizierten Konsistenthaltungssprachen entwickelt werden.

In dieser Dissertation haben wir vier bedeutende Herausforderungen identifiziert, die momentan nur unzureichend von Sprachen zur Entwicklung von Konsistenthaltungswerkzeugen adressiert werden. Erstens kombinieren diese Sprachen spezifische Unterstützung zur Konsistenthaltung nicht mit der Ausdrucksmächtigkeit und Flexibilität etablierter Allzweckprogrammiersprachen. Daher sind Entwickler entweder auf ausgewiesene Anwendungsfälle beschränkt, oder sie müssen wiederholt Lösungen für generische Konsistenthaltungsprobleme entwickeln. Zweitens unterstützen diese Sprachen *entweder* lösungs- oder problemorientierte Programmierparadigmen, sodass Entwickler gezwungen sind, Erhaltungsinstruktionen auch in Fällen anzugeben, in denen Konsistenzdeklarationen ausreichend wären. Drittens abstrahieren diese Sprachen nicht von genügend Konsistenthaltungsdetails, wodurch Entwickler explizit beispielsweise Erhaltungsrichtungen, Änderungstypen oder Übereinstimmungsprobleme berücksichtigen müssen. Viertens führen diese Sprachen zu Erhaltungsverhalten, das oft vom konkreten Anwendungsfall losgelöst zu sein scheint, wenn Interpreter und Übersetzer Code ausführen oder erzeugen, der zur Realisierung einer spezifischen Konsistenzspezifikation nicht benötigt wird.

Um diese Probleme aktueller Ansätze zu adressieren, leistet diese Dissertation die folgenden Beiträge: Erstens stellen wir eine Sammlung und Klassifizierung von Herausforderungen der Konsistenthaltung vor. Dabei diskutieren wir beispielsweise, welche Herausforderungen nicht bereits adressiert werden sollten, wenn Konsistenz spezifiziert wird, sondern erst wenn sie durchgesetzt wird. Zweitens führen wir einen Ansatz zur Erhaltung von Konsistenz gemäß abstrakter Spezifikationen ein und formalisieren ihn mengentheoretisch. Diese Formalisierung ist unabhängig davon wie Konsistenzdurchsetzungen letztendlich realisiert werden. Mit dem vorgestellten Ansatz wird Konsistenz immer anhand von beobachteten Editieroperationen bewahrt, um bekannte Probleme zur Berechnung von Übereinstimmungen und Differenzen zu vermeiden. Schließlich stellen wir drei neue Sprachen zur Entwicklung von Werkzeugen vor, die den vorgestellten, spezifikationsgeleiteten Ansatz verfolgen und welche wir im Folgenden kurz erläutern.

Wir präsentieren eine imperative Sprache, die verwendet werden kann, um präzise zu spezifizieren, wie Modelle in Reaktion auf spezifische Änderungen aktualisiert werden müssen, um Konsistenz in eine Richtung zu erhalten. Diese Reaktionssprache stellt Lösungen für häufige Probleme bereit, wie beispielsweise die Identifizierung und das Abrufen geänderter oder korrespondierender Modellelemente. Außerdem erreicht sie eine uneingeschränkte Ausdrucksmächtigkeit, indem sie Entwicklern ermöglicht, auf eine Allzweckprogrammiersprache zurückzugreifen. Eine zweite, bidirektionale Sprache für abstrakte Abbildungen kann für Fälle verwendet werden, in denen verschiedene Änderungsoperationen nicht unterschieden werden müssen und außerdem die Erhaltungsrichtung nicht immer eine Rolle spielt. Mit dieser Abbildungssprache können Entwickler Bedingungen deklarieren, die ausdrücken, wann Modellelemente als konsistent zueinander angesehen werden sollen, ohne sich um Details der Überprüfung oder Durchsetzung von Konsistenz bemühen zu müssen. Dazu leitet der Übersetzer automatisch Durchsetzungscode aus Überprüfungen ab und bidirektionalisiert Bedingungen, die für eine Richtung der Konsistenthaltung spezifiziert wurden. Diese Bidirektionalisierung basiert auf einer erweiterbaren Menge von komponierbaren, operatorspezifischen Invertierern, die verbreitete Round-trip-Anforderungen erfüllen. Infolgedessen können Entwickler häufig vorkommende Konsistenzanforderungen konzise ausdrücken und müssen keinen Quelltext für verschiedene Konsistenthaltungsrichtungen, Änderungstypen oder Eigenschaften von Modellelementen wiederholen. Eine dritte, normative Sprache kann verwendet werden, um die vorherigen Sprachen mit parametrisierbaren Konsistenzinvarianten zu ergänzen. Diese Invariantensprache übernimmt Operatoren und Iteratoren für Elementsammlungen von der Object Constraint Language (OCL). Außerdem nimmt sie Entwicklern das Schreiben von Quelltext zur Suche nach invariantenverletzenden Elementen ab, da Abfragen, welche diese Aufgaben übernehmen, automatisch anhand von Invariantenparametern abgeleitet werden. Die drei Sprachen können in Kombination und einzeln verwendet werden. Sie ermöglichen es Entwicklern, Konsistenz unter Verwendung verschiedener Programmierparadigmen und Sprachabstraktionen zu spezifizieren. Wir stellen auch prototypische Übersetzer und Editoren für die drei Konsistenzspezifikationssprachen vor, welche auf dem Vitruvius-Rahmenwerk für Multi-Sichten-Modellierung basieren. Mit diesem Rahmenwerk werden Änderungen in textuellen und graphischen Editoren automatisch beobachtet, um Reaktionen auszulösen, Abbildungen durchzusetzen und Invarianten zu überprüfen. Dies geschieht indem der von unseren Übersetzern erzeugte Java-Code ausgeführt wird.

Außerdem haben wir für alle Sprachen, die in dieser Dissertation vorgestellt werden, folgende theoretischen und praktischen Eigenschaften evaluiert: Vollständigkeit, Korrektheit, Anwendbarkeit, und Nutzen. So zeigen wir, dass die Sprachen ihre vorgesehenen Einsatzbereiche vollständig abdecken und analysieren ihre Berechnungsvollständigkeit. Außerdem diskutieren wir die Korrektheit jeder einzelnen Sprache sowie die Korrektheit einzelner Sprachmerkmale. Die operatorspezifischen Invertierer, die wir zur Bidirektionalisierung von Abbildungsbedingungen entwickelt haben, erfüllen beispielsweise immer das neu eingeführte Konzept *bestmöglich erzogener Round-trips*. Dieses basiert auf dem bewährten Konzept wohlerzogener Transformationen[4] und garantiert, dass übliche Round-trip-Gesetze erfüllt werden, wann immer dies möglich ist. Wir veranschaulichen die praktische Anwendbarkeit mit Fallstudien, in denen Konsistenz erfolgreich mit Hilfe von Werkzeugen erhalten wurde, die in den von uns vorgestellten Sprachen geschrieben wurden. Zum Schluss diskutieren wir den potenziellen Nutzen unserer Sprachen und vergleichen beispielsweise Konsistenthaltungswerk-

[4] J. N. Foster u. a. “Combinators for Bidirectional Tree Transformations: A Linguistic Approach to the View-update Problem”. In: *ACM Transactions on Programming Languages and Systems (TOPLAS)* 29.3 (Mai 2007).

zeuge die in zwei Fallstudien realisiert wurden. Die Werkzeuge, die mit der Reaktionssprache entwickelt wurden, benötigen zwischen 33% und 71% weniger Zeilen Quelltext als funktional gleichwertige Werkzeuge, die mit in Java oder dem Java-Dialekt Xtend entwickelt wurden.

Für Lotte

Contents

Acknowledgments

I am grateful to Jörg, who made me dream of a PhD, grateful to Jacques, because he made me start it, and grateful to Colin, as he made me discover an exciting research area for it.

My deepest thanks go to Ralf. He was an infinite source of inspiration and paved my way to a successful dissertation on many occasions and with great foresight.

Moreover, I am glad that my vitruvian colleagues Michael, Dominik, Heiko, and Erik supported me in many ways and on many days throughout the last years. Without them, I would have written a very different thesis or I would not have written a thesis at all!

In addition, much more people contributed to the content of this thesis, for example, as they were discussing ideas and developing prototypes with me. Others simply gave me invaluable feedback or accepted my responsibilities while I was writing this thesis. Representative for them, I thank Kirill, Nicolas, and Sebastian as well as all colleagues from the SDQ crew.

Part I.

Prologue

1. Introduction

In this thesis, we present languages that can be used to develop software engineering tools that keep models of different languages consistent during development. Before we explain which research goals and questions lead to the development of these languages, we briefly introduce the context of our research and explain how it is motivated.

1.1. Motivation

Complex IT systems are often developed using several programming and modelling languages. In order to support various development tasks, different languages can be used to represent parts of the system under development from several perspectives. As the system parts and the development tasks are usually not isolated but related, it cannot be avoided that system information is redundantly represented. Such partially redundant representations are not in themselves problematic, but they are usually not created one after the other and then never changed again. Instead, these representations often evolve during design and development and thus become inconsistent with other representations. Such inconsistencies can lead to wrong design decisions and faulty implementations, which may be costly to fix. For this problem of inconsistent redundancy in system representations, it is not important whether the information is textually or graphically represented and which other information is abstracted away. Instead, it is crucial which parts of the representations are related and to which rules these relations have to comply to achieve consistent representations. All representations—also those that describe the precise runtime behavior and are often called *code*—can be regarded and treated as *models* of the system. Therefore, the process of avoiding or repairing such inconsistencies can also be described as the process of *preserving consistency between models of different languages*, which is the last and biggest part of the title of this dissertation.

One possibility to avoid such inconsistencies between different models is to create a *central model that encompasses all information* so that all other models can be projected from it [ATM15]. Such a redundancy-free system representation is also called a Single Underlying Model (SUM) and used, for example, in the Orthographic Software Modeling approach [ASB10]. Before inconsistencies can be completely avoided using a SUM, a modelling language for this SUM has to be defined and transformations have to be developed for projecting SUM information into views and vice versa. If changes in the projective views are directly applied to the SUM, then such a SUM-based approach guarantees *consistency by construction*. It can, however, be complex to develop the modelling language for the SUM and the editable projections, especially if many different perspectives are needed. Furthermore, it is impossible to use editors without major modifications and it can be costly to develop new editors for existing languages in order to apply editor changes correctly to the SUM.

If redundant models cannot be avoided because existing languages or editors have to be used, then inconsistencies can still be evaded with strong *editability restrictions* for redundant information [Bur14]. One possibility is to support modifications of redundant information only in one model and to only allow reads but no writes for this information in all other views. This way, changes can always be propagated from the unique source to all other views by overriding the old version of the redundant information. It is, however, very difficult to decide which information may be modified in which models so that a piece of editable information is always completely isolated from other editable parts. This problem of isolating editable regions is similar to the problem of finding a redundancy-free SUM and has the effect that this approach can also not be used in all development contexts.

If neither projections from a redundancy-free SUM nor modification restrictions to unique information sources are feasible, then consistent models cannot be guaranteed, and consistency needs to be actively preserved. As consistency preservation is a time-consuming and error-prone task, special software engineering tools that update models during system development are often developed and used. These tools are responsible for keeping models of different languages consistent and can be seen as a special form of model transformations. If models become inconsistent or are at risk of becoming inconsistent with other models, then these tools update model elements in order to preserve consistency. When developers create such tools, they indirectly define under which conditions models are considered consistent, how consistency is checked, and how it is enforced in case of inconsistencies. These three parts of *specifying, checking, and enforcing consistency* are closely related, but they have very different characteristics. What is considered consistent is solely determined by the conceptual relations between the domains that are modelled and by the notation that is prescribed by the used languages. How this consistency should be checked is, however, also influenced by many technical concerns and not only by specifics of the used models and languages. Similarly, consistency enforcement mechanisms often mix issues of the technical solution with concerns of the modelling domain. Questions of when and how to enforce consistency can, for example, also be influenced by the way in which users modify models in editors.

Current approaches and languages that can be used to develop consistency preservation tools consider the above-mentioned specific characteristics of specifying, checking, and enforcing consistency insufficiently. With current approaches, developers are, for example, often forced to solve technical issues of *realizing* consistency checks and enforcement even if these issues are not related to the specific models and languages for which consistency is to be preserved. Furthermore, many approaches only support declarative consistency *specifications* for particular relations between model elements and are therefore limited to suitable consistency preservation contexts. Finally, developers that use such approaches cannot take all information on changes that were performed by users into account, and cannot request user feedback in order to decide how consistency has to be preserved.

In this thesis, we analyze challenges to consistency preservation and contribute new consistency specification languages for the development of tools that keep models of different languages consistent after changes. We identified four *Open Consistency Specification Language Challenges (OC-SLCs)*:

Specificity Limits Expressive Power: Specific consistency preservation support can only be used in certain contexts and for special consistency relations.

Either Solution- or Problem-Oriented Paradigms: This forces developers to realize all consistency requirements from one perspective and to provide preservation instructions where consistency declarations would be sufficient.

Missing Abstractions and Adaptations: Consistency preservation details often have to be considered although they are not needed to preserve consistency for a particular modelling language.

Detached Preservation Behavior: Interpreters with complex rules and compilers that produce much code that is not needed to realize a particular consistency specification.

The languages presented in this thesis address these open challenges and provide solutions for problems that occur in many contexts of consistency preservation. In order to explain how consistency can be preserved using the presented languages, we have formally defined fundamental concepts that describe consistency specifications and consistency preservation in a realization-independent way. To adequately support all possible contexts and requirements of consistency preservation for models of arbitrary languages, the presented languages support different programming paradigms and provide fallback mechanisms. If it is necessary, developers can use the *reactions language* to precisely define how models have to be updated in reaction to specific changes in order to preserve consistency in a certain direction. Common tasks, such as resolving corresponding elements, are supported with dedicated language constructs in order to relieve developers from repeatedly solving such generic problems. For cases where consistency never needs to be preserved in a change-specific way and not always in a direction-specific way, we present the *mappings language.* With it, developers can specify consistency conditions in a declarative way to abstract away from individual changes and details of checking and enforcing consistency. This abstraction is possible because enforcements are automatically derived from checks, and unidirectional enforcement code is automatically bidirectionalized using program inversion techniques. Both the imperative reactions language and the bidirectional mappings language are complemented by the normative *invariants language.* Developers can use it to specify consistency invariants in a notation that is closely aligned with the Object Constraint Language (OCL). To ease consistency preservation after violations of such invariants, the compiler of the invariants language automatically derives queries that return the model elements that violate an invariant. All three languages give developers various possibilities to declare which cases are considered consistency problems without providing instructions on how these problems are to be solved if this is not necessary.

We have realized all languages with prototypical compilers and evaluated theoretical and practical properties of the presented languages. For every language, we discuss completeness with respect to the intended range of use and correctness, for example, according to formal semantics or round-trip laws. For the inversion of mapping conditions, for example, we show that code for both consistency enforcement directions always fulfills a new notion of *best-possible behaved round-trips.* It guarantees that common round-trip laws are fulfilled whenever this is possible and is based on the established notion of well-behaved transformations [Fos+07]. Furthermore, we demonstrate the applicability of the languages using case studies in which consistency was successfully preserved with tools that were written using the presented languages. Finally, we discuss potential benefits of the presented languages. We discuss, for example, two case studies in which consistency preservation tools that were realized using the reactions language have between 33% and 71% fewer source lines of code than functionally equivalent realizations in Java or a Java dialect.

1.2. Problem Statement

To summarize the problems that we already presented in the preceding motivation, we formulate a problem statement in terms of a *research gap*: To our knowledge, all current approaches provide

no realization-independent notion of how consistency can be specified and preserved for models of arbitrary modelling languages

no change-driven consistency preservation that is triggered by user changes, depends on performed edit operations, and provides possibilities to interact with users in order to disambiguate the intended effects of their changes *no comprehensive language* for developing consistency preservation tools with support for all potential contexts and requirements of consistency preservation

1.3. Goals and Questions

The research presented in this thesis was guided by and is presented to achieve the following goal:

Goal: Identify recurring challenges of change-driven consistency preservation for models of different languages and *provide support* for specifying such consistency preservation.

As a first step towards operationalizing this goal, we rephrase it as a question. This will give the reader the possibility to determine whether we reached our goal by analyzing whether we provided a satisfactory answer to the question.

Question: What are recurring challenges of change-driven consistency preservation for models of different languages and *how can we* provide language support for specifying such consistency preservation?

As both the goal and the question already consist of two distinct parts, we have separated and refined these parts. For both parts we have formulated two more specific research questions, and we have created subquestions that pinpoint further details.

1.3.1. Identify Challenges and Define Consistency

For the first part of our overall goal, we formulated a research question, which does not only ask about challenges to consistency preservation but also about a definition that does not depend on how consistency is realized in the end. This research question is mainly answered in Part II of this thesis and stated as follows:

Research Question 1: How to define change-driven consistency preservation for models of different languages *in a realization-independent way* and *what are* recurring challenges to it?

In order to further operationalize our research, we have formulated four subquestions for this question:

Subquestion 1.1: What are recurring *challenges* of consistency preservation and how can they be *classified*, for example based on *when* they should be addressed?

Subquestion 1.2: Which of these challenges occur when consistency is *specified* and which challenges should be addressed by consistency *specification languages*?

Subquestion 1.3: Can we *formally define* how consistency can be specified in a realization-independent way and what are differences of such a specification-driven notion of consistency to *other notions* of consistency?

Subquestion 1.4: How to formally define whether this specification-driven notion of consistency is *preserved* after changes and how can we *check* this in a realization-independent way?

Answers to this question and its subquestions can help developers of consistency preservation tools to better understand which of the challenges that they are facing are not specific to their context and are therefore also addressed by other developers. Furthermore, developers of consistency specification languages or of other consistency preservation approaches can use such answers to put their work into relation and to embed it into an overall concept of consistency preservation. This kind of support is, however, rather conceptual, and therefore we have also formulated a second research question that asks for more practical consistency preservation support.

1.3.2. Support through Specification Languages

The second research question is concerned with the second part of the overall goal and particularly asks for specification languages that support developers by addressing those challenges that should be addressed on this language level. This research question is mainly answered in Part III of this thesis and states as follows:

Research Question 2: How to provide support for specifying change-driven consistency preservation for models of different languages *with specification languages* that address the challenges identified in subquestion 1.2?

For this question, we have also created four subquestions with further details. They are the direct result of our answer to subquestion 1.2, which asked about challenges for consistency specification languages. Every subquestion is a pendant to an OCSLC, which we will present in detail in section 3.5.

Subquestion 2.1: How to provide languages that combine *specific consistency specification* support with *unrestricted expressive power* and flexibility?

Subquestion 2.2: How to support *solution-oriented and problem-oriented* specifications of change-driven consistency with such languages?

Subquestion 2.3: How to *adapt* this language support to specific needs and *abstract away* from details that are not relevant for consistency preservation?

Subquestion 2.4: How to *preserve consistency* with such languages in a way that allows developers to *foresee* how consistency is enforced according to their specification?

1.4. Contributions

The contributions of this thesis are our answers to the previously presented two research questions, which we provide in chapter 3–8. Our answers to the second research question are not only textually described but also provided in terms of compilers and editors that realize the presented languages. The two central parts of this thesis, the research questions, the contribution chapters, and their relations are also illustrated in Figure 1.1.

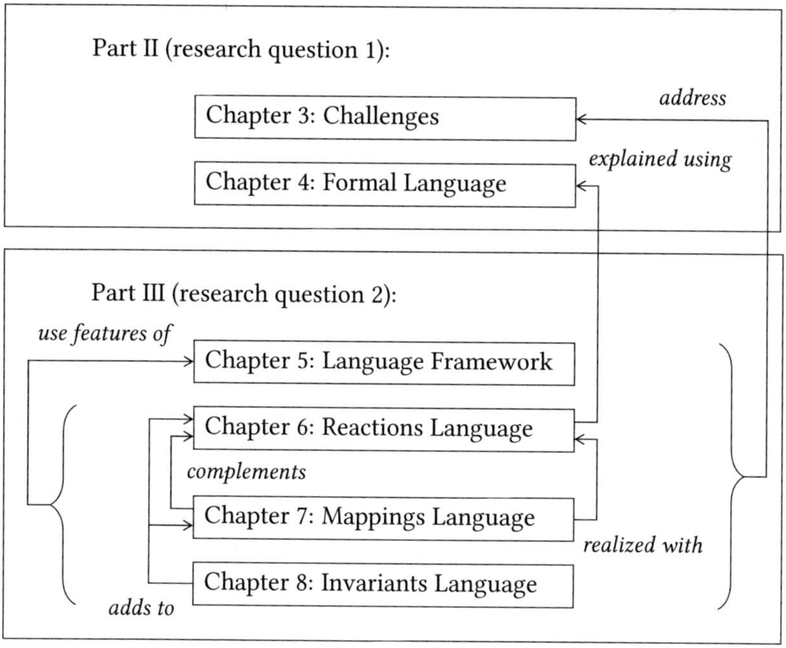

Figure 1.1.: Parts, research questions, and contribution chapters of this thesis

1.4.1. Consistency Challenges and Definitions

To answer the first research question, we provide a classification of challenges to consistency preservation and a formal language that defines how consistency can be specified and preserved after changes. More specifically, we contribute

a collection and classification of challenges that can occur when consistency is to be preserved for models of different languages. Developers of consistency preservation tools can encounter these challenges regardless of the used modelling languages and preservation techniques. The classification illustrates which consistency challenges should be addressed, for example, already when modelling languages are designed and which challenges should not be addressed when consistency is specified but only when it is enforced. Both, the collections of challenges and its classification are presented in chapter 3 as an answer to subquestion 1.1 and 1.2.

a formal language that introduces fundamental concepts of consistency preservation in a realization-independent way using set theory. It defines how consistency can be specified in such a way that it is possible to analyze whether consistency is preserved after changes. These specification-driven consistency concepts are also used to explain the semantics of the languages that can be used to develop consistency preservation tools. The formal language is presented in chapter 4 to answer subquestion 1.3 and 1.4

1.4.2. Specification Languages for Preserving Consistency

To answer the second research question, we present three new languages for developing consistency preservation tools based on specifications, and a language framework that integrates features that are provided by all three languages. These languages complement each other, and together they answer subquestion 2.1–2.4. More specifically, we contribute

a framework for languages that can be used to specify consistency in such a way that consistency according to a specification is semi-automatically preserved after user changes. These changes are monitored and can be universally processed by preservation programs as they are represented as instances of a generic change modelling language. The language framework provides a Java-based expression language that also supports well-known collection operators and iterators of OCL. It is presented in chapter 5 and especially answers subquestion 2.2 and 2.4.

an imperative language for universal consistency reactions that consist of preservation actions which are triggered for particular changes. To relieve developers from writing repetitive code, the reactions language provides declarative constructs for common consistency preservation tasks, such as resolving or creating corresponding elements. Furthermore, the language supports developers in structuring their code along three main steps of consistency preservation so that they develop manageable reactions without unwanted side-effects. The reactions language is presented in chapter 6 and especially answers subquestion 2.1 and 2.3.

a bidirectional language for abstract consistency mappings that complement the reactions language as they can be used if consistency does not need to be preserved in a change- or direction-specific way. In order to relieve developers from specifying symmetric consistency relations twice, the language automatically derives code that enforces conditions from a check specification and inverse enforcement code from bidirectionalizable conditions for the opposite preservation direction. To support many possible consistency relations, the mappings language gives developers the possibility to fallback to imperative, unidirectional code whenever this is necessary. It is presented in chapter 7 and especially answers subquestion 2.1 and 2.3.

a normative language for parameterized consistency invariants that can be used in addition to the reactions and the mappings language whenever constraints should be declared. If such invariants are violated the model elements that are responsible for the violation can be obtained using queries that are automatically derived for invariant parameters. The invariants language is presented in chapter 8 and especially answers subquestion 2.2.

1.5. Outline

The remainder of this thesis is structured as follows: First, we briefly introduce fundamental concepts and terms in chapter 2. This concludes the prelude part of this thesis. Then, we present our collection and classification of challenges to consistency preservation in chapter 3 and explain our formal language in chapter 4. Together, both chapters form the second part corresponding to research question 1. Subsequently, we introduce our language framework that also comprises the change modelling language and the OCL-aligned expression extension in chapter 5. Then, we present the reactions, mappings, and invariants language in chapter 6–8. This concludes the third part corresponding to research question 2. Next, we discuss how we evaluated our contributions in chapter 9 and describe related work in chapter 10. These chapters form the fourth part of this thesis. Finally, we conclude this dissertation and provide an outlook on possible directions for future work in chapter 11.

We suggest readers that cannot read the complete thesis to start with the framework chapter 5 and to follow back references to the challenges of chapter 3 and to the formal language of chapter 4 where necessary. As several parts of the chapters for the individual languages rely on the features provided by the framework, we do *not* suggest to directly start with one of these chapters. Apart from these features, each language chapter can also be read in isolation.

2. Foundations

In this chapter, we introduce fundamental concepts and terms that are used in the subsequent chapters of this thesis. First, we explain what models are, how they are used for software development, and how modelling languages can be built. Then, we briefly describe the multi-view modelling framework Vitruvius, which we have extended in this thesis, refer to the approach that inspired it and introduce the fundamental problem of multi-view consistency preservation. Finally, we formally define all modelling concepts on which our formal language for specification-driven consistency preservation is built (see chapter 4).

2.1. Models and Languages

In this thesis, we present programming languages that can be used to develop tools that preserve consistency between models that conform to different modelling languages. Therefore, models and modelling languages are central concepts of this thesis, which we will explain in the following.

2.1.1. Model Theory

Models are used in many engineering disciplines and in several fields of computer science. These models share many common properties, but what is considered a model can also be very different depending on the context. Therefore, we briefly introduce the so-called general model theory of Stachowiak [Sta73] before we explain models in the context of software development. Stachowiak defines the term *model* by postulating three main characteristics of models: representation, reduction, and pragmatics Stachowiak [Sta73, pp. 131–133]

According to Stachowiak, the *representation* characteristic is fulfilled if a model *represents originals* and their properties. These originals can be any “perceptiple” or “constructable” entities and they may be itself act as a model of another original [Sta73, p. 131]. We interpret the statement that “representation coincides with mapping properties of models to properties of originals” [Sta73, p. 132] in such a way that it is *required* that all properties of a model can be mapped to a property of an original. That is, a modelled property has to represent a property of an original and may not add any properties.

The *reduction* characteristic is fulfilled if not all but only those properties of an original “that seem relevant to the creator or user of a model” are represented [Sta73, p. 132]. This characteristic does not yet demand further requirements for those properties that are represented or not. It only requires that some properties are selected and others are not.

A model fulfills the last main characteristic, called *pragmatics*, if it replaces an original for certain subjects, for certain periods, and for certain functions to achieve a certain purpose [Sta73, p. 132]. This means, a model is no absolute representation of an original but a pragmatic replacement for a certain context and usage. The two other characteristics of representation and reduction should be considered relative to the pragmatics of a model. That is, how reduced properties of an original are represented and which other properties are abstracted away is determined by the pragmatics of a model.

2.1.2. Model-Driven Software Development

Model-Driven Software Development (MDSD) is a term that is not precisely defined but in many contexts, in which it is used, it stands for a development paradigm in which models are used in an *automated* way for *all* development tasks. Some of the goals that are often pursued using this paradigm by means of automation are an increase in development speed, improved software quality, and better productivity through reuse [VS06, pp. 13]. The central goal of automation in MDSD is also what is often used to distinguish MDSD from other software development approaches in which models are used, for example, for documentation purposes but not processed automatically.

To ease the automation, many concepts and tools for *model transformations* are used in MDSD.

The Model-Driven Architecture (MDA) approach of the Object Management Group (OMG) [OMG14] is a particular approach for developing software according to the MDSD paradigm. Similarly, the Unified Modeling Language (UML) [ISO12a] is a well-known modelling language that can be used to create models of software systems. Both are two prominent examples, but MDSD can also be realized according to other development approaches and using other modelling languages. It is also important to note that there is not always a clear border between concepts and tools that are used in compiler construction and MDSD. On the contrary, code is often also regarded as a model of the software and many MDSD tools use, for example, the parser generator ANTLR [PQ95].

2.1.2.1. Modelling Languages and Metamodels

To support model transformations, a modelling language has to specify which conditions have to be fulfilled by models of this language and what effects this has. Such a language specification is often separated into four parts [VS06, pp. 57–58]:

the abstract syntax of a modelling language specifies the represented concepts, their properties, and their relations

the concrete syntax defines how concepts, properties, and relations are represented in a textually or graphical way

the static semantics specify constraints that have to be fulfilled by all models but that cannot be defined in the abstract syntax

the dynamic semantics define the meaning of the models of the language for example by mapping them to models of other languages or to code

In MDSD the abstract syntax of a modelling language is often specified in terms of a metamodel. In this case all models of the modelling language are also called *instances* of the metamodel. A metamodel is usually itself a model of a meta-modelling language that is expressed as an instance of a meta-metamodel. A meta-modelling language can be self-descriptive. This possibility to define a meta-modelling language using its own concepts is, however, not mandatory and in general there may be an arbitrary number of meta-levels. The static semantics of a modelling language are often defined together with a metamodel or even added to it in order to have all rules that are necessary validating a model instance in one place.

2.1.2.2. Domain-Specific Languages

Standardized modelling languages, such as the UML, are well-supported and widely used but sometimes they are not well-suited, for example, to be automatically processed in a particular context. This can be the case if not all information that is needed to transform the models to models of another language can be modelled in a suitable way. An important concept of MDSD that can also be used to solve such problems is that of a Domain-Specific Language (DSL). Such a DSL can be tailored to represent the concepts of a particular domain with the level of detail that is needed for a specific development task. In this way, a DSL makes it possible to better achieve the model characteristics postulated by Stachowiak by tailoring the structure of *all* models to make them fit the pragmatics (see subsection 2.1.1).

The idea of tailoring a language to a specific context or domain can be used independent of the concrete syntax of the language and independent of the level of abstraction. Nevertheless, the term Domain-Specific Modelling Language (DSML) is often used to emphasize that the artefacts that are created using such a language are models and therefore support a particular abstraction. This term can, however, be misleading because many software developers associate the term modelling to a graphical syntax which is not characteristic for a model in contrast to, for example, a particular level of abstraction. Furthermore, we want to emphasize that the notion of models and of a DSL can also be used if the application domain is a particular area of software engineering, that is if the represented originals are pieces of software. The term DSL can be used to describe, for example, a language that is used to represent contracts of an insurance company. In the same way, languages that are used to represent, for example, design elements of mobile applications or rules for preserving consistency between development artefacts, can be considered DSLs. Finally, the concept of a DSL is independent of the question whether a concrete syntax of a host language is reused or whether a new concrete syntax is provided. Therefore, a library that can be used in an existing language can also be regarded as an *internal* DSL and distinguished from an *external* DSL.

There can be different reasons for using a DSL instead of a general language. We already mentioned the goal of developing or using a DSL to ease automated transformations. Another goal that is often pursued with a DSL is to relieve domain experts and software developers from performing certain tasks or to support them in performing tasks according to their field of expertise. A DSL can be used, for example, to give domain experts the possibility to express their concerns in a way that abstracts away from technical concerns that are encapsulated in the DSL. Furthermore, a DSL can be used to give domain experts possibilities to express concerns that would have to be considered by software developers if no DSL would be used.

2.1.2.3. Model-Driven Software Development Process

If several languages are used in a forward engineering process that follows the MDSD paradigm, we can distinguish between two general actions: On the one hand, models can be manually refined to lower the level of abstraction by adding additional details. On the other hand, models can be enriched with information of other models in automated transformations. Such manual refinements and automated transformations can be combined arbitrarily and can be repeated for models of different languages to finally obtain models that are detailed enough to serve their purpose. This purpose can be different depending on the usage context. One possibility is to directly execute models in interpreters. Another possibility is to generate code that can be directly or indirectly executed, for example, in a virtual machine.

Völter and Stahl presented a process for the development of a DSL using a code base that was developed without the DSL [VS06, pp. 14–16]. We illustrate this DSL development process using Figure 2.1, which we adopted from [VS06, p. 15]. In the first step, the code base is analyzed to identify three different code parts:

generic code , which does not need to be adapted to individual applications that are developed in the domain,

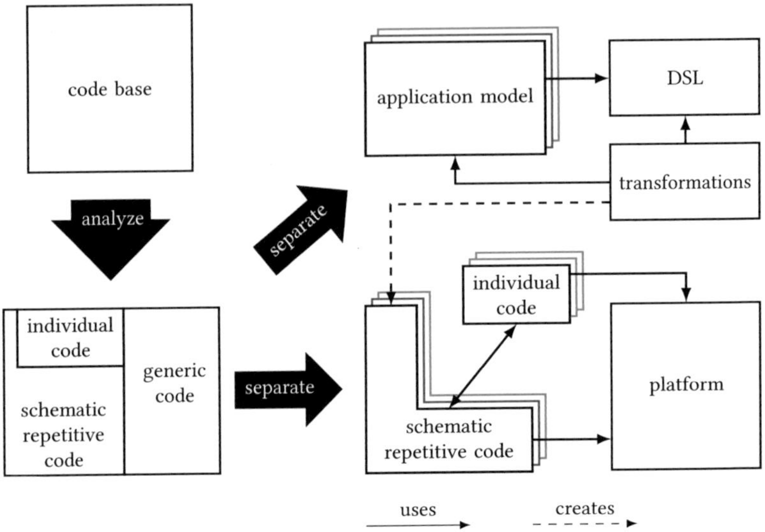

Figure 2.1.: Process for the development of a DSL based on an application code that was developed without the DSL, adapted from [VS06, p. 15]

schematic repetitive code , which is not identical for all applications but can be adapted in a systematic way, and

individual code , which is specific for a particular application and does not need to be generalized

During the development of the DSL these three parts of the code take different roles: Generic code becomes a single platform that can be used in all applications that are developed using the DSL. Schematic repetetive code is obtained by transforming application models that are created using the DSL. Individual code is deployed together with the code generated from the application models and both parts use each other as well as the platform code.

2.1.2.4. Eclipse Modeling Framework (EMF)

The Eclipse Modeling Framework (EMF) is a set of plug-ins for Eclipse, which is an Integrated Development Environment (IDE). It is also the technological base for further IDEs and for other software engineering tools in industry and academia. The EMF combines several tools that can be used to create, edit, analyze, and transform Java-based models that can be represented graphically and textually. It is mainly used to build Eclipse-based software engineering tools that can be applied in software development projects that follow the MDSD paradigm. It provides the meta-modelling language Ecore, which is often regarded as the reference implementation of the Essential Meta Object Facility (EMOF). We will briefly introduce the meta-modelling languages Ecore and EMOF later in this chapter.

2.1.2.5. Xtext Language Workbench

A well-known example for a tool that is built on top of EMF is the Xtext language workbench [EV06]. It is a set of Eclipse plug-ins that can be used to develop textual DSLs. It provides a grammar language that uses a syntax that is similar to the Extended Backus-Naur Form (EBNF) [Int96]. From a grammar that is created with this language a complete compiler toolchain can be generated to obtain extensible implementations of a lexer, a parser, a validator, and a code generator. Languages that are created with Xtext are programming languages and modelling languages at the same time: For every Xtext grammar a metamodel is created and the compiler creates instances of this metamodel. These model instances can be processed in the same way as any other EMF model. The metamodel that is created for a grammar can be influenced using the grammar language. It gives developers the possibility to specify, for example, which metaclass is to be instantiated when a parser rule is processed. In addition to compilers, Eclipse-based editors can also be generated for Xtext-based languages. These editors provide, for example, possibilities to influence auto-completion or to add quick-fixes that are suggested in case of common compilation errors.

To ease the development of DSLs that contain common expressions , the Xtext workbench provides the expression language Xbase [Eff+12]. The syntax of Xbase expressions is very similar to Java method body expressions and in large parts identical. Variable assignments, method invocations, and most expression operators, for example, are identical. Furthermore, language features that are not provided by Java, such as type inference for variable declarations, can be used when the Xbase grammar is integrated into the grammar of a Xtext-based DSL. Xtend[1] is an example of a language that was developed using Xtext and Xbase. It is a general purpose programming language that is similar to Java and it compiles to Java so that both languages are interoperable. Xtend provides, for example, lambdas for functional programming, template expressions for code generation and other features for working with EMF models. As Xtend is similar to Java but can deviate from it, it is also called a Java dialect.

We realized the compilers for the languages presented in this thesis using Xtext but will not show the Xtext-specific parts of the grammar rules. Instead we will use plain EBNF, which is a standardized notation for syntax definitions. In EBNF terminals are given in quotes and rule parts are explicitly concatenated with commas for denoting the concatenation operator. Therefore, it is possible to use spaces in identifiers of non-terminals and they do not have to be escaped. Furthermore, the following rules of EBNF are adopted from the original Backus-Naur Form (BNF):

- `[ ]` square brackets enclose optional rule parts,
- `|` the pipe character separates alternatives,
- `{}` rule parts in curly braces are repeated zero, one, or more times,
- `( )` parentheses group rule parts, and
- `;` the semi-colon denotes the end of a rule.

In addition, the minus character (`-`) is used to define exceptions as if symbol sequences would be removed from a previous set of symbol sequences. Therefore, symbol sequences that have to occur at least once can be achieved by removing the empty symbol sequence from a repeated rule part.

1 eclipse.org/xtend – A Java dialect based on Xtext and Xbase

2.1.3. Meta-Modelling Languages

To build MDSD tools it can be useful to have a common format for models of different modelling languages. One way to achieve this is to us a fixed meta-modelling language to create metamodels for modelling languages, no matter whether they are domain-specific or not. If such a meta-modelling language is used, tools, for example, for creating, editing, or transforming models of a particular modelling language can be built by adapting and extending generic tools that are based on the common meta-meta model. In the following, we will briefly present two meta-modelling languages. The consistency specification languages presented in this thesis can be used to preserve consistency between models that conform to arbitrary metamodels that were created using these two languages.

2.1.3.1. Essential Meta Object Facility (EMOF)

The Essential Meta Object Facility (EMOF) is one of two variants of the standardized meta-modelling language Meta Object Facility (MOF) [ISO14]. From a mathematical point of view, EMOF is a language for representing metamodels and models in a way that is equivalent to attributed, typed graphs with inheritance. MOF is a language of the OMG and it was initially developed by generalizing concepts of object-oriented UML class diagrams. It is self-descriptive as its concepts can be represented using a MOF-compliant metamodel. We illustrated the central concepts of EMOF in terms of a simplified class diagram in Figure 2.2 and briefly explain them in the following. Metamodels that are defined using EMOF consist of metaclasses that are instantiated by model elements which can also be called objects. Metaclasses have properties that are typed using metaclasses, primitive types and enumerations. The number of values that can be added to instances of a metaclass for a certain property can be restricted using lower and upper bounds for the multiplicity. Furthermore, properties can have a so-called composite aggregation kind. It denotes that the objects that are listed at an instance of the metaclass for the property are contained by the instance, which is therefore also called a container.

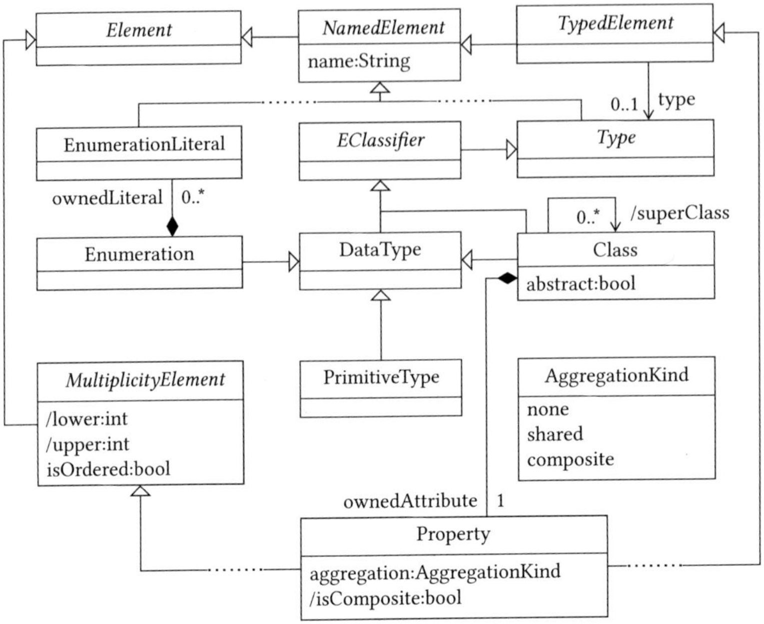

Figure 2.2.: Simplified class diagram showing central metaclasses of the EMOF metamodelling language [ISO14, p.27] (dotted lines denote indirect inheritance)

2.1.3.2. Ecore Metamodelling

A central part of EMF is the meta-modelling language Ecore, which is often regarded as the reference implementation of the EMOF standard. Some concepts of EMOF have, however, been refined in Ecore. We will briefly mention those refinements that are relevant for the languages presented in this thesis, but we ignore, for example, minor naming differences and the fact that Ecore has a simplified inheritance hierarchy. The central metaclasses of Ecore are also illustrated as a simplified class diagram in Figure 2.3. To emphasize the commonalities of EMOF and Ecore, we used the same layout as in Figure 2.2, where this was possible.

For this thesis, only the following differences between EMOF and Ecore are important: In Ecore, properties of metaclasses are called structural *features*.

Features that are typed using a primitive type or using an enumeration are called *attributes*, whereas features that are typed using a metaclass are called *references*. Instead of providing a composite aggregation kind, Ecore distinguishes between references that are marked as *containment reference* and non-containment references. In models conforming to an Ecore metamodel, the links that realize such containment references build a containment hierarchy. In this hierarchy every model element except for a root element is contained in exactly one container using one link for a containment reference. EMOF requires, however, only that all elements have at most one container [ISO14, pp. 31-32]. As with composite properties in EMOF and UML, the semantics of containment references in Ecore are that the existence of contained elements is bound to the existence of the container. Therefore, deletions have transitive effects [ISO12a, p. 36,p. 38]. We realized the prototypical compilers for the languages presented in this thesis using EMF so that they can be used for any models that conform to Ecore-based metamodels. Ecore can be seen as a refinement of EMOF, at least with respect to the differences that are relevant for the presented languages. Therefore, the concepts of the languages can also be used for any other EMOF-compliant modelling language. If our compilers would be ported to support other EMOF-compliant modelling languages the necessary modifications would mainly introduce additional checks to correctly treat properties with different types. Nevertheless, we use the Ecore terminology throughout this thesis. That is we write about features, attributes, and references instead of properties and call the container-containee relation containment instead of composition.

2.2. Multi-View Modelling

In the last informal section on foundations for this thesis, we briefly present two approaches for multi-view modelling. The first approach inspired our work on the second approach, which we extended using the languages presented in this thesis.

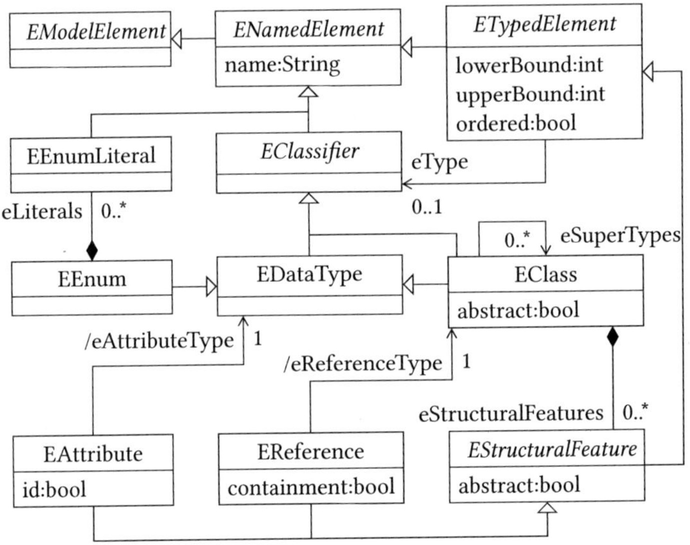

Figure 2.3.: Simplified class diagram showing central metaclasses of the Ecore metamodelling language according to [Ste+08, pp.97] and [Bur14, p.25]

2.2.1. Orthographic Software Modeling

Orthographic Software Modeling (OSM) is an approach for the development of software using multiple views and was presented by Atkinson et al. [ASB10]. It transferred the principle of othrographic projections to software development. All views in OSM are projections of a Single Underlying Model (SUM), which contains all information of the system under development [ISO11]. In OSM, the views and the metamodel for the SUM are created upfront by developers that take a special role called *methodologist*. Later on, developers only access information of the SUM via the projective views so that only these views have to be kept consistent with the SUM in a hub-and-spoke manner. To ease this consistency preservation between the views and the SUM, it should not contain any redundant information. In OSM views are dynamically generated using transformations. Furthermore, views can be navigated in a dimension-based way.

2.2.2. The Vitruvius Framework

In this thesis, we present three DSLs for developing consistency preservation tools based on the multi-view modelling framework Vitruvius [KBL13]. The development of this framework was strongly influenced by OSM but follows a hybrid approach that combines synthetic and projective elements (see also subsection 10.1.3). Instead of a SUM, the Vitruvius framework uses a Virtual Single Underlying Model (VSUM) to uniformly access models of different modelling languages. As this VSUM reuses existing modelling languages it usually contains redundant information. Vitruvius support developers in creating views for these languages and in preserving consistency between models of the VSUM in a change-driven way.. This way, they can reuse existing modelling languages and tools, such as editors. The overall goal of Vitruvius is to decouple views, modelling languages, and consistency preservation so that they can be reused in different combinations and for different projects. Currently, the Vitruvius framework

- monitors changes that are applied in Eclipse-based editors to models or code in order to trigger consistency preservation code [Lan17]
- processes these changes based on a generic change modelling language (see subsection 5.4.1)
- manages correspondences between models across languages based on temporarily unique identifiers (see subsubsection 5.5.1.1)
- supports the integration of code and models that were created without the framework for later consistency preservation [Lan17]
- can be used to create new views that combine information from several models using ModelJoin [Bur+14; Bur14]

2.2.3. The View-Update Problem

The need to preserve consistency between partially redundant information is not particular to MDSD or multi-view modelling. It has been discussed as the *view-update problem* in many publications and in different areas of computer science, for example databases [BS81]. We will only motivate this problem in a simplified way and informally introduce some desired properties for transformations between two models. A more formal discussion of these properties can be found in subsection 7.4.2 and a review on literature about the view-update problem is presented in subsection 10.1.1.

Broadly speaking, the problem of consistency preservation between two models that contain redundant pieces of information can be described in terms of the view-update problem. A possibility to achieve this, is to transfer the notion of a view on a database to the notion of two models that are related using two model transformations. Even if the problem does not need to be asymmetric, we usually call one model the source model and the other model the target model for a forward transformation from the source to the target. Analogous, the other transformation is usually called a backward transformation from the target to the source. In this asymmetric terminology, the roles of source and target are usually chosen in a particular way. The forward transformation, which is also called GET, only requires a new source value to compute a new target value. The backward transformation, however, may have to obtain the old source value in addition to the new target value in order to yield a desired new source value. Therefore, it is also called PUT.

To preserve consistency between two models, common laws for round-trip transformations can be used. These laws are concerned with cases in which a model is updated and GET and PUT transformations are executed to obtain values for the other model with partially redundant information. Foster et al. [Fos+07], for example, formulated a GETPUT law, and a PUTGET law (see also subsection 7.4.2). The informal idea of both laws is that roundtrips, in which no value was changed, should end up at the same value regardless of whether they started at the source model or at the target model. More specifically, the GETPUT law demands that invoking GET for an arbitrary source value and then PUT for the obtained target value and the source value always yields the initially used source value. Similarly, PUTGET demands that invoking PUT for arbitrary source and target values and then GET for the obtained source value always yields the initial target value.

2.3. Formal Foundations

In this section, we define fundamental concepts for a formal change-driven consistency preservation language, which is presented in chapter 4

We reused parts of existing formalizations for models and consistency constraints where this was possible, but had to create a specific notation in order to support the three specification languages appropriately. The formal language abstracts away from properties that are not needed for the reactions, invariants, or mappings language. It expresses only those properties that are central for the challenges tackled in this thesis. This is especially important for the explanation of the semantics of the three languages, which should not suffer from the accidental complexity of existing formalizations that also deal with concerns that are irrelevant for the languages. Those properties that are represented in our formal language are closely aligned to the implementation of the languages in order to avoid unnecessary gaps between formal descriptions of the semantics and implementation code. In this way, the formal language is itself a model for our specification languages with its own representation, reduction, and pragmatics (see subsection 2.1.1). Nevertheless, this formal representation of change-driven consistency is not entirely restricted to the three specification languages and could be reused for other approaches and languages for model consistency.

2.3.1. Notation, Conventions and Abstractions

Before we present the formal language that is the foundation for the three specification languages of this thesis, we explain the notation, conventions, abstractions and simplifications of it in this section. We also explain which formal descriptions of models or consistency are related to our formal language and why they are different.

2.3.1.1. Notation and Conventions

The formal language is based on set theory and uses the common notation for sets, elements, and operations, such as intersection. Therefore, we do not need to explain all these common notational elements. A notation that is worth mentioning is, however, the use of $\mathcal{P}(S)$ to denote the powerset of a set S, i.e. the set of all subsets of S. Furthermore, we explicitly mention when a set is infinite or a function is partial. Therefore, all sets that are not called infinite are finite and all functions that are not called partial are total.

Binary relations and their transitive closures on sets and functions are used in many definitions of the formal language. In order not to explain these central concepts at every usage, we briefly discuss them in general upfront: For a set S, the transitive closure of a binary relation $R \subseteq S \times S$ on a subset $B \subseteq S$ is denoted by

$$\begin{aligned} B^R := B \cup \{b_n \in S \mid \exists\,(b_1, b_2) \in B \times S \\ \wedge\ \exists\,(b_1, b_2), (b_2, b_3), \ldots, (b_{n-1}, b_n) \in R\ \wedge\ n > 1\} \end{aligned}$$

In this way, the transitive closure of a relation on a subset yields all elements of the subset and all elements of the superset that are directly or indirectly related to the elements of the subset. For two sets D, S, the transitive closure of a binary relation $R \subseteq S \times S$ on a function $\textsc{func}\colon D \rightarrow S$ is denoted by

$$\begin{aligned} \textsc{func}^R := d \rightarrow \{\textsc{func}(d)\} \cup \{s_n \in S \mid \\ \exists\,(\textsc{func}(d), s_1), (s_1, s_2), \ldots, (s_{n-1}, s_n) \in R\ \wedge\ n > 0\} \end{aligned}$$

In this way, the transitive closure of a relation on a function yields the function value and all elements of the codomain that are directly or indirectly related to the function value.

To ease the reading of our definitions, we established some conventions regarding the use of variables and fonts. All sets are denoted by a single character in upper case, e.g. O. All elements are denoted by single characters in lower case, e.g. $o \in O$. All functions and relations are denoted by a string in small capitals, e.g. $\textsc{foo}\colon O \rightarrow O$. For all concepts of the metamodel level, i.e. the level above model instances, which defines modelling languages based on metamodels, metaclasses etc., a blackboard bold font is used, e.g. $\mathbb{c} \in \mathbb{C}$. For all concepts that only pertain to specifications that define consistency for models using concepts of the metamodel level, a fraktur font is used, e.g. $\mathfrak{cr}$. To emphasize that a set contains sets, a calligraphic font is used for the single character denoting the set of sets, e.g. $\mathcal{O}$. Finally, to emphasize that a variable denotes a tuple, angled brackets surround the variable name, e.g. $\langle \mathbb{c} \rangle$ or $\langle o \rangle$.

2.3.1.2. Abstractions and Simplifications

There are several properties of EMOF-based models which are not relevant to formally define consistency and therefore not part of the formal language. These properties that are completely abstracted away are:

I. names, e.g. of metaclasses, attributes, or references

II. operations of metaclasses

III. abstractness of metaclasses

IV. attribute and reference multiplicities, i.e. lower and upper bounds

The reasons why we chose these abstractions are different: I.. Names are only descriptive and are not used to identify or retrieve elements because this is not necessary for sets. The membership relation between sets and elements is sufficient. II.. When operations are executed on models, they can only perform the same modifications that can be performed directly on the models. III.. It has to be ensured that abstract metaclasses cannot be directly instantiated, but they have the same effect on models like metaclasses that are not abstract. IV.. Restrictions on multiplicities of references are just a special form of restrictions and can be represented expressed with general invariant constraints for model validity.

In addition to properties that are not represented at all, there are also properties of models that are only represented in a simplified form in the formal language. These simplifications can also be interpreted as limitations on models that can be represented with the formal language. As long as the formal language is not extended to also support these cases, only a subset of all possible EMOF-based models can be represented with it. Our programming languages, which we describe using the formal language, do, however, *not* have these limiations. The current limitations of our formal language are:

1. References only refer to metaclasses of the same metamodel.

2. Links only link to objects of the same model.
3. No subtype relation between attribute types is defined.
4. No attribute types like strings or integers are predefined.
5. No types of attribute types, such as enumerations are defined.
6. An object is only linked once per reference and linking object.
7. An attribute value is only labeled once per attribute and object.
8. Links and attribute labels have no order.

Again, the reasons why we decided to make these simplifications are diverse: The simplifications 1 and 2 were made because the effect of dividing metamodels or models into parts are only syntactical. All three attribute type simplifications (3–5) were made because attribute values are always fixed in a metamodel. In contrast to reference values, which are model elements, attribute values are not instantiated in models but just referenced. Therefore, subtype relations, attribute types that are already predefined for all metamodels, and different types of attribute types like enums have no direct influence on models. Finally, the simplifications 6 – 8 were made in order to avoid the complexity of using tuples to express linked object and label values. Such multiplicities and the order of linked objects and label values could be used to specify or enforce consistency, but in our opinion the possible uses do not justify the added complexity for the presented formal language.

Furthermore, our definitions of model consistency only allow the specification and enforcement of consistency for two models that conform to two metamodels. Neither consistency for several models of two metamodels nor consistency for models of more than two metamodels can be expressed. The first restriction on two models is technical and does not limit the expressiveness of the formal language. We decided to accept this limitation in order not to complicate all definitions for consistency and enforcements without a conceptual benefit. The formal language could be easily extended by defining consistency for two sets of models for both metamodels instead of two models for both metamodels. Boundaries of models are technical as it makes no semantic difference whether an element is part of one or another model. Therefore, such an extension for more than two models would not allow any consistency specifications or enforcements that cannot be expressed with the presented formal language.

The second restriction that consistency can only be specified and enforced for models of two metamodels is, however, a major conceptual limitation. This limitation applies, however, also to the programming languages presented in the subsequent chapters of this thesis and to our approach to change-driven consistency in general . It will be targeted in future work (see also section 3.9) and will be analyzed in future case studies.

2.3.1.3. Foundations and Related Formalizations

We used parts of the formal semantics of the Object Constraint Language (OCL) [ISO12c, Annex A.1–A.3, pp. 193–201] as a basis for the definition of our formal language. As OCL is based on the Meta-Object Facility (MOF) [Obj06] it formally defines MOF-based metamodels and models[2]. An example of reuse is the general idea to define separate sets for attributes and associations of each metaclass. The majority of the formal MOF semantics of the OCL Annex, however, was not appropriate for our formal language. As the OCL supports all properties of MOF-based models the formal semantics of it are too detailed for our purposes. Therefore, the rationale for the abstractions and simplifications of the previous section are also rationale for our decision not to reuse the formal OCL semantics. In the formal OCL semantics names are, for example, used to identify elements instead of set-membership. This is necessary to precisely specify OCL for implementations of the language but unnecessary for the languages of this thesis.

Burger adapted the formal OCL semantics to specifics of the Ecore implementation of the Essential Meta-Object Facility (EMOF) in his dissertation [Bur14]. He restricted, for example, the MOF notion of associations with an arbitrary number of ends to the Ecore notion of references with two ends. As the formal OCL semantics are only adapted to Ecore but not simplified, they are also too detailed to be reused for our purposes. Rentschler used a formal definition of models as typed graphs with inheritance by Kleppe in his disseration [Kle08; Ren15]. The core of our formal

2 No relevant changes were performed in these parts of the new versions of OCL [Obj14] and MOF [ISO14]

language can be seen as a set-based alternative to attributed, typed graphs with inheritance, so the missing attributes or labels make it impossible to reuse this formalization. There are further formal definitions of models and consistency, such as those by Hettel and Macedo et al., but they were also defined with different reductions and pragmatics [Het10; MJC17].

2.3.2. Metamodels and Models

Before we can precisely define how consistency can be specified and enforced for two models, we have to define what a model is. We are not concerned with models that were created with a fixed modelling language. Instead, this thesis and the formal language of this chapter are concerned with models that conform to metamodels.

2.3.2.1. Metamodels and Types

Metamodels are models that define a modelling language, which can be used to create other models. In this sense, metamodels are itself ordinary models but the meta-modelling language, which is also often called meta-metamodel, is fixed. The formal language as well as the programming languages presented in this thesis are defined for metamodels that were created using the meta-modelling language EMOF. Therefore, we start by formally defining EMOF-based metamodels:

Definition 1 (Metamodel)
A metamodel $\mathbb{m}$ *is a tuple* $(\mathbb{C}, <, \mathbb{R}, \mathbb{A}, \mathbb{V})$*, where* $\mathbb{C}$ *is a set of metaclasses,* $< \subsetneq \mathbb{C} \times \mathbb{C}$ *is the partial order that represents the specialization hierarchy of metaclasses,* $\mathbb{R}$ *is a set of references,* $\mathbb{A}$ *is a set of attributes, and* $\mathbb{V}$ *is a possibly infinite set of attribute values.*

These five elements of a metamodel are sufficient to completely specify which models can be created using the metamodel. The references and attributes depend on metaclasses. Thus, it would also be possible to define that they are not directly a part of a metamodel but only of a metaclass. This would, however, make it complicated to access references and attributes across several metaclasses, e.g. in order to obtain all references or attributes that are defined for a metaclass or for its superclasses. Therefore, we directly define these second-class elements in a metamodel and not only in the metaclasses.

It would also be possible to define metamodels as many-sorted structures, which are a common concept used in mathematical logics. Then it would be necessary to explicitly define the arity of functions in terms of tuples of the sorts in order to explain which function has which domain. We decided to avoid this unnecessary complexity for the definition of metamodels and many subsequent definitions because tuples are sufficient for our formal language.

Some readers might expect attribute values to be part of models instead of metamodels. This is, however, misleading: A metamodel pre-defines which attribute values can be used in model instances. This set of allowed attribute values can be infinite but it is fixed and no model can use any further attribute values. Therefore, it is more precise to directly make these values part of the metamodel and not of models. Besides, the set of allowed attribute values is often finite in practice, e.g. because only numbers up to a certain size and strings up to a certain length are supported.

So far, we only defined that metamodels consist of metaclasses with a partial specialization order, references, attributes, and attributes values. In the next steps, we define what these elements of metamodels are and start with the central concept of metamodels: metaclasses.

Definition 2 (Metaclass)
Let $\mathbb{m} := (\mathbb{C}, \prec, \mathbb{R}, \mathbb{A}, \mathbb{V})$ be a metamodel.

A metaclass $\mathbb{c} \in \mathbb{C}$ *of* $\mathbb{m}$ *is a tuple* $(\mathbb{R}_\mathbb{c}, \mathbb{R}_{\mathbb{c},\blacklozenge}, \mathbb{A}_\mathbb{c})$ *where* $\mathbb{R}_\mathbb{c} \subseteq \mathbb{R}$ *are the references defined for* $\mathbb{c}$, $\mathbb{R}_{\mathbb{c},\blacklozenge} \subseteq \mathbb{R}_\mathbb{c}$ *are the containment references defined for* $\mathbb{c}$, *and* $\mathbb{A}_\mathbb{c} \subseteq \mathbb{A}$ *are the attributes defined for* $\mathbb{c}$ *such that the references and attributes of* $\mathbb{m}$ *are partitioned by* $\mathbb{C}$, *i.e.* $\forall\ \mathbb{c}_i, \mathbb{c}_j \in \mathbb{C}$ *with* $i \neq j$ *it holds that* $\mathbb{R}_{\mathbb{c}_i} \cup \mathbb{R}_{\mathbb{c}_j} = \emptyset = \mathbb{A}_{\mathbb{i}\mathbb{c}} \cup \mathbb{A}_{\mathbb{j}\mathbb{c}}.s$

Note that the containment references, which are special references that are used to serialize models, are a subset of the references of a metaclass. It would also be possible to define a set of non-containment and a set of containment reference with empty intersection. This would, however, make it more complicated to reason about references when it does not matter whether they are containment references or not.

Definition 3 (Specialization Relation)
Let $(\mathbb{C}, \prec, \mathbb{R}, \mathbb{A}, \mathbb{V})$ be a metamodel.

Two metaclasses $\mathbb{c}_1, \mathbb{c}_2 \in \mathbb{C}$ *are related using the metaclass specialization relation* $\prec$ *such that* $\mathbb{c}_1 \prec \mathbb{c}_2$ *iff* $\mathbb{c}_1$ *specializes* $\mathbb{c}_2$*. In such cases* $\mathbb{c}_1$ *is called a* subclass *of* $\mathbb{c}_2$ *and* $\mathbb{c}_2$ *is called a* superclass *of* $\mathbb{c}_1$.

The transitive closure of $\prec$ is denoted by $\preccurlyeq$. For $\mathbb{c}_1 \prec \mathbb{c}_2$, we also call $\mathbb{c}_1$ a direct subclass of $\mathbb{c}_2$ and $\mathbb{c}_2$ a direct superclass of $\mathbb{c}_1$. For $\mathbb{c}_1 \preccurlyeq \mathbb{c}_2 \wedge \mathbb{c}_1 \not\prec \mathbb{c}_2$, we call $\mathbb{c}_1$ an indirect subclass of $\mathbb{c}_2$ and $\mathbb{c}_2$ an indirect superclass of $\mathbb{c}_1$.

The effect of a direct ($\prec$) or indirect specialization relation ($\preccurlyeq$) between two metaclasses is well-known from object-oriented programming. Every property that is defined for a superclass is also present in all its subclasses. For models this means that every reference and attribute that is defined for a metaclass can be used in objects that instantiate the metaclass or one of its subclasses in order to link to other objects and in order to label it using attribute values. In other words a metaclass inherits all references and attributes of its superclass.

We call this relation between metaclasses a specialization relation and do not use the name generalization relation of the formal OCL semantics. The reason is that for two metaclasses $\mathbb{c}_1$,$\mathbb{c}_2$ the expression $\mathbb{c}_1 \prec \mathbb{c}_2$ can be read from left to right as "$\mathbb{c}_1$ specializes $\mathbb{c}_2$". For sentences in English this is more intuitive than reading "$\mathbb{c}_2$ generalizes $\mathbb{c}_1$" from right to left.

Definition 4 (Transitive References and Attributes)
Let $\mathbb{c} := (\mathbb{R}_{\mathbb{c}}, \mathbb{R}_{\mathbb{c},\blacklozenge}, \mathbb{A}_{\mathbb{c}})$ be a metaclass of a metamodel $\mathbb{m}$.

The transitive references, transitive containment references, and transitive attributes of $\mathbb{c}$ *are the closures of metaclass specialization* $\prec$ *on* $\mathbb{R}_{\mathbb{c}}$, $\mathbb{R}_{\mathbb{c},\blacklozenge}$, *and* $\mathbb{A}_{\mathbb{c}}$. *They are denoted by* $\mathbb{R}_{\mathbb{c}}^{\preccurlyeq}$, $\mathbb{R}_{\mathbb{c},\blacklozenge}^{\preccurlyeq}$, *and* $\mathbb{A}_{\mathbb{c}}^{\preccurlyeq}$ *and contain all references, containment references, and attributes that are defined for* $\mathbb{c}$ *or one of its superclasses.*

The definition of a transitive closure on a subset of the set on which a binary relation is defined was already given in subsubsection 2.3.1.1.

Definition 5 (Reference)
Let $\mathbb{c}_1 := (\mathbb{R}_{\mathbb{c}_1}, \mathbb{R}_{\mathbb{c}_1,\blacklozenge}, \mathbb{A}_{\mathbb{c}_1})$ be a metaclass of a metamodel $(\mathbb{C}, \prec, \mathbb{R}, \mathbb{A}, \mathbb{V})$.

A reference $\mathbb{r} \in \mathbb{R}_{\mathbb{c}_1}$ *has a target metaclass type* $\mathbb{c}_2 \in \mathbb{C}$.

References that are defined for a metaclass are used by objects that instantiate this metaclass or a subclass of it in order to link to other objects. These links can be seen as directed edges of a directed graph. We just call them links instead of edges to ease the discussion of linked objects and incoming or outgoing links.

We do not distinguish between a metaclass and a reference type but directly use the set of metaclasses as the codomain of RTYPE. Furthermore, metaclasses may define reflexive references, i.e. $\mathbb{c}_1 = \mathbb{c}_2$ may hold for Definition 5.

So far, we defined that a metamodel pre-defines all possible attribute values but we did not define which attribute values can be used for which attribute. To this end, we introduce attribute types before we define attributes, as they have no further properties than a type:

Definition 6 (Attribute Type System)
Let $\mathbb{m} := (\mathbb{C}, \prec, \mathbb{R}, \mathbb{A}, \mathbb{V})$ be a metamodel.

An attribute type system for $\mathbb{m}$ *is a tuple* $(\mathbb{T}, \mathbb{P}_{\mathbb{V}}^{\mathbb{T}}, \textit{ATYPE})$*, where* $\mathbb{T} := \{\mathbb{t}_1, \ldots, \mathbb{t}_{|\mathbb{T}|}\}$ *is a set of attribute types,* $\mathbb{P}_{\mathbb{V}}^{\mathbb{T}} := \{\mathbb{V}_{\mathbb{t}_1}, \ldots, \mathbb{V}_{\mathbb{t}_{|\mathbb{T}|}}\}$ *is a partition of* $\mathbb{V}$ *according to* $\mathbb{T}$*, i.e.* $\forall\, \mathbb{v}, \mathbb{w} \in \mathbb{V}\colon\ \exists\, \mathbb{t}_i, \mathbb{t}_j \in \mathbb{T}\colon\ \mathbb{v} \in \mathbb{V}_{\mathbb{t}_i}\ \wedge\ \mathbb{w} \in \mathbb{V}_{\mathbb{t}_j}\ \wedge\ (i \neq j \Rightarrow (\mathbb{t}_i \neq \mathbb{t}_j \wedge \mathbb{V}_{\mathbb{t}_i} \cap \mathbb{V}_{\mathbb{t}_j} = \emptyset))$*, and* $\textit{ATYPE}\colon \mathbb{A} \rightarrow \mathbb{T}$ *is a function that yields the type of an attribute.*

Attributes of metaclasses are used to label objects using attribute values that are pre-defined by the metamodel. The metamodel defines which attribute values can be used for models. The attribute types are used to define which of these values can be used for which attributes. To this end, an attribute type system simply partitions the set of attribute values into a partition for each attribute type.

To keep the definitions as simple as possible for our goals, we do not depict subtype relations as mentioned in subsubsection 2.3.1.2. This means that it cannot be expressed, for example, that the attribute type representing all natural numbers is a subtype of the attribute type representing all integers. An extension of Definition 6 and all dependent definitions would be straightforward but is not necessary for this thesis.

Different attribute values may have the same type, but a single attribute value has—as we discussed in the previous paragraph—only one type. Therefore, the expression defining the partition of $\mathbb{V}$ does not require that v and w are different. It uses the condition that i and j are different only as a precondition for the empty intersection of $\mathbb{V}_{\mathbb{t}_i}$ and $\mathbb{V}_{\mathbb{t}_j}$. The inclusion of $\mathbb{v}$ in $\mathbb{V}_{\mathbb{t}_i}$ and $\mathbb{w}$ in $\mathbb{V}_{\mathbb{t}_j}$ has, however, no such precondition. Therefore, it also holds for $v = w$, which leads to $\mathbb{t}_i = \mathbb{t}_j$ because $\mathbb{P}_{\mathbb{V}}^{\mathbb{T}}$ is a partition.

Based on the definition of attribute types, we can now extend our definition of metamodels to typed metamodels. We could have started directly with typed metamodels without the need to define a separate attribute type system. We decided, however, to introduce attribute types after an initial definition of metamodels and metaclasses in order keep the initial definitions small and simple.

Definition 7 (Typed Metamodel)
Let $\mathbb{m} := (\mathbb{C}, \prec, \mathbb{R}, \mathbb{A}, \mathbb{V})$ be a metamodel and let $\mathbb{s} := (\mathbb{T}, \mathbb{P}_{\mathbb{V}}^{\mathbb{T}}, \text{ATYPE})$ be an attribute type system for $\mathbb{m}$.

A typed metamodel $\widetilde{\mathbb{m}}$ *is a tuple* $(\mathbb{C}, \prec, \mathbb{R}, \mathbb{A}, \mathbb{V}, \textit{RTYPE}, \mathbb{T}, \mathbb{P}_{\mathbb{V}}^{\mathbb{T}}, \textit{ATYPE})$, *where* $\textit{RTYPE} : \mathbb{R} \rightarrow \mathbb{C}$ *is a function that yields the target metaclass of a reference.*

The transitive closure of metaclass specialization $\prec$ on RTYPE is denoted by $\text{RTYPE}^{\preccurlyeq}$. It contains the target metaclass of a reference and all direct and indirect superclasses of it. As $\mathbb{V}$, $\mathbb{T}$, and $\mathbb{P}_{\mathbb{V}}^{\mathbb{T}}$ are often not directly needed when ATYPE and RTYPE are given, we briefly write $(\mathbb{C}, \prec, \mathbb{R}, \mathbb{A}, \text{RTYPE}, \text{ATYPE})$ for $\widetilde{\mathbb{m}}$.

In contrast to metamodels, we do not list the set of attribute values $\mathbb{V}$ for typed metamodels. It is indirectly given by $\bigcup_{\mathbb{t}_\mathbb{s} \in \mathbb{T}} \mathbb{V}_{\mathbb{t}_\mathbb{s}}$. To focus on important parts, we will keep on using metamodels instead of typed metamodels where types are not necessary for subsequent definitions, even if metamodels are usually not used without types.

Definition 8 (Attribute)
Let $\mathbb{c} := (\mathbb{R}_\mathbb{c}, \mathbb{R}_{\mathbb{c},\blacklozenge}, \mathbb{A}_\mathbb{c})$ be a metaclass of a typed metamodel $\mathbb{m} := (\mathbb{C}, \prec, \mathbb{R}, \mathbb{A}, \mathbb{V}, \text{RTYPE}, \mathbb{T}, \mathbb{P}_{\mathbb{V}}^{\mathbb{T}}, \text{ATYPE})$.

An attribute $\mathbb{a} \in \mathbb{A}_\mathbb{c}$ *has a type* $\mathbb{t}$, *which can be obtained using the function* $\textit{ATYPE}: \mathbb{A} \rightarrow \mathbb{T}$.

An attribute of a typed metamodel only has one property: its type. It is unnecessary to define an attribute for an untyped metamodel because it would have no properties. A metaclass may have several attributes of the same type or inherit attributes with the same type from superclasses. Therefore, it is not possible to directly identify attributes with their types and the attribute elements are needed to relate metaclasses and attribute types.

2.3.2.2. Models and Objects

We have defined all concepts of metamodels that are necessary to define what a model is and what it consists of. For our formal language, a model is just a container for objects and it has no additional properties. Therefore, we first define objects before we define models:

Definition 9 (Object)
Let $\mathbb{c} := (\mathbb{R}_{\mathbb{c}}, \mathbb{R}_{\mathbb{c},\blacklozenge}, \mathbb{A}_{\mathbb{c}})$ be a metaclass of a metamodel $\mathbb{m} := (\mathbb{C}, \prec, \mathbb{R}, \mathbb{A}, \mathbb{V})$.

An object o that instantiates $\mathbb{c}$ *has links to other objects for references of* $\mathbb{c}$ *and for references of direct or indirect superclasses of* $\mathbb{c}$ *and label values for attributes of* $\mathbb{c}$ *and for attributes of direct or indirect superclasses of* $\mathbb{c}$*.*

We do not formally define sets of linked objects and labelled values for an object, because we only need them in combination with other objects of a model. Objects as well as their links and labels are always part of a model, for which we define functions to obtain linked objects and labelled values in the next definition. Because objects always depend on a model they are also called *model elements.*

Definition 10 (Model)
Let $\mathbb{m} := (\mathbb{C}, \prec, \mathbb{R}, \mathbb{A}, \mathbb{V})$ be a metamodel with $\mathbb{C} := \{\mathbb{c}_1, \ldots, \mathbb{c}_{|\mathbb{C}|}\}$.

A model that instantiates $\mathbb{m}$ *is a tuple* $(O_{\mathbb{c}_1}, \ldots, O_{\mathbb{c}_{|\mathbb{C}|}}, \textit{LINK}, \textit{LABEL})$*, where each* $O_{\mathbb{c}_i}$ *contains all objects that directly instantiate* $\mathbb{c}_i$*,* $\textit{LINK}\colon O \times \mathbb{R} \rightarrow \mathcal{P}(O)$ *is a function that yields objects that are linked from an object for a reference, and* $\textit{LABEL}\colon O \times \mathbb{A} \rightarrow \mathcal{P}(\mathbb{V})$ *is a function that yields values that are labeled to an object for an attribute.*

We briefly use the set $O := \bigcup_{\mathbb{c} \in \mathbb{C}} O_{\mathbb{c}}$ do denote the model $(O_{\mathbb{c}_1}, \ldots, O_{\mathbb{c}_{|\mathbb{C}|}}, \text{LINK}, \text{LABEL})$. All objects that directly or indirectly instantiate a metaclass $\mathbb{c}_2 \in \mathbb{C}$ are denoted by $O_{\mathbb{c}_2}^{\preccurlyeq} := \bigcup_{(c_1, c_2) \in \preccurlyeq} O_{\mathbb{c}_1}$.

Definition 10 does not enforce all restrictions of the given metamodel. It uses the metamodel to instantiate only objects of the given metaclasses but the domains and co-domains of the functions LINK and LABEL are not restrictive enough. LINK$(o, \mathbb{r})$ or LABEL$(o, \mathbb{a})$ can return objects or attribute values for $\mathbb{r}$ or $\mathbb{a}$ even if they are not defined for the metaclasses that are directly or indirectly instantiated by o. Furthermore, LINK can return objects that are not of the prescribed type. In order to keep our definitions simple, we separate the instantiation of a metamodel from the conformance to a metamodel:

Definition 11 (Model Conforming to a Metamodel)
Let $O := (O_{\mathbb{C}_1}, \ldots, O_{\mathbb{C}_{|\mathbb{C}|}}, \text{LINK}, \text{LABEL})$ be a model that instantiates a metamodel $\mathbb{m} := (\mathbb{C}, \prec, \mathbb{R}, \mathbb{A}, \mathbb{V})$

The model O conforms to $\mathbb{m}$ iff both LINK and LABEL are defined exactly for references and attributes that are defined for the metaclasses instantiated by the given object, i.e.

$$(\forall\, \mathbb{r} \in \mathbb{R}\colon\ \mathit{LINK}(o, \mathbb{r}) = \bot \Leftrightarrow \mathbb{r} \notin \mathbb{R}_{\mathbb{c}}^{\preccurlyeq})$$
$$\wedge\ (\forall\, \mathbb{a} \in \mathbb{A}\colon\ \mathit{LABEL}(o, \mathbb{a}) = \bot \Leftrightarrow \mathbb{a} \notin \mathbb{A}_{\mathbb{c}}^{\preccurlyeq})$$

The three conditions of Definition 11 ensure that the model adheres to all restrictions that are specified by the metamodel without attribute types. Definition 10 only required that every object of a model that instantiates a metamodel directly instantiates a single metaclass of the metamodel. For models conforming to a metamodel Definition 11 requires that the links and labels adhere to the restrictions of the references and attributes of the metamodel. In the first condition, we use $\text{RTYPE}^{\preccurlyeq}(\mathbb{r})$ to obtain all metaclasses that can be instantiated by objects that can be linked using the reference $\mathbb{r}$. Conformance to a typed metamodel with its attribute types has an additional condition for the labels:

Definition 12 (Conforming to a Typed Metamodel)
Let $O := (O_{\mathbb{c}_1}, \ldots, O_{\mathbb{c}_{|C|}}, \text{LINK}, \text{LABEL})$ be a model that conforms to a metamodel $\mathbb{m} := (\mathbb{C}, <, \mathbb{R}, \mathbb{A}, \mathbb{V})$ and let $\widetilde{\mathbb{m}} = (\mathbb{C}, <, \mathbb{R}, \mathbb{A}, \mathbb{V}, \text{RTYPE}, \mathbb{T}, \mathbb{P}_{\mathbb{V}}^{\mathbb{T}},$ ATYPE) be a typed metamodel.

The model O conforms to the typed metamodel $\widetilde{\mathbb{m}}$ iff it only links to objects that instantiate the type of the reference or a subclass of it and only has label values of the type of the attributes, i.e.

$$\forall \mathbb{c} \in \mathbb{C}: \forall o \in O_{\mathbb{c}}: (\forall \mathbb{r} \in \mathbb{R}_{\mathbb{c}}^{\preccurlyeq}: \textit{LINK}(o, \mathbb{r}) \subseteq \bigcup_{\mathbb{d} \in \textit{RTYPE}^{\preccurlyeq}(\mathbb{r})} O_{\mathbb{d}})$$

$$\forall \mathbb{c} \in \mathbb{C}: \forall o \in O_{\mathbb{c}}: \forall \mathbb{a} \in \mathbb{A}_{\mathbb{c}}^{\preccurlyeq}: \textit{LABEL}(o, \mathbb{a}) \subseteq \mathbb{V}_{\textit{ATYPE}(\mathbb{a})}$$

This label condition for models conforming to typed metamodels is the last piece of our general definitions for metamodels and models conforming to them. These definitions precisely show how metamodels can be used to restrict the links and labels of objects instantiating their metaclasses. These restrictions are, however, only very coarse-grained and therefore not sufficient for defining consistency specifications and enforcement. It is only possible to specify that objects instantiating certain metaclasses may link to *any* of the objects instantiating another metaclass or may be labelled using *any* of the values of certain attribute type. Before we can define how consistency can be specified and ensured, we provide a possibility to specify more precise conditions for valid models in the next section.

2.3.3. Conditions and Valid Models

In this section, we define how additional conditions can be specified to define which models are valid models. Such conditions for validity can be used to complete the restrictions of metamodels for all possible models conforming to them. In practice, models that do not fulfill such conditions are considered invalid and are therefore often not supported by modeling tools and development environments. We will reuse the following definitions for model conditions in the next section in order to specify additional conditions that have to be fulfilled for models that are consistent to other models.

2.3.3.1. Serializability and Supporting Tuples

Before we define concepts that allow the specification of custom conditions, we pre-define a serializability condition that is a prerequisite for many practical applications of EMOF-based models. It would be possible to support unserializable models for applications that do not need to serialize models because they only process them in memory. We decided, however, to make serializability a precondition for validity so that serializability does not need to be considered when consistency is checked or enforced on valid models.

Definition 13 (Serializable Model)
Let O be a model $(O_{\mathbb{c}_1}, \ldots, O_{\mathbb{c}_{|\mathbb{C}|}}, \text{LINK}, \text{LABEL})$ that conforms to a typed metamodel $\mathbb{m} := (\mathbb{C}, \prec, \mathbb{R}, \mathbb{A}, \text{RTYPE}, \text{ATYPE})$.

The model O is serializable iff three conditions are fullfilled:
1. O has no cyclic containment links, i.e.

$$\forall\, \mathbb{c}_1, \ldots, \mathbb{c}_{n+1} \in \mathbb{C}\colon\ \forall\, o_1 \in O_{\mathbb{c}_1}, \ldots, o_{n+1} \in O_{\mathbb{c}_{n+1}}\colon$$
$$\forall\, \mathbb{r}_1 \in \mathbb{R}^{\preccurlyeq}_{\mathbb{c}_1,\blacklozenge}, \ldots, \mathbb{r}_n \in \mathbb{R}^{\preccurlyeq}_{\mathbb{c}_n,\blacklozenge}\colon$$
$$(\mathit{LINK}(o_1, \mathbb{r}_1) = o_2\ \wedge\ \ldots\ \wedge\ \mathit{LINK}(o_n, \mathbb{r}_n) = o_{n+1}) \Rightarrow o_1 \neq o_n$$

2. One object has no incoming containment link, i.e.

$$\exists_1\, \mathbb{c} \in \mathbb{C}\colon\ \exists_1\, o \in O_{\mathbb{c}}\colon$$
$$\Big|\bigcup_{\mathbb{c}_2 \in \mathbb{C}} \{(o_2, \mathbb{r}) \in O_{\mathbb{c}_2} \times \mathbb{R}^{\preccurlyeq}_{\mathbb{c}_2,\blacklozenge} \mid \mathit{LINK}(o_2, \mathbb{r}) = o\}\Big| = 0$$

3. All other objects have one incoming containment link, i.e.

$$\forall\, \mathbb{c}_1 \in \mathbb{C}\colon\ \forall\, o_1 \in O_{\mathbb{c}_1} \setminus \{o\}\colon$$
$$\Big|\bigcup_{\mathbb{c}_2 \in \mathbb{C}} \{(o_2, \mathbb{r}) \in O_{\mathbb{c}_2} \times \mathbb{R}^{\preccurlyeq}_{\mathbb{c}_2,\blacklozenge} \mid \textit{LINK}(o_2, \mathbb{r}) = o_1\}\Big| = 1$$

The objects and links of a model can be represented as the nodes and edges of a directed graph. If we only consider containment links, then the three serializability constraints ensure that serializable models can be represented as a special form of a directed acyclic graph, which is called a rooted out-tree. The first serializability constraint ensures that the containment graph has no cycles. This means an object of a model can never directly or indirectly contain itself. For this constraint, it is not necessary to directly require that $o_1, \ldots, o_{n+1}$ are pair-wise disjunct, because this is indirectly required for o_1 and o_{n+1} and for *any* n. The second constraint ensures that there is a root node with an indegree of 0. It is for the object o without an incoming containment link of the model. The last constraint ensures that all other nodes have an indegree of 1. This means all objects except o have exactly one container, i.e. an object with a containment link pointing to them. As a result, all nodes are connected to each other and for every non-root node there is exactly one path from the root node to it. This makes it possible to easily serialize and deserialize such models using the containment links.

As a last preparatory step for defining custom models conditions, we define tuples of metaclasses and tuples of objects that instantiate these metaclasses element-wise. We use these two concepts in order to define a condition in two-steps: 1. Which metaclasses have to be instantiated by objects that could fulfill the condition? 2. For which objects of these metaclasses is the condition fulfilled?

Definition 14 (Metaclass Tuple of Metamodel)
Let $\mathbb{m} := (\mathbb{C}, \prec, \mathbb{R}, \mathbb{A}, \mathbb{V})$ be a metamodel.

A tuple $(\mathbb{c}_{i_1}, \ldots, \mathbb{c}_{i_n})$ *such that* $\mathbb{c}_{i_1}, \ldots, \mathbb{c}_{i_n} \in \mathbb{C}$ *is called a metaclass tuple of* $\mathbb{m}$.

A metaclass tuple contains an arbitrary multiset of the metaclasses of a metamodel in arbitrary order. We do not use an ordered set instead of a multiset because custom conditions should be specifiable for objects that do not necessarily instantiate different metaclasses. Therefore, Definition 14 uses a sequence of indices $i_1, \ldots, i_n$, for which $i_j = i_k$ may hold for $1 \leq j, k \leq n$.

Definition 15 (Universe of a Metamodel)
Let $\mathbb{m}$ be a metamodel.

The universe of the metamodel $\mathbb{m}$ *is the infinite set of all models that instantiate* $\mathbb{m}$ *and denoted by* $\mathcal{O}_{\mathbb{m}}$. *The infinite set of all serializable models of* $\mathbb{m}$ *is called universe of serializable models of* $\mathbb{m}$ *and denoted by* $\mathcal{O}^{\star}_{\mathbb{m}} \subsetneq \mathcal{O}_{\mathbb{m}}$.

The concept of a universe of a metamodel makes subsequent definitions more compact. Such a universe contains every model that instantiates the metamodel. Every model in the universe is finite because it has a fixed number of objects with a fixed number of links and labels. The universe of the metamodel, however, is infinite because it contains every model that instantiates the metamodel and the size of a model is not limited.

Definition 16 (Instance Tuple for Metaclass Tuple)
Let O be a model that instantiates a metamodel $\mathbb{m}$ and let $\langle \mathbb{c} \rangle := (\mathbb{c}_{i_1}, \ldots, \mathbb{c}_{i_n})$ be a metaclass tuple of $\mathbb{m}$.

A tuple $\langle o \rangle := (o_{j_1}, \ldots, o_{j_n}) \in O^{\preccurlyeq}_{\mathbb{c}_{i_1}} \times \ldots \times O^{\preccurlyeq}_{\mathbb{c}_{i_n}}$ *is an instance tuple for* $\langle \mathbb{c} \rangle$ *in* O.

The set of all instance tuples for $\langle \mathbb{c} \rangle$ in O is denoted by $O_{\langle \mathbb{c} \rangle} := \{\langle o \rangle \in O^{\preccurlyeq}_{\mathbb{c}_{i_1}} \times \ldots \times O^{\preccurlyeq}_{\mathbb{c}_{i_n}}\}$.

An instance tuple of a metaclass tuple in a model is nothing else than an ordered multiset of objects of the model with the same length like the metaclass tuple and an additional constraint: Every object of the instance tuple has to directly or indirectly instantiate the metaclass at the same position in the metaclass tuple. We already mentioned for Definition 14 that metaclass tuples may list the same metaclass multiple times. Similarly, an instance tuple may list the same object multiple times. Furthermore, the same object may be listed for different metaclasses of the metaclass tuple, i.e. $o_{j_k} = o_{j_l}$ may hold for $1 \leq j_k, j_l \leq n$ even if $i_k \neq i_l$ as long as $O^{\preccurlyeq}_{\mathbb{c}_{i_k}} \ni o_{j_k} \in O^{\preccurlyeq}_{\mathbb{c}_{i_l}}$.

Definition 17 (Universe of a Metaclass Tuple)
Let $\langle \mathbb{c} \rangle := (\mathbb{c}_{i_1}, \ldots, \mathbb{c}_{i_n})$ be a metaclass tuple of a metamodel $\mathbb{m}$.

The universe of $\langle \mathbb{c} \rangle$ is the infinite set of all instance tuples for $\langle \mathbb{c} \rangle$ in all models that instantiate $\mathbb{m}$. It is defined as $\mathcal{O}_{\langle \mathbb{c} \rangle} := \bigcup_{O \in \mathcal{O}_{\mathbb{m}}} O_{\langle \mathbb{c} \rangle}$ using the universe $\mathcal{O}_{\mathbb{m}}$ of the metamodel $\mathbb{m}$.

Every instance tuple in the universe of a metaclass tuple is finite because the metaclass tuple lists a fixed number of metaclasses that have to be instantiated by the objects of every instance tuple. The universe of a metaclass tuple, however, is infinite because the universe of the metamodel, from which the instance tuples are created, is infinite.

2.3.3.2. Conditions and Validity

With the support of serializability, metaclass tuples, and instance tuples we are now able to take the next steps towards formal model consistency by defining conditions for metamodels and when they are valid in a model.

Definition 18 (Condition for a Metaclass Tuple)
Let $\langle \mathbb{c} \rangle$ be a metaclass tuple of a metamodel $\mathbb{m}$ and let $O_{\mathbb{m}}$ be the universe of $\mathbb{m}$.

A condition for $\langle \mathbb{c} \rangle$ is a unary relation COND *on the universe of $\langle \mathbb{m} \rangle$, i.e.* COND $\subseteq O_{\langle \mathbb{c} \rangle}$.

A condition is simply represented by a possibly infinite set of tuples that list objects that fulfill the condition. The metaclass tuple for which a condition is defined, indicates which metaclasses have to be instantiated by objects that can fulfill the condition. Therefore, the metaclass tuple represents a type restriction for the condition which makes it possible to directly see which objects of a model are candidates that can fulfill the condition and which are not. The possibly infinite set COND contains all instance tuples $\langle o \rangle$, which list such candidate objects, for which the condition is fulfilled. For such instance tuples $\langle o \rangle \in$ COND, we say that COND is valid for $\langle o \rangle$.

Definition 19 (Condition Valid in a Model)
Let O be a model that instantiates a metamodel $\mathbb{m}$ and let COND be a condition for a metaclass tuple $\langle \mathbb{c} \rangle$ of $\mathbb{m}$.

The condition COND *is valid in O iff the relation holds for all instance tuples of $\langle \mathbb{c} \rangle$ in O, i.e. $O_{\langle \mathbb{c} \rangle} \subseteq$* COND

The simple idea of this definition is that a condition holds for a complete model iff it holds for all possible combinations of objects in the model. More precisely, a condition for a metaclass tuple is valid in a model if it is valid for all possible instance tuples that can be created for the metaclass tuple of the condition in the model. This can also be re-formulated as a constraint for every object of the model that could be part of a combination of objects that fulfill the condition: Every combination of such candidate objects has to fulfill the condition.

With the above reformulation of the constraint for the validity of a condition in a model, we can demonstrate that it would also be possible to define a weaker notion validity for complete models. It would be possible, for example, to require for every of these candidate objects, which could be part of a fulfillment, that there is at least one combination of objects for which the condition is fulfilled. More precisely, such a weaker notion of validity would require for every object that is listed in a possible instance tuple that there is at least one instance tuple for which the condition holds. Such a weaker notion of validity for complete models would make consistency checks more complex than with the strong notion of Definition 19. For the weaker notion checks would either not be stateless or would have at least quadratic complexity, because it would be necessary to either keep track of the condition fulfilling instance tuples for every object or to always iterate over all of them.

Based on these definitions, which codify how custom conditions can be specified, we can now define how such conditions can be used. We begin with a usage that is not yet specific for consistency checks or enforcement: General conditions that always have to hold for every instance of a metamodel can be specified in order to complete the implicit constraints of the metamodel. Such additional metamodel conditions are also called invariants.

Definition 20 (Constrained Metamodel)
Let $\mathbb{m} := (\mathbb{C}, <, \mathbb{R}, \mathbb{A}, \textsc{rtype}, \textsc{atype})$ be a typed metamodel.

A constrained metamodel is a tuple $\widetilde{\mathbb{m}} := (\mathbb{C}, <, \mathbb{R}, \mathbb{A}, \textit{RTYPE}, \textit{ATYPE}, \mathbb{I})$ *where* $\mathbb{I}$ *is a set of conditions for metaclass tuples of* $\mathbb{m}$ *called invariants.*

A model conforms to $\widetilde{\mathbb{m}}$ if it conforms to $(\mathbb{C}, <, \mathbb{R}, \mathbb{A}, \textsc{rtype}, \textsc{atype})$.

Instead of extending the definition of metamodels to constrained metamodels, we could have made the set of invariants $\mathbb{I}$ directly part of the metamodel definition. This would not have changed which metamodels could be specified, because $\mathbb{I}$ can always be empty. We decided, however, not to do this in order not to distract the reader from the more central concepts, such as metaclasses.

Definition 21 (Valid Model)
Let O be a serializable model that conforms to a constrained metamodel $\mathbb{m} := (\mathbb{C}, \prec, \mathbb{R}, \mathbb{A}, \textsc{rtype}, \textsc{atype}, \mathbb{I})$.

The model O is a valid model of $\mathbb{m}$ iff all invariant conditions in $\mathbb{I}$ are valid in O.

This definition of model validity concludes our preparatory definitions for model consistency: A serializable model is valid iff all invariant conditions are valid, i.e. iff all invariants hold for all possible object combinations. As we already mentioned in the introduction of this section, we made serializability a prerequisite for validity. This relieves us from the necessity to demand respectively check serializability whenever we want to persist valid models.

The most important definitions that we presented so far are also depicted in Figure 2.4. It relates our five definitions for models to our three metamodel definitions and to attribute type systems. At the very end of this conformance hierarchy are valid models, which depend on all other definitions as they are serializable models that conform to a constrained metamodel and fulfill invariants.

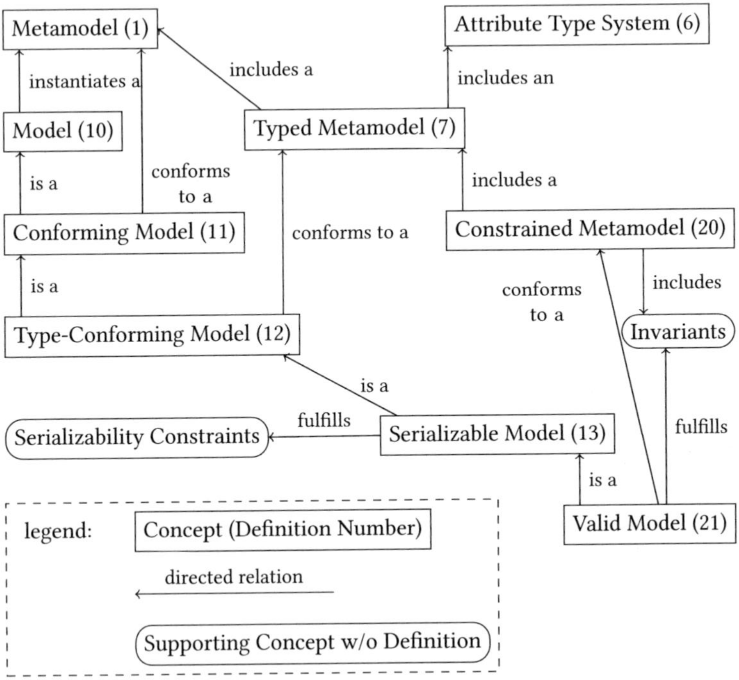

Figure 2.4.: Hierarchy of models that instantiate a metamodel, conform to a metamodel, conform to type restrictions, or fulfill additional serializability constraints and invariants

Part II.

Consistency Preservation Challenges and Formalization

3. Challenges to Consistency Preservation

Before we provide reusable solutions to some recurring challenges to change-driven consistency preservation, we present an analysis and classification of challenges. With this challenge classification we provide answers to the first part of our research question 1 and to the subquestions 1.1 and 1.2, which we presented in section 1.3.

3.1. Classification and Terminology

We briefly present how we have classified the challenges that we identified and introduce general terms that are necessary to discuss the individual challenges.

3.1.1. Classification According to Origin and Abstraction

We identified five classes of challenges to consistency based on their origin. These classes range from conceptual to implementation challenges and are sorted by the level of abstraction at which the challenges arise. We start with the class of challenges at the highest level of abstraction. It contains conceptual challenges to consistency, which stem from the relationship between modelled originals regardless of how models and consistency specifications are expressed. Our classification continues with modelling language challenges, which result from the way modelling languages are designed and realized, often without a special focus on consistency with models of other languages. Next, we discuss the most important class of consistency challenges for this thesis: *specification challenges.* These challenges

1. conceptual challenges
2. modelling language challenges
3. specification challenges
4. enforcement challenges
5. implementation challenges

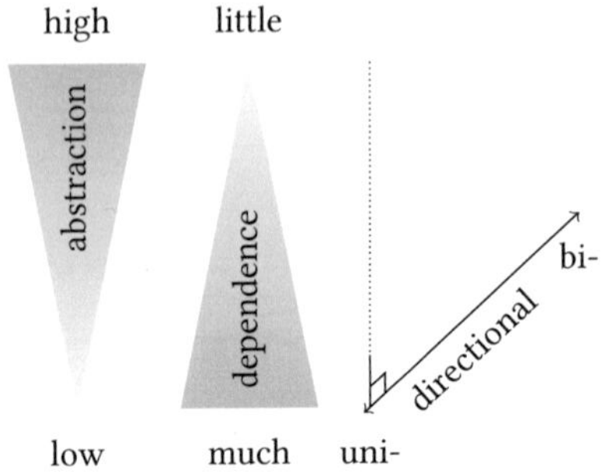

Figure 3.1.: Classes of challenges to consistency preservation with their level of abstraction, their dependence on challenges of other classes, and the orthogonal dimension of directionality

arise when consistency shall be specified for models of given languages in a way that makes it possible to check and possibly also enforce consistency but that does not fix how checking and enforcement are performed. Then, we present a separate class of Open Consistency Specification Language Challenges, which we address with the languages that we present in thesis. After this, our classification continues along the abstraction dimension with enforcement challenges, which occur if consistency according to a given specification can be achieved in different ways. The last class of challenges deals with implementation issues, which are related to technical properties of the languages and tools that are used to implement a given checking or enforcement strategy. In addition to this five classes that correspond to different levels of abstractions and the class for specification language challenges, we also discuss challenges to bidirectionality as an orthogonal dimension. The five abstraction-related classes of challenges and the orhogonal dimension of directionality are also depicted in Figure 3.1. It also illustrates how the level of abstraction decreases with every class of challenges and how the dependence on other classes increases.

Some challenges to consistency reappear in different forms at different levels of abstraction. We divide these challenges into individual challenges for each level and relate them to their counterparts on the other levels. An alternative would be to describe bigger challenges for which different aspects are discussed at different levels of abstraction. Some challenges at one level are, however, related to several challenges at other levels, which would be difficult to describe in terms of level-spanning challenges. Therefore, we take a more fine-grained approach with challenges that are always assigned to a single level of abstraction but that can be part of a bigger group of related challenges on several levels. Many challenges at the specification level, for example, can reappear at the enforcement level if they are not completely addressed in consistency specifications.

Our five challenge classes can be used for many other approaches for consistency preservation, but the exemplary challenges that we present are influenced by the perspective on consistency that we describe in this thesis and realize with our approach. More specifically, we only consider challenges to consistency between models of two languages to which a sequence of changes is performed by a single user. Challenges of circular change propagation and concurrent editing, for example, are not discussed.

3.1.2. Fundamental Terms of Consistency Preservation

We introduce some central terms in order to have the necessary vocabulary to discuss the challenges to change-driven consistency preservation that we identified. In order to keep the discussion general and as straightforward as possible, we introduce these terms only informally and refer the reader to the next chapter for a more formal and precise discussion of consistency.

The most important term for our perspective on consistency is *consistency specification*. It denotes a description of consistency for a given set of modelling languages in an arbitrary format or representation that is precise enough for unambiguous consistency checks or even enforcement. This means that for any given set of models of the concerned languages a *consistency check specification* always has to clearly specify whether the models are consistent with each other. In analogy, a *consistency enforcement specification* always has to specify what has to be done to achieve consistency. The latter of these two *types* of consistency specifications is a specialization of the first: Because an enforcement specification can always be used to check consistency, every consistency enforcement specification is also a consistency check specification. Our notion of a consistency specification implies that it can be used as the only source for checking and enforcing consistency in addition to the models to be kept consistent. We call an approach that fulfils this restriction *specification-driven*. Note that consistency specifications have to specify unambiguously *what* is consistent or *which* actions have to be performed in order achieve consistency, but *how* consistency can be checked or enforced should be left open as specifications should be more abstract than realizations of consistency mechanisms.

A property of consistency specifications that should not be confused with the role that specifications can play in consistency preservation approaches is its nature: The nature of a consistency specification can be *prescriptive* or *descriptive*. A prescriptive specification dictates consistency that did not exists without it and does not exist alongside. A descriptive specification is an additional representation of consistency that already exists. Therefore, specifications used in specification-driven approaches can be prescriptive or descriptive.

In analogy to the prescriptive and descriptive nature of consistency specifications, we call those specifications that are used to enforce consistency *executive* and those that are used to check consistency *analytic*. With these two terms we distinguish different *usages* of consistency specifications that is not bound to their type: Even a consistency check specification can not only be used in an analytic way but also in an executive way. Examples for this are approaches that check consistency for many candidate models, which are exhaustively derived by manipulating initial models.

Consistency specifications describe a single *consistency relationship* that can be present between models of two modelling languages by defining several *consistency relations* between elements of these two languages. They relate language elements by implicitly or explicitly specifying the *conditions* that have to hold if instances of these elements shall be considered consistent. When consistency is checked on concrete models according to a specification, it is analyzed whether the consistency relations that are defined for the language elements are *realized* by instances of these language elements according to the conditions. For consistency it is not necessary that all possible combinations of language element instances for every relation realize the relation by fulfilling the conditions. A specification can require that consistency relations only have to be realized for a subset of combinations by specifying appropriate restrictions.

To denote consistency not only for complete models but also for their elements, we introduce a *correspondence* relation between them. A set of elements of models of one modelling language *corresponds* to another set of elements of models of another modelling language with respect to a relation of a consistency specification for these languages if the relation is specified for the instantiated language elements and if all conditions of it are fulfilled. If several relations are defined for the same combination of language elements, then it is also possible that two sets of model elements correspond to each other with respect to more than one of these relations. In other words: several consistency relations can be realized by the same sets of model elements. It is important that correspondence is only determined by those relations of a consistency specification that are defined exactly for the combination of language elements that are instantiated. As a result, only those sets of model elements for which consistency is explicitly specified can correspond to each other. This is different from the notion of *consistency for elements* with respect to a consistency specification: Combinations of two sets of model elements for which no conditions are specified cannot be *inconsistent* because specification conditions that do not exist can also not be violated. Therefore, such sets of model elements are always *consistent* but do not correspond to each other.

To increase the readability, we often do not write about a modelling language of a consistency specification or about a set of model elements of this language but simply call such a language or such a set a *side*. Unless stated otherwise, we always discuss consistency for both sides in a *symmetric* way where both sides are equally treated. Nevertheless, we use the terms *left side* and *right side* in order to be able to refer to them with distinct names even if the assignment could be initially swapped.

To handle consistency for models that are changed we introduce the notions of model *state* and change *operations*. A model that is changed is going from one state to another as an effect of the change operations that are applied to it. If an approach for consistency preservation requires several model states as input it is called *state-based*. If it requires a description of the performed change operations it is called *operation-based*. We distinguish between two types of change operations: *user change operations* are performed by individuals and may lead to *enforcement change operations*, which are performed in order to preserve consistency.

For the act of performing change operations to enforce consistency after user change operations, we use the term *consistency preservation*. Such enforcement operations can also be performed if a user change did not yet violate the consistency relationship between models, e.g. in order to prevent future inconsistencies. Therefore, we use the term consistency preservation instead of consistency restoration, which implies that consistency is only restored after it was destroyed. We consider this implication more misleading than the fact that we use the term preservation even if consistency does not need to be preserved at all times because there may be cases in which temporal inconsistencies occur for a short period of time.

3.2. Conceptual Challenges

Our first class of challenges to consistency contains challenges that arise on the highest level of abstraction. These challenges directly result from the properties of modelled originals and the relations between them. Whether they arise and how they can be addressed is not influenced by the way these originals are represented using a modelling language. Therefore, understanding the reasons for these challenges and developing potential solutions can be beneficial for a variety of systems in which these elements are modelled and processed.

3.2.1. Diverse Consistency

For many pairs of modelling languages, there is not a single notion of consistency but diverse possibilities how models can be related in a way that can be deemed consistent. This freedom to choose and define consistency for two modelling languages can be challenging already on a conceptual level regardless of issues, for example, on the specification or enforcement level.

If two modelling languages describe properties of modelled originals in a way that allows different co-occurrences that are deemed consistent, then they do not induce a canonical notion of consistency. In such cases, the decision to restrict the notion of consistency to one or several possibilities and certain conditions can have a strong impact. Therefore, the freedom to define consistency for two modelling languages can be indirectly restricted in several ways.

For example, the way the modelling languages are used to develop systems in certain project contexts can influence our definition of consistency. Furthermore, the benefits of consistency preservation for the models of these languages—may it be automated or not—can vary with the chosen notion of consistency. In addition, the way consistency diversity is approached can influence whether and how it is possible to specify, check, or enforce consistency.

3.2.2. Tolerating Inconsistency and Wanted Inconsistency

Consistency that can be described for models of a set of modelling languages does not always need to be enforced immediately or at all. In some cases, it can be desired to tolerate inconsistencies, for example, as long as they are restricted to certain model elements, certain model regions, or certain intermediate model states. But, there are also cases in which consistency should never be enforced. Inconsistencies are generally tolerated, for example, in cases where inconsistencies were deliberately introduced and these decisions shall be documented. This can be necessary if violations of consistency specifications are not only allowed but also have an impact on system development or if uncertainty cannot be expressed in a consistent way.

Conditionally or generally tolerated inconsistencies are not only a question of consistency enforcement, but have conceptual implications. On the one hand, tolerated inconsistencies make it possible to apply strategies that cannot be used if consistency always has to be achieved. Examples are postponed or delegated consistency checks and enforcements. On the other hand, tolerated inconsistencies can also impede consistency preservation: If some consistency conditions are not strict because their violation is tolerated, then the checks and enforcement of all other conditions also have to deal with these tolerated inconsistencies. We cannot profit from tolerated inconsistencies if checks and enforcement for a consistency condition assume that all other conditions hold. Therefore, it has to be explicitly specified for which conditions inconsistencies can be tolerated and whether preconditions can deal with that. Such precautions have to be taken when inconsistencies are tolerated in order not to turn analyses useless due to the general rule in classical logic that anything can be deduced from contradictions.

In some cases, inconsistencies only need to be tolerated if changes are performed on a specific side, but not if the corresponding elements are changed on the other side. One possibility to address such a requirement without tolerating inconsistencies would be to only allow changes on the other side. The classical relation between code on the one side and tests or contracts on the other side is an example for such a requirement for tolerating inconsistencies or no changes: Let us consider a change to a test that makes the code inconsistent with it, e.g. because a new method signature is prescribed by the test. A strategy could be to repair consistency by adapting the method signature in the code accordingly. If an analog change is performed in the code, e.g. a method signature is modified, it could be erroneous to adapt the tests if they fix the signatures that have to be provided. In such a case, one could tolerate the inconsistency until somebody revokes the change or modifies the contractually specified tests. Or, one could simply decide that method signatures are prescribed by the tests and therefore can only be changed in the tests. If all signature changes are propagated to the code, this would not reduce the power of developers but would prescribe for some changes where they have to be performed.

The idea of "tolerating inconsistency" has been prominently discussed in an article by Balzer [Bal91]. He has introduced an approach for inconsistency resolution by marking tolerated inconsistencies and storing the values leading to them. The principle of explosion, which states that anything can be followed from contradictions, has also been used to motivate an article by Finkelstein et al. [Fin+94]. They have presented an approach in which inconsistencies in databases are not repaired but it is specified with an "action-based meta-language based on linear-time temporal logic" [Fin+94, p. 574] how to act depending on the context. Two reasons that are similar to the reasons for generally tolerated inconsistencies that we mentioned in the first paragraph of this section, have been discussed in an article by Nuseibeh et al. [NER01]: They have stated that "inconsistency may indicate deviations from a process model" and that "inconsistency can be used to identify areas of uncertainty" Nuseibeh et al. [NER01, p. 173]. Furthermore, they have presented a general framework for managing inconsistency based on a loop with four steps of monitoring, diagnosing, and handling inconsistencies as well as monitoring the consequences of this handling.

3.2.3. Evolving Consistency

What is deemed consistent for a given pair of modelling languages is not always fixed for all times, but can evolve on its own, and may need to be adapted to evolving modelling languages. This evolution of consistency specifications and modelling languages is not only difficult to realize in practice, but can already be conceptually challenging.

We can decide, for example, to follow a backward compatible way of consistency preservation. Then, we have to allow the coexistence of model elements that were consistent according to an old specification, and of elements that are consistent according to a new specification. On the one hand, this relieves us from solving problems like the migration of old consistent models. On the other hand, it forces us to be explicit with regards to preconditions and dependencies, if we do not separate the elements that are consistent according to the old specification from the remaining model elements.

If a modelling language evolves, this always has technical implications for the coevolution of model of the language, but it can also influence consistency with models of another modelling language in a conceptual way. Concepts or properties that are also represented in the other language may be introduced, modified, or removed so that consistency can newly, differently, or no longer be checked or enforced. Therefore, all challenges that can occur initially may reappear when one of the modelling languages evolves. But, such an evolution can also pose new challenges that do not need to be addressed, if modelling languages are fixed. An example is the challenge to reuse or even adapt parts of a consistency specification for an old version of a modelling language in order to obtain a specification for a new version. Another example is the challenge to ensure backward compatibility. For this compatibility, everything that can still be expressed with a new language version and that was consistent according to the specification for an old language version is of interest. Such models should still be consistent according to the specification for the new language version.

3.2.4. Totality of Consistency

In the context of consistency for models of two modelling languages the notion of totality can be discussed in three ways:

Totality of the relationship for the consistency relationship between models as defined by a complete specification,

Totality of relations for individual consistency relations specified on the language level, and

Totality of correspondences for the correspondence relations that realize them for model elements on the instance level.

There may be other names for it, but this question whether there is a consistent counterpart for every model, for every possible set of elements of a relation, or for every concrete element has strong implications.

The consistency relationship between models, which is defined by a consistency specification, is left-total respectively right-total, iff there is a consistent counterpart for every possible left model respectively right model. If a relationship is not left-total, for example, then there are changes that can be performed on a left model so that no consistent right model exists. In such a case, it can be interesting to investigate whether and how it is possible to avoid such dead ends if reverting changes on the left side is not an accepted or desired option. One possibility for this is to analyze which changes lead to a dead end and to disallow these exact changes on specific elements or even complete change types for all elements. For this, a specification that allows such analyses is needed.

A consistency relation for two sets of language elements of the two languages of its consistency specification is left-total respectively right-total, iff it relates every possible set of instances of the left respectively right set of language elements for which its conditions hold to a set of instances of the other set of language elements. If a consistency relation is left-total, for example, then it is sufficient to check its conditions for the elements on the left side to know whether it can be enforced by only modifying elements on the right side. This can be important, for example, if consistency shall only be enforced on the unchanged side, e.g. in order to avoid unexpected overrides of user changes.

The correspondence relations for the consistency relations of a consistency specification for two languages are left-total respectively right-total, iff every possible model element of the left respectively right language corresponds to at least one element of the other side. Therefore, left-total respectively right-total correspondence relations of a consistency specification indicate that no element on the left respectively right side can be modified independent of the other side. A consistency specification between a language and a superset language, for example, should always have left-total correspondence relations to preserve consistency according to the superset relation between the languages.

3.2.5. Dependencies between Consistency Relations

It is often not only the case that the elements and conditions of several consistency relations of a consistency specification are related to each other, but that they depend on each other. More specifically, a consistency relation depends on another consistency relation if at least one of the conditions of the first relation can only hold for elements that are related to consistent elements using the other relation. No matter if such a dependency is made explicit in the specification or not, it has an effect on how consistency can be checked and enforced.

On the one hand, dependencies between consistency relations can be exploited to improve the structure and execution of consistency enforcement and checking code. On the other hand, such dependencies can make it more complex to understand or process consistency specifications and can cause problems. Mutual exclusions or cyclic dependencies, for example, can result in specifications that cannot be enforced. Therefore, automated dependency analyses can be necessary to detect and avoid such cases.

In order to work with dependencies between consistency relations, it is often beneficial to identify sets of relations that have dependencies within a set but no dependencies to relations outside the set. One possibility is to search for sets of relations that are minimal in the sense that every subset has at least one relation that depends on a relation that is not in the set. This notion of minimalism can, however, only provide a lower bound for sets of relations that should be specified and processed together because it relies on our strict notion of dependency: If some language elements, for example, are affected by two relations but the satisfaction of the conditions of one of them is not always a prerequisite for the satisfaction of a condition of the other, it can be very beneficial to treat them together even if they have no formal dependency.

3.2.6. Identification of Elements

A crucial requirement for consistency preservation is the possibility to identify model elements. It is a prerequisite for determining and modifying corresponding elements in order to preserve consistency. If elements cannot always be identified, then it is possible, for example, that a change operation on a model element leads to an enforcement operation that is performed on a wrong element with the same identifier.

Identifiers can only be used to check and enforce consistency according to a specification, if the element identification complies with the consistency conditions of it. Let us consider, for example, two elements that have the same identifier and appear in one model of a certain metamodel. For another model of another metamodel, it has to make no difference in terms of consistency to which of the two elements a consistency is established. More specifically, specification compliance means that two elements on one model side that have the same identifier do not need to have identical properties but every condition of every consistency relation that is fulfilled by one of the elements also has to be fulfilled by the other and vice-versa. As a result of the consistency compliance requirement, it is possible that the identification of elements of a single modelling language has to be performed differently for two specifications that define consistency to elements of two different modelling languages.

Because user change and enforcement operations can always change properties that are not used for identification, it is necessary that the element identification used for consistency preservation is robust with respect to such contextual changes. More precisely, contextual robustness means that every change or enforcement operation that results in a change from an old to a new identifier for a model element, for example, has to result in the same identifier change, if it is performed on an arbitrary element with the same identifier regardless of the context, i.e. properties that did not cause an initially different identifier.

For practical consistency preservation, all identifiers of model elements for consistency preservation have to be temporally unique for any given model state but not globally unique across all possible model states. That is, if two elements of a model state share the same consistency identifier, they can be treated as equivalent during consistency checking and preservation. The temporal relaxation of uniqueness concerns individual identifiers and the set of all identifiers in two ways: An identifier for an individual element can change during the lifetime of an element, and an individual identifier may identify different elements throughout different model states.

The identification of model elements for consistency preservation can also be challenging, because the identifier of a single element may not only depend on the properties of this element but also on properties of other elements. In such cases, user change and enforcement operations on a single model element may lead to new identifiers for several dependent elements. Because of such identifier dependencies and the consistency compliance of identifiers as discussed above, a single change can lead to many enforcement operations. One reason, why this can be challenging, is that users may not always anticipate such series of reactions. Another reason is that the management of correspondence relations has to rely on identifiers and has to process such series.

3.2.7. Information for Determining Corresponding Elements

The identification of a model element is only the first step for determining which elements correspond to it according to the consistency relations defined in a consistency specification. First, we have to know whether we have enough information to determine corresponding elements. If this is not the case, we have to know how we can obtain the necessary information or how we can deal with its lack.

If information that is required for determining corresponding elements is not directly available in a model, then we have to derive it from the available information or have to obtain it from additional sources. Both possibilities to obtain the required information have implications on further consistency preservation. If the information that is required for determining or enforcing correspondences can be derived from available information, then we either have to recompute these derivations if the input changed or we also have to preserve the consistency of the derivation results. The same applies to information from additional sources: If such information is necessary for consistency preservation, then it also has to be kept consistent just as models have to be kept consistent.

In case the information required for determining corresponding elements cannot be derived from available information nor be obtained from additional sources, it is possible to acquire it from the user or to suppose default values for it. Asking the user to provide such information has the advantage that we may obtain more suitable information for specific cases. This is more difficult to achieve with fixed or dynamically computed default values, but it has the advantage that no interaction with the user is required, which may disturb the workflow or not be available after a change.

If the information required for determining and preserving correspondences cannot be derived, obtained, acquired, nor supposed, the only remaining option is to postpone consistency preservation until the information is available. The difficulty with this is that the correct point in time at which the information is available or can be obtained has to be detected. Furthermore, there may be abortion criteria, which specify under which conditions consistency cannot be enforced anymore so that postponing is no longer possible.

3.3. Modelling Language Challenges

The challenges to consistency of the second class, which we present in this section, arise at the second but highest level of abstraction, which is the level of modelling languages. These challenges directly result from the way modelled originals and the relations between them can be represented using a given modelling language. How a modelling language is used and defined in terms of abstract syntax can have many implications on how consistency to another modelling language can be checked or enforced. If it is possible to shape a modelling language according to consistency preservation needs, it can be beneficial to directly address the following challenges during this language definition process so that some consistency challenges on lower levels of abstractions are less likely to occur. But, often it is necessary to preserve consistency for models of given modelling languages which cannot be changed. In such cases, the challenges presented in this section may only be addressed during consistency specification, enforcement, or implementation.

3.3.1. Consistency-Enabling Abstraction

Modelling languages for which models shall be kept consistent with models of other languages, have to provide abstractions that are detailed enough with respect to the abstractions of the other languages. Different modelling languages are often designed for models that are used for different tasks (see also pragmatics in subsection 2.1.1). To support these tasks only with the required information, the languages can use different levels of abstraction. If the languages are used in combination and consistency between its models shall be enforced automatically, it is often necessary to overcome such abstraction differences.

If a modelling language abstracts away from details that are necessary for consistency preservation, these details can either be obtained from other models, from additional sources or the user. The first case refines the conceptual challenge of the previous section subsection 3.2.7 which does not take into account which modelling language is used for the model that provides the required information. If the necessary details are available in models of another modelling language, these models can be used to implicitly or explicitly augment the models that abstracted away from the details. In case of an *implicit augmentation* the model that abstracts away from the necessary details is left unchanged and the details are always retrieved from the models of the other languages. To ease this retrieval references from the elements missing the details to the elements providing it are often stored in so called *witness structures*. An *explicit augmentation* adds the necessary details to the models requiring them, so that they can be directly used without following any references etc. As we already discussed above for conceptually determining correspondences using explicitly added additional information, such solutions have the disadvantage that the information that is added has to be kept consistent afterwards.

3.3.2. Different Roles for Models

Whether models have a prescriptive or descriptive nature (see also page 58) and which role they play during system development is often already given by the modelling language and it has an influence on consistency preservation. The role played by a model can, for example, be described with a level of *rigidity*. Models can be used in a rigid way, e.g. in automated processes or with a catalogue of manually performed but inevitable consequences, or in a flexible way where they are rather guidelines than rules. Furthermore, models can have different *origins* as they can be automatically derived from existing development artifacts or manually created by developers. Models from both origins can have faults depending on the regulation of the automated or manual derivation or creation process.

The nature, rigidity, and origin of models can influence consistency preservation, especially in terms of *precedence*. For the enforcement of consistency it can be beneficial if the used modelling languages lead to models that play complementary roles. Prescriptive models and models that are automatically implemented in a rigid way, e.g. using code generation or model execution techniques, may, for example, take precedence over descriptive models or over models that are manually created to express additional but uncertain information on a best-effort basis. Incompatible roles can, however, hinder consistency enforcement. Consider, for example, a descriptive model that is automatically derived and a prescriptive model that is manually created and rigidly used to generate code. If these models are inconsistent, it can be argued that the descriptive model takes precedence because the derivation process is assumed to be correct. But it can also be argued that the prescriptive model should take precedence because the intent of the developer should be preserved and it is assumed that no unintentional changes are performed.

3.3.3. Different Usage of Types and Identity

If different notions of types and identity are used in two modelling languages for which models should be kept consistent, these differences have to be taken into account during consistency preservation. Elements or values that are considered fixed or identifying on the type level in one language, may be considered flexible or common in the other language. In such cases, consistency preservation also has to preserve these notions and has to translate flexible instances to the corresponding types. This can be especially challenging, if both modelling languages do not fix the possible set of types on the language level but postpone this to the instance level. These belatedly defined types can be explicitly provided using hard-wired particular models that contain these types or implicitly during their usage as a matter of modelling conventions. Some modelling languages, such as the Unified Modeling Language (UML) [ISO12a; ISO12b], even provide distinct language constructs to support types on the instance level, e.g. stereotypes or powertypes.

An example for different notions of types is the combination of a modelling language that has a fixed set of possible enumeration literals to represent a certain property of an original with another modelling language that uses a metaclass with an unlimited number of different instances with an own identity to represent the same property. Preserving consistency is straightforward if only the first modelling language is used to model this property, because a unique instance of the metaclass of the second language can be automatically created for every enumeration literal. But, if new instances of the metaclass of the second language are manually created by developers, then we may have to map several such instances of the second language to a single literal of the first language and the correct instance has to be chosen when a literal is used in the first language.

A similar problem occurs, if one modelling language uses a certain property value to uniquely identify instances that represent an original but another modelling language represents the same original using instances that have no identity so that the same property value can be used several times. The challenge is to establish a notion of identity for the combination of both languages, which may identify instances based on the combination of their properties in both languages. This also means that it is not always possible to determine the identity of elements by only taking one of both languages into account, which can be difficult for developers that only work on models of one of the languages.

3.3.4. Other Representation Variations

Modelling languages can use many different ways that influence consistency preservation to represent further properties of modelled originals in addition to types and identity. Such variations can either differ only in syntactic terms with restricted consequences for consistency preservation, or they also represent semantic differences, which can be more difficult for consistency preservation. Whether modelling language variations have semantic consequences is not directly determined by the variations itself, but it depends on the usage of the language and the semantics of it.

A variation that may have semantic consequences is, for example, the representation of several simple-typed attributes or references to model elements as an unordered collection or as an ordered list. If one modelling language has an unordered collection and the other has not, consistency preservation has to take the consequences of a change in order into account. In models of the first language, different orders of such a collection make no difference or cannot even be represented. But the order of a corresponding collection in a model of the second language may be interpreted by automated processes or developers. Therefore, consistency preservation has to ensure that the correct order in the model of the second language is used when changes are applied to models of the first language.

Another possibility for variation that may have semantic consequences for consistency preservation is whether a property of a modelled original is represented using a single model element respectively attribute or several elements and attributes. Such variations can be challenging during consistency preservation in terms of atomicity. If a single element or attribute in a model of one language is kept consistent with several elements or attributes in a model of another language, then changes to some but not all elements of the second model can be difficult to propagate to the single element of the first model.

Purely syntactic variations in modelling languages present no challenges to consistency preservation semantics but have to be addressed nevertheless. Type-safe enumerations in one modelling language, for example, may have to be kept consistent with attributes of model elements of another language that are not statically checked. In such a case, attribute values that cannot be translated to one of the fixed enumeration literals have to be avoided in models of the second language. Other syntactic variations can, for example, occur if the navigability or opposition of references to other model elements is handled differently. Limitations of navigability for references in one modelling language can be technically overcome if consistency preservation with models of another modelling language cannot be achieved without it. If model elements of one language always have a reference to another element that references it but the corresponding elements of another language only exhibit one of these opposite references or both but without such a constraint, then consistency preservation has to ensure that references changes in models of the second language can be correctly propagate to both references of the first modelling language.

3.4. Specification Challenges

This section presents the third class of challenges to consistency after conceptual and modelling language challenges. It contains challenges that may occur when consistency for two fixed languages is specified so that consistency can later be checked or enforced according to this specification. These challenges are still independent of the mechanisms that are used to check or enforce consistency.

3.4.1. Unspecifiable Consistency

Not all consistency relations that should exist between models of different languages can be specified in such a way that it can be unambiguously decided for any given input models whether they are consistent or how consistency can be achieved. For such ambiguous cases, an imprecise consistency description can be provided in addition to a specification for the unambiguous cases. Such a description can be used as a guideline even if it is too ambiguous to serve as a specification for these cases. Whether and how such cases occur can depend on the involved modelling languages and on the language for specifying consistency.

Two types of unspecifiable consistency relations can be distinguished based on the expressivity of the specification language. First, consistency relations that cannot be expressed unambiguously with any specification language because the ambiguity is induced by the relation itself. Second, consistency relations that cannot be expressed unambiguously with a given specification language but with another one. Such cases only have an influence on consistency, if the specification language cannot be extended or replaced. In practice both types of unspecifiable consistency relations are likely to be ignored: If it cannot be specified whether models have this relation or how they should obtain it, then it is hard to imagine that parts of the developed system or of development process are influenced by it.

3.4.2. Complex Consistency Relations

A major challenge for specifying consistency is the complexity of the consistency relations that shall be checked or enforced. These relations do not always directly map identical information, but may involve complex conditional computations and conversions. On the one hand, such complex consistency relations have to be described in a way that is precise enough to serve as specification for all possible cases. On the other hand, specifications only serve their purpose, if they are easy to write and understand and do not describe more than is needed. Furthermore, the efforts for both specifying and checking or enforcing consistency should be kept minimal. For simple consistency relations, there are not many different ways of specifying and checking or enforcing them. Complex relations, however, can be specified in various ways and the conflicting goals discussed above make it difficult to decide on it.

Let us consider, for example, a consistency relation for two model elements of two modelling languages that represent information in different formats. There are several possibilities for specifying the conversion of the representation formats and the conditions for the overall relation and specific conversion steps. Different cases, for example, can be integrated into a single conversion description with conditional computations, subroutines and intermediate results. This could reduce the specification effort and later maintenance because no statements have to be unnecessarily repeated. Checking and enforcing such a specification could, however, be more complicated regardless of the degree of automation. An alternative would be to specify independent and complete conversions for each case. This could make it easier to understand and execute the specification, but it could increase the efforts for maintaining the consistency specification.

3.4.3. Consistency for a Flexible Number of Elements

Specifying consistency for a set of elements with a size that may vary from case to case is challenging. One reason is, for example, that the number of model elements and the number of references between them may vary independently. Therefore, such consistency specifications have to define precisely which model parts that are involved in a consistency relation may have a flexible size and which parts have to be of a fixed size. In this context, references between flexible and fixed parts are especially challenging, for example, because cardinality constraints of a reference from a fixed element to flexible elements may indirectly restrict the possible number of flexible elements.

Flexible numbers of elements are also addressed by different graph transformation approaches. For example, using a collection operator for Triple Graph Grammars (TGGs) [GKM11, pp.123f]. This operator matches an arbitrary number of subgraphs that fulfill optionally specified cardinality constraints on the left side of a graph rule. The changes that are specified by the right side of the rule are applied to every subgraph that was matched by the collection operator based on shared identifiers. Another approach for dealing with flexible numbers of elements is multi-amalgamation [Leb+15, pp.92ff]. So-called multi-rules are applied to a kernel rule in a way that depends on the number of matches for the multi-rules. This makes it possible to define multi-amalgamated rules for which the number of involved elements is determined at transformation time.

3.4.4. Consistency for Specific Instances

Consistency relations are usually specified on the language or type level, but there may be cases in which specific element instances should be considered. A specification for a consistency relation on the language level defined conditions for consistency in terms of properties that are defined for model elements of a certain type. This means, such relations hold whenever the conditions are satisfied by those elements and different elements with the same values for the relevant properties are treated identically. There are, however, two cases in which such pre-defined consistency relations based on element types may not be sufficient.

In the first case, the properties defined for elements of a certain type do not allow a precise identification of the right element instances for consistency preservation. More specifically, these properties defined in one language are not sufficient to always select those element instances of the first language that shall correspond to element instances of another language, which may have more information. This means more information is necessary to automatically distinguishing these element instances of the first language. If this information cannot be retrieved from other models or be derived and added to the models, a possible solution is to ask the user to perform the distinction.

In the second case, it cannot be fixed upfront which property values shall be kept consistent in which way. This means the problem in this case is not a limited amount of information available in the models, but a limited amount of information available in the consistency specification. Therefore, the only way to address this lack of specification information is to let the user chose specific element instances at runtime. It is not guaranteed that the information available at runtime while be sufficient to choose the right instances, but it is strictly more information than at compile time.

3.4.5. Abstract Consistency Specifications

Consistency specifications should abstract away from model details that are not needed to check or possibly enforce consistency (see OCSLC 3 in section 1.2). If specifications contain such unnecessary details, they may be less concise and more difficult to understand, execute, and maintain than needed. Therefore, specifications should only mention those attributes of model elements for which different values may have a different impact on consistency preservation. Similarly, only references to elements that are relevant for a consistency relation should be mentioned. This is, however, especially challenging because there can be transitive relations that involve intermediate elements that are not relevant. In such a case, the fact that there is a sequence of references and intermediate elements that links two elements is relevant. All properties of the intermediate elements are, however, irrelevant, except for the references forming the transitive relation. This demonstrates that partial abstractions may be helpful for consistency specifications, but can be difficult to define.

Abstract consistency specifications may choose different ways to deal with the information that is abstracted away. One possibility is to specify abstract patterns of relevant elements and implicitly match them to complete models. With this approach, everything that is not specified in a pattern can be present in different ways or not. Therefore, we call this pattern-based approach *open-world abstraction.* An example is the star operator for TGGs [Lin+07, pp.3f], which is analog to the star operator in Kleene algebra [Koz94, pp.369f]. This operator finds an arbitrary number of matches of a subpattern between two other subpatterns that are isomorph to each other.

Another possibility to achieve abstract consistency specifications is to define abstract queries and explicitly match requested elements. In this case, everything that is not specified in a query cannot be present and we call this *closed-world abstraction.* The advantage of this approach, is that unintentional implicit matchings can be excluded and that the matching process can be influenced. A prominent example for this is the query-based model transformation framework Viatra [Ber+11], which also uses patterns. It also demonstrates that both abstraction possibilities, patterns and queries, can be combined. Implicit abstraction and explicit matching instructions as well as no or full control over the matching process are just the ends of a continuous range of abstraction possibilities.

3.4.6. Redundancy in Specifications

The amount of redundant information in consistency specifications—and in any other development artifact—should be minimized in order to reduce the efforts necessary for evolving and maintaining them. This is especially challenging because two characteristics of consistency preservation between models of two languages are inherently prone to redundancies: the commonalities of *checking or enforcing* consistency and the symmetry of preserving consistency after changes in *forward or backward* direction.

Every consistency enforcement specification can also be used to check consistency. Consistency check specifications, however, usually do not define what has to be changed, if a check is not successful (see also page 57). This one-way dependency means that enforcement could theoretically be specified by referring to a check specification and providing only redundancy-free enforcement details that are not necessary for checks. In practice, this is not always the case. Those parts of a consistency specification that describe enforcements, can repeat information that is already given in parts that define consistency checks. A specification may, for example, define how a value for a property that is declared for an abstract metaclass should be checked and may repeat this value in another part that specifies how consistency is enforced for concrete subclasses of this metaclass. This redundancy could be avoided if the enforcement specification only added details for the subclasses and referred to the check for the value of the superclass as it also implies that this value should be set during enforcement.

The symmetry of enforcing consistency in forward or backward direction is the second consistency characteristic that is prone to redundancy. In this context, we use the term *forward direction* for enforcement change operations that are performed on the right side in reaction to user change operations on the left side. Likewise, the term *backward direction* is used for changes on the left side in reaction to changes on the right side. These directions are never completely isolated. More specifically, there is always a reaction to a previous reaction to an initial change that has something to do with the initial change. Therefore, redundancy cannot be avoided if both directions are specified separately. Even if both directions are specified at once, it is challenging to find redundancy-free definitions for all possible consistency relations.

3.4.7. Reuse in Specifications

The reuse of complete specifications and parts of it is a challenge that is closely related to redundancy in specifications and also the Open Consistency Specification Language Challenge 1 (see section 1.2). Redundant parts in consistency specifications that are hard or impossible to avoid are often due to the consistency relations itself and not due to specification deficits. In these cases, a major challenge is to find ways to explicitly reuse parts of specifications instead of repeating them. Such reuse mechanisms are mainly constrained by two factors: the support of variability and the relation between initial efforts for introducing reusability and eliminated efforts for maintaining redundant parts.

If specification parts that are not identical but structurally similar should be expressed together for reuse, then variations between these parts have to be expressible using a reuse mechanism. For this, points of variability have to be defined in the reused specification parts and bindings for these points have to be specified where they are reused. These definitions and usages of variation possibilities should be described in a way that renders reusable specifications more beneficial than alternatives with redundant parts. If consistency specifications with reusable instead of redundant parts are not easier to use or maintain, the reuse mechanisms should be put into question. Even more, the benefits for the maintenance of reusable specifications should not be eliminated by the initial effort to write a specification with reusable parts.

3.4.8. Scope of Consistency Relations

Implicit and explicit restrictions on the sets of used modelling language elements and property values are challenges for specifying consistency. Such restrictions limit the scope of consistency relations, which is not always bad but often just necessary. If the scope of a consistency relation is, however, unintentionally to narrow or to wide, this may impede the reuse for several development projects or for specifications of consistency with other modelling languages.

Consistency specifications can implicitly inherit the limited scope defined by the development context and may implicitly further restrict it. In many software development projects only some of the elements types and relations that are defined by a modelling language are used in model instances. Large and standardized modelling languages can, for example, be a reason for this. If consistency between two modelling languages is specified for such a project, it may be implicitly assumed that only certain element types and relations are used. The specification may implicitly inherit the limited scope and may impose further restrictions, for example, by not mentioning irrelevant subclasses etc. Such a specification should not be used outside its scope for models with instances of excluded element types to avoid unexpected results.

It is difficult to build mechanisms for defining explicit scope limitations that do not only restrict relations but that can also be enforced to move elements into the scope. Individual consistency relations often need to be restricted to certain parts of modelling languages or to elements fulfilling special conditions. There are many different ways to directly or indirectly express such restrictions, which have an influence on how easy the resulting scope limitation can be determined. For consistency enforcement specifications it is, however, especially challenging to provide facilities for specifying limitations that can also be enforced. A consistency relation may, for example, take the form that only those elements that do *not* have a certain value correspond to other elements with a certain value. The value of one of the later elements can be changed so that it should no longer correspond to one of the former elements. It is clear that these two elements are no longer in the scope, but it is unclear how the value of the former element should be changed. The scope limitation that this element should *not* have a certain value is not sufficiently described to be enforced.

3.4.9. Referring to Changes and States

If a specification is used to check or enforce consistency after a change, it can be beneficial to have the possibility to refer to the change or to the state of models before or after the change. In this context it can be challenging to decide which information about a change should be accessible in which way and which model information shall be provided for which state. These decisions can influence the way specifications are written and how they are checked and enforced.

The possibility to refer to changes in consistency specifications is not always needed, but if it is provided for change-driven specifications, then its representation and the access to it influences specifications. Change representations can, for example, be designed in a way that emphasizes the uniformity of different change types by providing similar types of information in the same way. Explicitly changing a value to an identity element, such as the empty string, can be represented in the same way like the removal of a value in order to ease a uniform treatment of these two cases. But it can also be a goal to allow as much differentiation between different change types and contexts as possible by distinguishing even very similar changes. The explicit removal of a model element together with its only incoming reference, for example, can be represented in a different way than the removal of a last reference to such an element, if both changes require different consistency checks or enforcements although they can have the same initial effect. The representation of model changes is also important for composite changes that can be presented as a composition of atomic changes.

If a specification is used to check or enforce consistency after a change, it is possible to provide access to model information from the old state before the change happened and from the new state after it happened. As long as complete information about a change and about one of the two states is provided, it is theoretically possible to derive all information about the other state. But in practice information about one state may be more appropriate for specifying consistency than the other. If a new state can be reached from several old states using the same change—or the other way round—, then consistency specifications can be more complex or less precise than needed if the wrong state is provided.

Together, a change and one or both model states can be used for change-driven consistency specifications and complement each other. Information that is needed for specifying consistency but not available from a change representation has to be obtained from a model state and the other way round. If the old state is provided together with a description of a change that can be executed on this old state, this is usually called a *forward change description*. In analogy, the combination of the new state and a change description that can be executed on it is usually called a *backward change description*. If both states are provided together with a change description that can be executed on both states, we call this a *bothward change description*.

3.5. Specification Language Challenges

In this section, we do *not* present challenges at another level of abstraction. Instead, we introduce four special challenges of consistency specification *languages*. This means, that these challenges can occur when consistency is specified—like the challenges of the previous section—but instead of being readdressed for every individual specification, they should be addressed by languages for consistency specifications. Furthermore, these challenges are not yet sufficiently addressed in current specification languages. Therefore, they are central to this thesis and we name them *Open* Consistency Specification Language Challenges (OCSLCs). These challenges are the basis for the research subquestions of research question 2, which we have presented in subsection 1.3.2. The goal of each of these subquestions is to explore how the following open challenges can be addresses by new specification languages, which we will present in chapter 6–8.

The four OCSLCs that we identified are:

1. *Specificity Limits Expressive Power*: Current consistency specificaton languages hardly combine specific support for consistency preservation with full expressive power. Instead, developers often have to decide whether the cases supported by dedicated languages for consistency specifications are sufficient for their needs or whether they have to use a general-purpose language to express their needs with unlimited expressive power. That is, more specific support for important or frequently occurring cases is often traded against limitations in terms of expressive power. As a result, developers are either restricted to certain use cases or forced to also apply general-purpose languages to cases in which full expressive power would not be needed and specific languages could be applied.

2. *Either Solution- or Problem-Oriented Paradigms*: Many consistency relations can be preserved based on specifications that only define problems of consistency without specifying how these problems can be solved or have to be solved. To preserve other consistency relations, it is often necessary to specify exactly how inconsistencies are to be resolved. Current languages often support programming paradigms that either allow solution-oriented or

problem-oriented consistency specifications but not both. Therefore, developers are forced to address all consistency requirements and problems for all modelling parts and relations from one perspective.

3. *Missing Abstractions and Adaptations*: To preserve consistency between models of two modelling languages, not all concerns and details that are represented in the models are relevant. Different variants of modelling related concepts, for example, can often be treated uniformly when consistency to less detailed models is specified. Moreover, it is not always necessary to consider all possibilities of how and where consistency can be preserved. Current languages, however, only provide insufficient means to abstract away from such modelling and preservation details when consistency is specified. If abstraction is achieved, the level of abstraction can often not be adapted to specify consistency for different model elements and relations using different abstractions. As a result, irrelevant details often have to be considered so that it becomes unnecessarily complex for domain experts or developers to specify consistency.

4. *Detached Preservation Behaviour*: Many consistency specification languages make it difficult for developers to understand how consistency is going to be preserved according to their specification. It is often difficult to foresee how different specification possibilities affect the resulting consistency preservation behaviour in different situations. Interpretative realizations of consistency specifications languages, for example, burden developers with complex engines in which the behavior of many routines can hardly be related to a particular part of a consistency specification. Similarly, many compilers generate a lot of code for which developers may find it difficult to trace the instructions back to consistency specification parts. This makes it difficult to assess upfront whether a specification will preserve consistency as required.

3.6. Enforcement Challenges

In this section, we present challenges to change-driven consistency preservation that occur if a consistency specification is enforced. The presented challenges are concerned with general properties, such as the time, space, and automation of consistency enforcement. They are independent of the implementation for a given consistency enforcement technique.

3.6.1. Enforcement Time and Granularity

The first subclass of consistency enforcement challenges is concerned with the point of time at which consistency enforcement takes place and the distance between these points of time, which is also called granularity.

3.6.1.1. When to Enforce

The identification and selection of points of time at which consistency is enforced is fundamental for change-driven consistency enforcement. First, we have to identify times at which it is possible to enforce a consistency specification, e.g. when all enforcement pre-conditions are fulfilled. Second, if different points of times were identified as candidates for enforcing consistency after a change, we have to select one. These two steps for identifying and selecting enforcement *times* have equivalents in terms of *change grouping*: First, we have to identify groups of changes with which consistency for a given change can be enforced. These groups can also be considered change compositions. Second, if different groupings are possible, we have to select one to decide for which changes consistency shall be enforced together. Both steps are closely related to the conceptual challenge of deciding how much inconsistency shall be tolerated at the time of enforcement, which we discussed in subsection 3.2.2. Furthermore, both steps do not only depend on the modelling language of the changed elements but also on the language of the models to which consistency is enforced. Consistency specifications for different target languages can lead to different decisions on enforcement times and change groups.

3.6.1.2. What Information is Needed to Enforce

To enforce consistency after a change, it has to be determined which information is necessary for the enforcement. For example, information about decisions on enforcement times and change groups has to be provided if their results influence the enforcement because different times or groups would lead to different enforcements. Like these decisions on enforcement times and groups, the general challenge of determining the information necessary for enforcement also depends on the target language. Therefore, different information may be provided for enforcing consistency to different target modelling languages.

An important group of information, which can be necessary for change-driven consistency enforcement is all information that describes the context of a change and that is not present in the changed models. Such additional context information may, for example, convey who performed a change or how it was performed, if this is relevant for consistency enforcement. Consistency after a change by a developer that was trained in the subject of a special model part, for example, could be enforced differently than after a change by a developer that was not trained accordingly. Furthermore, consistency could be enforced differently after two different change operations leading to the same model state, if one operation copies a certain value from another model part and the other sets the same value without such a relation. If such context information is not obtained upfront and provided as an input to consistency enforcement, it may be difficult to restore it after consistency enforcement started.

A possible solution for the challenge of deciding which change grouping or composition information should be provided is a greedy two-phased approach: When changes occur, all available information about the composition of changes is preserved without any analysis of its necessity. During enforcement of consistency after these changes to models of each target language, this information is ignored or removed per default as if no composition information would be available. Only for those languages and enforcement cases for which such information is required, the available information is used to correctly enforce consistency for these change compositions.

3.6.1.3. When and How to Undo Enforcement

If consistency enforcement operations can fail, then mechanisms for detecting such failures and undoing the enforcement change are necessary. A consistency specification may, for example, define post-conditions that have to hold when consistency was enforced after a user change operation. If they are violated, the specification may require that only the enforcement change operation or also the user change operation are undone in order to reach a consistent state.

Undoing enforcements is not necessary if a consistency specification makes it possible to determine for each user change whether consistency can be successfully enforced or not. For this, the specification may directly specify conditions for changes that can be enforced, which only have to be evaluated. If such conditions are not given, it is still possible to analyze upfront if the result of an enforcement change operation and the fulfillment of post-conditions can be determined. In cases where this analysis is not possible, it may still be possible to simulate enforcement, e.g. on model copies, in order to avoid undoing enforcements.

Enforcements can be undone by executing reverse operations for each enforcement change operation or by restoring an old version of the model state. Reverse operations can be performed based on the user change operations and the enforcement change operations. They can inspect both changes to indirectly obtain all old values. In this way, the old model state can be reached again but no additional bookkeeping for this old model state is necessary. Such bookkeeping is necessary if old versions should directly be restored. The advantage is, however, that the complexity of enforcement change operations and user change operations has no influence on version restoration. Restoring and old model state and discarding the state after a failed enforcement can always be performed the same way regardless of what happened. Both undo mechanisms of change reversion and version restoration have to guarantee that enforcement that did not happen cannot be distinguished from an enforcement that was undone.

If different ways of grouping user change operations influence consistency enforcement as discussed above, then enforcement operations for such change groups may have to be undone in a transactional manner. A consistency specification may, for example, require that consistency after two subsequent changes is either successfully enforced for both changes or for none of them. If the first enforcement is successful but the second enforcement fails, both enforcements have to be undone. A change reversion mechanism has to perform reverse operations for both enforcements and a version restoration mechanism has to go back to the version before both enforcements. This is, however, only a simple example for transactional undoing of enforcements, which may be much more challenging. It may, for example, be necessary that user change operations are also undone or that users are requested to repeatedly disambiguate their changes with a limited set of possibilities in order to find a way to successfully enforce consistency.

3.6.2. Enforcement Space and Boundaries

The second subclass of consistency enforcement challenges is related to the boundaries of the model space in which enforcement takes place.

3.6.2.1. Enforce on One or Both Sides

An important question of enforcement is whether it is sufficient to enforce consistency only on the side that was not changed with a user change operation. Such a strict boundary between the side at which a change originated and the side at which consistency is enforced is preferable because it avoids conflicts between user operations and enforcement operations. The question whether such a boundary is possible is closely related to the totality of consistency, which we discussed in subsection 3.2.4. It was also discussed in a survey paper on bidirectional transformations [Ste08, p.413], but it is relevant for all types of consistency transformations.

If a consistency relation is not left- or not right-total, then there can be changes to a consistent state that cannot be made consistent by only modifying one side. Either such changes have to be undone as discussed before, or consistency enforcement operations that modify both sides have to be performed. If enforcement operations can modify both sides, then manually performed changes can conflict with the effects of an enforcement operation. Such conflicts of manual changes and automated consistency enforcement can be avoided if enforcement operations modify only the other side. A simple approach, for example, is to enforce consistency before changes are performed on the other side. That is, for a sequence of changes that individually occur on either of both sides, consistency is enforced after every maximal subsequence of changes that modified only one side.

3.6.2.2. Where to Enforce

A consistency specification may not always directly define which model elements have to modified, created, or deleted in order to enforce consistency after a change. In such cases, these locations at which consistency enforcement has to take place have to be determined because enforcement change operations can be performed. This question of identifying enforcement locations can be functionally relevant if different locations would yield different enforcement results. If consistency has to be enforced at several locations, then even the order in which enforcement operations are performed at these locations may make a difference. Determining enforcement locations can also be relevant if non-functional properties of the consistency preservation, such as performance, are important. Consider, for example, a consistency specification for which references to other elements have to be checked on every model element of a certain type to determine enforcement locations regardless of the user change. If these possible enforcement locations cannot be restricted, then the worst-case runtime of consistency enforcement may be quadratic in the number of model elements.

The locations at which consistency has to be enforced may be indirectly given by the context of a change, e.g. by the correspondence of a changed model element. Such indirect specifications of enforcement locations may result in consistency specifications that are less verbose and complex than specifications that explicitly define enforcement locations. This requires mechanism that determine locations for consistency enforcement, e.g. by analyzing correspondences of elements at which consistency conditions were violated.

3.6.3. Automated Enforcement

The last subclass of consistency enforcement challenges deals with possibilities and degrees of automated consistency enforcement. We already discussed the conceptual challenge that models do not always contain all information that is necessary to decide whether they are consistent in subsection 3.2.7. The automation challenges on the enforcement level have a similar cause: How much automation can be performed and how it can be performed depends on the amount and unambiguousness of information contained in the models *and* in the consistency specification.

3.6.3.1. How Much Automation

The degree of consistency enforcement automation that is possible increases if the ambiguity of the information in models and consistency specifications decreases. We introduce six degrees of automation from no automation, over automated checking of consistency, automated change impact analysis, automated enforcement suggestions, and semi-automated repair with user interaction, to fully automated consistency repair. The borders between these degrees are only precise for a consistency approach in general but not for parts of it or for individual executions on specific models. If a user performs, for example, a selection from a list of enforcement suggestions after a change but not every suggestion can be executed automatically, this interaction can already be seen as semi-automated repair. Furthermore, an enforcement process that is in general semi-automated can be performed without a single user interaction for some input models and changes. We will now briefly present the six automation degrees, which are also illustrated in Figure 3.2, and we will discuss three further automation challenges in the next sections.

In the worst case, *no automation* can be achieved at all because the information in models and consistency specifications is not sufficient for automated checking of consistency so that. This is the lowest degree of consistency enforcement automation. The next possibility is that the information is sufficient for *automated checking*, but not for automatically determining which model parts could need to be modified to enforce consistency after an inevitable change that breaks consistency. Such an *automated change*

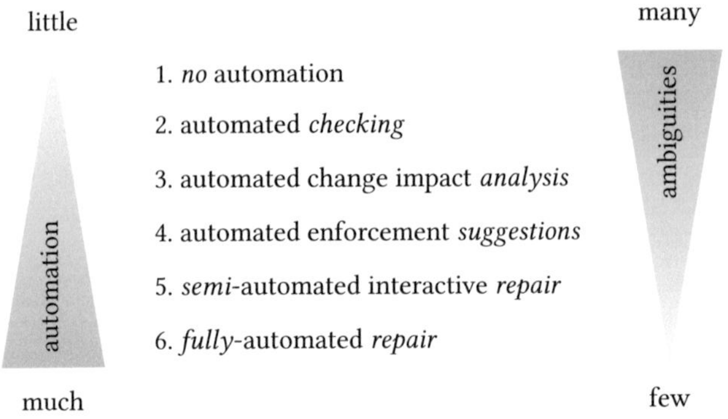

Figure 3.2.: Increasing degrees of *achievable* consistency enforcement automation with their relation to a decreasing number of ambiguities in the consistency specification

impact analysis that only computes which elements could need to be modified but not how this could be done is the next degree of consistency enforcement automation. After this, *automated enforcement suggestions* that describe which operations can be performed to enforce consistency but cannot be automatically executed are the next degree. Theoretically, a way to automatically check consistency can always be used to analyse the change impact or to obtain enforcement suggestions with brute force. Practically, we suggest to define upper bounds for the time neeed to perform a change impact analysis and for the time needed to compute enforcement suggestions as well as for the number of provided suggestions. This would ensure that these three degrees do not always coincide. The remaining two degrees *semi-automated interactive repair* and *fully automated repair* are the only two degrees of consistency enforcement automation that also automate the execution of enforcement operations. On the second highest degree of semi-automation all operations for enforcing consistency are performed automatically but the user can still be prompted interactively to decide which operations are performed or to provide values for parameters of the automated execution. This is not necessary for the highest degree: a fully automated consistency enforcement approach can only be influenced with a previously defined configuration.

These degrees of consistency enforcement automation can be used to classify consistency problems and solutions. If a certain degree of automation is theoretically *achievable* for a given set of modelling languages to enforce consistency according to a given specification, there can, however, be reasons why one may decide to realize a lower degree of automation in practice. The effort for reaching a certain degree of automation may, for example, not be in an appropriate or desired relation to the benefits resulting from it.

3.6.3.2. How to Obtain Enforcement Options

If the models and the consistency specification make it possible to automatically check consistency but do not determine how it can be enforced, it can be challenging to compute enforcement options. One possibility to use an automated consistency check to enforce consistency is to perform arbitrary modifications until a model state that passes the consistency check is found.

To improve the performance of such a brute-force approach one can try to direct the search for consistent models. One can control *where* modifications are performed e.g. by starting at elements that were changed when consistency broke. Furthermore, one can control *which* modifications are performed e.g. by inspecting which properties are analyzed during the automated consistency check.

Regardless of performance it can be challenging to find models that are not only consistent according to a given specification but also satisfy further requirements that are not encoded in the specification. Such requirements can, for example, state that certain modifications are more desired than others e.g. to prefer additions over deletions. Therefore, the applicability of an approach that enforces consistency by finding consistent models strongly depends on the restrictiveness of the modelling languages and of the consistency specification. A decreasing amount of freedom increases the chances and speed for finding not only any consistent models but the right ones.

In the literature, three approaches for deriving consistent models from constraints and relational transformations using answer set programming

[Era+12], satisfiability solving [MC13; MGC13; CGR15], or abduction [HLR09; Het10] are described. With these approaches consistent models are found by formulating search problems, checking the satisfiability of relations, or by inferring modifications for which the given transformation rules would induce the observed change.

If several possible enforcement options are computed, one either has to ask the user to manually choose, as discussed in the next section, or one has to choose automatically, as discussed in the last automation challenge section.

3.6.3.3. When and How to Interact with the User

A challenge that is closely related to the previous automation challenge is whether and how users can be involved in order to provide information that is required to enforce consistency. If the information in involved models *and* the consistency specification is not sufficient to determine how consistency should be enforced, then the user can be asked for this information.

The missing information that leads to a user interaction can have different reasons. Either the consistency specification deliberately allows different ways to enforce consistency, or the specification is faulty. Often, there are several valid ways to enforce consistency because a modelling language forces a developer to choose from several ways to represent information even if the choice has no influence on inter-language consistency. Even in such cases, it can be beneficial to let the user decide in order to avoid that models contain many default values or elements for which it is unclear whether they were created on purpose or not. If the choice of an enforcement option has an influence on consistency, then user interaction can hardly be avoided.

There are different possibilities for interactive user influence on consistency enforcement. We briefly discuss different points of time and types of interaction but avoid discussing, for example, interface and design options.

The information required for consistency enforcement can be provided by the user in advance, when needed, or afterwards. The first case, in which the information is provided in advance, can be seen as an interactive reconfiguration of consistency enforcement. In the second case, consistency enforcement information is interactively provided by a user. Such an interaction has to happen after a change made it necessary but before a next change happens. This case can be seen as the highest level of interaction but it may lead to requests for consistency enforcement information that could be avoided if the interaction would be postponed. The last case of postponed interaction can avoid such requests and makes it possible to delegate information requests to other users. This can be beneficial if different users play different roles during development, but it also bears the risk of wasting efforts if complex sequences of changes prove to be unnecessary after they already have been performed.

Interactive request for information that is needed to enforce consistency can ask users to choose an enforcement option or to provide values to complete or influence enforcement. In the first type of interaction, a user is asked to choose from a fixed set of different enforcement operation where each specific operation in the set is always performed in the same way. In the second type of interaction, a user can provide input values that either only complete the result of a fixed enforcement operation or influence a parameterized enforcement operation. Both, the set of options in the first case and the input in the second case, can be realized in very different ways so that it may be hard to see whether the enforcement is fixed or not. Let us consider, for example, a request for change disambiguation that is used to obtain a name for an element that was newly created in a model of one language but has to be kept consistent with a list of names in a model of another language. If the user simply enters a name it can be unclear whether this will choose, complete, or influence an enforcement option. The set of allowed names is usually fixed because the number of allowed characters and possibilities for each character is usually fixed. But, it is not obvious, whether the enforcement result—apart from the chosen name—is the same for every possible choice, or if the enforcement will, for example, create additional elements in the model of the other language depending on the name. The first case with a result that only differs by the chosen name can theoretically be realized as interaction of both types, but in practice users will probably not be forced to choose a name longer than a few characters from a complete list.

3.6.3.4. How to Choose from Enforcement Options

To decide how consistency should be enforced if the consistency specification leaves several options, it is also possible to automatically choose an enforcement option instead of interacting with the user. In this case, a major challenge is to define and implement criteria according to which the selection is performed. First, one needs to decide which properties of a consistent result should have an influence on the selection process. Then, one has to define metrics that analyze these properties so that different results can be automatically compared. Last, one has to develop an algorithm that determines which comparisons are performed and how an enforcement option is chosen based on the metrics results.

Several approaches address this challenge by measuring the difference before and after an enforcement operation has been performed and by choosing the enforcement result representing the least change [Mee98]. It is also possible to attempt to measure the difference to concurrently performed modifications as least surprise [Che+15]. Another possibility for bidirectional consistency would be to measure an inverse propagation distance to minimize round-tripping differences. For a change on one side with several enforcement possibilities on the other side, one could perform every enforcement option as if it was a manual update to the second side and measure the distance between every possible enforcement result on the first side and the state after the original update on that side.

3.7. Implementation Challenges

The last class of challenges to consistency contains challenges that arise on the lowest level of abstraction when consistency enforcement is implemented.

3.7.1. Consistency between Checks and Enforcements

Checks and enforcement of consistency are inter-dependent: First, consistency checks have to fail, if and only if consistency enforcement is needed. Second, all consistency checks have to pass after executing all necessary consistency enforcement operations. These two constraints for consistency checks and enforcement either have to be guaranteed by the developer or by the consistency preservation tool.

Whenever the tool obtains separate check and enforcement specifications from the developer, these specifications have to fit together. The tool can support the developer by verifying whether the specifications fit in order to issue error messages, or it can even replace parts of the specifications to make them fit. If the tool is capable of fixing some check and enforce specifications that do not fit, it should be investigated, whether check and enforcement can be derived from a single specification in some cases as described in subsection 3.4.6.

If the tool performs consistency checks and enforcement based on a single specification, the tool bears all responsibility to make them fit. It can be designed in such a way that the two constraints for checks and enforcement hold for all possible input specifications and models. If this is not the case, it can perform dynamic checks to avoid illegal states, e.g. by evaluating and asserting that all consistency checks pass after every successful enforcement. Both options for correctly realizing checks and enforcement have advantages and disadvantages: Static guarantees for fitting checks and enforcement can be difficult to achieve or proof or may impose restrictions on how specifications can be described. Dynamic checks, however, can be cheap to develop at design time but may turn out to be costly in terms of execution at runtime.

3.7.2. Debugging Consistency Preservation

Several factors make it difficult to debug implementations of change-driven consistency preservation mechanisms. The construction of change descriptions, for example, may have to be debugged both for state-based and operation-based preservation mechanisms. Furthermore, debugging the enforcement itself can be difficult, e.g. when specifications are enforced using interpreters or using generated code that calls platform routines.

Change-driven consistency preservation begins with the computation of change-representation that serve as input and that may also have to be debugged. For state-based approaches the comparison of old and new model states and the computation of differences may have to be debugged. This can be challenging, for example, because many combinations of new and old properties of model elements are possible. If an operation-based approach is used, then the monitoring of user change operations and construction of appropriate operation descriptions may have to be debugged. The simulation of user changes may, for example, present challenges to systematic debugging of this process.

It can be difficult to debug code that enforces consistency according to a specification if this code depends on a lot of other code that is not particular for this specification. A declarative consistency specification, for example, may be interpreted so that the code of an interpreter may also have to be debugged to analyze the effects of the specification. In such cases, it may be difficult to identify those code parts of such general interpreters that may be relevant for a given consistency specification. If a specification is not interpreted but used as input for a generator, it is sufficient to analyze the code that was particularly generated for the specification. Such generated consistency enforcement code can, however, call general platform routines (see subsubsection 2.1.2.3). These calls in generated code may also be difficult to debug if a lot of irrelevant code has to be inspected. Altogether, the difficulty of debugging consistency preservation is an important part of the Open Consistency Specification Language Challenge 4, which is about the general difficulty to relate observed enforcement behavior to a consistency specifications (see section 1.2).

3.7.3. Keeping Associated Information

If a change is performed in one model but consistency is automatically enforced in other models that are not in sight of the user, then it is possible that information in these models is removed but the user does not take note of it. This is one of the reasons why facilities for rolling back changes and change propagations as described in subsubsection 3.6.1.3 can be desired. But, even in cases where an original change should not be undone and the initial information removal is wanted, it can be desired to keep such information in other models in the long run.

A reason for keeping such information can be the dependency between information containers that are deleted during consistency enforcement and contained information that is not automatically re-created but indirectly destroyed during consistency enforcement. If the initial deletion of such a consistency container is implicitly undone by recreating the corresponding elements, then the same or an equivalent container may be recreated during enforcement but the information that was initially removed can still be lost. To keep this information it either has to be restored automatically or the user has to be asked whether this should be done. Regardless of automated restoration decisions, it is already challenging to decide which information shall be stored for restoration in which cases and how long. It can be sufficient to only keep certain and not all removed information for restoration and it can be adequate to keep it only for a certain time or until a certain number of further changes were performed.

An example for an approach that strives to keep such information is the synchronization technique for TGGs by Greenyer et al. [GPR11]. During a synchronization step, they mark element for deletion instead of directly deleting them in one rule application in order to reuse these elements in the matching process of subsequent rule applications. Only those elements that are marked for deletion and not reused are deleted at the end of the synchronization step. By this, it can be avoided that elements are deleted and re-created in reaction to a single change but not in reaction to several changes.

3.7.4. Retrieving the Right Correspondence

If more than one correspondence may exist for a model element, mechanisms for retrieving the correct correspondence are necessary for successful consistency enforcement. We already discussed in subsection 3.2.7 how the information that is required to identify correspondences can be obtained. On the implementation level it can be challenging to design mechanisms for retrieving correspondences based on this information.

Consistency specifications may treat several correspondences between the same set of model elements differently if these correspondences were established, for example, under different conditions or for separately specified consistency relations. In such cases, it is not sufficient to implement correspondence retrieval mechanisms that only inspect the corresponding elements. They may also have to take into account which conditions were fulfilled when the correspondence was established and with respect to which consistency relation this happened. For this, there has to be a way to identify relations of a consistency specification and the conditions or subcases they define. All factors that distinguish correspondences on the specification level have to be considered when correspondences are established or retrieved in the implementation.

3.7.5. Partial Evaluation and Execution

Change-driven consistency preservation can be implemented in an incremental way to avoid unnecessary overhead in terms of runtime for the implementation and debugging complexity for developers. Such incremental implementations have to determine which parts of a consistency specification are not relevant after a change. With such knowledge it is possible to perform only partially evaluate consistency checks and only partially execute enforcements.

Partial evaluation can be performed if it can be determined which conditions of which consistency relations of a specification might be no longer or newly fulfilled after a change. Depending on the language that is used for the specifications of such conditions, it may be necessary to evaluate conditions for which it cannot be decided upfront whether their fulfillment may change. Consistency enforcement specifications can be partially enforced if it can be determined which executions cannot change the current model state. Again, the computational power of the used languages may restrict the possibilities to statically analyze which enforcement operations do not need to be executed.

3.8. Orthogonal Bidirectionality Challenges

In addition to the five classes of challenges to change-driven consistency, we present challenges to bidirectionality, which are orthogonal to the levels of abstractions represented by the five previous classes. We describe these bidirectionality challenges for the conceptual, specification, and enforcement level, but they also influence other levels such as the implementation. They are relevant for all consistency preservation mechanisms that allow changes to model elements at both sides and require both preservation directions to work appropriately together.

3.8.1. Bidirectionality without Bijectivity

A major conceptual challenge to bidirectional consistency preservation is to achieve bidirectionality without bijectivity. This is crucial because many consistency relations cannot be specified in terms of bijections even if the modelling languages can be adapted accordingly. The reason is that many common mappings from values of an attribute of a model element on one side to values of an attribute of a model element on the other side are not left-unique (injective). Basic examples for such mappings are the string concatenation or integer division, which are both fundamental parts of many consistency relationships.

One possibility to achieve bidirectional consistency even for mappings that are not bijective is to restrict the set of possible values or the changes that can be applied. The goal of such techniques is to avoid exactly those cases that are not left-unique. Consider, for example, a mapping that maps two values l_1 and l_2 of an attribute of a model element on the left side to the same value r of an attribute of a model element on the right side. If it is not possible to set the value r on the right side, but l_1 and l_2 can both be used on the left side, then such a mapping can still be treated in a bidirectional way if the decision for either l_1 or l_2 is correctly preserved.

3.8.2. Single or Double Specification

Another central challenge to bidirectionality is concerned with the advantages and disadvantages of a single specification for both directions (see also [Ste08, p. 412]). Bidirectionality only requires that consistency can be enforced in both directions. It is not necessary that the specification used for this enforcement never distinguishes between these directions.

Single specifications can be written using languages with a special focus on bidirectionality in order to statically guarantee that certain bidirectional properties are fulfilled. This can make it easier to avoid incorrect specifications. It should, however, be ensured that simple specifications are not more difficult to define than without such precautions. Nevertheless, the fact that bidirectionality is guaranteed can be easier to detect with single specifications. Therefore, the benefits of single specifications for bidirectional consistency relations should take both the efforts for writing and for using or maintaining specifications into account.

If both directions are specified separately no special constructs for bidirectional specifications have to be used. In this way, it is possible to reuse specification parts that already existed before and to use unidirectional languages. The available possibilities for automatically checking and guaranteeing the coherence of both specifications are, however, more restricted than with a single specification with special bidirectional constructs and predefined coherence checks. Therefore, the responsibility for achieving bidirectionality as desired remains with the person writing the double specification and not with the tool that implements a single specification in a bidirectional way. Furthermore, the coherence of both directions has to be preserved during the maintenance of evolving specifications for both directions. To achieve this additional requirement for double specifications there are, however, techniques for automatically verifying the coherence of separate specifications for both directions. For example, additional constraints can be provided for two sets of graph transformation rules [Pos+14]. Despite these disadvantages, double specifications provide the flexibility to deliberately deviate from bidirectionality requirements when necessary.

3.8.3. Well-Behaved Roundtrip Enforcement

Bidirectional enforcement should usually fulfill requirements for well-behavedness in order to avoid problems during roundtrip consistency preservation. Such requirements may, for example, demand symmetry properties or avoid unexpected effects, such as oscillations. Their fulfillment can guarantee that both sides may be treated and modified in the same way.

Some classical requirements for so-called *well-behaved bidirectional transformations* are the round-trip laws GetPut, PutGet, and PutPut [Fos+07] (see also subsection 2.2.3). They can also be applied to bidirectional change-driven consistency preservation: All three laws distinguish between a source side and a target side. Informally, they are concerned with consistency enforcements on the target side that may retrieve views on values from the source side (get), from which the change originated, and may update source values according to target views (put). The *GetPut* law demands that every roundtrip that first retrieves a target view on a source value and then updates the source value according to the unmodified target value, has to end at the original source value. Similarly, the *PutGet* law demands that every roundtrip that first updates a source value according to a target value and then retrieves a target view on the updated source value, has to end at the original target value. The *PutPut* law is for so-called *very well-behavedness* and demands that two updates of a source value according to the same target value result in the same source value as a single update with this target value.

Further requirements for bidirectional transformations that can be applied to bidirectional change-driven consistency preservation have been described in the literature. We translate three such requirements to our consistency preservation terminology based on the discussion by Xiong et al. [Xio+11]: First, consistency enforcement operations are *correct with respect to a consistency relation* if they establish this relation [Ste10]. Second, they are *hippocratic* if they leave consistent models consistent [Ste10]. Finally, they are *undoable* if undoing a change on one side also undoes the effects of the enforcement operations on the other side [Dis08]. The first and the second of these three requirements also apply to unidirectional consistency enforcement.

3.9. Future Challenges

In this chapter's last section, we present two exemplary challenges that are out of scope of this thesis as they only occur if models cannot be kept consistent when pairs of modelling languages are considered in isolation of other pairs. These challenges should be addressed in future work as soon as this restriction is dropped.

3.9.1. Propagating Propagations without Cycles

If more than two modelling languages are used, then it has to be ensured that transitive effects do not lead to propagation cycles. Let us consider a general case in which three models of three languages contain elements such that elements of the first model can be in a consistency relation with the second model, elements of the second model can be in a consistency relation with elements of the third model, and elements of the third model can be in a consistency relation with elements of the first model. In such a case, a change to the first model has to be propagated to the second model. Next, this change in the second model has to be propagated to the third model. Finally, this change in the third model has to be propagated back to the first model, where the change initially occurred. This need to transitively propagate propagations is challenging in two ways: First, enforcement change operations have to be monitored like user change operations in order to propagate their effects, perhaps even using the same mechanisms as for propagating effects of user change operations. Second, it must not be the case that a transitive change in the first model leads again to the same propagation to the second model or to any other type of propagation cycle.

In some cases it may be sufficient to partition the set of element types of modelling languages. More specifically, if the possible consistency relations between models of three or more modelling languages can be specified in such a way that they always concern different model elements, the problems can be avoided. It is, however, questionable how often the consistency relationships between modelling languages induce such a partition.

3.9.2. Order of Multi-Directional Propagations

If a modelling language has more than one consistency relationships with other languages, the order in which changes to instances of this language are propagated to instances of the other languages may make a difference. Let us consider a general case in which three models of three languages contain elements such that elements of the first model can be in a consistency relation with both other models. In such a case, a change to the first model has to be propagated to both other models, but is in unclear in which order these propagations should happen. This order is important if elements of both propagation targets can be in turn in a direct consistency relation or in an indirect consistency relationship that involves models of the first language or of other languages. Thus, the elements and their consistency relations form a diamond. For such a diamond, the final enforcement result may be different if the enforcements for one of these direct or indirect relationships were already perfirned or will be performed later. Even if no further consistency relations exist, the order may have an effect on consistency if the user is demanded for input during consistency enforcement but may behave differently for different orders.

3.10. Conclusions

In this chapter, we have presented a collection and classification of challenges that can occur when consistency has to be preserved between models of different modelling languages. We have informally introduced general terms of specification-driven consistency preservation to ease the discussion. Based on this, we have presented a collection of challenges that occur in this context as an answer to subquestion 1.1, which we presented in section 1.3. We have classified these challenges according to the level of abstraction at which they occur. These levels range from conceptual challenges that are even independent of the used modelling languages to implementation challenges. We have also presented a special class of open challenges that should be addressed by consistency specification languages. These *Open Consistency Specification Language Challenges* are our answer to subquestion 1.2 and the reason why we have developed the consistency preservation languages that we will present in Part III of this thesis. Many challenges that we have presented are related to other challenges on the same or on different levels of abstraction. For such challenges, we have explained which parts should be addressed on which level in order to relieve developers of consistency preservation tools. Many concerns of general challenges to consistency enforcement, for example, should already be addressed by preservation tools so that developers can choose from appropriate enforcement options when they specify consistency for particular modelling languages. We have also presented challenges to bidirectional consistency preservation as a separate class of challenges because the direction in which consistency is preserved is not related to the level of abstraction. Finally, we have discussed challenges that occur if consistency has to preserved for more than two languages. We have called them future challenges because this thesis only discusses consistency preservation for models of two languages.

4. A Formal Language for Change-Driven Model Consistency

In this chapter, we present a formal language for change-driven consistency preservation based on set theory and all the definitions that we have already provided in section 2.3 of the chapter on foundations for this thesis. This formal language is the foundation for the change-driven languages for consistency preservation specifications, which we present in the subsequent chapters. It was designed to enable precise explanations of the semantics of the specification languages, which are implemented by the compilers of these languages. The formal language is a prerequisite for these explanations, which we will provide in section 6.7 and 7.7, and therefore one of the ways in which we address the Open Consistency Specification Language Challenge 4. With this language, we provide answers to our research question 1 and to the subquestions 1.3 and 1.4, which we presented in section 1.3.

In the foundations chapter of this thesis, we defined basic concepts for models that fulfill the restrictions of a metamodel and additional conditions called invariants (see section 2.3). These conditions are added to a single metamodel in order to impose further restrictions on all models that conform to it. In this chapter, we will define how consistency can be specified and enforced for models of two metamodels based on conditions that are specified for such a pair of metamodels. All definitions together provide the neccessary precision for our specification-driven notion of consistency for models of different languages, which we introduced in subsection 3.1.2.

4.1. Consistency Rules and Specifications

In the first section of this chapter, we will define how consistency can be specified and checked using rules, before we define how consistency can be enforced in the second section.

4.1.1. Rules and Correspondences

Before we can define how consistency specifications can be checked for two complete models, we have to define individual consistency rules and correspondences for individual combinations of objects.

Definition 22 (Consistency Rule)
Let $\langle \mathbb{C}_l \rangle$ and $\langle \mathbb{C}_r \rangle$ be two metaclass tuples of two typed metamodels $\mathbb{m}_l$ and $\mathbb{m}_r$, let $\mathcal{O}_{\langle \mathbb{C}_l \rangle}$ and $\mathcal{O}_{\langle \mathbb{C}_r \rangle}$ denote the universes of $\langle \mathbb{C}_l \rangle$ and $\langle \mathbb{C}_r \rangle$, let $\text{COND}_{\langle \mathbb{C}_l \rangle} \subseteq \mathcal{O}_{\langle \mathbb{C}_l \rangle}$ be a condition for $\langle \mathbb{C}_l \rangle$, and let $\text{COND}_{\langle \mathbb{C}_r \rangle} \subseteq \mathcal{O}_{\langle \mathbb{C}_r \rangle}$ be a condition for $\langle \mathbb{C}_r \rangle$.

A consistency rule for the metaclass tuples $\langle \mathbb{C}_l \rangle$ and $\langle \mathbb{C}_r \rangle$ is a set $\mathfrak{R}_{\mathbb{C}_l, \mathbb{C}_r} \subseteq \mathcal{P}(\text{COND}_{\langle \mathbb{C}_l \rangle} \times \text{COND}_{\langle \mathbb{C}_r \rangle})$ which contains pairs of co-occuring instances tuples for $\langle \mathbb{C}_l \rangle$ respectively $\langle \mathbb{C}_r \rangle$ that fulfill the conditions of $\text{COND}_{\langle \mathbb{C}_l \rangle}$ respectively $\text{COND}_{\langle \mathbb{C}_r \rangle}$.

To make this relationship between a rule and its condition sets explicit, we briefly write $\mathfrak{R}_{\mathbb{C}_l, \mathbb{C}_r}$ *binds* the conditions $\text{COND}_{\langle \mathbb{C}_l \rangle}$ and $\text{COND}_{\langle \mathbb{C}_r \rangle}$.

A consistency rule for two metaclass tuples of two typed metamodels is a possibly infinite set of pairs of instance tuples for these metaclass tuples. Every instance tuple in such a pair has to fulfill an appropriate consistency condition. More specifically, every pair consists of an instance tuple that fulfills a condition for the left metaclass tuple and of an instance tuple that fulfills a condition for the right metaclass tuple. Note that there is no need to define explicit dependencies between consistency rules, because the same effect can be achieved if a rule is directly restricted to pairs that are also listed in the set of the other rule. To have a name for the relationship between the conditions and the consistency rule, we say that a consistency rule binds the conditions.

A consistency rule specifies which instance tuples always have to occur together with another instance tuple. It does, however, not specify that a certain instance tuple has to be present in a model that is to be considered consistent. Consider, for example, a consistency rule that expresses that the name of an instance of a left metaclass always has to be identical to the name of an instance of right metaclass if some further constraints are satisfied. The set of the rule contains all pairs of objects that have the same name and fullfill the further constraints. As a long as none of these objects occurs, the consistency rule does not require anything, but if such an object occurs in a model then the other object of the pair has to occur in another model of the other metamodel. To keep track of those pairs of consistency rules that occur in two specific models, we introduce the concept of so-called correspondences that witness consistency. Our notion of change-driven consistency, which we introduce gradually in this chapter, is not absolute but always defined relative to these correspondences. We will now define these correspondences, which are of central importance to the conceptual approach and to the three programming languages of this thesis.

Definition 23 (Correspondence for a Consistency Rule)
Let $\mathfrak{R}_{\mathbb{c}_l,\mathbb{c}_r}$ be a consistency rule that binds two conditions $\textsc{cond}_{\langle\mathbb{c}_l\rangle}$ and $\textsc{cond}_{\langle\mathbb{c}_r\rangle}$, which are defined for two metaclass tuples $\langle\mathbb{c}_l\rangle$ and $\langle\mathbb{c}_r\rangle$ of two typed metamodels $\mathbb{m}_l$ and $\mathbb{m}_r$, and let O_l and O_r be two serializable models of $\mathbb{m}_l$ and $\mathbb{m}_r$.

A correspondence $\mathfrak{c}$ for the consistency rule $\mathfrak{R}_{\mathbb{c}_l,\mathbb{c}_r}$ in O_l and O_r is a pair of two instance tuples for $\langle\mathbb{c}_l\rangle$ and $\langle\mathbb{c}_r\rangle$ in O_l and O_r that adheres to the consistency rule $\mathfrak{R}_{\mathbb{c}_l,\mathbb{c}_r}$, i.e. $O_{\langle\mathbb{c}_l\rangle} \times O_{\langle\mathbb{c}_r\rangle} \in \mathfrak{c} \ni \mathfrak{R}_{\mathbb{c}_l,\mathbb{c}_r}$.

Correspondences are central to many subsequent definitions but simple: They only list objects that instantiate metaclasses of one metamodel and fulfill the condition of a consistency rule for that metamodel. Additionaly, they list objects that instantiate metaclasses of the other metamodel and fulfill the other condition of the rule. As we already mentioned above, the motivation for this definition of correspondence is that we want to define a relative notion of consistency. This relative consistency can only be checked and enforced with respect to correspondences, which are meant to witness consistency.

Similar to the prerequisite of serializability for validity, we make serializability a prerequisite for consistency. This relieves us from dealing with all cases in which serializability may be fulfilled or not. To achieve this, we only define correspondences in serializable models, even if we do not directly use this precondition in the next definition.

4.1.2. Prescriptive Consistency

Based on our notion of individual consistency rules and correspondences, we will now define consistency according to a rule and consistency according to specification, which bundles rules and their correspondences. This notion of consistency and all subsequent definitions are intended for approaches with prescriptive consistency specifications (see page 58 of subsection 3.1.2).

Definition 24 (Consistency According to a Rule)
Let $\mathfrak{R}_{\mathbb{c}_l,\mathbb{c}_r}$ be a consistency rule that binds two conditions $\text{COND}_{\langle\mathbb{c}_l\rangle}$ and $\text{COND}_{\langle\mathbb{c}_r\rangle}$, which are defined for two metaclass tuples $\langle\mathbb{c}_l\rangle$ and $\langle\mathbb{c}_r\rangle$ of two typed metamodels $\mathbb{m}_l$ and $\mathbb{m}_r$, let O_l and O_r be two serializable models of $\mathbb{m}_l$ and $\mathbb{m}_r$, and let $\mathfrak{C} \subseteq O_{\langle\mathbb{c}_l\rangle} \cap \text{COND}_{\langle\mathbb{c}_l\rangle} \times O_{\langle\mathbb{c}_r\rangle} \cap \text{COND}_{\langle\mathbb{c}_r\rangle}$ be a set of correspondence candidates for $\mathfrak{R}$ in O_l and O_r.

The models O_l and O_r are consistent according to the consistency rule $\mathfrak{R}_{\mathbb{c}_l,\mathbb{c}_r}$ with respect to $\mathfrak{C}$ iff all elements in $\mathfrak{C}$ are correspondences and there is at least one correspondence for every instance tuple for which the condition is valid:

$$\forall \langle o_l\rangle \in O_{\langle\mathbb{c}_l\rangle} \cap \mathit{COND}_{\langle\mathbb{c}_l\rangle}: \exists \langle o_r\rangle \in O_{\langle\mathbb{c}_r\rangle}: (\langle o_l\rangle, \langle o_r\rangle) \in \mathfrak{C}$$
$$\wedge\ \forall \langle o_r\rangle \in O_{\langle\mathbb{c}_r\rangle} \cap \mathit{COND}_{\langle\mathbb{c}_r\rangle}: \exists \langle o_l\rangle \in O_{\langle\mathbb{c}_l\rangle}: (\langle o_l\rangle, \langle o_r\rangle) \in \mathfrak{C}$$

By Definition 24, two models are consistent according to a consistency rule with respect to a set of correspondence candidates if every fulfillment of the conditions of the rule is witnessed by at least one correspondence. This witnessing is required for every combination of objects in one of the two models that fulfills the condition for the instantiated metamodel of the consistency rule: The set of correspondences has to contain at least one pair with these condition fulfilling objects and objects of the other model. It is not necessary to impose any constraints on these pairs in addition to the requirement that they are correspondences because Definition 23 and Definition 22 already require that they fulfill the other condition for the other metamodel, i.e. $(\langle o_l \rangle, \langle o_r \rangle) \in \mathfrak{C} \subsetneq \text{COND}_{\langle \mathbb{C}_l \rangle} \times \text{COND}_{\langle \mathbb{C}_r \rangle}$.

Our notion of consistency neither requires that only one correspondence exists for a fulfillment of a condition, nor that every pair of fulfillments for both conditions of a rule has to be witnessed. This means the role of a correspondence is more than just a pointer to objects that fulfill the conditions of a rule. Because of these flexible multiplicities, a set of correspondences can also be seen as a selection of object combinations for which consistency shall be documented. The goal of selecting correspondences from all possible fulfillment combinations is to have a possibility to specify where consistency has to be preserved after changes even if these changes may remove objects. Therefore, it is possible to meet the requirements of our definition of consistency with a subset of all possible correspondences, i.e. $O_{\langle \mathbb{C}_l \rangle} \cap \text{COND}_{\langle \mathbb{C}_l \rangle} \times O_{\langle \mathbb{C}_r \rangle} \cap \text{COND}_{\langle \mathbb{C}_r \rangle}$ does not *need* to be a subset of $\mathfrak{C}$. The reason is that it is not necessary that every left instance tuple for which the left condition is valid has to correspond to every right instance tuple for which the right condition is valid. If this is, however, the case, then $\mathfrak{C}$ encompasses *all pairs* of instance tuples in O_l and O_r that fullfill the conditions, i.e. $O_{\langle \mathbb{C}_l \rangle} \cap \text{COND}_{\langle \mathbb{C}_l \rangle} \times O_{\langle \mathbb{C}_r \rangle} \cap \text{COND}_{\langle \mathbb{C}_r \rangle} = \mathfrak{C}$ because of Definition 23 (see previous paragraph).

As correspondences fulfill the conditions on both sides by definition they can only witness consistency but not inconsistency. That is, if all correspondence candidates are correspondences, then the two models can only be inconsistent according to the rule and with respect to the correspondences if a correspondence is missing but not because a correspondence lists two instance tuples for which one does not fulfill the appropriate condition. Therefore, we define consistency not for a set of correspondences but for a set of correspondence candidates. Consider, for example, a case in which a model is changed in such a way that two instance tuples that formed a correspondence before the change are no longer corresponding because one of both does no longer fulfill the appropriate condition. To detect this inconsistency, we only have to check for all former correspondence candidates whether they are (still) fulfilling the conditions.

Definition 25 (Consistency Specification)
Let O_l and O_r be two serializable models of two typed metamodels $\mathbb{m}_l$ and $\mathbb{m}_r$.

A consistency specification $\mathfrak{cs}$ *for* O_l *and* O_r *is a tuple* $(\mathfrak{R}_{\mathbb{C}_{1,l},\mathbb{C}_{1,r}}, \mathfrak{C}_1, \ldots, \mathfrak{R}_n, \mathfrak{R}_{\mathbb{C}_{n,l},\mathbb{C}_{n,r}})$ *where* $\mathfrak{R}_{\mathbb{C}_{1,l},\mathbb{C}_{1,r}}, \ldots, \mathfrak{R}_{\mathbb{C}_{n,l},\mathbb{C}_{n,r}}$ *are consistency rules for metaclass tuples of* $\mathbb{m}_l$ *and* $\mathbb{m}_r$*, and where every* $\mathfrak{C}_i \subseteq O_{\langle \mathbb{C}_{i,l} \rangle} \cap COND_{\langle \mathbb{C}_{i,l} \rangle} \times O_{\langle \mathbb{C}_{i,r} \rangle} \cap COND_{\langle \mathbb{C}_{i,r} \rangle}$ *is a set of correspondence candidates in* O_l *and* O_r *for the rule* $\mathfrak{R}_{\mathbb{C}_{i,l},\mathbb{C}_{i,r}}$.

A consistency specification for two models lists consistency rules for the two metamodels of the models and a set of correspondences in the two models for each consistency rule. It would also be possible to define a notion of consistency specification purely on the metamodel level for two metamodels and without correspondences for concrete models. Such a specification term is, however, not necessary for our purposes and could mislead the reader to a notion of absolute consistency instead of our concept of correspondence-relative consistency.

Definition 26 (Consistency According to a Specification)
Let $\mathfrak{cs} := (\mathfrak{R}_1, \mathfrak{C}_1, \ldots, \mathfrak{R}_n, \mathfrak{C}_n)$ be a consistency specification for two serializable models O_l and O_r.

The models O_l *and* O_r *are consistent according to the consistency specification* $\mathfrak{cs}$ *iff* O_l *and* O_r *are consistent according to every rule* $\mathfrak{R}_i$ *with respect to* $\mathfrak{C}_i$.

The notion of consistency according to a complete specification is a straightforward continuation of the notion of consistency for a single consistency rule with respect to a set of correspondences: It is sufficient if two models are consistent with respect to every consistency rule of a consistency specification with respect to the according set of correspondences. All rules and correspondences contribute independently and equally to the notion of specification consistency.

So far, we defined how consistency can be specified in terms of rules and correspondences and defined under which conditions two models are considered consistent. In the next section, we define how models can be updated to enforce consistency and which updates are consistency preserving.

4.2. Consistency Updates and Preservation

In the last part of our formal language for consistency preservation, we define how models can be updated to enforce consistency. We also define which conditions have to be fulfilled by updates that correctly preserve consistency.

4.2.1. Updates of Links, Labels, and Models

In order to preserve consistency it is necessary to update models. Therefore, we will now define link updates and label updates for objects as well as model updates.

Definition 27 (Link Update for an Object)
Let $o \in O_{\mathbb{c}}$ be an object that instantiates a metaclass $\mathbb{c} := (\mathbb{R}_{\mathbb{c}}, \mathbb{R}_{\mathbb{c},\blacklozenge}, \mathbb{A}_{\mathbb{c}})$ of a typed metamodel $\mathbb{m}$ in a serializable model $O := (O_{\mathbb{c}_1}, \ldots, O_{\mathbb{c}_{|\mathbb{C}|}}, \text{LINK}, \text{LABEL})$ of $\mathbb{m}$.

A link update for the object o in the model O is a tuple $(o, \mathbb{r}, O^-, O^+)$, where $\mathbb{r} \in \mathbb{R}_{\mathbb{c}}^{\preccurlyeq}$ is a reference of $\mathbb{c}$ or one of its superclasses, O^- and O^+ are sets of objects to be removed and added from and to the links of o for $\mathbb{r}$, i.e. $O^- \subseteq \textit{LINK}(o, \mathbb{r}) \land O^+ \subseteq \bigcup_{\mathbb{d} \in \textit{RTYPE}^{\preccurlyeq}(\mathbb{r})} O_{\mathbb{d}} \setminus \textit{LINK}(o, \mathbb{r})$.

A link update only affects the set of objects that are linked by an object for a reference that is defined for one of the metaclasses instantiated by the object. Links can be removed by removing objects from this set and can be added by adding new objects to the set. Such added objects have to directly or indirectly instantiate the metaclass of the type that is specified by the reference and have to be from the model to which the object for which the links are updated belongs. This is necessary to ensure that a link update does not break metamodel conformance.

Definition 28 (Label Update for an Object)
Let $o \in O_{\mathbb{c}}$ be an object that instantiates a metaclass $\mathbb{c} := (\mathbb{R}_{\mathbb{c}}, \mathbb{R}_{\mathbb{c},\blacklozenge}, \mathbb{A}_{\mathbb{c}})$ of a typed metamodel $\mathbb{m}$ in a serializable model $O := (O_{\mathbb{c}_1}, \ldots, O_{\mathbb{c}_{|\mathbb{C}|}}, \text{LINK}, \text{LABEL})$ of $\mathbb{m}$.

A label update for the object o in the model O is a tuple $(o, \mathbb{a}, \mathbb{V}^-, \mathbb{V}^+)$, *where* $\mathbb{a} \in \mathbb{A}_{\mathbb{c}}^{\preccurlyeq}$ *is an attribute of* $\mathbb{c}$ *or one of its superclasses,* $\mathbb{V}^-$ *and* $\mathbb{V}^+$ *are sets of attribute values to be removed and added from and to the labels of o for* $\mathbb{a}$*, i.e.* $\mathbb{V}^- \subseteq \textit{LABEL}(o, \mathbb{a}) \land \mathbb{V}^+ \subseteq \mathbb{V}_{\textit{ATYPE}(\mathbb{a})} \setminus \textit{LABEL}(o, \mathbb{a})$.

Analog to a link update, a label update only affects the set of attribute values that are labelled to an object for an attribute that is defined for one of the metaclasses instantiated by the object. Labels can be removed by removing attribute values from this set and can be added by adding new attribute values to the set. Such added attribute values have to be of the type that is specified by the attribute. The only structural difference to Definition 27 is that attribute types have no hierarchy and all attribute values are defined for the metamodel so that no constraint for their origin is needed.

Definition 29 (Object Update)
Let $O := (O_{\mathbb{c}_1}, \ldots, O_{\mathbb{c}_{|\mathbb{C}|}}, \text{LINK}, \text{LABEL})$ be a serializable model of a typed metamodel $\mathbb{m} := (\mathbb{C}, \prec, \mathbb{R}, \mathbb{A}, \text{RTYPE}, \text{ATYPE})$.

An object update in the model O is a tuple $(o, \mathbb{c}_i, k_\pm)$*, where o is an object that directly instantiates the metaclass* $\mathbb{c}_i \in \mathbb{C}$ *and* $k_\pm \in \{k_+, k_-\}$ *is the* *update kind, which indicates whether o will be added to O or removed from O, i.e.* $o \in O_{\mathbb{C}_i} \Leftrightarrow k_\pm = k_-$.

An object update in a model lists a single object to be removed from the model or to be added to the model together with the metaclass that is directly instantiated by the object. This definition is not intended to give the reader any further insights. It is a supporting definition that gives us a counterpart of link updates and label updates, which is used in later definitions of consistency preservation after an update.

Definition 30 (Model Update for a Consistency Rule)
Let $\mathfrak{C}$ be a set of correspondences for a consistency rule $\mathfrak{R}$ in two serializable models O_l and $O_r := (O_{\mathbb{C}_1}, \ldots, O_{\mathbb{C}_{|\mathbb{C}|}}, \text{LINK}, \text{LABEL})$ of two typed metamodels $\mathbb{m}_l$ and $\mathbb{m}_r$.

A model update for the consistency rule $\mathfrak{R}$ *in the model* O_r *based on the correspondences* $\mathfrak{C}$ *is a tuple* $(\mathfrak{C}^-, \mathfrak{C}^+, \mathfrak{O}, \mathfrak{I}, \mathfrak{A})$*, where* $\mathfrak{C}^-$ *and* $\mathfrak{C}^+$ *are sets of correspondences to be removed and added from and to* $\mathfrak{C}$*, where* $\mathfrak{O}$ *is a set of object updates in* O_r*. where* $\mathfrak{I}$ *is a set of link updates, and where* $\mathfrak{A}$ *is a set of label updates. The link and label updates in* $\mathfrak{I}$ *and* $\mathfrak{A}$ *update objects of* O_r *after the object removals and additions, i.e. objects in* $(O_r \setminus \bigcup_{\mathfrak{o} \in \mathfrak{O}} \{o \mid \mathfrak{o} = (o, \mathbb{c}_i, k_-)\}) \cup \bigcup_{\mathfrak{o} \in \mathfrak{O}} \{o \mid \mathfrak{o} = (o, \mathbb{c}_i, k_+)\}$.

A model update is called empty if all sets of it are empty. All model updates for $\mathfrak{R}$ in all serializable models of $\mathbb{m}_r$ based on arbitrary correspondences for $\mathfrak{R}$ are denoted by $\mathcal{U}_{\mathfrak{R}}^{\mathbb{m}_r}$. We call a model update for $\mathfrak{R}$ in O_r also briefly an update in O_r.

Updates in O_l are defined analogously by replacing the direction-specific occurrences of O_r with O_l and $\mathbb{C}_r$ with $\mathbb{C}_l$ in Definition 30.

A model update brings several object updates, which remove and add objects from the model, together with links and label updates for different objects. It is only defined for a specific consistency rule and lists correspondences to be removed and added for this rule. Such correspondences require a second model of a second metamodel. Therefore, a model update is indirectly based on both models of the correspondences, even if updates are only performed in one of these two models.

Definition 30 imposes no constraints on the linked objects and labelled attribute values that are removed or added using link and label updates. The link and label updates of a model update may, however, only update objects that are not removed. It would not cause any problems to also allow link or label updates for objects to be removed. This could, however, be misleading and the result of a model update would not be different if objects were updated before removal. This constraint on the targets of link and label updates are best explained using the implied order of execution: Link and label updates are performed after the object removals and additions.

The metaclass tuples for which the consistency rule $\mathfrak{R}$ is defined, are irrelevant for our definition of a model update. By Definition 23 it is already given that the consistency rule $\mathfrak{R}$ is defined for two metaclass tuples of the correct metamodels $\mathbb{m}_l$ and $\mathbb{m}_r$. Therefore, we do not have to make this an additional requirement for Definition 30. Furthermore, it does not need to be mentioned in the definition which metaclasses are listed in these metaclass tuples. The sets of correspondences to be removed and added, however, are affected by them as they contain objects as required by them.

4.2.2. Results and Consistency Preservation

In this section, we define results of model updates for consistency rules and conditions for consistency-preserving updates.

Definition 31 (Result of a Model Update)
Let $\vec{\mathfrak{u}}_r := (\mathfrak{C}^-, \mathfrak{C}^+, \mathfrak{O}, \mathfrak{I}, \mathfrak{A})$ be a model update for a consistency rule $\mathfrak{R}$ in a serializable model $O_r := (O_{\mathbb{C}_1}, \ldots, O_{\mathbb{C}_{|\mathbb{C}|}}, \textsc{link}, \textsc{label})$ of a typed metamodel $\mathbb{m}_r := (\mathbb{C}, \prec, \mathbb{R}, \mathbb{A}, \textsc{rtype}, \textsc{atype})$ based on correspondences $\mathfrak{C}$.

The result of the model update $\vec{\mathfrak{u}}_r$ *is a tuple* $(\widetilde{\mathfrak{C}}, \widetilde{O_r})$*, where* $\widetilde{\mathfrak{C}} := (\mathfrak{C} \setminus \mathfrak{C}^-) \cup \mathfrak{C}^+$ *is the resulting set of correspondence candidates and* $\widetilde{O_r} := (\widetilde{O_{\mathbb{c}_1}}, \ldots, \widetilde{O_{\mathbb{c}_{|\mathbb{C}|}}}, \widetilde{LINK}, \widetilde{LABEL})$ *is the model conforming to* $\mathbb{m}_r$ *resulting from the object removals and additions, i.e.*

$$\forall\, \mathbb{c} \in \mathbb{C}\colon\ \widetilde{O_{\mathbb{c}}} := (O_{\mathbb{c}} \setminus \bigcup_{\mathfrak{o} \in \mathfrak{O}} \{o \mid \mathfrak{o} = (o, \mathbb{c}, k_-)\}) \cup \bigcup_{\mathfrak{o} \in \mathfrak{O}} \{o \mid \mathfrak{o} = (o, \mathbb{c}, k_+)\}$$

with $\widetilde{LINK}\colon \widetilde{O_r} \times \mathbb{R}_{\mathbb{C}}^{\preccurlyeq} \to \mathcal{P}(\widetilde{O})$ *and* $\widetilde{LABEL}\colon \widetilde{O_r} \times \mathbb{A}_{\mathbb{C}}^{\preccurlyeq} \to \mathcal{P}(\mathbb{V})$ *according to the link and label updates, i.e.*

$$\widetilde{LINK}(o, \mathbb{r}) := \begin{cases} (LINK(o, \mathbb{r}) \setminus O^-) \cup O^+ & \text{if} \exists\, (o, \mathbb{r}, O^-, O^+) \in \mathfrak{I} \\ LINK(o, \mathbb{r}) & \text{else} \end{cases}$$

$$\widetilde{LABEL}(o, \mathbb{a}) := \begin{cases} (LABEL(o, \mathbb{a}) \setminus \mathbb{V}^-) \cup \mathbb{V}^+ & \text{if} \exists\, (o, \mathbb{a}, \mathbb{V}^-, \mathbb{V}^+) \in \mathfrak{A} \\ LABEL(o, \mathbb{a}) & \text{else} \end{cases}$$

Results of updates $\overleftarrow{\mathfrak{u}}_l$ in the left model are defined analogously by replacing the direction-specific occurrences of the index r with l and the forward arrow with the backward arrow in Definition 31.

A model update results in a new model, which is obtained by executing the link, label, and object updates. It also results in a new set of correspondence candidates, which is obtained by removing and adding the correspondences directly given by the model update. The resulting model is completely defined by the given updates. No further constraints are necessary and no degrees of freedom remain. The resulting model is identical to the model in which the model update is performed, except for the modifications precisely prescribed by the model update. In this sense, the definition of a result of model update provides the semantics for a model update.

By Definition 30 it is already given that the elements in $\mathfrak{C}$ are correspondences for $\mathfrak{R}$ in a serializable model of a typed metamodel and in O_r. This other model, which we usually name O_l, and its metamodel are not needed in Definition 31. They have, however, an indirect influence on the result of a model update, as the old and new correspondences are based on them.

Definition 32 (Serializability-Preserving Model Update)
Let $\vec{\mathfrak{ur}}_r := (\widetilde{\mathfrak{C}}, \widetilde{O_r})$ be the result of a model update $\vec{\mathfrak{u}}_r := (\mathfrak{C}^-, \mathfrak{C}^+, \mathfrak{D}, \mathfrak{I}, \mathfrak{A})$ for a consistency rule $\mathfrak{R}$ in a serializable model O_r of a typed metamodel $\mathbb{m}_r := (\mathbb{C}, \prec, \mathbb{R}, \mathbb{A}, \text{RTYPE}, \text{ATYPE}_r)$ based on correspondences $\mathfrak{C}$.

The model update $\vec{\mathfrak{u}}_r$ is serializability preserving iff the resulting model $\widetilde{O_r} = (\widetilde{O_{\mathbb{c}_1}}, \ldots, \widetilde{O_{\mathbb{c}_{|\mathbb{C}|}}}, \widetilde{\mathit{LINK}}, \widetilde{\mathit{LABEL}})$ is a serializable model of $\mathbb{m}_r$ without correspondence candidate pairs that contain removed objects and without links to removed objects, i.e. for $O_r^- := \bigcup_{\mathfrak{o} \in \mathfrak{D}} \{o \mid \mathfrak{o} = (o, \mathbb{c}_j, k_-)\}$:

$$\forall\, (\langle o_l \rangle, (\widetilde{o_{r,1}}, \ldots, \widetilde{o_{r,m}})) \in \widetilde{\mathfrak{C}}\colon \forall\, 1 \leq i \leq m\colon \widetilde{o_{r,i}} \notin O_r^-$$
$$\wedge\ \forall\, \mathbb{c}_i \in \mathbb{C}_r\colon \forall\, \widetilde{o_1} \in \widetilde{O_{\mathbb{c}_i}}, \mathbb{r} \in \mathbb{R}_{\mathbb{c}_i}\colon \forall\, \widetilde{o_2} \in \widetilde{\mathit{LINK}}(\widetilde{o_1}, \mathbb{r})\colon \widetilde{o_2} \notin O_r^-$$

Serializability-preserving updates $\overleftarrow{\mathfrak{u}}_l$ in the left model are defined analogously by replacing the direction-specific occurrences of the index r with l and the forward arrow with the backward arrow in Definition 32.

Serializability-preserving model updates are updates which result in serializable models and correspondence candidates such that no correspondence candidate pair contains a removed object and no links to removed objects remain. This means that the model update has to ensure that all correspondences and all links to removed objects are removed as well. It also means that no cyclic containment references or multiple containers for an object may be introduced by the model update. There are, however, no requirements for the conditions of the consistency rule for which the model update is performed. Such a requirement is added in the next definition which deals with consistency preservation.

As in Definition 30, the correspondences in $\mathfrak{C}$ are for the consistency rule $\mathfrak{R}$ and they are based on O_r and another serializable model of a typed metamodel. Both, the other model and metamodel are not directly relevant for Definition 32 and therefore omitted. In other words, whether a model update is serializability preserving or not cannot be influenced by changing the other model or metamodel. It only depends on the updated model and on those halves of the correspondences that are related to the updated model.

Definition 33 (Consistency Rule Preserving)
Let $\vec{\mathrm{ur}}_r := (\widetilde{\mathfrak{C}}, \widetilde{O_r})$ be the result of a serializability-preserving model update $\vec{\mathrm{u}}_r$ for a consistency rule $\mathfrak{R}$ in a serializable model O_r based on correspondences $\mathfrak{C}$ in a serializable model O_l and in O_r such that O_l and O_r are consistent according to $\mathfrak{R}$ with respect to $\mathfrak{C}$.

The model update $\vec{\mathrm{u}}_r$ is consistency preserving according to $\mathfrak{R}$ with respect to $\mathfrak{C}$ iff O_l and the resulting serializable model $\widetilde{O_r}$ are consistent according to $\mathfrak{R}$ with respect to $\widetilde{\mathfrak{C}}$.

Updates $\overleftarrow{\mathrm{u}}_l$ in O_l that preserve consistency according to a rule are defined analogously by replacing the direction-specific occurrences of the index r with l and the forward arrow with the backward arrow in Definition 33.

A model update preserves consistency according to a consistency rule if the resulting model is consistent with the other model, for which correspondences were given, according to the rule. This definition of consistency preservation demands only that the resulting model has to be consistent with the other model with respect to the resulting correspondences. It is not further restricted how this consistency is achieved. This minimal definition of consistency preservation is only possible because the combination of two other definitions imposes enough constraints. Our notion of consistency (see Definition 24) contains strong requirements for the correspondences, and a model update (see Definition 30) may only update one of both models. In particular, the instance tuples of the correspondences from the model that is not updated are still present after an update and still fulfill the condition of the consistency rule. Thus, the definition of consistency requires that there is at least one correspondence for these instance tuples, which witnesses consistency with objects in the updated model. Therefore, a consistency-preserving model update has to add new correspondences for all removed correspondences that were not optional because there are several correspondences for the same instance tuples of the other side.

We only define consistency *preservation* for updates of models that are already consistent. A model update that results in consistent models when the initial models were not consistent could be called *consistency establishing*. If the initial models can be consistent or not, then a model update that results in consistent models could also be called *consistency achieving* in order to emphasize that it is not specified whether consistency was preserved or newly established. For our change-driven approach it is, however, not necessary to define such concepts because we are always working based on a former model state that was already consistent.

As before, there are some details that follow from other definitions but that are not central to our definition of consistency preservation according to a rule. By Definition 31 and Definition 23, for example, it is already given that O_r and O_l are serializable models of typed metamodels. These metamodels, which we usually name $\mathbb{m}_l$ and $\mathbb{m}_r$, are not relevant for Definition 33, so we do not mention them in the definition.

4.3. Change-Driven Consistency Preservation

In order to keep two models consistent after changes, it is not sufficient to preserve consistency for two models that are already consistent as in our last definition. A key concept of the change-driven consistency preservation approach presented in this thesis, is to re-establish consistency after a change that renders two previously consistent models inconsistent. To this end, we will first define what a model change is and when it is considered consistency-breaking. Then, we introduce a change-relative notion of consistency preservation. Note, however, that we will only define consistency preservation for changes that break consistency according to at most one rule at once.

4.3.1. Consistency-Breaking Model Changes

In this section, we define model changes, explain the difference to model updates and define which changes are considered consistency-breaking.

Definition 34 (Model Change)
Let O be a serializable model of a typed metamodel $\mathbb{m}$.

A model change in O is either a link update for an object in O, a label update for an object in O, or an object update in O.

We call a model change in O also briefly a change in O.

A model change only affects a single object and changes exactly one part of the model: It either adds or removes linked objects for a single reference, adds or removes labelled values for a single attribute, or it adds or removes the object. Therefore, it is very different from a model update, which may combine several link, label, and object updates. Furthermore, a model change is neither directly nor indirectly related to another model or to a consistency rule. A model update, however, is only defined for a consistency rule and based on correspondences with another model.

Definition 35 (Result of a Model Change)
Let $\mathfrak{c}$ be a change in a serializable model O of a typed metamodel $\mathbb{m}$.

The result of a model change $\mathfrak{c}$ is a model $\widetilde{O}$, which conforms to $\mathbb{m}$ and results from executing $\mathfrak{c}$ in O analogous to Definition 31, i.e. $\widetilde{O} := (O_{\mathbb{C}_1}, \ldots, O_{\mathbb{C}_{i-1}}, \widetilde{O_{\mathbb{C}_i}}, O_{\mathbb{C}_{i+1}}, \ldots, O_{\mathbb{C}_{|\mathbb{C}|}}, \widetilde{LINK}, \widetilde{LABEL})$ with

$$
\begin{array}{ll}
\widetilde{LINK}(o, \mathbb{r}) := (LINK(o, \mathbb{r}) \setminus O^-) \cup O^+ & \textit{if } \mathfrak{c} = (o, \mathbb{r}, O^-, O^+) \\
\widetilde{LABEL}(o, \mathbb{a}) := (LABEL(o, \mathbb{a}) \setminus \mathbb{V}^-) \cup \mathbb{V}^+ & \textit{if } \mathfrak{c} = (o, \mathbb{a}, \mathbb{V}^-, \mathbb{V}^+) \\
\widetilde{O_{\mathbb{C}_i}} := O_{\mathbb{C}_i} \cup \{o\} & \textit{if } \mathfrak{c} = (o, \mathbb{C}_i, k_+) \\
\widetilde{O_{\mathbb{C}_i}} := O_{\mathbb{C}_i} \setminus \{o\} & \textit{if } \mathfrak{c} = (o, \mathbb{C}_i, k_-)
\end{array}
$$

and unchanged $\widetilde{O_{\mathbb{C}_i}}$, $\widetilde{LINK}$, and $\widetilde{LABEL}$ in all other cases.

The result of a model change is the model that we obtain by executing the change on the model for which it is defined: In case of a link or label update, the given objects or attribute values are removed and added to the set of linked objects or labelled values. If the model change is an object update, the given object is added or removed depending on the given update kind. This definition provides the semantics for a model change and is analogous to the definition of a result of a model update (Definition 31).

Our goal is to re-establish consistency directly after two models became inconsistent through a model change. To achieve this, we want to distinguish such model changes from other changes. We are not interested in changes that preserve consistency for two models that were already consistent, because no model update is necessary to preserve consistency in such a case. Furthermore, we are not interested in changes that re-establish consistency for two models that were inconsistent, because no model update is needed in this case either. Finally, we are not interested in changes that preserve inconsistency for two models that were already inconsistent, because we want to avoid such cases, which can be difficult to handle as nothing is known about the inconsistencies. We are only interested in those changes that break consistency, because they can be considered as witnesses of the reasons for inconsistency. Therefore, we define which model changes have this consistency-breaking property:

Definition 36 (Consistency-Breaking Change)
Let O_l and O_r be two serializable models that are consistent according to a consistency rule $\mathfrak{R}$ with respect to a set of correspondences $\mathfrak{C}$ and let $\mathfrak{c}_l$ be a change in O_l.

The model change $\mathfrak{c}_l$ in O_l is consistency breaking for O_r according to $\mathfrak{R}$ with respect to $\mathfrak{C}$ iff the result $\widetilde{O_l}$ of $\mathfrak{c}_l$ and O_r are not consistent according to $\mathfrak{R}$ with respect to $\mathfrak{C}$ and $\widetilde{O_l}$ is serializable.

A consistency-breaking change renders two previously consistent models inconsistent but preserves the serializability of the changed model. Therefore, all consisteny-breaking changes are serializability-preserving changes. We could distinguish these changes from changes that break not only consistency, but also serializability and we could differentiate between changes that do or do not break validity if it was given before. Such *serializability-breaking* or *validity-preserving* changes are, however, not necessary for our approach to change-driven consistency. First, we do not support changes that break serializability, because they should be avoided by the editors in which models are changed. Second, we do not distinguish between validity-breaking, validity-preserving, or invalidity-preserving changes, because we react with model updates in all cases. These updates have to re-establish consistency with respect to consistency rules for both metamodels and can only influence the validity of the unchanged model.

4.3.2. Model Updates After a Change

Based on the definition of a consistency-breaking change, we will now introduce a concept for preserving consistency after such changes through model updates.

Definition 37 (Consistency Preserving After Change)
Let $\widetilde{O_l}$ be the result of a model change $\mathfrak{c}_l$ in a serializable model O_l that is consistency-breaking for a serializable model O_r according to a consistency rule $\mathfrak{R}$ with respect to a set of correspondences $\mathfrak{C}$ and let $\vec{\mathfrak{ur}}_r := (\widetilde{\mathfrak{C}}, \widetilde{O_r})$ be the result of a serializability-preserving model update $\vec{\mathfrak{u}}_r$ for $\mathfrak{R}$ in O_r based on $\mathfrak{C}$.

The model update $\vec{\mathfrak{u}}_r$ is consistency preserving after the model change $\mathfrak{c}_l$ according to $\mathfrak{R}$ with respect to $\mathfrak{C}$ iff the models $\widetilde{O_l}$ and $\widetilde{O_r}$ resulting from the change $\mathfrak{c}_l$ and the update $\vec{\mathfrak{u}}_r$ are consistent according to $\mathfrak{R}$ with respect to $\widetilde{\mathfrak{C}}$.

Consistency-preserving updates $\overleftarrow{\mathfrak{u}}_l$ in O_l after changes in O_r are defined analogously by replacing the direction-specific occurrences of the index r with l and the forward arrow with the backward arrow in Definition 37.

This refined notion of consistency preservation after a model change brings all central concepts of our approach to change-driven consistency preservation together. It starts with two models that are consistent according to a rule with respect to certain correspondences, which witness this consistency. Then, a *single* change occurrs in one of the models, which renders both models inconsistent. We want to update only the unchanged second model in order to preserve consistency after this change. Therefore, we are interested in those updates of the second model that result in an updated second model that is consistent with the changed first model. These updates are exactly those that are defined as consistency preserving after a change by Definition 37. Note, however, that it does not define a notion of consistency preservation if *several* changes occurr.

Similar to our definition of consistency preservation without a change (Definition 24), this definition of consistency preservation after a change imposes no additional constraints on the model update. Every model update, for which the models resulting from the change and the update are consistent, is allowed. Again, this is only possible because our definition of consistency (Definition 24) makes strong requirements and the update only affects the unchanged model: For every instance tuple of the changed first model that was part of a correspondence before the change and is still present after the change, there has to be at least one correspondence which involves objects of the updated second model. Therefore, it is, for example, not possible that a model update that preserves consistency after a change simply deletes all inconsistent elements in the second model and removes all correspondences to them. The change may only have deleted a single object. Thus, all objects of the first halves of the removed correspondences except for at most one object are still present and still fulfill the condition of the consistency rule. Therefore, the definition of consistency requires that there are correspondences for these objects of the changed first model that witness consistency with objects in the updated second model.

Of course, consistency according to a single consistency rule is not enough, because several such rules may be necessary to specify consistency for two metamodels. Therefore, we define consistency preservation according to a complete consistency specification, i.e. according to several rules:

Definition 38 (Consistency Specification Preserving)
Let O_l and O_r be two serializable models that are consistent according to a consistency specification $\mathfrak{cs} := (\mathfrak{R}_1, \mathfrak{C}_1, \ldots, \mathfrak{R}_n, \mathfrak{C}_n)$, let $\widetilde{O}_l$ be the result of a change $\mathfrak{c}_l$ in O_l that is consistency-breaking for O_r according to $\mathfrak{R}_i$ with respect to $\mathfrak{C}_i$, and let $\vec{\mathfrak{ur}}_r := (\widetilde{\mathfrak{C}}_i, \widetilde{O_r})$ be the result of a serializability-preserving model update $\vec{\mathfrak{u}}_r$ for $\mathfrak{R}_i$ in O_r based on $\mathfrak{C}_i$.

The model update $\vec{\mathfrak{u}}_r$ is consistency preserving after $\mathfrak{c}_l$ according to $\mathfrak{cs}$ iff the models $\widetilde{O_l}$ and $\widetilde{O_r}$ resulting from the change $\mathfrak{c}_l$ and the model update $\vec{\mathfrak{u}}_r$ are consistent according to $\widetilde{\mathfrak{cs}} := (\mathfrak{R}_1, \mathfrak{C}_1, \ldots, \mathfrak{R}_{i-1}, \mathfrak{C}_{i-1}, \mathfrak{R}_i, \widetilde{\mathfrak{C}_i}, \mathfrak{R}_{i+1}, \mathfrak{C}_{i+1}, \ldots, \mathfrak{R}_n, \mathfrak{C}_n)$.

Consistency specification preserving updates $\overleftarrow{\mathfrak{u}}_l$ in O_l after changes in O_r are defined analogously by replacing the direction-specific occurrences of the index r with l and the forward arrow with the backward arrow in Definition 38.

In Definition 38, it can already be seen that an update in a model preserves consistency after a change to another model according to a rule with respect to a set of correspondences regardless of any additional consistency rules and correspondences. This is a direct consequence of our definition of consistency according to a specification (Definition 26), which deduces consistency according to several rules from independent consistency according to a single rule. To demonstrate this independence, we present a corollary, which shows that all other rules have no influence on the consistency preservation property of an update for a single rule:

Corollary 1 (*Rule Preserving is Enough*)
Let O_l and O_r be two serializable models of two typed metamodels $\mathfrak{m}_l$ and $\mathfrak{m}_r$, let $\vec{\mathfrak{ur}}_r := (\widetilde{\mathfrak{C}}, \widetilde{O_r})$ be the result of a model update $\vec{\mathfrak{u}}_r$ in O_r that is consistency preserving after a change $\mathfrak{c}_l$ in O_l according to a consistency rule $\mathfrak{R}$ with respect to correspondences $\mathfrak{C}$, and let $\widetilde{O_l}$ be the result of the change $\mathfrak{c}_l$.

The model update $\vec{\mathfrak{u}}_r$ is consistency preserving after the change $\mathfrak{c}_l$ according to every consistency specification $\mathfrak{cs} := (\mathfrak{R}, \mathfrak{C}, \mathfrak{R}_1, \mathfrak{C}_1, \ldots, \mathfrak{R}_n, \mathfrak{C}_n)$ for $\mathfrak{m}_l$ and $\mathfrak{m}_r$, with arbitrary additional consistency rules $\mathfrak{R}_i$ and arbitrary additional correspondences $\mathfrak{C}_i$, iff both the original models O_l and O_r as well as the models $\widetilde{O_l}$ and $\widetilde{O_r}$, which result from the change $\mathfrak{c}_l$ and the model update $\vec{\mathfrak{u}}_r$, are consistent according to $(\mathfrak{R}_1, \mathfrak{C}_1, \ldots, \mathfrak{R}_n, \mathfrak{C}_n)$.

Proof 1
"$\Rightarrow$"

Given:

$\vec{\mathfrak{u}}_r$ *consistency preserving after* $\mathfrak{c}_l$ *according to* $\mathfrak{cs}$
with Definition 38 this yields
$\widetilde{O}_l$ *and* $\widetilde{O_r}$ *consistent according to* $(\mathfrak{R}, \widetilde{\mathfrak{C}}, \mathfrak{R}_1, \mathfrak{C}_1, \ldots, \mathfrak{R}_n, \mathfrak{C}_n)$
and with Definition 26 this yields
$\widetilde{O}_l$ *and* $\widetilde{O_r}$ *consistent according to* $(\mathfrak{R}_1, \mathfrak{C}_1, \ldots, \mathfrak{R}_n, \mathfrak{C}_n)$.

From the given and Definition 38 we obtain
O_l *and* O_r *consistent according to* $(\mathfrak{R}, \mathfrak{C}, \mathfrak{R}_1, \mathfrak{C}_1, \ldots, \mathfrak{R}_n, \mathfrak{C}_n)$
and with Definition 26 this yields
O_l *and* O_r *consistent according to* $(\mathfrak{R}_1, \mathfrak{C}_1, \ldots, \mathfrak{R}_n, \mathfrak{C}_n)$.

"$\Leftarrow$"

Given:
$\widetilde{O}_l$ *and* $\widetilde{O_r}$ *consistent according to* $(\mathfrak{R}_1, \mathfrak{C}_1, \ldots, \mathfrak{R}_n, \mathfrak{C}_n)$

Prerequisite of Corollary 1:
$\vec{\mathfrak{u}}_r$ *consistency preserving after* $\mathfrak{c}_l$ *acc. to* $\mathfrak{R}$ *with respect to* $\mathfrak{C}$
with Definition 37 this yields
$\widetilde{O}_l$ *and* $\widetilde{O_r}$ *consistent according to* $\mathfrak{R}$ *with respect to* $\widetilde{\mathfrak{C}}$
with Definition 26 and the given this yields
$\widetilde{O}_l$ *and* $\widetilde{O_r}$ *consistent according to* $(\mathfrak{R}, \widetilde{\mathfrak{C}}, \mathfrak{R}_1, \mathfrak{C}_1, \ldots, \mathfrak{R}_n, \mathfrak{C}_n)$ (1)

Also given:

O_l *and* O_r *consistent according to* $(\mathfrak{R}_1, \mathfrak{C}_1, \ldots, \mathfrak{R}_n, \mathfrak{C}_n)$ (2)

with Definition 38 the previous facts (1) and (2) yield

$\vec{\mathfrak{u}}_r$ *consistency preserving after* $\mathfrak{c}_l$ *according to* $\mathfrak{cs}$

■

This corollary shows that an update that is consistency preserving for a single rule only has to ensure that it does not break consistency for any other rules in order to be consistency preserving for them too. More specifically, every update that is consistency preserving after a change for a single rule is consistency preserving after the change for any consistency specification that contains this rule iff the original models and the models resulting from the change and the update are consistent according to all other rules of the specification. A key requirement is that the original models were already consistent according the other rules. This means that a single update for a single rule is enough to preserve consistency for a complete specification after a change iff neither the change nor the update breaks consistency for the other rules. Therefore, the corollary demonstrates that consistency can be achieved in a way that deals with individual rules in isolation by updating models directly after changes that only break consistency for an individual rule.

4.3.3. Update Functions for Consistency Rules

The goal of the formal language presented in this chapter is to represent a change-driven approach to consistency preservation, which starts with empty—and thus trivially consistent—models and always updates one of these models after a consistency-breaking change in the other model. In order to reach this goal of automated consistency preservation it is not enough to only consider an update for two fixed models and a single change. Therefore, we define functions that yield an update that shall preserve consistency after a change as output if we provide two models, a change, and correspondences for these models as input:

Definition 39 (Update Function for a Consistency Rule)
Let $\mathfrak{R}_{\mathbb{C}_l,\mathbb{C}_r}$ be a consistency rule for two metaclass tuples $\langle\mathbb{C}_l\rangle$ and $\langle\mathbb{C}_r\rangle$ of two typed metamodels $\mathbb{m}_l$ and $\mathbb{m}_r$ and let $O^{\star}_{\mathbb{m}_l}$ and $O^{\star}_{\mathbb{m}_r}$ denote the universes of serializable models of $\mathbb{m}_l$ and $\mathbb{m}_r$.

An update function for the consistency rule $\mathfrak{R}_{\mathbb{C}_l,\mathbb{C}_r}$ is a function $\overrightarrow{\text{UF}}_{\langle\mathbb{C}_l\rangle,\langle\mathbb{C}_r\rangle}$: $O^{\star}_{\mathbb{m}_l} \times O^{\star}_{\mathbb{m}_r} \times C^{\mathbb{m}_l} \times \mathcal{P}(O_{\langle\mathbb{C}_l\rangle} \times O_{\langle\mathbb{C}_r\rangle}) \rightarrow \mathcal{U}^{\mathbb{m}_r}_{\mathfrak{R}_{\mathbb{C}_l,\mathbb{C}_r}}$, which takes two serializable models of $\mathbb{m}_l$ and $\mathbb{m}_r$, a change in a model of $\mathbb{m}_l$, and a set of correspondence candidates in $O_{\langle\mathbb{C}_l\rangle} \times O_{\langle\mathbb{C}_r\rangle}$ as input and yields a model update for $\mathfrak{R}_{\mathbb{C}_l,\mathbb{C}_r}$ in the given model of $\mathbb{m}_r$ as output, i.e. $C^{\mathbb{m}_l}$ denotes the infinite set of changes in all serializable models of $\mathbb{m}_l$ and $\mathcal{U}^{\mathbb{m}_r}_{\mathfrak{R}_{\mathbb{C}_l,\mathbb{C}_r}}$ denotes the infinite set of updates for $\mathfrak{R}_{\mathbb{C}_l,\mathbb{C}_r}$ in all serializable models of $\mathbb{m}_r$ based on arbitrary correspondences for $\mathfrak{R}_{\mathbb{C}_l,\mathbb{C}_r}$.

Backward update functions $\overleftarrow{\text{UF}}_{\langle\mathbb{C}_l\rangle,\langle\mathbb{C}_r\rangle}: O^{\star}_{\mathbb{m}_l} \times O^{\star}_{\mathbb{m}_r} \times C^{\mathbb{m}_r} \times \mathcal{P}(O_{\langle\mathbb{C}_l\rangle} \times O_{\langle\mathbb{C}_r\rangle}) \rightarrow \mathcal{U}^{\mathbb{m}_l}_{\mathfrak{R}_{\mathbb{C}_l,\mathbb{C}_r}}$ for $\mathfrak{R}_{\mathbb{C}_l,\mathbb{C}_r}$ are defined analogously by replacing the direction-specific occurrences of the index r with l and the forward arrow with the backward arrow in Definition 39.

Update functions take two models, a change in the first model, and instance tuples that could be correspondences for these models as input and output an update for the second model. This definition is only the basis for subsequent definitions of special update functions that yield serializability-preserving or even consistency-preserving updates for inputs that fulfill certain constraints. We could have incorporated these constraints in our definition of update functions, but refrained from it in order to avoid additional complexity. The domain $\mathcal{P}(O_{\langle\mathbb{C}_l\rangle} \times O_{\langle\mathbb{C}_r\rangle})$ for the correspondence candidates, for example, could have been restricted to those instance tuples that occur in the two models that are provided as first and second input. This would, however, make Definition 39 even more complex and would still not be enough as we are finally only interested in consistency-breaking changes and consistency-preserving updates. Therefore, we extend our definition of update functions with additional constraints and guarantees in two separate steps and define serializability-preserving update functions before we define consistency-preserving update functions:

Definition 40 (Serializability-Preserving Function)
Let $\vec{\text{UF}}_{\langle \mathbb{c}_l \rangle, \langle \mathbb{c}_r \rangle} : O^{\star}_{\mathbb{m}_l} \times O^{\star}_{\mathbb{m}_r} \times C^{\mathbb{m}_l} \times \mathcal{P}(O_{\langle \mathbb{c}_l \rangle} \times O_{\langle \mathbb{c}_r \rangle}) \rightarrow \mathcal{U}^{\mathbb{m}_r}_{\mathfrak{R}_{\mathbb{c}_l, \mathbb{c}_r}}$ be an update function for a consistency rule $\mathfrak{R}_{\mathbb{c}_l, \mathbb{c}_r}$ for two metaclass tuples $\langle \mathbb{c}_l \rangle := (\mathbb{c}_{i_1}, \ldots, \mathbb{c}_{i_n})$ and $\langle \mathbb{c}_r \rangle$ of two typed metamodels $\mathbb{m}_l$ and $\mathbb{m}_r$.

The update function $\vec{\text{UF}}_{\langle \mathbb{c}_l \rangle, \langle \mathbb{c}_r \rangle}$ is serializability preserving iff it yields serializability-preserving model updates for $\mathfrak{R}_{\mathbb{c}_l, \mathbb{c}_r}$ in the given right model based on the given pairs of instance tuples if these are correspondences for $\mathfrak{R}_{\mathbb{c}_l, \mathbb{c}_r}$ in the given models and the given change results in a serializable model, but is undefined otherwise, i.e. for $\mathcal{U}^{O_r}_{\mathfrak{R}_{\mathbb{c}_l, \mathbb{c}_r} \star}(\mathfrak{C})$ denoting the infinite set of serializability-preserving model updates for $\mathfrak{R}_{\mathbb{c}_l, \mathbb{c}_r}$ in O_r based on correspondences $\mathfrak{C} := \{(\langle o_{l,1} \rangle, \langle o_{r,1} \rangle), \ldots, (\langle o_{l,n_i} \rangle, \langle o_{r,n_i} \rangle)\}$ and $C^{\mathbb{m}_l}_{\star}$ denoting the infinite set of all changes in all serializable models of $\mathbb{m}_l$ with serializable result model:

$$\vec{\text{UF}}_{\langle \mathbb{c}_l \rangle, \langle \mathbb{c}_r \rangle}(O_l, O_r, \mathfrak{c}_l, \mathfrak{C}) :=$$

$$\begin{cases} \mathfrak{e} \in \mathcal{U}^{O_r}_{\mathfrak{R}_{\mathbb{c}_l, \mathbb{c}_r} \star}(\mathfrak{C}) & \text{if } \mathfrak{c}_l \in C^{\mathbb{m}_l}_{\star} \ \wedge \ \forall\, 1 \leq i \leq n: \\ & \quad (\langle o_{l,i} \rangle, \langle o_{r,i} \rangle) \in \text{COND}_{\langle \mathbb{c}_l \rangle} \times \text{COND}_{\langle \mathbb{c}_r \rangle} \\ \bot & \text{otherwise} \end{cases}$$

Serializability-preserving backward update functions $\overleftarrow{\text{UF}}_{\langle \mathbb{c}_l \rangle, \langle \mathbb{c}_r \rangle}$ for $\mathfrak{R}_{\mathbb{c}_l, \mathbb{c}_r}$ are defined analogously by replacing the direction-specific occurrences of the index r with l and the forward arrow with the backward arrow in Definition 40.

A serializability-preserving update function yields a serializability-preserving model update as output if it is given a serializability-preserving change and correspondences for the considered rule. It is undefined in all other cases, i.e. if the change results in a model that is not serializable, or the given pairs of instance tuples are not correspondences for the given models and the considered rule, or both. Furthermore, it is only required that the provided instance tuples are correspondences for the considered rule in the given models. By Definition 23 this means that these tuples have to fulfill the conditions of the considered rule but no completeness as in our definition of consistency (see Definition 24) is required. Therefore, a serializability-preserving update function contains no constraints and guarantees for consistency and consistency preservation. It only provides guarantees regarding the serializability: If the function returns an update, then the provided change preserves serializability from the model O_l to the changed model $\widetilde{O_l}$. Every returned update preserves serializability from the model O_r to the updated model $\widetilde{O_r}$. Altogether, this means that for all cases for which a serializability-preserving update function is defined, the change input preserves serializability for the changed model and the update output preserves serializability for the updated model.

Definition 41 (Consistency-Preserving Function)
Let $\vec{\text{UF}}_{\langle \mathbb{C}_l \rangle, \langle \mathbb{C}_r \rangle} : O^{\star}_{\mathbb{m}_l} \times O^{\star}_{\mathbb{m}_r} \times C^{\mathbb{m}_l} \times \mathcal{P}(O_{\langle \mathbb{C}_l \rangle} \times O_{\langle \mathbb{C}_r \rangle}) \rightarrow \mathcal{U}^{\mathbb{m}_r}_{\mathfrak{R}_{\mathbb{C}_l,\mathbb{C}_r}}$ be a serializability-preserving update function for a consistency rule $\mathfrak{R}_{\mathbb{C}_l,\mathbb{C}_r}$.

The update function $\vec{\text{UF}}_{\langle \mathbb{C}_l \rangle, \langle \mathbb{C}_r \rangle}$ is consistency preserving according to $\mathfrak{R}_{\mathbb{C}_l,\mathbb{C}_r}$ iff $\vec{\text{UF}}_{\langle \mathbb{C}_l \rangle, \langle \mathbb{C}_r \rangle}(O_l, O_r, \mathfrak{c}_l, \mathfrak{C})$ yields updates for the given right model O_r that are consistency preserving after $\mathfrak{c}_l$ according to $\mathfrak{R}_{\mathbb{C}_l,\mathbb{C}_r}$ with respect to the given pairs of instance tuples $\mathfrak{C}$ if these are correspondences for $\mathfrak{R}_{\mathbb{C}_l,\mathbb{C}_r}$ in the given models and $\mathfrak{c}$ is consistency-breaking for the given models according to the considered $\mathfrak{R}_{\mathbb{C}_l,\mathbb{C}_r}$ with respect to the given $\mathfrak{C}$, but is undefined otherwise.

Consistency-preserving backward update functions $\overleftarrow{\text{UF}}_{\langle \mathbb{C}_l \rangle, \langle \mathbb{C}_r \rangle}$ for $\mathfrak{R}_{\mathbb{C}_l,\mathbb{C}_r}$ are defined analogously by replacing the direction-specific occurrences of the index r with l and the forward arrow with the backward arrow in Definition 41.

A consistency-preserving function yields a consistency-preserving update iff it is given a consistency-breaking change and correspondences that witness the broken consistency. Similar to a serializability-preserving function, it is undefined in all other cases. More precisely, in addition to all cases for which a serializability-preserving function is undefined, a consistency-preserving function is also undefined in the following cases: If the given change results in a serializable model that does not break consistency, or the set of correspondences is incomplete because not all condition fulfillments are witnessed, or both. This means a consistency-preserving function makes stronger requirements for inputs for which it is defined than serializability-preserving functions.

In the same way a consistency-preserving function also provides stronger guarantees for its outputs than a serializability-preserving function. It preserves serializability for *both* models individually and consistency for the combination of both models. Therefore, a longer description for consistency-preserving functions, which emphasizes the stronger requirements and guarantees would be as follow: Functions that yield updates that preserve consistency, which also guarantees serializability, after changes that break consistency but preserve serializability of the changed model if they obtain all correspondences that witness the broken consistency.

4.3.4. Consistency-Preserving Update Specifications

As consistency specifications consist of several consistency rules, a single update function for one of these rules is not enough to preserve consistency according to the specification. Therefore, we will define consistency update specifications with several consistency update functions in this section. Prior to that, we will show that update functions that yield updates that preserve consistency for a single rule independent of other rules, are sufficient to preserve consistency for all rules:

Corollary 2 (*Rule Preserving is Still Enough*)
Let O_l and O_r be two serializable models of two typed metamodels $\mathbb{m}_l$ and $\mathbb{m}_r$ that are consistent according to a consistency rule $\mathfrak{R}$ with respect to correspondences $\mathfrak{C}$ and let $\vec{\text{UF}}_{\langle \mathbb{c}_l \rangle, \langle \mathbb{c}_r \rangle}$ be an update function that is consistency preserving for $\mathfrak{R}$.

The update function $\vec{\text{UF}}_{\langle \mathbb{c}_l \rangle, \langle \mathbb{c}_r \rangle}(O_l, O_r, \mathfrak{c}_l, \mathfrak{C})$ *yields updates* $\vec{\mathfrak{u}}_r$ *that are consistency preserving after* $\mathfrak{c}_l$ *according to every consistency specification* $\mathfrak{cs} := (\mathfrak{R}, \mathfrak{C}, \mathfrak{R}_1, \mathfrak{C}_1, \ldots, \mathfrak{R}_n, \mathfrak{C}_n)$ *for* $\mathbb{m}_l$ *and* $\mathbb{m}_r$*, with arbitrary additional consistency rules* $\mathfrak{R}_i$ *and arbitrary additional correspondences* $\mathfrak{C}_i$ *iff both the original models* O_l *and* O_r *as well as the models* $\widetilde{O_l}$ *and* $\widetilde{O_r}$*, which result from the change* $\mathfrak{c}_l$ *and the model update* $\vec{\mathfrak{u}}_r$*, are consistent according to* $(\mathfrak{R}_1, \mathfrak{C}_1, \ldots, \mathfrak{R}_n, \mathfrak{C}_n)$*, and is undefined in all other cases.*

Proof 2
"$\Rightarrow$"

Given:

$\vec{\mathfrak{u}}_r$ *consistency preserving after* $\mathfrak{c}_l$ *according to* $\mathfrak{cs}$
with Definition 38 this yields
$\widetilde{O}_l$ *and* $\widetilde{O_r}$ *consistent according to* $(\mathfrak{R}, \widetilde{\mathfrak{C}}, \mathfrak{R}_1, \mathfrak{C}_1, \ldots, \mathfrak{R}_n, \mathfrak{C}_n)$
with Definition 26 this yields
$\widetilde{O}_l$ *and* $\widetilde{O_r}$ *consistent according to* $(\mathfrak{R}_1, \mathfrak{C}_1, \ldots, \mathfrak{R}_n, \mathfrak{C}_n)$ (1)

From the given we also obtain with Definition 38 and 36
O_l *and* O_r *consistent according to* $(\mathfrak{R}, \widetilde{\mathfrak{C}}, \mathfrak{R}_1, \mathfrak{C}_1, \ldots, \mathfrak{R}_n, \mathfrak{C}_n)$
with Definition 26 this yields
O_l *and* O_r *consistent according to* $(\mathfrak{R}_1, \mathfrak{C}_1, \ldots, \mathfrak{R}_n, \mathfrak{C}_n)$ (2)

Together, (1) and (2) show the required forward implication.

"$\Leftarrow$"

Given:
O_l *and* O_r *consistent according to* $(\mathfrak{R}_1, \mathfrak{C}_1, \ldots, \mathfrak{R}_n, \mathfrak{C}_n)$ (1)
and also given:
$\widetilde{O}_l$ *and* $\widetilde{O_r}$ *consistent according to* $(\mathfrak{R}_1, \mathfrak{C}_1, \ldots, \mathfrak{R}_n, \mathfrak{C}_n)$. (2)

Prerequisite of Corollary 2:

$\vec{UF}_{\langle \mathbb{c}_l \rangle, \langle \mathbb{c}_r \rangle}$ *consistency preserving for* $\mathfrak{R}$

with $\vec{UF}_{\langle \mathbb{c}_l \rangle, \langle \mathbb{c}_r \rangle}(O_l, O_r, \mathfrak{c}_l, \mathfrak{C}) = \vec{\mathfrak{u}}_r$ *this yields*

$\vec{\mathfrak{u}}_r$ *consistency preserving after* $\mathfrak{c}_l$ *acc. to* $\mathfrak{R}$ *with respect to* $\mathfrak{C}$ (3)

With Corollary 1 the previous facts (1), (2), and (3) yield

$\vec{\mathfrak{u}}_r$ *consistency preserving after* $\mathfrak{c}_l$ *according to* $\mathfrak{cs}$.

■

This corollary demonstrates that we can consider update functions, which yield consistency-preserving changes for every consistency-breaking change, instead of updates for specific changes without losing the advantage that we can deal with individual consistency rules in separation. It is still enough to preserve consistency for an individual rule to preserve consistency according to a complete specification iff the original models and the models resulting from the change and the update are consistent according to all other rules of the specification. As a result, it is sufficient to have a separate update function for each rule of a consistency specification:

Definition 42 (Consistency Update Specification)
Let $\mathfrak{cs} := (\mathfrak{R}_{\mathbb{c}_{1,l}, \mathbb{c}_{1,r}}, \mathfrak{C}_1, \ldots, \mathfrak{R}_n, \mathfrak{R}_{\mathbb{c}_{n,l}, \mathbb{c}_{n,r}})$ be a consistency specification for two typed metamodels $\mathbb{m}_l$ and $\mathbb{m}_r$.

A consistency update specification for $\mathfrak{cs}$ *is a tuple* $(\vec{UF}_{\langle \mathbb{c}_{1,l} \rangle, \langle \mathbb{c}_{1,r} \rangle}, \ldots, \vec{UF}_{\langle \mathbb{c}_{n,l} \rangle, \langle \mathbb{c}_{n,r} \rangle})$, *where every* $\vec{UF}_{\langle \mathbb{c}_{i,l} \rangle, \langle \mathbb{c}_{i,r} \rangle}$ *is an update function for* $\mathfrak{R}_{\mathbb{c}_{i,l}, \mathbb{c}_{i,r}}$.

Backward update specifications are defined analogously.

A consistency update specification is just a list that contains an update functions for every consistency rule of a consistency specification in the same order as the rules. It only requires that the update functions are defined for models and changes of the correct metamodels and for pairs of instance tuples that could be correspondences of the considered rule.

Definition 43 (Consistency Preserving Specifications)
Let $\mathfrak{us} := (\vec{\text{UF}}_{\langle \mathbb{c}_{1,l}\rangle, \langle \mathbb{c}_{1,r}\rangle}, \ldots, \vec{\text{UF}}_{\langle \mathbb{c}_{n,l}\rangle, \langle \mathbb{c}_{n,r}\rangle})$ be an update specification for a consistency specification $\mathfrak{cs} := (\mathfrak{R}_{\mathbb{c}_{1,l}, \mathbb{c}_{1,r}}, \mathfrak{C}_1, \ldots, \mathfrak{R}_n, \mathfrak{R}_{\mathbb{c}_{n,l}, \mathbb{c}_{n,r}})$.

The update specification $\mathfrak{us}$ *is consistency preserving iff every update function* $\vec{UF}_{\langle \mathbb{c}_{i,l}\rangle, \langle \mathbb{c}_{i,r}\rangle}$ *is consistency preserving according to* $\mathfrak{R}_{\mathbb{c}_{i,l}, \mathbb{c}_{i,r}}$.

Consistency-preserving backward update specifications are defined analogously.

A complete consistency update specification is consistency preserving iff every individual update function preserves consistency for its rule. Because of Corollary 2, this means that it is possible to preserve consistency for any two serializable models that conform to two metamodels using a consistency-preserving forward update specification and a consistency-preserving backward update specification for both models. This can be done by starting with two empty models, which are trivially consistent, and performing an update in one of the two models after every consistency-breaking change in the other model. These updates can be obtained by invoking the update function for the consistency rule for which a condition is no longer fulfilled after the change. All definitions and corollaries of this chapter were presented in order to guarantee that such a consistency-preservation strategy always results in consistent models if no serializability-breaking updates are performed and if no change breaks the conditions of more than one consistency rule at once. But even in such a case, it could be possible that a subsequent execution of several updates for a single change results in models that are consistent according to the complete specification. This can, however, not be guaranteed with the presented formalization.

4.4. Conclusions

In this chapter, we have presented a formal language that defines realization-independent concepts of specification-driven consistency preservation using set theory. It is based on definitions for fundamental concepts, such as metamodels, models, or conditions, which we have presented in section 2.3. First, we have introduced concepts for consistency rules and for correspondences, which are used as witness structures for the fulfillment of consistency conditions. Then, we have defined how updates of model elements, links, and labels can be formally represented and we have explained their semantics in terms of the results of such updates. Next, we have specified which conditions have to be fulfilled by an update to preserve consistency according to a rule or a set of rules. Subsequently, we have introduced atomic changes and we have discussed the conditions under which such changes break consistency. Based on this, we have presented a refined definition of consistency preservation after a consistency-breaking change. Then, we have introduced functions that output consistency-preserving updates when they obtain two given models, a change, and correspondence candidates as input. Finally, we have discussed circumstances in which it is sufficient to always preserve consistency after a single change and according to a single rule in order to preserve consistency inductively and for all rules. Altogether, the presented definitions and explanations represent answers to subquestion 1.3 and 1.4, which we presented in section 1.3.

Part III.

Languages for Consistency Preservation Specifications

5. A Language Framework for Consistency Preservation Specifications

In this chapter, we present and explain a language framework, which is the foundation of the three languages for consistency preservation specifications, which we present in the next chapters. First, we explain the key concept of preserving consistency based on specifications that do not need to explicitly prescribe *how* consistency is to be preserved but mainly *what* is considered consistent. Then, we present the concept of change-driven consistency preservation and discuss why we decided to provide reusable solutions in the form of purpose-built languages. Next, we explain how the language framework is used by the three languages for reactions, invariants, and mappings. Then, we show how languages for changes, expressions, and constraints are integrated into all languages created with the framework. Finally, we describe how we realized the identification of elements, triggering of updates, and generation of code technically.

Each of the previous two chapters on challenges and on our formal language answered two subquestions of our first research question. This chapter and the next three chapters presenting our three languages have, however, a more complex relation to our second research question and its subquestions. We formulated each subquestion in order to find answers to the Open Consistency Specification Language Challenges that we identified. These problems are addressed in different ways with several language constructs and code generation techniques. In this chapter, we briefly mention some of these constructs and techniques. They will be presented and explained in a comprehensive and detailed way in the next chapters. Therefore, this chapter mostly provides an outlook on how we will answer subquestions 2.1 to 2.4 in the next chapters.

5.1. Consistency Preservation Specifications

The framework described in this chapter is the basis for our three languages for developing tools that preserve consistency between models of different modeling languages by performing automated model updates in reaction to changes that were performed by developers. Before we explain the common foundation of the three languages in the next sections, we have to introduce the concepts of consistency preservation and consistency specifications.

5.1.1. Preserving Consistency

We already discussed why it is challenging to preserve consistency between models of different languages in chapter 3. These challenges are an important motivation for the languages presented in this thesis and the language framework described in this chapter. In order to demonstrate the need for the languages and the framework, we have, however, to briefly repeat why we cannot achieve consistency differently in some development contexts (see section 1.1).

Often consistency is needed for models that were created using modelling languages for which existing editors or other tools have to be reused as black boxes. In such a situation, projective views on central models of a single modelling language that combine all information are often infeasible. Consistency cannot be achieved using editors that directly perform changes in all models in the background because the editors cannot be altered. Therefore, it is necessary to develop a new modelling language that incorporates all information of all used modelling languages. To completely avoid inconsistencies with this new language while supporting existing languages, projective views have to be created. These views have to output models for the existing tools and have to propagate every change to the central models.

If projective approaches cannot be used because existing tools have to be supported, then consistency has to be achieved in a synthetic way. This means, consistency has to be achieved by directly checking and modifying the models of the different languages. Often, models with inconsistencies cannot be used for further development until consistency is restored again.

Therefore, consistency has to be achieved continuously while models evolve during development. To highlight, that inconsistencies are only temporarily tolerated in such a process, we call it *consistency preservation* (see also page 59).

5.1.2. Specifying Consistency

In chapter 4, we formally defined how consistency can be specified, checked, and updated according to consistency rules. The conditions for such rules are simply defined by listing all combinations of elements of all possible models for which the conditions hold. This is very precise, but only theoretically relevant because listing all elements that are considered consistent is infeasible when consistency shall be specified for two realistic modelling languages. In order to allow automated consistency preservation, a precise *and* practical specification of what shall be considered consistent is needed. The main goal of the language framework presented in this chapter is to support the development of languages that allow such specifications.

A key concept of our approach to consistency preservation is to provide languages that enable developers to specify consistency in a *problem-oriented* way if this is possible and in a *solution-oriented* way if this is necessary. This means a developer can specify consistency by defining in which cases consistency is a problem or not and only has to specify how consistency is achieved by solving these problems if this cannot be avoided. To make this possible, we created a language framework for consistency preservation specifications that supports declarative and imperative language constructs. For *declarative* languages, which focus on the problem of defining consistency or identifying inconsistencies, we rely on code generation. This makes it possible to realize complex control flow during code generation for language constructs that do not support direct control flow instructions. If *imperative* language constructs are needed for consistency preservation, they can be newly defined or existing constructs of the imperative target language can be reused. Such constructs are, however, not provided per default because the language framework is intended for consistency *specification* languages that are specific with respect to *what* is defined as consistent but unspecific with respect to *how* consistency is achieved. We introduced the Open Consistency Specification Language Challenge 2 of supporting several programming paradigms in section 1.2 and we will explain the paradigms supported by the three languages presented in this thesis in subsection 5.3.2.

5.2. Change-Driven Languages

In the previous section, we explained what we mean by preserving and specifying consistency and why these concepts are central to our approach and language framework. We continue by describing two more central characteristics: The preservation of consistency in reaction to changes performed by developers and the provision of reusable and adaptable solutions to common problems in the form of a purpose-built language.

5.2.1. Change-Driven Consistency Preservation

Our language framework and therefore also the three languages realized with it preserve consistency in reaction to and according to model changes that are performed by developers during the design and implementation of an IT system. Such model changes are not only used to trigger the consistency preservation process but they are also the central input for it. The changes are the central driver for consistency preservation and the language framework is built around them. It provides, for example, language constructs to describe and analyze changes regardless of the used modelling language and editor. Furthermore, the code generator of the language framework uses changes to structure the control flow of the generated code and to integrate it with the change monitoring process. As a result, whether and how consistency is checked and enforced is mainly influenced by what has changed or how a change was performed, and not, for example, by the complete model or by a comparison of an old and a new model state. Therefore, we use the term *change-driven* to emphasize that changes drive the preservation process like tests drive the development process in test-driven development. In the literature, the term change-driven [RVV09; Ber+12] is already used when changes are *used* as input or output but nothing is stated about the *role* that these changes play, for example, if they are used as the only input. Similarly, the term reactive programming [Bai+13] is

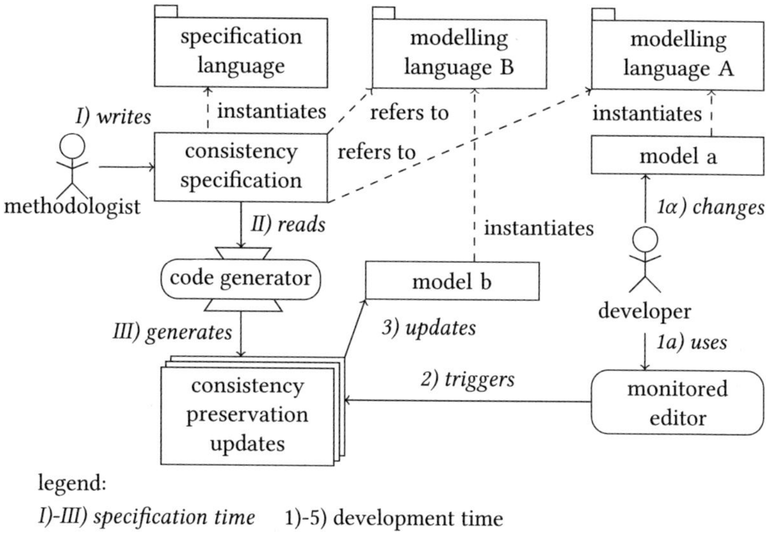

Figure 5.1.: Process for writing consistency specifications using a language of the framework and for updating models according to these specifications to preserve consistency

used to denote that developers *can* express reactions to changes but it is not stated whether everything *has to* be expressed in reaction to changes.

The change-driven consistency preservation process for an arbitrary consistency specification language created with our language framework is shown in Figure 5.1. Before models are created and updated, a so-called methodologist writes a consistency specification using the language (step I) for models of two modelling languages. When the code generator is executed (step II), it reads the specification (step III) and produces a consistency preservation program that contains updates for different possible changes (step IV). This concludes the general preparations that have to be performed before a concrete system is developed. If a developer changes a model that was created with one of the languages (step 1α), the monitored editor, which records all changes, has to be used (step 1a). This monitor triggers the previously generated consistency preservation update that reacts to the performed change (step 2). It may update a model of the other modelling language to restore consistency after the change according to the specification (step 3). This process of recording changes and performing according updates is continuously repeated during system development and starts with empty models, which are trivially consistent.

5.2.2. Languages Providing Reusable Solutions

The last key characteristic of our approach is that we provide reusable and adaptable solutions to common problems of consistency preservation in the form of languages. These consistency specification languages are built for change-driven consistency preservation and are not suited for other purposes. In this sense, they are so-called external domain-specific languages for the domain of change-driven consistency preservation. Instead of creating such languages, we could also have provided, for example, a fixed library with an advanced programming interface (API), which is sometimes also called an internal domain-specific language (see subsubsection 2.1.2.3).

We decided to create external languages with a custom syntax and code generation step in order to address two Open Consistency Specification Language Challenges. By defining a custom syntax for a consistency specification language we can abstract away from details of models or changes that are not relevant for consistency preservation (OCSLC 3). During code generation, the reused solutions, which are encapsulated in language constructs, can be adapted to the current usage and to the modelling languages for which consistency is specified. It is possible to generate only those code snippets that are necessary and to use, for example, usage-specific identifiers for generic elements. These techniques cannot be used if the code is fixed before use and we support them in our language framework to ease the understanding and debugging of consistency enforcement (OCSLC 4).

5.3. Usage of the Language Framework

We used the language framework to create three languages for specifying consistency in terms of imperative reactions, bidirectional mappings, and normative invariants. The primary reason for developing the language framework was not to support the creation of arbitrary languages but to have a common foundation for these three particular languages. In this section, we briefly explain why we designed three separate languages and discuss how they complement each other. Furthermore, we present the programming paradigms supported by the languages and explain what can be expressed with which language.

5.3.1. Complementary Languages for Reactions, Invariants, and Mappings

Different modelling languages can be in very different relationships and may therefore benefit from different support for specifying what is deemed consistent and how consistency can be preserved. It is, however, always possible to specify imperatively which updates shall be performed in reaction to changes. Therefore, the reactions language is the central language of this thesis. For many combinations of modelling languages, consistency can also be specified in terms of invariants. Such invariants declare which constraints have to hold but do not specify how consistency shall be enforced. Therefore, reactions can be triggered if an invariant is newly violated or no longer violated after a change. In this way, the invariants language complements the reactions language with constraint-based programming. Finally, some consistency relationships are symmetric so that two unidirectional specifications would exhibit redundant parts that can be avoided with bidirectional specifications. For such cases, the bidirectional mappings language provides the possibility to declare in a direction-agnostic way how model elements, attributes, and references shall correspond. Developers can specify such mappings without considering whether updates shall be performed in one or the other direction. They do not need to convert checks to enforcements, or forward- to backward-assignments, because this is done automatically when unidirectional reactions are generated from the bidirectional mappings. In this way, the mappings language complements the reactions language with bidirectionalization techniques.

The reactions language or any other Turing-complete language is expressive enough to preserve consistency in a change-driven way. Constraints of invariants can be formulated in terms of check and bidirectional consistency relationships can be formulated using two unidirectional specifications.

This forces, however, developers to specify redundantly how invariants shall be checked and elements that violate them shall be retrieved or how consistency shall be preservation in each direction. In such redundant specification parts, developers need to address challenges that are not specific for the modelling languages for which consistency is specified. The invariants language and mappings language provide reusable solutions for such generic challenges of consistency checking and bidirectionalization. With these two languages, developers can specify invariants and mappings that complement reactions while abstracting away from details that are only relevant if invariant violations are inspected manually or propagation directions are made explicit. This is one of the ways in which we address the Open Consistency Specification Language Challenge 3, which is about missing abstractions (see section 1.2).

Abstractions that relieve developers from details of consistency preservation are not only provided by the complementary invariants and mappings languages but also by the reactions language. It offers constructs that make it possible to declare which model elements and correspondences shall be retrieved, created, or deleted without specifying how models and correspondences are navigated and filtered. These constructs also abstract away from technical details such as necessary clean-up steps to deleted model links and correspondence links to deleted elements. Such steps always have to be performed during consistency preservation regardless of the used modelling languages. Therefore, we relieve developers from writing explicit calls to methods that perform such steps by providing declarative language constructs for which we generate code that performs all necessary steps.

5.3.2. Supported Programming Paradigms

The reactions, mappings, and invariants languages support several programming paradigms to ease the development of consistency preservation tools. We already explained in section 1.2 that languages that only support either solution- or problem-oriented programming paradigms force developers to address challenges of consistency preservation only from one perspective (OCSLC 2). We address this problem by supporting solution- and problem-oriented programming paradigms in our three languages. This makes it possible to adapt the way how consistency is specified to the context in which models are used and evolved.

Together, the three languages provide constructs that support the imperative programming paradigm, the reactive programming paradigm, the declarative programming paradigm, and the constraint programming paradigm. In the following, we will briefly explain how these paradigms are supported by which constructs of the three languages. Detailed presentations of all language constructs are given in the according chapters for every language.

The reactions language supports solution-oriented, imperative programming but is influenced by ideas of reactive programming and also provides problem-oriented declarative constructs: Routines for automatically updating models to restore consistency after user changes are always defined in reaction to these changes. Some of the actions of such routines can be defined using declarative language constructs as mentioned in the previous section. Attribute values and links of model elements can, however, only be updated with imperative code, which may contain variable definitions, calls to helper methods etc.

The mappings language supports problem-oriented declarative programming to preserve bidirectional consistency relationships and provides a fallback to imperative code. It provides constructs to declare how model elements, attributes and references shall be mapped to other elements, attributes, and references. How these mappings are checked and enforced cannot be specified with imperative language constructs but is automatically derived from the mappings. It is only possible to fall back to imperative code for specifying checks or enforcements that involve attributes and references of one or both sides, if the provided declarative language constructs are not sufficient. The code generator of the language bidirectionalizes mapping specifications that are given in a direction-agnostic way. An attribute mapping, for example, is specified using the common syntax of assignment statements with an equals-sign, which assign the value of an expression at the right of the sign to an attribute at the left of a sign. Such an attribute mapping looks like an imperative assignment but is in fact declarative because an assignment for the direction opposing the notational direction is automatically derived using program inversion techniques as explain in section 7.4.

The normative invariants language supports the problem-oriented constraint programming paradigm. It supports no further paradigms, and no other language supports this paradigm. The invariants language can only be used to define consistency constraints that always have to hold for every instance of a given metaclass and are therefore called invariants. The language is closely aligned to a subset of the Object Constraint Language (OCL) and constraints only consist of a sequence of calls to methods that have no side-effects and finally return a boolean value. In contrast to OCL, we cannot only evaluate whether an invariant holds but also provide a mechanism to automatically obtain those model elements that are responsible for an invariant violation as explained in section 8.2. These elements can be used in consistency preservation updates that are defined with the reactions language which makes the invariants language a constraint *programming* and not only a constraint *checking* language.

5.3.3. Expressive Power and Restrictions

Our three programming languages provide language constructs with limited expressive power in order to enable code generation and static analyzes based on these limitations. If these language constructs would not enforce these restrictions, it would not be possible to generate code for all possible usages or to analyse them statically. In such cases, it is necessary to limit the expressive power of a language part in order to provide consistency preservation functionality that cannot be provided if everything can be expressed. It is, however, not necessary to limit the expressive power of the complete specification language. On the contrary, it should be possible to specify arbitrary consistency relationships even if the language can only provide restricted support for some of them. Therefore, we decided to make the reactions and the mappings language Turing-complete by also providing language constructs with full expressive power but limited assistance. In this way, we address the Open Consistency Specification Language Challenge 1, which describes the usual dilemma of either providing particular solutions with a restricted language or supporting all cases with powerful but unspecific languages (see section 1.2). We will show in chapter 10 that many languages that only provide constructs with limited expressivity provide solutions to many recurring problems but are also often too restrictive to be used in all cases.

The expressive power of the three languages presented in this thesis ranges from Turing-complete to primitive recursive. Our central reactions language is Turing-complete because it is possible to define reactions to arbitrary changes that do not match or retrieve elements or correspondences and only contain an update block for the changed element with arbitrary Java code. The declarative language constructs of the reactions language, which we already presented in the previous section, have, however, a limited expressive power. Consider, for example, trigger statements for selecting changes after which a reaction is to be executed or match statements for retrieving elements corresponding to changed elements or related elements. In both statements declarative language constructs can be used together with blocks of almost arbitrary code but expressions with side-effects are not supported. This restriction to expressions without side-effects also applies to the conditions that can be defined in the invariants language. Furthermore, it is not possible to express while-programs with it, but loop-programs can be expressed with it. Therefore, the invariants language can only be used to define primitive recursive functions, which will be shown in detail in subsection 9.2.6. Finally, the mappings language is also Turing-complete because it can simulate every single-taped Turing machine using mappings for all metaclasses in which we fall back to custom code for checking and enforcing consistency. This code can be arbitrary Java code and therefore we are able to simulate any Turing machine with it. The declarative language constructs for specifying bidirectional relationships using direction-agnostic mappings are, however, much more limited in terms of expressive in order to enable bidirectionalization.

5.4. Language Integration and Alignment

The language framework, which we created for the three consistency preservation specification languages presented in this thesis, supports the integration of existing languages and alignment of new languages to existing languages. In this section, we explain how we integrated a newly developed modelling language for representing model changes into our reactions language. We also describe how we integrated an existing language for Java-based method body expressions into all three languages presented in this thesis. Finally, we explain how we extended this expression language to obtain a side-effect free constraint language that is equivalent to a subset of OCL.

5.4.1. A Language for Representing Model Changes

In order to perform the correct model updates after a model was changed by a user, the reactions and the mappings language need to process an abstract representation of the changes that are recorded by the used model editor. These representations have to be independent of the used modelling language and editor in order to make our languages applicable to different modelling languages and editors. Furthermore, the representations have to express which edit operations where performed by a user because consistency may need to be preserved differently for different edit operations that result in the same model state. In the literature, such representations are called edit-based [Wag14; JR16] and contrasted to state-based and delta-based representations of changes. Therefore, we developed a modelling language that fulfills these requirements by supporting edit-based change modelling in a generic way. This language is used to model changes that can be processed by the code generated for reactions and mappings. It was necessary to design a new change modelling language because existing representations were developed with different pragmatics and therefore do not provide exactly the edit operation information that should be available in a change-oriented language.

A developer that uses a change-oriented language to specify which model updates have to be performed after a change needs appropriate possibilities to access all necessary change information but no more. That is, technical details that are only relevant for the editor monitoring a change or for the code generated for a specification should not be part of such a change model. Furthermore, information that is required for change-driven consistency specifications does not only need to be available in any form. All change information should be conveniently accessible but all precision and type-safety that is provided by the modelling languages of the changed model has to be sustained. This is necessary because we cannot know in advance whether it is necessary to perform fine-grained case distinctions to specify consistency correctly with our languages. It is, for example, possible that a developer does not only need to know whether a model element was created and added to a model but has to distinguish different possible insertion targets. Such possible insertion targets can be distinguished by all properties of the existing model element that links to the new element and by the all properties of the reference defining this link.

5.4.1.1. Different Requirements for EMOF- and Ecore-Based Models

Different information and case distinctions are necessary to describe all possible model changes for modelling languages that follow the Essential Meta Object Facility (EMOF) standard or the Ecore variant. Both meta-modelling languages and the differences between them are described in subsubsection 2.1.3.1 and 2.1.3.2. Only two differences have a major effect on our change modelling language and the specifications language that use them:

1. In EMOF, properties can be typed using metaclasses or using other data types, but in Ecore these are distinguished as references and attributes.
2. Ecore requires that all elements except for a root element are contained in exactly one container and EMOF only requires that all elements have at most one container [ISO14, pp. 31-32].

If we only consider these two differences, then Ecore can be seen as a refinement of EMOF, which only adds a more fine-grained distinction of properties and further containment restrictions. Because of this refinement relation, we will first describe which information is necessary to represent model changes of EMOF-based models and then add further information and distinctions for Ecore-based models. Finally, we briefly explain how we made all this information available in practice using a change modelling language.

5.4.1.2. Changes in EMOF-based Models

The generic change modelling language, which we use in our consistency specification languages, has to be able to represent all changes that can occur in models that conform to EMOF-based metamodels. We already mentioned above, that different information of different type has to be provided for different cases of changes. The case distinctions that are necessary to correctly represent changes in EMOF-based models are illustrated using a feature model in Figure 5.2. Cases are only distinguished if different information is needed to represent a change or if different types can be distinguished for this information. First, we distinguish between atomic change representations and compound change representations. This distinction is not imposed by EMOF but due to goal to support representations of all possible changes in models that may conform to arbitrary EMOF-based metamodels. As different editors may use different composition of changes to modify models, we solely base our distinction on the change representation: A compound change representation solely composes representations of other changes. Change representations that are not compound according to this definition are atomic change representations. A change in which a model element is moved from one container to another, for example, is represented as a compound change that consists of two atomic representations for subtracting and adding the moved element. Often several changes can be represented both as several unrelated changes with atomic representations or as a single change with composite representation. Our change modelling language provides the possibility to choose between both representations in order to convey information on how changes occurred and how they can be processed. This way we sustain information not only on the result of a change but also on the edit operation that was performed to obtain the result. If an editor monitored a single action that can be represented in both ways, then it can choose a compound representation with several atomic representations to sustain the information that these atomic changes occurred together. Let us consider, for example, a subtraction of an element from one container that precedes and addition of the same element to another container in a representation of a move change. If consistency has to be preserved differently depending on the type of the new container, then the information that both changes occured together may ease the development of an appropriate preservation routine. The current compiler of the reactions language does, however, not yet directly support compound change representations but still handles the composed atomic changes in isolation.

All case distinctions that are necessary for atomic changes are directly given by EMOF. EMOF only defines classes with properties which can be ordered and have a lower and upper bound. Elements and property values can be

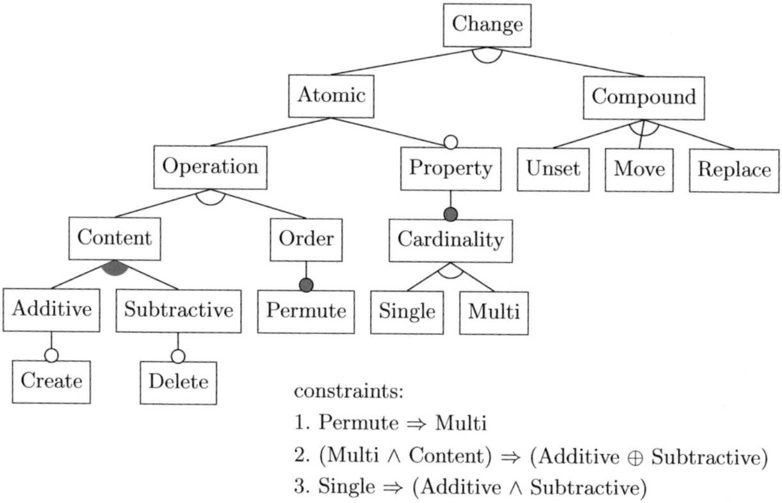

Figure 5.2.: Feature model for all changes in EMOF-based models that require different information or information of different types

added or subtracted but property values can also be permuted if they may hold multiple values (constraint 1). A change of a property that can only hold a single value always replaces a previous value even if this previous value may be undefined. Therefore, it is not necessary to represent changes that only add or only subtract a value of such a property. Thus, all changes of such properties with single cardinality are additions and subtractions (constraint 2). Additions and subtractions of values of properties that may hold multiple values, however, can occur independent of each other. If they occur together, this is not an atomic change according to our definition. Therefore the only atomic changes of such properties either add or subtract a value (constraint 3). New elements can be created and existing elements can be deleted. Because EMOF imposes no appropriate constraints on composite properties, such creations and deletions may but do not need to coincide with a change of an appropriately typed composite property. All elements can also just be added or subtracted directly from the model. Therefore, creation or deletion is an optional feature of additive or subtractive content changes.

During change-driven consistency preservation it is only necessary to react to changes that result in a model that differs from the model before the change. It would be possible to represent changes that have no effect and leave a model unchanged with our change modelling language. Such changes can, however, simply be discarded in the monitored editor or during the conversion from an editor-specific change representation to our modelling language.

5.4.1.3. Changes in Ecore-based Models

As we explained above, further cases have to be distinguished when changes in Ecore-based models shall be represented with maximal type-safety based on descriptions of changes for EMOF-based models. Consistency after a change for a simple-typed attribute, for example, is usually preserved in a more local way than consistency after a change for a reference. The reason is that such a changed link to another model element for a reference may also indirectly influence additional elements that link to the same element. The additional case distinctions that are necessary for Ecore-based models are illustrated as a feature model together with those case distinctions that we already used for changes of EMOF-based model in Figure 5.3. Changes of attributes and references have to be distinguished because they have to represented using old and new values of the correct complex or simple types. Ecore distinguishes between a single root element without an incoming containment link and all other non-root elements with exactly one incoming containment link. Therefore, changes in which a root element is added, replaced, or removed cannot be handled like changes to containment references in which non-root elements are added, replaced, or removed. Furthermore, attribute values have no mutable properties and therefore do not need to be created nor deleted. Values of references, however, are model elements with mutable properties so they need to be distinguished from other elements with currently equivalent properties and can also be created and deleted. Therefore, creations and deletions only occur when an appropriately typed containment reference is changed but not when attribute values are added or subtracted (constraint 4). If an element is created, a reference value or root element was added (constraint 5). Similarly, if an element is deleted, a reference value or root element was subtracted (constraint 6). Other root changes than additions or subtractions

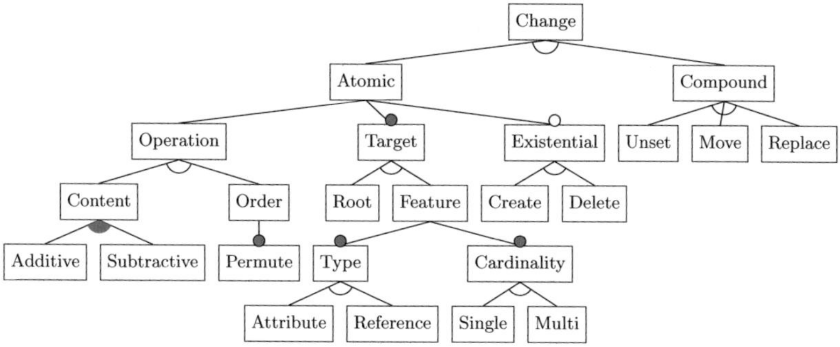

constraints:
1. Permute ⇒ Multi
2. (Multi ∧ Content) ⇒ (Additive ⊕ Subtractive)
3. Single ⇒ (Additive ∧ Subtractive)
4. Existential ⇒ (Root ⊕ Reference)
5. Create ⇒ (Additive ⊕ Root)
6. Delete ⇒ (Subtractive ⊕ Root)
7. Root ⇒ (Additive ⊕ Subtractive)

Figure 5.3.: Feature model for all changes in Ecore-based models that require different information or information of different types

of elements are not possible (constraint 7). Whether a containment or non-containment reference was changed is not explicitly distinguished in Figure 5.3 because this information can be obtained from the reference. If we would have displayed feature attributes such as new values or a containment flag for references, we would have needed to state in constraint 4 that existential changes can only be applied to containment references.

5.4.1.4. Realizing the Change Modelling Language

In the previous sections we described which cases have to be distinguished when changes in EMOF- or Ecore-based models have to be represented. It is, however, more complicated to explain which information of what type is necessary in which cases. Therefore, we provide two class diagrams and a textual description that explain the change modelling language from different perspectives. The class diagrams are structured using the different cases and list for each case which information is necessary. Figure 5.4 shows all 12 metaclasses that are not abstract together with the information they provide regardless of the hierarchy of abstract metaclasses that is used to introduce this information using inheritance. The complete metamodel, which we provide in ?? in the appendix, shows this hierarchy and therefore does not repeat inherited attributes, references, and operations.

The following textual description is not structured by the distinguished cases but by the provided information. For all information carried by an attribute or a reference in the metamodel, we list all cases that are represented as atomic changes in which the information is provided. Operations are omitted for the sake of brevity. The element and feature that are affected by a feature change, are provided in all atomic change descriptions except for the two changes of inserting or removing a root element. A new value is provided, if an attribute value or reference link is inserted in a list of multiple values, or if a single attribute value or reference link is replaced. Similarly, the old value is provided, if an attribute value or reference link is removed from a list of multiple values or if a single attribute value or reference link is replaced. The information at which index an attribute value or reference links were inserted or removed in a list, is provided in exactly these cases. A new index for all items at every former place, is provided if lists of multiple attribute values or reference links are changed. If a reference link is inserted in a list of multiple values or if a single reference link is replaced, then a flag isCreate is used to state whether the newly linked element already existed before. Similarly, a flag isDelete is used to denote whether the removed element still exist afterwards. Both flags are necessary because a change of a containment references may be part of a compound change, such as a move operation, and does not always need to imply a creation or deletion of an element. Finally, a unique resource identifier is provided if root elements are added or removed.

For compound change representations, it is not beneficial to structure the description along the provided information because it is different for each compound change except for an operation that simply returns all atomic change descriptions. Therefore, we explain the provided information for each change with compound representation. If a feature of a model element is explicitly unset, then a change for every value that is subtracted due to the unset change is provided. In case of a subsequent removal and insertion of a value at the same position in a list, these two atomic changes are provided together in a compound replace in list change. Finally, if a model element is moved, then four atomic changes that represent which model element links no longer or newly to the moved element using which reference are provided.

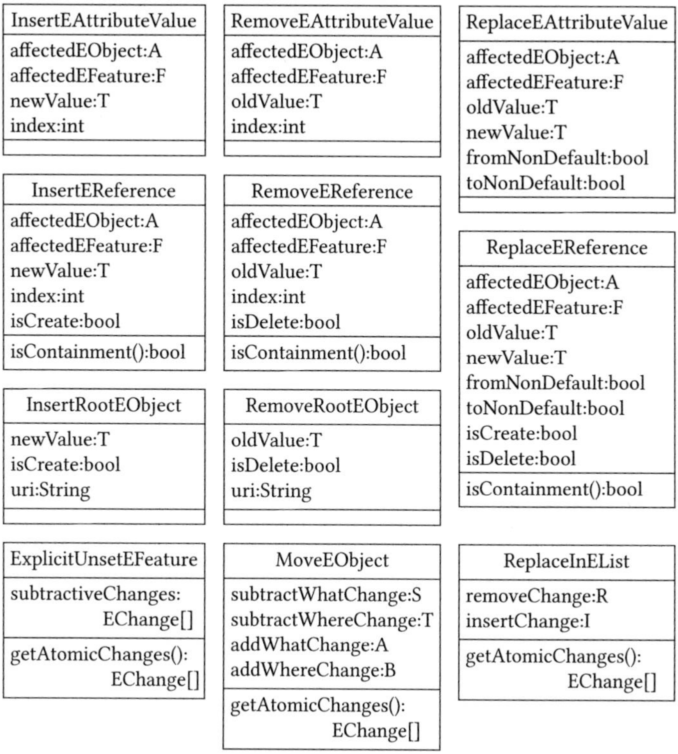

Figure 5.4.: Metaclasses of the change modelling language that are not abstract with all features directly and indirectly declared for them (simplified names and types, no permutation changes)

5.4.2. Reusing a Java-Based Expression Language

To relieve developers from learning completely new programming languages and to keep our languages small, we reuse an existing Java-based expression language. This reuse allows developers to write expressions using a syntax and semantics that they are already familiar with. By embedding the reused expressions language into the grammars for our consistency preservation languages the size of these grammars is reduced. This also reduced the effort to realize the compilers for the languages.

The reused expression language is called Xbase [EV06] as it can be used as a base language for all languages that are created using the language development framework Xtext [Eff+12]. We call it Java-based because the compiler directly produces Java code and because the language syntax is based on the syntax of Java. Some parts of this reused Xbase language, such as variable assignments or method invocations, are identical to the statements and expression in Java methods. Other parts, such as variable or field declarations, are almost identical. Additional language features without counterparts in Java, such as type inference or null-safe field access and method invocations, are provided in an optional way. This way, developers that learn to use the languages presented in this thesis can start writing expressions that are almost identical to Java. When they become more familiar with additional features of the reused expression language, they can start to gradually use these features to write simpler expressions, e.g. without explicit types or null checks. Because of the similarity to Java and the possibility for flexible deviation from it, Xbase can also be seen as a dialect for Java method body expressions.

The main difference between the reused Xbase language and Java is that it does not distinguish between statements that do not return a value and expressions that do return a value. Everything in the reused expression language Xbase is an expression and all expressions except for variable declarations do return a value. The control flow, for example, is influenced using loops and conditional branches like in Java, but these language constructs are also expressions that return the value that is returned by the last expression in their block. Such blocks may also contain variable declarations, which do not return a value as mentioned above. Therefore, the last expression of a block may not be a variable declaration.

We reuse single expressions and expression blocks of the Xbase language in two ways in our languages. Single expressions, which may not be variable declarations, are used in many places but expression blocks are only used to fallback to imperative code in special places as mentioned in subsection 5.3.3. The reason is that the consistency preservation specifications that are created with our languages should use declarative language constructs whenever this is possible in order not to repeat code that could be generated. Basic expressions, such as value comparisons or assignments of variables, however, would result in the same Java code regardless of the language constructs that we provide for them. Therefore, we decided to reuse the Xbase language for such single expressions in our languages because implementing particular language constructs with the same functionality would not provide any benefit. When we fall back to complete expression blocks in the reactions and mappings language, the reason for reuse is, however, different. Developers can write such fallback blocks because we intentionally did not design declarative language constructs for every possible way to achieve what is considered consistent in a certain context. We reuse expression blocks when consistency specifications need to be expressed in a way for which we did not *design* language constructs with *different* functionality and not because we did not *implement* single expressions with the *same* functionality.

Because of these two different ways of reusing expressions where it is possible and expression blocks where it cannot be avoided, their usage in consistency specifications can have different meaning. Single expressions are no pointer to potential deficits of our languages and cannot be overused. Expression blocks, however, may be used in situations where additional language features could be useful and they can be misused when declarative language features are available.

5.4.3. An OCL-Aligned Expression Extension

We extended the expression language to provide possibilities for navigating and inspecting models without side-effects similar to OCL. This extension was developed for the invariants language, but it can be used in all three consistency specification languages. It provides the functionality of many OCL operation body expressions [ISO12c, pp.42] and uses a similar concrete syntax. This way, developers that are already familiar with OCL do not have to learn many differences. Furthermore existing OCL expressions are automatically converted to expressions of the extended language (see subsection 9.4.3). In contrast to OCL, our OCL-aligned expression extension does not need to be interpreted based on a given model instance. The compiler produces Java code for all OCL-aligned extensions, which allows static analyses and direct debugging.

The main focus of our OCL-aligned extension was to create equivalent methods for collection operators [ISO12c, pp.156–168] and iterators of OCL [ISO12c, pp. 168–174] and make them available in all expressions. In

<table>
<tr><th>OCL</th><th>Xbase</th><th>Expression in extension method</th></tr>
<tr><td>=</td><td>==</td><td>-</td></tr>
<tr><td><></td><td>!=</td><td>-</td></tr>
<tr><td>size</td><td>size</td><td>-</td></tr>
<tr><td>includes</td><td>contains</td><td>-</td></tr>
<tr><td>excludes</td><td>-</td><td>!coll.contains(elem)</td></tr>
<tr><td>includesAll</td><td>containsAll</td><td>-</td></tr>
<tr><td>excludesAll</td><td>-</td><td>coll2.forAll[!coll1.contains(it)]</td></tr>
<tr><td>isEmpty</td><td>empty</td><td>-</td></tr>
<tr><td>notEmpty</td><td>-</td><td>!coll.empty</td></tr>
<tr><td>max</td><td>max</td><td>-</td></tr>
<tr><td>min</td><td>min</td><td>-</td></tr>
<tr><td>product</td><td>-</td><td>coll1.forEach[e1|
 coll2.forEach[result.put(e1,it)]
]</td></tr>
</table>

Table 5.1.: OCL collection operators and corresponding methods of the reused Xbase language and our OCL-aligned extension

the UML metamodel, more than 80% of the OCL invariants consists of such collection operator expressions, iterator expressions, or of feature access expressions that can be trivially expressed with the reused expression language [Fis15, p.40][FKL16, p.201]. An overview of the provided collection operators and iterators is given in Table 5.1 and Table 5.2 in the order in which they appear in the OCL standard. For every OCL operator or iterator in these tables, we either provide the equivalent method of the reused Xbase language or the expression with which we implemented an extension method that provides the same functionality using the same name. We do not show parameter declarations for collection parameters `coll`, `coll1`, or `coll2` and for element parameters `elem`. The only parameters that we make explicit are predicates for a single element `p`, double predicates for two elements `dp`, and functions `f`. Both tables list methods that we implemented using lambda expressions, which allow in-line definitions of methods. In the reused Xbase language these lambda expressions are enclosed in square brackets `[...]` in order to distinguish them from arguments of method invocations, which are enclosed in parentheses as in Java. Lambda expression either have an implicit parameter `it` or explicit parameters that are

OCL	Xbase	Expression in extension method
`iterate`	`fold`	-
`exists`	`exists`	-
`exists(dp)`	-	`coll.product(coll).exists[dp]`
`forAll`	`forAll`	-
`forAll(dp)`	-	`coll.product(coll).forAll[dp]`
`isUnique(f)`	-	`coll.groupBy[f.apply(it)]` `.values.forAll[it.size == 1]`
`any`	`findFirst`	-
`one(p)`	-	`coll.filter(p).size == 1`
`collect`	`flatten` ∘ `map`	-
`select`	`filter`	-
`reject(p)`	-	`coll.filter[!p.apply(it)]`
`collectNested`	`map`	-
`sortedBy`	`sortBy`	-

Table 5.2.: OCL iterators and corresponding methods of of the reused Xbase language and our OCL-aligned extension

declared at the beginning of a lambda expression and separated using a pipe character `|`.

We make the methods that are equivalent to collection operators and iterators of OCL available using an syntactic extension mechanism of the reused Xbase expression language. With this extension mechanism we can invoke a static utility method of another class as if it was a non-static method that is available in the class of the first argument. As a result, a developer does not need to distinguish between methods that are directly available for fields or variables of a certain type and methods that extend such a type using this mechanism. Technically, the extension mechanism can be seen as the counterpart of how non-static methods are invoked on the Java Virtual Machine (JVM) by passing the object on which a method is invoked as the implicit first argument [Lin+14, p.52]. We implicitly import the methods equivalent to collection operators and iterators whenever one of our three languages is used. This way, it is possible to invoke these OCL-aligned methods on collections as if they were defined in the collections API of the Java language or as if they were provided using special language constructs.

The collection operators and iterators provided in the OCL-aligned expressions extension can be used to write code that should have no side-effects just like OCL code would. Although the reused expression language Xbase is not restricted in this way, it provides an annotation `@Pure` that can be used to mark methods that have no side-effects. We are using this annotation and a user-defined whitelist with methods that have no side-effects but cannot be annotated with this annotation, for example, because they are part of a library. Our current compiler prototypese produce warnings if it is not certain that code that should not have any side-effects only calls such pure methods. Both, the static code analysis and the inital whitelist entries of library methods will be improved in future work to reduce the number of false alarms.

5.5. Technical Realization and Code Generation

In this section, we explain how we realized the identification and retrieval of corresponding elements as well as code generation for languages of our framework. These steps are important because without our specification languages developers often have to implement their own retrieval mechanisms or have to understand a lot of generated code.

5.5.1. Retrieving Model Elements and Correspondences

To preserve consistency between elements of different models and modelling languages, they have to be accessed and corresponding elements have to be retrieved. For this, model elements have to be uniquely identified, which we will explain in the following.

5.5.1.1. Temporarily Unique Identifiers

If consistency has to be preserved between model elements, it is necessary to keep track of elements that are already consistent to each other. To this end, every model element has to be uniquely identified throughout consistency preservation independent of the question whether and how models are persisted. Appropriate identifiers are, however, not always directly available for models of every modelling language. A common reason is, for example, the use of a textual syntax for models or code. In such cases, additional mechanisms are needed to identify model elements. If explicit identifiers cannot be added to existing models or code, then implicit identifiers have to be derived from properties of model elements.

An identifier for a java method, for example, can be derived from the identifier of the class that declares the method, the return type, the method name and the parameter types. According to the Java language specification this identifier has to be unique[1]. If a method is, for example, renamed, its identity has to be preserved if additional information in other models that are kept consistent should not be lost [LK14]. The new identifier of the method has again to be unique, but it is different from the old identifier. Therefore, it is not sufficient to derive the identifier once from the current properties of a model element. Instead, identifiers have to be recomputed after changes that affect properties that were used to derive the identifier.

Often identifiers are hierarchical, that is an identifier of one element can influence many identifiers of elements that depend on it. A package in Java, for example, is used when the identifiers of all classifiers in all direct and indirect subpackages are derived. Even worse, a package identifier indirectly influences the identifiers of all fields and methods of these classifiers. Therefore, a renamed package results in new identifiers for all these subpackages, classifiers, fields and methods. This demonstrates that a local change of a single property that is used to derive an identifier may change identifiers of many other elements if these identifiers are hierarchically constructed.

A common non-functional requirement for code that reacts to a model change is that the performance of the code only depends on the size of the change and not on the size of the model. As we explained above, the worst case for a single model change is that the number of changed identifiers is only limited by the total number of model elements. Therefore, such requirements can only be fulfilled if several identifiers can be changed in a single computation step. One possibility to achieve this is to use a data structure that links identifier substrings to common predecessors and provides fast forward identifier resolution, for example, based on hashes. In

[1] see docs.oracle.com/javase/specs/jls/se7/html/jls-8.html#jls-8.4.2

our current prototype, we use such a data structure to store all temporarily unique identifiers of model elements.

5.5.1.2. Correspondences for Witnessing Consistency

The model element identifiers described above are used to document which elements are already consistent to which other elements. We call such a witness structure for consistency correspondence and already formally introduced this term in Definition 23 of subsection 4.1.1. In our prototype, such correspondences for model elements are registered and persisted using identifiers. This is used to retrieve corresponding model elements, i.e. elements of models that were created using other modelling languages and for which a correspondence is registered. For this, an identifier is derived for the given element and the identifiers of corresponding elements are resolved to obtain these elements. In most cases, developers that use the specification languages of our framework do not need to take into account when and how temporarily unique identifiers are derived, updated, or resolved. Furthermore, they do not need to ensure, for example, that correspondences for deleted elements are deleted as well or how multiplicities of corresponding elements and string tags that mark correspondences are handled.

5.5.1.3. Accessing Elements of Different Models

Another important are in which developers can be relieved from technical details during consistency specification is model persistence and model boundaries. To preserve consistency between model elements technical details of model persistence are mostly irrelevant. Of course, all model elements have to be persisted, but a developer that specifies which elements have to co-occurr should not need to consider where and how these elements are persisted. Therefore, our prototype gives developers the possibility to add elements a model by only specifying a file path for the model and an identifier for a container element in the model. They do not need to consider whether the model already exists at the given path, whether it is currently loaded, or when it is saved because this is not relevant. Instead, all models are automatically created, loaded, and saved whenever this is necessary for consistency preservation.

In the future, we also want to relieve developers from considering model boundaries and file paths. Model elements should only have global identifiers and automatically be added to models that are persisted at predefined paths. This should be realized with rules for metaclasses for which instances may be root elements that define how a file path is obtained for such a root element. Such a technique would be especially helpful for modeling languages with model boundaries that have no semantics, e.g. compilation units of textual languages. In Java, for example, a classifier of a compilation unit refers to other classifiers in other compilation units. These compilation units act as model boundaries and define a file path for the classifiers. For consistency preservation, they have, however, no semantics as developers only need to specify which classifiers of which packages should be kept consistent regardless of compilation units.

5.5.2. Generating and Executing Consistency Preservation Code

We already explained the process of change-driven consistency preservation from the perspective of developers that specify consistency and users that change models in subsection 5.2.1. In this section, we will briefly describe important steps of code generation and execution that are not noticed by developers until they start to debug their consistency specifications.

So far, we only explained that changes that are performed by a user on a model are monitored to trigger consistency preservation updates on a model of another modelling language according to a specification. This explanation skips, however, intermediate steps of the consistency preservation process. Therefore, we provide and explain an extended extract of Figure 5.1 in Figure 5.5. It refines how a monitored editor triggers consistency preservation updates and that these updates do not only update a model but also correspondences. The input for consistency preservation updates are generic change models. These models are created from change descriptions that are specific for monitored editors with different technical realizations. Consistency preservation updates have no explicit

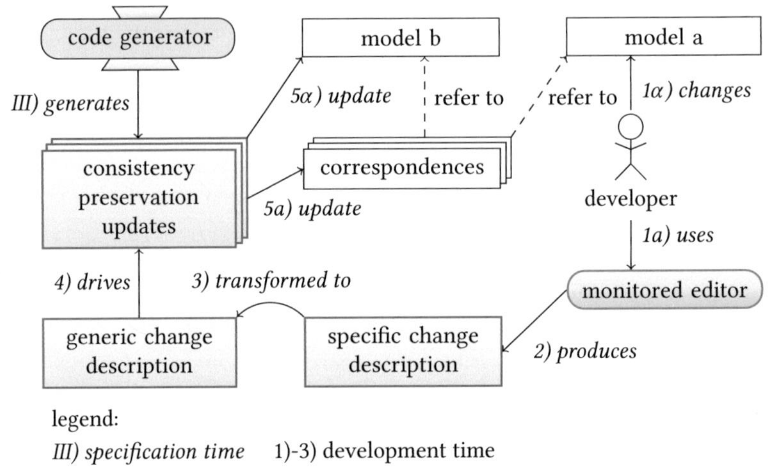

Figure 5.5.: Process for executing consistency preservation updates based on change descriptions and correspondences

output but directly perform updates on models and correspondences. These correspondences are created or updated between elements of models that were created using the two modelling languages for which consistency is specified. A single change may lead to the execution of several consistency preservation updates, which may alter several models with elements that directly or indirectly correspond to the originally changed element. We will, however, not explain in this thesis how the updates to be executed are technically selected for a given change.

All code that is executed to preserve consistency according to specifications that were created using a language of our framework can be separated into three parts according to Völter and Stahl [VS06, p. 15].

1. Generic code, which is independent of the modelling languages for which consistency is preserved and independent of the specifications according to which consistency is preserved.
2. Repetitive code, which depends on the modelling languages and specifications but can be generated from usages of declarative language constructs in the specifications.

3. Individual code, which is copied from expressions and fallback code blocks of specifications during code generation.

To address Open Consistency Specification Language Challenge 4 we strictly separated these code parts during code generation. Individual code is directly copied with as few modifications as possible so that developers can easily debug these code parts in the way that they would expect from a general purpose programming language. During the generation of repetitive code we try sustain type and naming information. The goal is that developers can easily understand which parts of the consistency specifications they develop result in which code and what a potential change in a specification would mean for the generated code. Finally, generic code is not generated for every specification but only realized once as part of the framework and called from generated code. This gives developers the possibility to comprehend which consistency preservation behavior is generic and can only be indirectly influenced when other calls to generic code are generated for specification alternatives.

5.6. Conclusions and Future Work

In this chapter, we have presented a framework for the consistency preservation languages of this thesis. We have introduced central concepts for preserving consistency in reaction to changes and according to consistency specifications. To explain how we address the Open Consistency Specification Language Challenge 3 and 4, we have discussed why we developed new languages instead of providing libraries for existing languages. Furthermore, we have explained how the languages for consistency preservation specifications complete each other in order to support several programming paradigms to counter Open Consistency Specification Language Challenge 2. We have also shown how we extend an existing expression language and how we integrate this language and a change modelling language into our framework. This way, we have demonstrated how to combine the advantages of a powerful general purpose language and of specific solutions for change-driven consistency preservation to counter Open Consistency Specification Language Challenge 1. Finally, we have explained how we realize the retrieval of corresponding elements and how code is generated and executed to preserve consistency according to specifications.

Altogether, this chapter makes first contributions to answering our research question 2 and its subquestions 2.1–2.4 (see section 1.3). In the following three chapters, we will present each language individually and we will discuss how we designed these languages to address challenges of current consistency specification languages. This way, we will complete and further explain the initial answers to research question 2, which we presented in this chapter.

We suggest to put the focus of future work for the language framework especially on two topics: compound changes and code validation. The current prototype handles an individual change that is part of a compound change representation without considering sibling changes, as we already mentioned above. In the future, we want to give developers the possibility to specify consistency preservation for compound change representations *and* for the atomic change representations they contain. We are planning to realize further static code analyses in order to validate that restrictions on the usage of the powerful expression language are respected. This way, we will support the developer in avoiding unwanted side-effects even if no special language constructs but ordinary expressions or helper methods are used.

6. An Imperative Language for Universal Consistency Preservation Reactions

In this chapter, we present our change-oriented language for consistency preservation reactions, which is also the basis of the two other languages for invariants and mappings. It can be used to specify reactions that preserve consistency by updating models of one language after a user changed a model of another language. The reactions language provides declarative elements for typical consistency preservation actions, such as the management of corresponding elements. It also includes check expressions and imperative model manipulations, which are based on the expression language Xbase [EV06] and our OCL-aligned extension (see subsection 5.4.2 and 5.4.3). Therefore, the reactions language is a universal language for unidirectional consistency preservation reactions. It can be complemented with invariants and bidirectional mappings using the two languages presented in the next chapters.

We designed the reactions language together with Heiko Klare, who also implemented a compiler and generator for the language using the language development framework Xtext [Eff+12]. His master's thesis [Kla16], which was supervised by the author of this dissertation, provides further background information on how we realized the reactions language and also additional rationale for fundamental design decisions.

6.1. Overview: Triggers, Retrievals, and Actions

The reactions language separates change-driven consistency preservation into three main steps with different objectives and restrictions:

1. Triggering reactions according to the type and properties of a user change
2. Retrieving model elements that correspond to elements of the changed model
3. Performing actions on retrieved elements and managing correspondences

For the first *trigger* step, the developer specifies for which changes a reaction is responsible by inspecting the occurred change. The models of the two modelling languages do not need to be taken into account in this first step. If the reaction is responsible for the change in a model of one language, then the *retrieval* step is used to obtain elements of models of the other language, for which correspondences were established in previous reactions. *Actions* are only performed if all elements that are necessary for a reaction and that fulfill the optional retrieval conditions were successfully retrieved. Only in this last step, the retrieved model elements and all elements accessible through them may be modified. The model in which the change occurred and all other models of that language cannot be modified in any of these steps. This is necessary to prevent endless cycles of changes and consistency preservation reactions. The individual language constructs for these three steps are already sketched in Listing 6.1.

The goal of partitioning all activities of a reaction in this way, is to reduce the risk for developers to develop reactions with unwanted side-effects or code that is unnecessarily complex. We carefully designed the language in a way that imposes restrictions on exactly these reaction activities that may be restricted without compromising the expressive power of the complete language. These restrictions give developers the possibility to choose from a limited number of building blocks for each step of consistency preservation reactions but also allow arbitrary actions in the last step. In this way, developers can be guided through the process of specifying consistency preservation reactions without restricting the language to certain use cases. The restrictions make it impossible to alter models while checking the

```
reactions ConsistentOOorADL
  in reaction to changes in adl
  execute actions in oo

reaction {
  after // trigger definition ...
  call aSpecificRoutine(...)
}

routine aSpecificRoutine(...) {
  match {
    // retrieve corresponding elements ...
  }
  action {
    // perform actions and manage correspondences ...
  }
}
```

Listing 6.1: Stub of a reaction illustrating the main language constructs and three steps of change-driven consistency preservation

responsibility of a reaction or while checking conditions on candidate elements for correspondence retrievals. In this sense, developers are protected during the specification of triggers and retrievals. The need for providing specific language support and full expressive power was motivated as Open Consistency Specification Language Challenge 1 in section 1.2. Semi-formal sketches for proving that the constructs of our reactions language cover all possible cases will be provided in subsection 9.2.4.

6.2. Running Example: Component Models and Object-Oriented Design

In this section, we introduce a scenario, in which component-based architecture models are kept consistent with an object-oriented design, as a running example of consistency preservation. This example is inspired from a case study, in which we preserved consistency between models that are created using an Architectural Description Language (ADL) and Java code (see subsubsection 9.4.4.1). We do, however, leave out details of the original case study that are not necessary to explain the syntax and semantics of the reactions language. Thus, the modelling languages and consistency requirements of our running example represent a simplified subset of the languages and requirements used in the case study.

6.2.1. Component-Based Architecture Models

In the running example, we represent component-based architecture models using an ADL for which we present a metamodel in Figure 6.1. Such a model contains a *repository*, which has a name. A repository contains component interfaces which declare service signatures, and reusable components, which provide and require these services. Components and component interfaces are both identified using unique names. A *component interface* groups services that are required or provided together. For each of these *services*, the component interface declares a signature. Such a *service signature* consists of an optional return type, a service name and parameters that have a name and a type. These return and parameter *data types* can either be simple types, such as integer types, or complex types. A complex type either represents a collection of several values of the same data type or a composition of values of different data type. Apart from the name and the signatures, a component interface contains no further information, for example, on how a service shall be realized. A *component* references component interfaces to denote which services are provided by the component and which services are required. Two service signatures of two different component interfaces can be identical and a component interface can be provided or required by several components [Rhi07]. In our running example a component has no further properties than its name and these provides and requires relations. The reason for this simple component representation is that we do not need, for example, components that are internally realized by composing components. Information on the ADL used in the case study that inspired this running example, is provided in subsubsection 9.4.4.1.

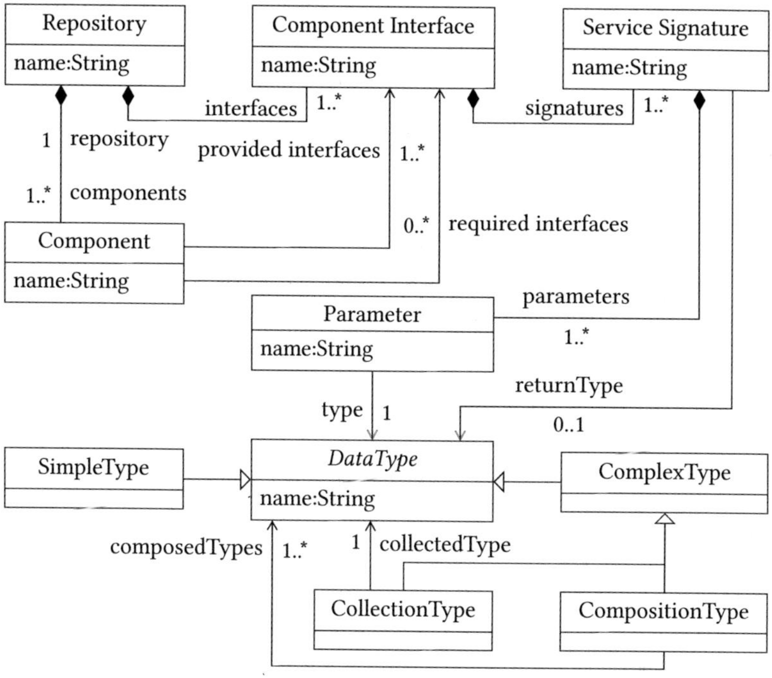

Figure 6.1.: Class diagram showing a simplified metamodel for models of component-based software architectures

6.2.2. Object-Oriented Design

The object-oriented design of a system is represented in our running example using classes and interfaces as shown with a metamodel in Figure 6.2. These interfaces and classes are two different types of classifiers and are always contained in a package. For the running example it is irrelevant whether these classifiers and packages are defined in text files using an object-oriented programming language, such as Java, or in models using a modelling language, such as the Unified Modeling Language (UML). A package has a name and may have a parent package. In such a case the package is called a subpackage of its parent package and this parent package references all its subpackages. An interface in the object-oriented design

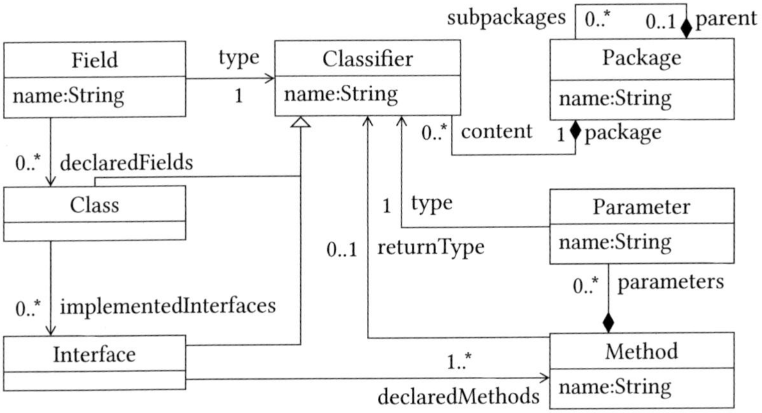

Figure 6.2.: Class diagram showing a metamodel for object-oriented designs that is simplified as needed for our running example

declares methods with a method name, parameters, and an optional return type, which is a classifier. A parameter is typed using a classifier and has a name. Classes have a name and declare which interfaces they implement. They also declare fields, which have a name and are also typed using a classifier. In our running example, classes only define methods that are declared in the interfaces implemented by the class. Other methods and constructors as well as other essential concepts of object-orientation, such as class inheritance or interface extension, are not necessary in our running example. In subsubsection 9.4.4.1, we explain how we reused a special printer and parser for Java in order to treat Java code like any other model.

6.2.3. Consistency Requirements

The consistency requirements of our running example demand correspondences between repositories and packages, between components and packages, between components and classes, and between component interfaces and interfaces of the object-oriented design. A repository corresponds to a root package with the same name that has three subpackages for component interfaces, data types, and components. Every component corresponds to a subpackage in the components subpackage of its repository and to a *component-realization class.* The component interfaces of a repository correspond to an interface in the subpackage for component interfaces of the repository root package. Service signatures in component interfaces correspond to method declarations in the interfaces of the object-oriented design. Simple data types have equivalent counterparts in the object-oriented design and complex data types correspond to classes in the data types subpackage of the repository root package. A class corresponding to a collection data type extends an existing collection class of the object-oriented language using the class corresponding to the inner type of the collection data type as type parameter for the extension. Classes that correspond to a composite data type declare a field for every inner type of the composite data type that is types using the class corresponding to the inner type. A provides relation between a component and a component interface corresponds to a implements relation between the corresponding component-realization class and the corresponding interface of the object-oriented design. Finally, every requires relation between a component and a component interface corresponds to a field declaration in the corresponding component-realization class that is typed using the corresponding interface. The original consistency requirements for the case study, which inspired this running example, were presented in a conference article [Kra+15]. They are explained in more detail by Klare [Kla16] and Langhammer [Lan17].

6.3. Reactions and Separate Reaction Routines

Before we introduce the features of our reactions language, we explain the overall structure of consistency preservation specifications that are created with it. With our reactions language, consistency preservation is specified in terms of reactions that define a trigger and call reaction routines. In these reaction routines, elements are retrieved and actions are performed in two subsequent routine parts. The main steps of consistency preservation reactions, which we introduced in section 6.1, are expressed as triggers of reactions and as retrieve and action parts of called reactions routines. This relation between reactions, triggers, routines, retrievals, and actions is also depicted in Figure 6.3. A reactions specification defines reactions

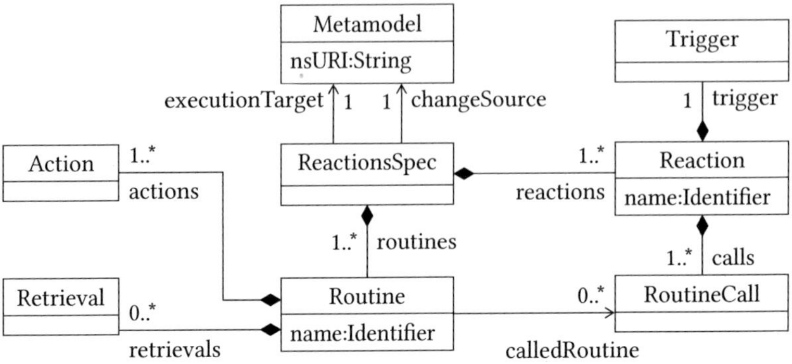

Figure 6.3.: Simplified class diagram with central metaclasses for representing consistency preservation reactions in an AST

and routines that are executed in instances of one metamodel in reaction to changes that occurred in instances of another metamodel. The first of these metamodels is called *execution target* metamodel and the second is called *change source* metamodel Metamodels are identified using the unique resource identifier of their namespace and reaction routines are identified using their unique names. A reaction has a trigger and calls one or several reaction routines. These reactions routines can but do not need to retrieve elements in instances of the execution target metamodel that correspond to elements in instances of the change source metamodel. Every reaction routine has to define at least one action to be executed.

For our running example, which we introduced in the previous section, we can create a reaction to preserve consistency after a creation of a component in the architectural model. This reaction only has to be triggered whenever a component is created. Apart from this trigger definition it only contains a call to a reaction routine. This routine specifies the retrieval of a package for components which corresponds to the repository in which the component was created. After this, it defines an action that has to be executed to create the subpackage and component-realization class in the object-oriented design as corresponding elements for the component of the architectural model.

It is not necessary to separate triggers from retrievals and actions to support the definition of arbitrary consistency preservation reactions. Reactions could also directly contain triggers, retrievals, and actions. And it would be possible to support reactions with calls to explicit routines and reactions with direct retrievals and actions that are implicitly put into a nested routine that is implicitly called. We had initially chosen to support these two reaction types with our language. Finally, we decided to only support explicit routines in order to keep the reactions language simple and to always benefit from names and type restrictions of explicit routine parameters. Explicit reaction routines give developers the possibility to declare parameters with names that are meaningful for the specific reaction routine. In a reaction definition, all change information is available and can be used to decide whether the reaction should be triggered and as arguments for calls to reaction routines. During the retrievals and actions of a reaction routine, change information is only available if it was provided as an argument in the call of the reaction routine. With implicit reaction routines, retrievals and actions have to obtain direct access to all generic change information and developers do not need to provide names and type restrictions for this information.

The reaction for our running example, which we described above, can also benefit from separated reaction routines. Exemplary code for the reaction to a component creation is given in Listing 6.2. Instead of calling a single routine that retrieves the package for components, creates a subpackage corresponding to the created component, and creates a component-realization class, we call a separate routine that calls two further routines named `createSubpackage` and `createClass`. For this, we have to obtain the created element, which is a component, from the change for which we define a reaction (line 7). The first routine (line 10) has a parameter for this component and retrieves the package for components that corresponds to the repository of the given component (line 11–15). It passes this components package and the component to a call of a second routine (line 18) to create a subpackage corresponding to the created component. The called routine returns the created subpackage (line 17). This subpackage is passed as an argument to a call to a third routine that creates a component-realization class (line 19). Further arguments of this call are the created component and a suffix "Impl" that is appended to the name of component to obtain the name of the component-realization-class. As the component is provided as

```
reactions ConsistentOOorADL
  in reaction to changes in adl
  execute actions in oo

reaction {
  after element adl::Component created
  call createSubpackageAndClass(change.newValue)
}

routine createSubpackageAndClass(adl::Component component) {
  match {
    val componentsPkg = retrieve oo::Package
    corresponding to component.repository
    tagged with "componentsPackage"
  }
  action {
    val subPkg =
      createSubpackage(componentsPkg, component, component.name, "")
    call createClass(subPkg, component, "Impl")
  }
}
```

Listing 6.2: Reaction to the creation of a component in an architecture model by creating a package and a class in the object-oriented design

an argument, the routine `createSubpackageAndClass` is not concerned with the change that led to a call of this routine and which change properties were used to yield this argument.

To demonstrate that routines can be called to achieve different reactions for different changes, we also provide the code for the two called routines `createSubpackage` and `createClass` in Listing 6.3. The first routine is a general routine for creating a package. It does not only create the package but also initializes attributes and references of the new package in order to add it as a subpackage to a given parent package and to set its name a given string (line 4–7). Furthermore, it registers a new correspondence between a given element of an architectural model and the newly created subpackage for a given string tag (line 8–9). The routine is even used to create the root package in the object oriented design (see line 7 of Listing 6.4 on page 183). This is possible because the parent package reference initialization has no effect if no parent package is provided (line 5). The second routine

```
1 routine createSubpackage(oo::Package parentPkg,
2  adl::Element correspElem, String name, String newTag) {
3    action {
4      val subPkg = create oo::Package and initialize {
5        subPkg.parent = parentPkg
6        subPkg.name = name
7      }
8      add correspondence between correspElem and subPkg
9        tag with newTag
10   }
11   return subPkg
12 }
13
14 routine createClass(oo::Package parentPkg,
15  adl::NamedElement namedElem, String nameSuffix) {
16   action {
17     val class = create oo::Class and initialize {
18       class.package = parentPkg
19       class.name = namedElem.name + nameSuffix
20     }
21     add correspondence between namedElem and class
22   }
23 }
```

Listing 6.3: Reaction routines that create a package and a class in the object-oriented design in correspondence with a named element of the architectural model

is responsible for creating a component-realization class and for three additional steps. First, it adds the class to a given package (line 18). Then, the routine sets the name of the class to the string that results from appending a given suffix to the name of a given element of an architectural model (line 19). Finally, it registers a new correspondence between this architectural element and the new class (line 21).

6.4. Change Triggers, Restrictions, and Routine Calls

So far, we explained that consistency preservation specifications that are created with the reactions language contain reactions and reactions routines. In this section, we will explain the language constructs for defining which reactions are triggered according to the type and properties of a user change. Furthermore, we mention how reaction routines can be called. The language constructs that are available in these routines for retrieving corresponding model elements and for performing actions on them will be introduced in the next section.

6.4.1. Triggering Reactions Based on Change Descriptions

After an optional reaction name, which is only used in the generated code to ease debugging, the first element of every reaction definition is a trigger definition. Such a trigger definition states in reaction to which changes the reaction is going to be executed and whether this execution is going to happen before or after the change. In addition to this trigger time, a trigger definition has two parts in which trigger restrictions can be defined based on change types and based on change properties. We will now describe all three trigger parts in detail.

The definition of the *time of execution* in a trigger also determines whether we obtain a state representing the changed model before or after the change happened. If a reaction is triggered before a change, then the actions can inspect properties of the changed model in the state before the change happened. Similarly, reactions after a change can inspect the changed model in the state after the change happened. In both cases, it is also possible to reconstruct the other state using the provided change information. The goal of this language feature is, however, to relieve developers from performing change applications or reversals by doing this in the background according to the given trigger time.

An important goal during the design of the reactions language was to provide an easy and precise way of defining before or after which *types of changes* a reaction has to be executed. Therefore, we created a special concrete syntax to denote types of changes in the second part of a trigger definition. These types can be defined for changes that are represented using the change modelling language, which we introduced in subsection 5.4.1. The concrete syntax for change types relieves developers from performing explicit type checks on the obtained change model element. Without this syntax for change types, even simple trigger definitions can be quite complex because type checks can refer to thirteen concrete metaclasses as well as to the twentytwo abstract metaclasses. The concrete syntax for defining a change type in the reactions language is illustrated as a syntax diagram for the non-terminal change type in Figure 6.4. We provide five main change type distinctions:

1. a replacement of a single attribute or reference value
2. list changes, that affect the whole list or a single entry
3. insertions and removal of root elements
4. creation or deletions of model elements
5. any change, which subsumes 1–4

Insertions respectively removals of list entries or root elements may go along with a creation respectively deletion of a model element. Therefore, the change types 2 and 3 can be combined with change type 4. Our implementation currently decomposes compound change representations into atomic representations and we do not yet provide keywords for all compound changes. Future work should provide a possibility to directly specify updates in reaction to changes that are represented as compound changes by supporting appropriate keywords for the change type of triggers. The semantics of such reactions could be that compound change representations are only decomposed if no reaction would be triggered before decomposition.

6.4.2. Restricting Reactions Based on Change Properties

In the third and last part of a trigger definition, it is possible to restrict a reaction based on values of properties of the change description. Such restrictions are called *change properties checks* and they are defined in terms of an expression which may inspect change properties and call side-effect change type:

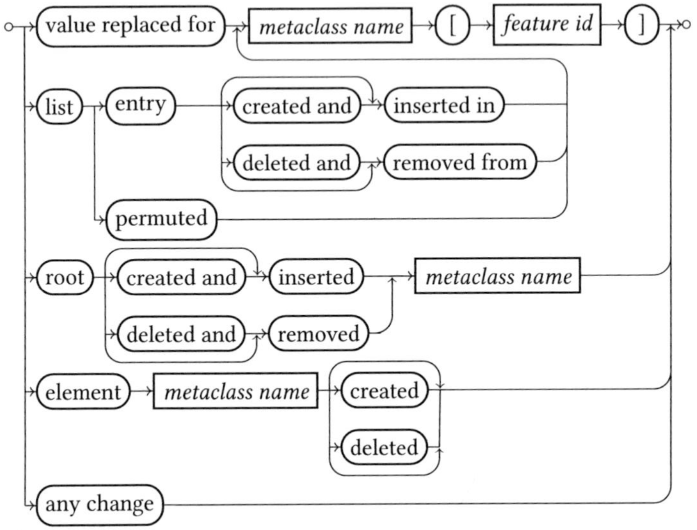

constraints:

1. feature has to have an upper bound < 1 after "value replaced for"
2. feature has to have an upper bound > 1 after "list"
3. "list"…"created"/"deleted"… to be followed by containment ref.

Figure 6.4.: Syntax diagram showing all possible change types that can be given in a trigger definition and additional validation constraints

free methods. It is necessary that these checks have no side-effects, because developers can only control whether a trigger condition is evaluated by defining appropriate change type restrictions. The order in which change properties checks are performed for several reactions if the change type checks passed, for example, cannot be controlled. Therefore, it is important that models are not altered while the responsibility of a reaction is checked. Furthermore, change properties checks do not have access to elements of models of the execution target metamodel. They also do not have access to elements of models of the change source metamodel that are not directly or indirectly accessible from the change information. The goal of restricting change properties checks to information of the change was to reduce the number of possibilities in which consistency preservation reactions can be specified. It is sufficient to perform checks on model elements during their retrieval after a successful evaluation of the change type restrictions and change properties checks. With this restriction of reaction definitions to change properties, we also enforce the partition of consistency preservation reactions into three main steps as introduced in section 6.1.

The change type restrictions of a trigger definition determine which properties of a change are available in a change properties check expression. In every change properties check expression a variable `change` is available, but the type of this variable is adapted according to the change type restrictions. As a result, a new value that was inserted in a list, for example, can only be obtained from this change variable if the type was restricted accordingly. The type of this new value depends in turn on the type of the feature for which the value was inserted. This type information is available from the change source metamodel to which the changed model is conforming. The usage of the change type information of the trigger and of the type information in the change source metamodel, relieves developers from explicitly performing type casts because all necessary type checks and type casts are automatically performed in the generated code. An overview on the properties that are available for different change types was given in Figure 5.4 on page 155.

Trigger definitions with their change type and change property restrictions represent a part of the reactions language that follows the reactive programming paradigm (see subsection 5.3.2). This paradigm was described by Bainomugisha et al. as a paradigm that "facilitates the declarative development of event-driven applications by allowing developers to express programs in terms of what to do, and let the language automatically manage when to do it" [Bai+13, p.52:3]. In the reactions language, the management of when actions are executed according to a trigger definition is done in the code that is generated for trigger definitions. This code obtains a representation of a change that was monitored in an editor. The representation is an instance of a metaclass of our change modeling language (see subsection 5.4.1). On this representation type checks and methods are invoked according to the change type and change property check of the trigger definition. If all type checks and the overall change property check is successful, then all routine calls of the reaction are called and an appropriately typed change description is passed as implicit argument. More details on how code is generated and executed are provided in subsection 6.6.2.

6.4.3. Calling Reaction Routines

The second and last part of every reaction definition contains calls to reactions routines, which encapsulate element retrievals and actions. We already explained in section 6.3 why reactions call separated reaction routines. Therefore, we only have to provide explanations of how reactions can be called.

Every reaction definition either ends with a single reaction routine call or with a code block for reaction routine calls. A single reaction routine call is performed like a method call in Java: The name of the routine to be called is followed by an opening parenthesis. Then, arguments for each parameter of the called routine have to be provided and followed by a closing parenthesis. A code block for reaction routine calls can contain several such reaction calls and arbitrary Xbase expressions that cause no side-effects.

It would not be necessary to allow arbitrary side-effect free expressions in routine call blocks in addition to routine calls. The reason is that it is always possible to call a new routine that only contains a single call action with arbitrary code. In such a call action for defining trigger decisions it would, however, also be possible to modify model elements. This is problematic with respect to our partition of change-driven consistency preservation into three main steps (see section 6.1). Developers that create such routines for trigger decisions can cause unintentional side-effects in them. This means that they can move from the first main step, which is about triggering reactions, to the third step of performing actions without noticing it. Therefore, we decided to make it unnecessary to define trigger decisions in a separate routine with a powerful call action by providing the possibility to define such trigger decisions directly in the call block of a reaction. In many cases, it is, however, not necessary to perform very complex trigger decisions. Often, it is already sufficient to declare and assign final variables that can be used as arguments for routine calls or to cast the type of such variables. We will explain these two frequent types of helper expressions for routine call blocks in the following.

```
1 reaction {
2   after element adl::Repository created
3   action {
4     call {
5       val repo = change.newValue
6       val rootPkg =
7         createSubpackage(null, repo, repo.name, "rootPackage")
8       createSubpackagesForRepository(repo, rootPkg)
9     }
10  }
11 }
```

Listing 6.4: Reaction to the creation of a repository in an architecture model by creating packages in the object-oriented design

If a final variable is declared in a routine call block, then it can be used in argument expressions of subsequent reaction routine calls. This can make these routine calls more readable because specific names can be used instead of generic names, such as `newValue`. In our running example, we can call two different routines in reaction to the creation of a new component repository in the architectural model as shown in Listing 6.4. Before these two routine calls, we declare a final variable for the created repository and assign the appropriate value of the obtained change to it (line 5). Then, the value of this final variable is used as an argument for a call to a routine that creates a root package for the repository (line 7). The return value of this call is assigned to a new final variable that stores the newly created root package. Both variables are then used as arguments in a call to a routine that creates subpackages that will contain all elements that correspond to component interfaces, data types, and components (line 8).

If the type of a value that is available from the change description was checked during the trigger, it can be necessary to cast such a value before it can be correctly used as an argument of routine call. In our running example, this is necessary to correctly react to deletions of composite data types as shown in Listing 6.5. In the trigger, we require that the data type that was deleted from a repository was a composite data type (line 3). In the routine call block, we cast this general data type to a composite data type (line 6). Then, we call a routine for deleting class that corresponds to the data type using the correctly typed value as an argument (line 7).

```
reaction {
  after list entry removed from adl::Repository[dataTypes]
    with change.oldValue instanceof CompositeDataType
  action {
    call {
      val compositeDataType = change.oldValue as CompositeDataType
      deleteClassifier(compositeDataType)
    }
  }
}
```

Listing 6.5: Reaction to the deletion of a composite data type in an architecture model by deleting the corresponding class

The complete concrete syntax for reaction definitions will be provided in terms of a grammar in Listing 6.6 in subsubsection 6.6.1.2 to complete the information provided in the class diagram and the syntax diagram of this section.

6.5. Encapsulating Matching and Actions in Reaction Routines

Apart from reaction definitions with triggers and routine calls, reactions specifications also contain reaction routine definitions, which we present in this section. Every reaction routine definition specifies the name of the routine and optional parameters. Furthermore, it may contain a match block in which retrieval expressions can be used to obtain elements of models that conform to the execution target metamodel of the reactions specification. Additionally, the match block can also specify arbitrary match checks that may not have any side-effects. After the optional match block, the routine definition lists the actions to be performed in single action block that contains at least one action. These actions are only performed if all retrievals and checks of a matcher are successful. Finally, a reaction routine may end with a return statement in order to provide a value to the reactions and reactions routines that call it.

The signature of a reaction routine is specified analogue to method signatures in Java using a routine name and routine parameters. After the reaction definition keyword `reaction`, the name of the routine to be defined is followed by an opening parenthesis. Then, parameters can be defined by specifying pairs of parameter types and parameter names, which are separated by commas. The signature of a reaction routine definition is ended by a closing parenthesis and followed by a reaction routine block that lists optional retrievals and mandatory actions enclosed by curly braces. In contrast to Java, no access modifiers or keywords for final or static methods can be given for reaction routines. Access modifiers could be added in future work together with further infrastructure for reusing reaction routines, e.g. through routine refinement or parameterized types. Only after such an extension to the reactions language, a final modifier would make sense to indicate which reactions cannot be overridden. Currently, all reaction routines are static in the sense that there is no possibility to define routine objects to keep and modify values between different routine invocations. Therefore, a keyword static for routines would only make sense if such routine objects would be introduced. We have no plans for such a language extension in the future, as we are convinced that this would make routines for consistency preservation reactions unnecessarily complex.

6.5.1. Retrieving Corresponding Elements

In the first part of a reaction routine definition it can be specified which elements and conditions have to be matched before actions are executed. For this presence and absence retrievals can be combined with arbitrary match checks. Both language constructs are used in a block that is introduced with the keyword `match`. In a retrieval, it can be declaratively specified which elements of models that conform to the execution target metamodel of the reactions specification shall be retrieved based on correspondences. This can be done in a retrieval block which may contain one or several retrievals. These retrievals can have three different types. *Presence retrievals*, on the one hand, define which elements have to be present. They have two subtypes for the retrieval of required and optional elements. The first subtype is used to define which elements have to be retrieved before actions are performed and the second subtype is used to define retrievals that do not need to be successful but are attempted before actions are performed.

Absence retrievals, on the other hand, define which elements have to be absent. This is done by specifying which retrievals have to be impossible before actions can be performed. Such an absence retrieval can be used, for example, to ensure that a container element, such as a package, is not created twice as it is only needed once for all contained classifiers. For such cases, absence retrievals are a convenient means. They are, however, usually not needed as often as presence retrievals. Required presence retrievals are the default in the reactions language because they are the most frequent type of retrieval. Optional presence retrievals are indicated using the keyword `optional` and absence retrievals are denoted with `require absence of`.

All retrievals specify the type of the element to be retrieved and a *source element expression* that returns an element for which the correspondences are inspected during the retrieval. The purpose of a retrieval statement is to check whether an element of a given type of the execution target metamodel corresponds to a given element of a model that conforms to the change source metamodel. Therefore, the type of the element to be retrieved has to be an abstract or concrete metaclass of the execution target metamodel. The element to be retrieved needs to instantiate this metaclass directly or indirectly. In addition to this target type, all retrievals also have to specify an expression that returns an element of a model conforming to the change source metamodel. This source element is used to retrieve the desired target element by inspecting the correspondences that were created during the execution of previous consistency preservation reactions. For all correspondences that exist for the given source element and an arbitrary target element, it is evaluated whether these target elements instantiate the given target metaclass. We call such an evaluation a *retrieval condition evaluation* and explain in the next paragraph which consequences are possible for these evaluations.

Depending on the retrieval type the retrieval condition evaluations have different consequences. A presence retrieval is successful, if exactly one of the corresponding target elements fulfills the retrieval condition. If all other retrievals are also successful, then the retrieved element can be used during the execution of the actions of the reaction routine. If none of the corresponding elements fulfills this condition, then a presence retrieval fails and no actions will be executed for the reaction routine. An absence retrieval, however, is only successful in exactly this case, as it was impossible to retrieve an element that fulfills the specified retrieval condition.

Therefore, an absence retrieval only influences whether the actions of the reaction routine will be executed, but it provides no elements that could be used during this execution.

In order to make the retrieved element accessible, optional and required presence retrievals have to be combined with a variable declaration and assignment. This final variable can be accessed in all actions of the reaction routine to obtain the retrieved element. Altogether, the match keyword, the variable declaration and assignment, the retrieve keyword, the type of the element to be retrieved, the correspondence keywords, and the source element expression can almost be read like English sentences. We illustrate this with the reaction to the creation of a component of our running example (see Listing 6.2, line 11–15):

```
11  match {
12    val componentsPkg = retrieve oo::Package
13    corresponding to component.repository
14    tagged with "componentsPackage"
15  }
```

This can be read as "Match a repository package: retrieve the package corresponding to the component's repository.

We provide declarative retrieval statements in order to relieve developers from considering many technical details that have to be considered if correspondences are inspected manually to obtain corresponding elements. With these retrieval statements we also address the Open Consistency Specification Language Challenge 3. The code generated for retrievals contains type checks, type cast, variable declarations, assignments, and case distinctions if several retrievals are combined. In this way, we can also abstract away from multiplicities of corresponding elements. The generated code performs all necessary operations if an element has one or more several corresponding elements before or after type restrictions were applied. A retrieval statement, however, can always be formulated in the same way as it does not need to differentiate between these cases.

6.5.2. Retrieval and Match Restrictions

The conditions under which actions shall be executed are restricted by presence or absence retrievals as their success or failure is a precondition for the execution of the actions of a reaction routine. Whether actions are executed or not can also be restricted by providing specifying check restrictions for retrievals or for the complete matching process. It is not sufficient to only allow further restrictions for retrievals because conditions may have to be formulated for combinations of several elements.

The retrieval conditions, which are created for a given target type and a given source element expression, can be further restricted in two ways. On the one hand, it is possible to restrict the target elements that are to be retrieved using a *retrieve properties check*, which has to be preceded by the keyword `with`. Such an expression can inspect any of the properties of an element that is to be retrieved and may call any helper methods that have no side-effects. This is necessary because neither successful nor failed retrieval attempts should have an influence on other retrievals (see also subsection 6.4.2). On the other hand, the correspondences of the elements returned by the source element expression can be restricted with a *tag expression*, which has to be preceded by the keywords `tagged with`. Such a tag expression specifies which string tag had to be used to register the correspondence in one of the previous executions of a reaction routine. To this end, any expression that returns a string value and has no side-effect can be used.

The check expressions resulting from both possibilities to further restrict retrievals are conjunctively added to the retrieval condition obtained for the target type and source element expression. This means the definition of success and failure for a presence or absence retrieval as well as the consequences of such a success or failure remain the same. Only the retrieval condition evaluation that is performed for every retrieval statement is extended. If a retrieve properties check is specified, then it is conjunctively added to the retrieval condition. Independent of this, a check for tag equivalence is conjunctively added to the retrieval condition if a tag expression is provided.

The concrete syntax for all three different types of retrievals with their two additional restriction possibilities is depicted in Figure 6.5 as a syntax diagram. It shows that the optional keyword can only be specified for presence retrievals and that both additional retrieval restrictions can be specified in all cases.

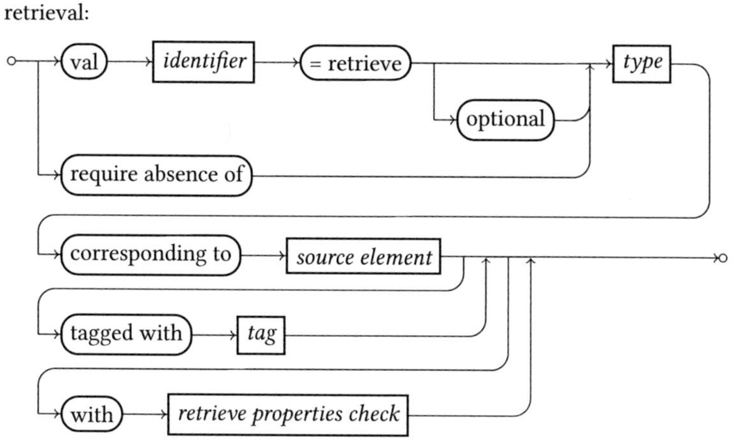

Figure 6.5.: Syntax diagram showing all possible correspondence retrievals that can be given in a match block

If further retrieval restrictions based on tags or properties checks are not sufficient, then developers can also specify arbitrary match checks. As for trigger definitions and retrieval restrictions, match checks also have to be side-effect free in order to free developers from considering when and in which order matching is performed. Both, retrievals and match checks can be combined in any order in a match block and none of them is necessary for a reaction routine.

6.5.3. Add and Remove Actions for Correspondences

The second part of a reaction routine definition lists all actions that have to be performed to preserve consistency. These actions can have three different types, which are illustrated in Figure 6.6 using classes that are used to build an Abstract Syntax Tree (AST). The first type of actions register or de-register correspondences, which can be seen as a witness structure or trace model for consistency (see subsubsection 5.5.1.2 and Definition 23 in subsection 4.1.1). With the second type of actions, model elements can be created, deleted, or updated. In third type of action, other reaction routines or arbitrary code can be called.

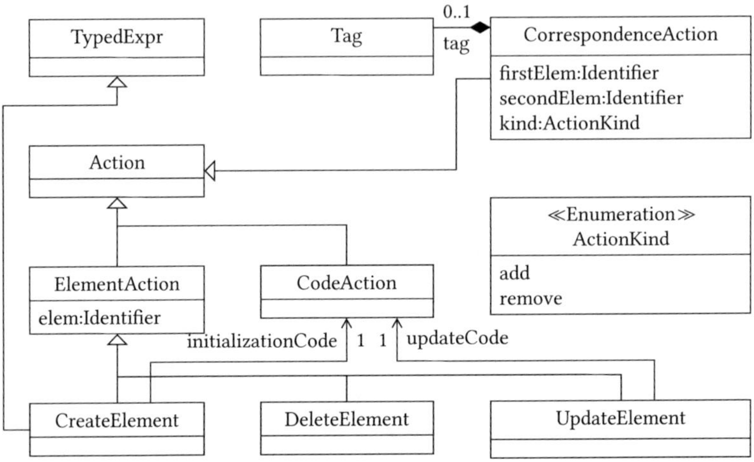

Figure 6.6.: Simplified class diagram for metaclasses for representing actions of the consistency preservation reactions language in an AST

An action for adding or removing a correspondence can be specified by providing the two model elements that should newly or no longer correspond. One of these elements has to instantiate a metaclass of the change source metamodel and the other element has to instantiate a metaclass of the execution target metamodel. To simplify the use of these actions, the order in which the elements are given does not matter. That is, it does not need to be the same order as in the reactions specification header. The result of a correspondence addition action is that a new correspondence is registered and persisted for the two given elements. This happens regardless of any other correspondences that may or may not already exist for one or both elements. Similarly, the result of a correspondence removal action is that the registered correspondence for the given elements is removed regardless of any other correspondences for one or both elements. An exception is thrown if no correspondence for the given elements exists or if more than one correspondence exists for this element combination when the action is executed.

For cases in which several correspondences shall be registered for a single element and several other elements, it is possible to specify a string tag to identify different correspondences. This tag is used to identify the correspondence during addition, retrieval, and removal. As we described in the previous section, the retrieval of corresponding elements can be restricted to correspondences that were registered using a given tag. If a tag is provided, a correspondence removal only leads to an exception if no correspondence or several correspondences with the given tag are registered for the given elements. In our running example, we use such tags to differentiate between the four different packages in the object-oriented design that correspond to a single component repository in the architectural model. The correspondence to the root package for the repository, which contains all subpackages, is tagged "rootPackage". Its subpackages have correspondences that are tagged "interfacesPackage", "dataTypesPackage", and "componentsPackage" to denote the type of the elements for which they contain corresponding elements.

A correspondence is identified using the two elements for which it is registered and optionally using the tag that was used during registration. It has no other properties and thus no own identity. That is why it makes no sense to speak of a correspondence creation or deletion. Therefore, we use the keywords `add` or `remove` to specify actions in which correspondence are registered or de-registered. The keywords `create` and `delete` are only used to specify the creation or deletion of model elements, which have an own identity. We describe these actions and element update actions in the next section.

6.5.4. Create, Delete, and Update Element Actions

With the second type of reaction routine actions instances of metaclasses of the execution target metamodel can be created, deleted, or updated. This could also be done with imperative code that navigates through the models, calls factory methods, and sets reference or attribute values. We decided, however, to provide declarative language constructs for these actions in order to give developers a possibility to structure reaction code and to reduce the amount of boilerplate code that has to be written.

An element creation action has to provide the metaclass that is to be instantiated and may be combined with a variable declaration and assignment as well as with optional initialization code. For such an element creation action, the code generator produces a call to a factory method for the given metaclass of the execution target metamodel. This factory method is always available because our consistency preservation prototype is built on top of the Eclipse Modeling Framework (EMF), which requires metamodels to provide appropriate factory classes. If a new variable shall be declared to hold the created element, then the respective keyword `val` or `val` has to provided together with an identifier for the variable and an equals-sign to denote an assignment to this variable. As in variable declarations in Xbase, `val` denotes a declaration of a final variable and `var` denotes a declaration of a non-final variable. If an element creation action is combined with such a variable declaration and assignment, then the code generator simply produces an identical variable declaration in the Xtend code and an assignment from the result of the factory method call to the variable. Finally, an element creation action may be combined with a block of initialization code for the created element. In this initialization code, values of attributes and references can be set for the newly created element. If initialization code is provided, then the element creation action has to be combined with a variable declaration and assignment. This is necessary in order to have a possibility access the attributes and references of the newly created element. In the generated code the initialization code is re-produced without any changes directly after the declaration and assignment of the variable to the call to the factory method.

Instead of or in addition to the variable identifier for a newly created element, we could have provided other ways to access it in initialization code. It would have been possible, for example, to provide a keyword such as `this` or `it` to refer to the newly created element in initialization code even if no variable is created for it. The first solution could, however, mislead developers to think that they also obtain access to private fields and methods in the initialization code. In order not to confuse developers, the second solution would require an explicit lambda expression, which would add unnecessary complexity to the reactions language.

With an element deletion action, an existing element of a model that conforms to the execution target metamodel can be deleted by simply listing its identifier. The generated code for such an action ensures that all incoming reference links to this element are also deleted. This is necessary to ensure that no model contains dangling references. Furthermore, all elements that are directly or indirectly contained by the element to be deleted are also recursively deleted together with their incoming links.

Finally, an element update action provides the possibility to update values for attributes and references of an existing model element. To this end, the identifier for the existing variable has to provided together with a block of update code. This syntax and semantics of this code block is identical to the initialization code block of an element creation action. The attributes and variables are again accessed using the element identifier and the code is also re-produced without any changes in the generated code. Both, the initialization code of an element creation action and the code of an element update action give developers a possibility to structure their code. If values for several attributes or references are initially set or updated in a single reaction routine, then the code blocks of both actions make it possible to group all code for an individual element. Other code, such as calls to helper methods that may compute new attribute or reference values without any changes on model elements, can be separated from these blocks. This can make it easier for developers to identify how model elements are finally initialized or updated in a consistency preservation reaction.

We are currently not restricting initialization code or update code to only call side-effects on the given model elements, but we want to consider this option in future work. Such a restriction could provide developers an additional protection that ensures that their initialization or update code only has the intended effects. Furthermore, it could make it easier to understand code of other developers if it is guaranteed that every updated element is explicitly mentioned. A possible drawback could, however, be that syntactically different model elements with a common consistency relation to elements of an instance of the change source metamodel would have to be updated in separate update actions.

The concrete syntax for all correspondence and element actions is depicted as a syntax diagram in Figure 6.7. We also added the non-terminals execute action block and call action block to provide the complete syntax for all action types of reaction routine definitions. Both are syntactically equivalent to a routine call block, for which we will present the concrete syntax in Listing 6.6 on page 197 of subsection 6.4.3. The semantics and the rationale behind these last two types of action are explained in the next section.

action:

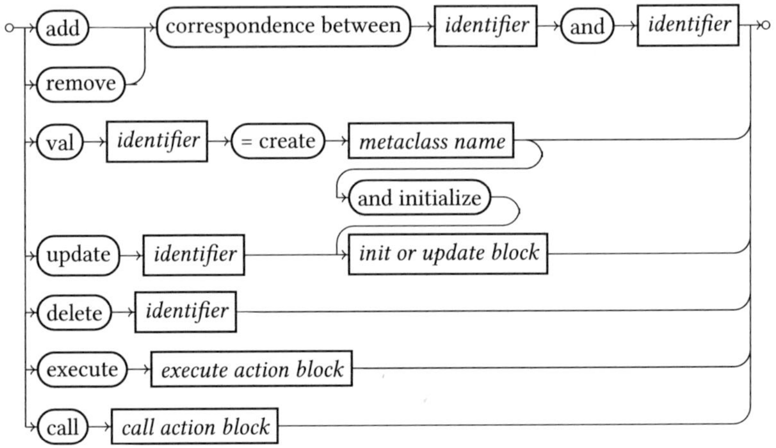

constraint:

1. "= create" to be followed by a metaclass that is not abstract

Figure 6.7.: Syntax diagram showing all possible actions that can be given in an action block of a reaction routine definition

6.5.5. Executing Arbitrary Code and Calling Routines

The last two type of actions that can be specified in routines for consistency preservation reactions can be used to execute arbitrary code and to call other routines. Both actions are specified in blocks, which are called *execute action blocks* and *call action blocks*. These blocks are syntactically identical to the routine call block of reaction definitions (see subsection 6.4.3). The only semantic difference is that execute action blocks may cause side-effects. The goal of providing this fallback in execute action blocks is to equip the reactions language with unrestricted expressive power (see subsection 5.3.3). It can be argued, that the initialization and update code blocks of the appropriate actions already provide such a fallback. We are, however, convinced that developers should not be forced to pollute initialization or update code blocks for individual elements with complex computations and manipulations of arbitrary model elements, even if we do not automatically enforce this.

After retrievals, and actions, the third and last part of a reaction routine is an optional return statement. This return statement can be used, for example, in order to provide callers of a reaction routine access to a model element that was newly created in the routine. In the generated code, this statement is directly re-produced and no additional code, for example, to declare the return type of a reaction routine is necessary. This is possible because we generate Xtend code, which does not require an explicit return types for methods because it implicitly infers it by computing the type of the value that is returned in the return statement.

6.5.6. User Change Disambiguation

The reactions that should be performed to preserve consistency after a certain change cannot always be completely fixed upfront. In order to also preserve consistency in such cases, we give developers the possibility to define that the user that performs such a change is to be involved in the consistency preservation process in order to resolve ambiguities [LK14]. The developer can, for example, decide to let the user select from a given set of options or to require additional input. Further actions of a reaction can then be based on the results of such interactions. We are currently not providing any dedicated language constructs for user change disambiguation and directly call appropriate API methods of the Vitruvius framework in call action blocks [Lan17]. In our running example, users are asked to disambiguate their change after the creation of a collection data type in the architectural model. They can select from different collection implementations, such as those of a hash set or an array list. The selected collection implementation is used as a superclass for the class that is created in the object-oriented design and registered as corresponding to the collection data type.

In future work, we want to investigate whether calling API methods for user change disambiguation is sufficient or if additional language constructs should be provided. Such constructs could, for example, make it easier to define which options should be possible or which kind of interaction should be used. Currently, all options have to be explicitly passed as arguments to the API calls. This could be simplified in the future if some or all possible options can be derived, for example, by analyzing the routines to be called and the input they require. At the moment the supported kinds of interaction are blocking dialogs, non-blocking dialogs, and additions to task lists for lazy interactions. The input and return values for these interaction kinds could also be supported with dedicated language constructs if necessary.

Further information on the concrete syntax of routine definitions with the reactions language will be provided in terms of a grammar in Listing 6.7 in subsubsection 6.6.1.2 to complete the information provided in the class diagram and syntax diagrams of this section.

6.6. Realizing a Compiler for the Reactions Language

We will now complete the information on the syntax of the reactions language that we provided so far and briefly explain how we realized it in terms of a prototypical compiler.

6.6.1. Reactions Language Syntax

In the previous sections, we have only presented parts of the syntax of the reactions language using examples and in order to explain how it can be used by developers. We have showed class diagrams that represent parts of the abstract syntax and syntax diagrams to illustrate the concrete syntax. In the following, we will explain the complete abstract syntax and provide grammar rules for parts that we have not yet presented in a visual form.

6.6.1.1. Complete Abstract Syntax

From the explanations of the previous sections it would be possible to derive the abstract syntax of the reactions language. This would, however, be cumbersome and error-prone. Therefore, we present a class diagram that

```
reaction = "reaction" , [xbase identifier] , "{" ,
  execution time , change type , ["with" , change properties check] ,
  "call" , (routine call | routine call block) ,
"}";
execution time = "before" | "after";
change properties check = xbase expression;
routine call = xbase identifier , "(" , [arguments] , ")";
arguments = argument expression , {"," , argument expression};
argument expression = xbase expression;
routine call block = "{" ,
  {[routine call | routine call expression]} - ,
"}";
routine call expression = xbase expression;
```

Listing 6.6: Part of the grammar of the reactions language with rules for reaction definitions in EBNF (without rules for change types)

covers the complete syntax in Figure 6.8 to explicitly summarize the language structure on one page. It shows metaclasses that can be instantiated to represent any reactions code in terms of an AST. Such instances of an AST metamodel are produced by the prototypical compiler of the reactions language (see subsection 6.6.2). As this metamodel is generated from an enriched grammar, parts of it do, however, not abstract away from all details of the concrete syntax. Therefore, we decided to present a simplified class diagram to represent the abstract syntax of the language.

6.6.1.2. Concrete Syntax for Reactions and Routines

To complete the information that we have provided in section 6.3 and subsection 6.4.1 we present grammar rules for the concrete syntax of reactions definitions. The rules are complete except for the rules for change type expressions, which we already visualized in Figure 6.4, and except for the reused rules from the Xbase expression language for identifiers, expressions, and type expressions. Three trivial rules simply define change properties checks, argument expressions, and routine call expressions as Xbase expressions. These rules ease the validation that these expressions have no side-effects and return values of the correct type. For this grammar listing,

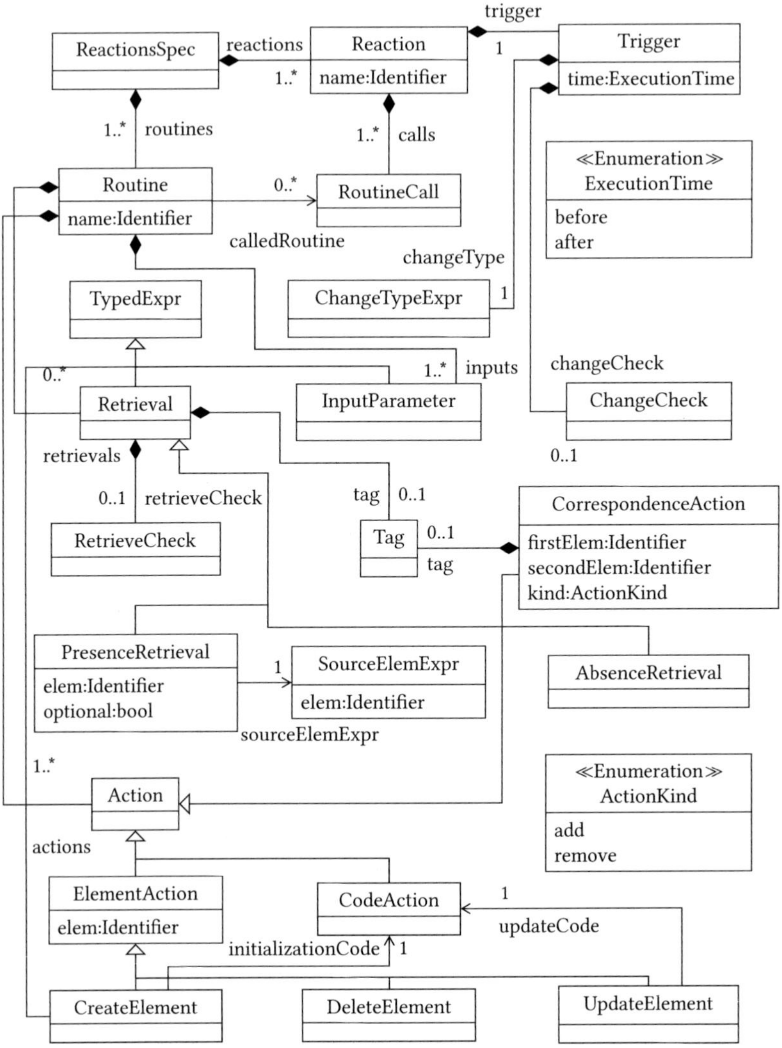

Figure 6.8.: Simplified class diagram with metaclasses for completely representing reactions in terms of an AST

```
routine definition = "routine" , xbase identifier , "(" ,
  [parameters] , ")" , "{" ,
    {["match" , match block] ,
    "action" , "{" ,
      {action} - ,
    "}" ,
"}";
parameters = typed identifier , {"," , typed identifier};
typed identifier = type expression , xbase identifier;
type expression = xbase identifier , "::" , xbase identifier;
match block = "{" ,
  {(retrieval | match check block)} - ,
"}";
retrieval = (["val" , xbase identifier , "="] , "retrieve" ,
          ["optional"]) | ("require␣absence␣of") ,
  type expression , "corresponding␣to" ,
  source element expression ,
  ["tagged␣with" tag expression] ,
  ["with" retrieve properties check];
type expression = xbase identifier , "::" , xbase identifier;
tag expression = xbase expression;
source element expression = xbase expression;
retrieve properties check = xbase expression;
match check block = "check" , "{" ,
  {match check} - ,
"}";
match check = xbase expression;
```

Listing 6.7: Part of the grammar of the reactions language with rules for routine definitions in EBNF (without rules for

we use the Extended Backus-Naur Form (EBNF) [Int96], which we have already introduced in subsubsection 2.1.2.5.

To complete the information on the concrete syntax reaction routine definitions, which we have provided in section 6.5, we present simplified grammar rules for this part of the reactions language in Listing 6.7. We do not show the rules for actions because we already visualized them in Figure 6.7 on page 194 of subsection 6.5.4. Again, trivial rules simply define tag expressions, source element expressions, retrieve properties checks, and match checks as Xbase expressions. This makes it easier to validate that these expressions return a value of the correct type and that they have no side-effects.

6.6.2. Editing, Compiling, and Executing Reactions

The prototypical compiler for the reactions language was developed using the Xtext language workbench [Eff+12]. With it, a lexer, parser, validator, editor, and code generator were partly generated from a grammar definition. This grammar is specified in an EBNF-like syntax with additional information to influence the automated generation of a metamodel for the grammar. For each parser rule in the grammar, it can be specified which metaclass is to be instantiated when the rule is processed by the parser. The result of parsing is always a model that instantiates the metamodel for the grammar to represent an AST of the parsed code. Before code is generated for such an AST model of reactions code, it is validated. Parts of the validation, scoping, linking and code generation are realized by mapping models of the reactions code to Java code models. Other parts are customized for the reactions language, for example, to realize special scoping rules that restrict the features that can be used to define a change trigger in terms of a list entry change. In the prototype, the mapping to Java code is also used to realize auto-completion in an editor for the Eclipse Integrated Development Environment (IDE) and to perform type checks during the validation.

For each reaction and each reaction routine a separate Java class is generated. In these classes methods are generated for triggers, checks, actions etc. Method parameters are generated to realize the explicit routine parameters and, for example, to pass retrieved model elements. Finally, mostly calls to platform methods are generated for element matching and routine actions. This way, we separate the code and the preservation behavior that results from a specific reaction from the code and behavior that is identical for all reactions. The goal of this separation is to make it easier for developers to understand and debug the generated code in order to address Open Consistency Specification Language Challenge 4. More details on code generation can be found in Heiko Klare's master's thesis [Kla16, pp. 102–106]. The overall process for generating and executing reactions code is explained in general in subsection 5.5.2.

6.7. Semantics of Consistency Preservation Reactions

In previous sections, we have informally explained the semantics of the reactions language by describing the behavior of the code that is generated for individual language constructs. To complete these descriptions from a formal perspective, we will sketch how to map the reactions language to the formal language, which we have introduced in chapter 4 based on section 2.3. We explain how consistency rules and update functions can be created for reactions and routines in such a way that consistency is always preserved by construction if the reactions are appropriately designed. This demonstrates how the reactions language relates to our formal definitions.

6.7.1. An Explanatory On-Demand Construction

The construction process that we will describe in the following explains how and why the reactions language can be used to preserve consistency. In the prototypical compiler, a different construction is, however, used. The reason is that the goal of the construction presented in this chapter and the goal of implementing a compiler are different. We have already explained in section 2.3 that the formal language is a model that represents concepts of our change-driven consistency preservation language. It was designed to convey the central ideas in a precise way and not to support an implementation in which the defined consistency preserving updates can directly be executed and debugged. Based on this formal language, the goal of the construction presented in this chapter is to explain the semantics of the reactions language in a way that abstracts away from many technical concerns, for example by using appropriate sets instead of other data structures. Directly implementing this set-based notation and the abstractions of the formal language in the prototypical compiler would, however, introduce accidental complexity. Furthermore, it would conflict with the goal that developers shall obtain code that can easily be traced back to the specific reactions they developed. Moreover, general consistency preservation behavior shall not be explained or illustrated but encapsulated in calls to platform code.

In general, it would be necessary to create a possible infinite set of tuples of objects that fulfill a condition as required by Definition 18. To avoid this and analogous problems for rules and update functions, we will only create snapshots of conditions, rules, and update functions on-demand after we obtained two given models and correspondences. The two models have to be consistent according to the specification that is implied by a set of reactions and reaction routines. In practice, this means the models either have to be empty or they have to be the result of a previous consistency preservation step after a single consistency-breaking change. The snapshots are finite but sufficiently represent the possibly infinite counterparts. This on-demand snapshot creation has, however, to be repeated for any two given models, for every possible update, and after every subsequent change. A current snapshot only considers elements of the current models and of the models that can be obtained by performing the actions of reaction routines. This is sufficient, because elements of inconsistent models are not contained in the originals and therefore also not in the snapshots. For correctness, it is only necessary that all tuples of objects that have to be in the possibly infinite originals are added to the finite snapshots before we check whether they are contained.

In the following three sections, we will describe how a consistency update specification can be created for a set of reactions and routines by creating consistency rules and update functions for every reaction. First, we will explain how consistency rules can be created for every reaction. These consistency rules express which conditions have to be fulfilled in the right model if certain conditions are fulfilled in the left model before or after a change depending on the time of execution that is specified in the trigger of the reaction. Then, we will describe how an update function can be created for every of these consistency rules by simulating the execution of the reaction for every possible change in the given left model. Finally, we will discuss why the resulting consistency update specification is consistency preserving by construction and which cases are not covered by the according formal definition.

6.7.2. From Reactions to Consistency Rules

Consistency rules can be constructed for two consistent models and a reaction that was expressed using the reactions language by analyzing which model elements are checked in which cases. For every possible change in the left model, all model elements that would be checked on a way to a successful entry in an action block of a reaction routine have to be collected. Whether the action block performs any updates is not relevant because the rules also have to cover cases in which a reaction only checks consistency but does not need to enforce it. Otherwise the rule would wrongly consider models consistent that do not fulfill such conditions that are only checked. Therefore, it would not be sufficient to perform a backward-construction of a rule by solely inspecting cases in which updates are performed and capturing conditions for the model states before these update.

Before we can explain how consistency rules can be constructed for reactions, we have to define the context. With the reactions language, a set of reactions and reaction routines is always specified for a change source metamodel, which is denoted by $\mathbb{m}_l$, and an execution target metamodel, which is denoted by $\mathbb{m}_r$. Accordingly, the input models for the on-demand construction are denoted by O_l and O_r. The tuple with sets of correspondences for these models is denoted by $(\mathfrak{C}_1, \dots, \mathfrak{C}_n)$. Altogether, our construction process yields a snapshot for a consistency update specification $\mathbb{us} := (\overrightarrow{\mathrm{UF}}_{\langle \mathbb{c}_{1,l} \rangle, \langle \mathbb{c}_{1,r} \rangle}, \dots, \overrightarrow{\mathrm{UF}}_{\langle \mathbb{c}_{n,l} \rangle, \langle \mathbb{c}_{n,r} \rangle})$ for the two metamodels $\mathbb{m}_l$ and $\mathbb{m}_r$ (see Definition 42) which only captures updates for O_l, O_r based on $(\mathfrak{C}_1, \dots, \mathfrak{C}_n)$. The update functions of $\mathbb{us}$ are denoted by $\overrightarrow{\mathrm{UF}}_{\langle \mathbb{c}_{i,l} \rangle, \langle \mathbb{c}_{i,r} \rangle}$ and constructed for consistency rules. These rules $\mathfrak{R}_{\mathbb{c}_{i,l}, \mathbb{c}_{i,r}}$ are based on metaclass tuples $\langle \mathbb{c}_l \rangle$ and $\langle \mathbb{c}_r \rangle$, which have to be created first.

To construct a consistency rule $\mathfrak{R}_{\mathbb{c}_{i,l}, \mathbb{c}_{i,r}}$ according to Definition 22 for a reaction, we first have to construct appropriate metaclass tuples according to Definition 14. The metaclasses for the left metaclass tuple $\langle \mathbb{c}_{i,l} \rangle$ are collected by determining all metaclasses that are directly instantiated by the objects of the left model that would be checked if the currently considered reaction would be executed for the currently considered change. To obtain these metaclasses, we have to inspect the change properties check and the routine call block of the reaction. Furthermore, we have to inspect all retrievals, match checks, and actions in all reaction routines that are directly or indirectly called in the reaction. It is not sufficient to only inspect the parameters of the routines because source element expressions and retrieve properties checks of retrievals may also check properties of instances of other metaclasses. This can be done by navigating from one of the objects that was provided as an argument for a parameter in the routine call. This navigation to instances of metaclasses that are not provided as a parameter type is also possible in several forms in the different types of actions so they have to be inspected as well. To obtain $\langle \mathbb{C}_{i,l} \rangle$, we create a tuple that contains the collected metaclasses in a fixed but arbitrary order. The right metaclass tuple $\langle \mathbb{C}_{i,r} \rangle$ is created differently as it will be used for the conditions that have to be fulfilled after the updates that are specified by a reaction were performed. All those metaclasses that are instantiated by the objects that are retrieved from the right model have to be collected. Furthermore, all those metaclasses are collected that are directly instantiated by the objects of the right model that are directly or indirectly accessed in a match check or in an action. Finally, the same step as for the left metaclass tuples is performed to obtain $\langle \mathbb{C}_{i,r} \rangle$ with a fixed but arbitrary order for the metaclasses that were collected for the right side.

To construct the conditions for a consistency rule, we have to simulate the reaction to every possible change in the given left model O_l. The resulting left model $\widetilde{O_l}$ for such a change can be obtained by executing the change in the given left model O_l (see Definition 35). Depending on the time of execution that is specified for the reaction, we have to simulate the execution of the reaction based on O_l (before) or $\widetilde{O_l}$ (after). To create a consistency rule $\mathfrak{R}_{\mathbb{C}_{i,l},\mathbb{C}_{i,r}}$ for a reaction, we have to create pairs that contain instance tuples (see Definition 16) for the metaclass tuples that are constructed for the reaction as described above. For all those objects that were inspected to obtain the metaclass tuples, we have to check during every simulation for every change whether an execution of the currently considered reaction would be aborted or not. This means, we have to determine whether such an object is checked in at least one change properties check, routine call block, retrieval, or match check during the simulation of an execution for a change for which an action block would be successfully reached. If this is the case, then we have to add the object to an instance tuple $\langle o_l \rangle$ for the change for which we currently simulate the reaction. Similarly, we have to determine for every object that is retrieved or checked in a match check whether the retrieval or match check would be part of an execution that would lead to the execution of an action block. All those objects for which this is the case and all objects of the right model that are directly or indirectly accessed in an action that would be reached have to be added to an instance tuple $\langle o_r \rangle$ for the change for which we currently simulate the reaction. To decide whether, we have to add the instance tuples $\langle o_l \rangle$ to the left condition $\text{COND}_{\langle \mathbb{C}_l \rangle}$ and $\langle o_r \rangle$ to the right condition $\text{COND}_{\langle \mathbb{C}_r \rangle}$ we have to distinguish the following six cases:

1. If the current simulation for a change yields correspondence additions but no correspondence removals, then a pair with $\langle o_l \rangle$ and $\langle o_r \rangle$ is added to the consistency rule to denote that the objects for which consistency was checked always have to co-occurr with the objects for which consistency was enforced.
2. If the simulation yields no correspondence additions but correspondence removals, then *no* pair with the tuples is added to the rule because no co-occurrence has to be required.
3. If the simulation yields neither correspondence additions nor correspondence removals but actions to be executed and at least one presence retrieval was simulated, then a pair with the tuples is also added to the rule as in case 1.
4. If the simulation yields neither correspondence additions nor correspondence removals but actions to be executed and at *no* presence retrieval was simulated, then then the reaction has to be rejected and the developer has to be asked to add a presence retrieval because our formal semantics cannot support this case.
5. If the simulation yields neither correspondence additions, nor correspondence removals, nor actions, then the right tuple is empty and *no* pair with the tuples is added to the rule because nothing could be required as co-occurring on the right side.
6. If the simulation yields correspondence additions *and* correspondence removals, then the reaction has to be rejected and the developer has to be asked to split the additions and removals into two separate reactions because our formal semantics cannot support this case.

The last part of the construction to formally represent reactions as consistency rules deals with correspondences. We will only explain the construction of update functions that also yield correspondence updates in the next section. Before this, we cannot explain why the on-demand construction of correspondences will fulfill the requirements of Definition 23. We can only argue that these requirements are initially fulfilled because we start with empty input models and an empty tuple of correspondence sets for each consistency rule. The initially empty correspondence sets for the empty models fulfill our definition of consistency according to a consistency rule (see Definition 24). Correspondences will always be added to or removed from these sets when the construction is extended to represent the execution of a reaction after a single consistency-breaking change.

The construction that we described so far yields a consistency specification $\mathfrak{cs} := (\mathfrak{R}_1, \mathfrak{C}_1, \ldots, \mathfrak{R}_n, \mathfrak{C}_n)$. Its consistency rules $\mathfrak{R}_{\mathbb{C}_{i,l},\mathbb{C}_{i,r}}$ specify which instance tuples in the left model and in the right model have to occur together. For those instance tuples that occur in the left model before or after a change occurs there have to be corresponding instance tuples in the right model after at least one action was taken by the reaction to restore consistency if the change was consistency breaking. Together, all consistency rules with their instance tuples for every reaction specify what should be considered consistent because the reactions language is designed for *prescriptive consistency specifications* (see also subsection 4.1.2 or page 58 of subsection 3.1.2). This means, by writing a reaction a developer does not only implement consistency preservation but also prescribes that those models that are obtained by executing the reactions are consistent.

6.7.3. Constructing an Update Function for a Reaction

So far, we explained how consistency rules can be constructed to describe formally how consistency is checked using reactions. Now, we will extend the construction in order to show formally in terms of update functions and update specifications how consistency is enforced using reactions.

We describe how to construct a consistency update specification $\mathfrak{us}$ for a consistency specification $\mathfrak{cs} := (\mathfrak{R}_1, \mathfrak{C}_1, \ldots, \mathfrak{R}_n, \mathfrak{C}_n)$ that was constructed for a set of reactions and reaction routines. Our formal language composes the notion of consistency preservation for a complete specification from the notion of consistency preservation for an individual rule (see Corollary 1 and 2). Therefore, it is sufficient to construct an update function $\vec{\text{UF}}_{\langle \mathbb{c}_{i,l} \rangle, \langle \mathbb{c}_{i,r} \rangle}$ (see Definition 42) for every individual consistency rule $\mathfrak{R}_{\mathbb{c}_{i,l},\mathbb{c}_{i,r}}$ that was constructed for a reaction. As before, we will only construct a snapshot of such an update function and define it exactly for those inputs that are relevant when two models and correspondences in these models are given for the currently considered $\mathfrak{R}_{\mathbb{c}_{i,l},\mathbb{c}_{i,r}}$. In general, an update function takes four inputs: a left model, a right model, a change in the left model, and a set of correspondence candidates, which are pairs of instance tuples for the metaclass tuples of the conditions of the consistency rule (see Definition 39). We only have to consider the two given models O_l and O_r and preserve consistency for the consistency rule $\mathfrak{R}_{\mathbb{c}_{i,l},\mathbb{c}_{i,r}}$ with respect to the given $\mathfrak{C}_i$ after a single change. Furthermore, we have to define updates exactly for those changes in O_l that are consistency breaking according to $\mathfrak{R}_{\mathbb{c}_{i,l},\mathbb{c}_{i,r}}$ with respect to $\mathfrak{C}_i$ (see Definition 41). Therefore, it is sufficient to define $\vec{\text{UF}}_{\langle \mathbb{c}_{i,l} \rangle, \langle \mathbb{c}_{i,r} \rangle}$ only for inputs that provide exactly the two given models, an arbitrary consistency-breaking change in the left model, and the given correspondences as correspondence candidates. In this case, the effective domain of the partial function $\vec{\text{UF}}_{\langle \mathbb{c}_{i,l} \rangle, \langle \mathbb{c}_{i,r} \rangle}$ will be $\{O_l\} \times \{O_r\} \times C^{\lightning,O_l}_{\mathfrak{R}_{\mathbb{c}_{i,l},\mathbb{c}_{i,r}}}(\mathfrak{C}_i) \times \{\mathfrak{C}_i\}$, where $C^{\lightning,O_l}_{\mathfrak{R}_{\mathbb{c}_{i,l},\mathbb{c}_{i,r}}}(\mathfrak{C}_i)$ is the set of all changes in O_l that are consistency-breaking according to $\mathfrak{R}_{\mathbb{c}_{i,l},\mathbb{c}_{i,r}}$ with respect to $\mathfrak{C}_i$. This set of changes is finite because we only have to check for every single change that is possible in the finite model O_l whether it breaks consistency by checking whether the reaction would lead to the execution of an action. We could extend the update function by repeating this construction for every set of correspondences for $\mathfrak{R}_{\mathbb{c}_{i,l},\mathbb{c}_{i,r}}$ in O_l and O_r in order to fulfill the requirements of Definition 41. As the update function will only be evaluated for the given correspondences $\mathfrak{C}_i$, this is possible but not necessary.

Having explained the input to an update function $\vec{\text{UF}}_{\langle \mathbb{c}_{i,l} \rangle, \langle \mathbb{c}_{i,r} \rangle}$, we will now explain how to determine the outputs from the reaction for which the consistency rule $\mathfrak{R}_{\mathbb{c}_{i,l},\mathbb{c}_{i,r}}$ was constructed. Such an output is always a model update $(\mathfrak{C}^-, \mathfrak{C}^+, \mathfrak{O}, \mathfrak{I}, \mathfrak{A})$ in O_r, which groups correspondences to be removed and added as well as updates of objects, links, and labels (see Definition 30). From now on, we have to distinguish informal and formal correspondences. Informal correspondences are pairs of model elements with an optional string tag for which retrievals, removals, and additions are specified in reactions. Formal correspondences are pairs in the condition sets of a consistency rule that contain two instance tuples with all objects that were checked or updated in a simulated reaction execution. In our construction, we can construct several formal correspondences for a single informal correspondence. Furthermore, we register dependencies from formal correspondences to informal correspondences in order to know which formal correspondences have to be removed when a removal of an informal correspondence is specified in a reaction routine. To compute model updates, we extend the simulation that we described in the previous section to construct conditions. During this simulation, we collect the informal correspondences to be removed and added in the correspondence actions of called reactions. As we simulate the execution of the reaction and called reaction routines based on the inputs, we only inspect those actions that would finally be executed after all successful properties checks, retrievals, and match checks on the way. We also collect the sets of object updates $\mathfrak{O}$, link updates $\mathfrak{I}$, and label updates $\mathfrak{A}$ by inspecting the simulated element actions and execute actions. These actions are the only potential source for such updates because side-effects are not allowed anywhere else in the reactions language.

So far, we only described how some of the sets that are needed for a model update ($\mathfrak{C}^-, \mathfrak{C}^+, \mathfrak{O}, \mathfrak{I}, \mathfrak{A}$) are constructed. Now, we will explain how the missing sets of formal correspondences to be added and removed $\mathfrak{C}^-$ and $\mathfrak{C}^+$ are constructed. For this, we have to distinguish the first three of the cases that we described for the construction of conditions for the consistency rule on page 205 of section 6.7.2. In case 1, we add a formal correspondence to $\mathfrak{C}^+$ and register a dependency from it to all informal correspondences for which successful presence retrievals or correspondence addition actions were simulated. The formal correspondence tuple can be constructed by selecting the appropriate instance tuples that were created for the simulation of this change. In case 2, we mark all formal correspondences that depend at least one of the informal correspondences for which correspondence removal actions were simulated as to be removed by adding them to $\mathfrak{C}^-$. Finally, in case 3, we add a formal correspondence to $\mathfrak{C}^+$ and register a dependency from it to all informal correspondences for which successful presence retrievals were simulated. Again, this formal correspondence only lists the appropriate instance tuples that were already constructed. If the simulation shows that the reaction would not update anything, then all five sets of the constructed model update are empty. In such a case, the change for which we currently simulate the execution of the given reaction is not consistency breaking and therefore $\vec{\text{UF}}_{\langle \mathbb{C}_{i,l} \rangle, \langle \mathbb{C}_{i,r} \rangle}$ has to be undefined for this change (see Definition 41). In all other cases, we extend the definition of $\vec{\text{UF}}_{\langle \mathbb{C}_{i,l} \rangle, \langle \mathbb{C}_{i,r} \rangle}$ to return the model update $(\mathfrak{C}^-, \mathfrak{C}^+, \mathfrak{D}, \mathfrak{I}, \mathfrak{A})$ for the given models, correspondences, and the currently simulated change.

The correspondences in $\mathfrak{C}^-$ and $\mathfrak{C}^+$, which are collected during the simulation, are only to be removed from $\mathfrak{C}_i$ or added to it. All other sets of correspondences can remain unchanged because of the above mentioned notion of consistency for a specification that composes consistency for each rule. If this construction is performed to obtain an update function for every reaction, then correspondences are always added to the right set of correspondences in the tuple of the consistency specification. The question whether the correspondence additions and removals fulfill the requirements for consistency according to a rule (see Definition 24) is discussed in the next section.

6.7.4. Consistency Preserving by Construction

To conclude the explanatory mapping from reactions to our formal language, we discuss which requirements have to be fulfilled by reactions if they should formally preserve consistency. The goal for the development of the reactions language was *not* to have a restricted language for which it can be formally proven that consistency is preserved. Instead, we wanted to provide a language for specifying consistency preservations that is restrictive enough to yield semantics that can be precisely explained but powerful and general enough to be applicable in many cases (see also OCSLC 1 in section 1.2). Therefore, we have to require that some possibilities of the reactions language are not used for reactions for which it shall be formally explained why they preserve consistency.

Let us briefly recap the two requirements that we indirectly described on page 205 of section 6.7.2 in terms of two cases of simulations for which a reaction has to be rejected. The first requirement is that every execution of an action in reaction to a change has to be preceded by at least one presence retrieval of a correspondence (case 4) The second requirement is that no execution of a reaction may combine correspondence additions and correspondence removals (case 6). Both requirements are only technical and not difficult to fulfill for a developer. To avoid case 4, a presence retrieval for a correspondence has to be added, which should be no problem as the executed actions clearly show that consistency is preserved and could be witnessed. Case 6, can be avoided by defining two reactions such that one reaction performs all necessary additions and the other reaction performs all necessary removals. The combination of correspondence additions and removals shows that some consistency for certain elements is replaced by some other consistency. In such a case, it should be no problem to define separate reactions and most redundant checks can easily be avoided if both reactions call some common reaction routines.

In addition to these two technical requirements, developers have the responsibility to fulfill three fundamental properties when specifying reactions. These fundamental properties are concerned with conditions that are fulfilled when an informal correspondence is successfully retrieved before an action is executed or when an informal correspondence is added.

I. Such conditions have to be rechecked after every change that could lead to a new fulfillment of them.

II. Informal correspondences for such conditions have to be removed whenever the conditions are no longer fulfilled.

III. Such conditions may only check whether an object has a certain attribute value or a certain reference link if this is necessary for the fulfillment of the condition.

We have to assume that the two technical requirements and the three fundamental properties are fulfilled to explain that our construction yields a consistency-preserving update specification (see Definition 43). For this, three steps are necessary for an arbitrary update function because our construction is identical for all update functions. First, we have to explain that the update function is only defined for changes that are consistency breaking (see Definition 36 and 41). Then, we have to argue why the update function yields for a consistency-breaking change a model update that is consistency preserving after the change (see Definition 37). This is achieved by discussing why the models after the update is performed are consistent according to the consistency rule for which the update function is defined (see Definition 24).

By the construction of the conditions for a consistency rule of a reaction and the cases in which we add or remove formal correspondences, actions are only executed in the reaction if conditions are newly or no longer fulfilled. More specifically, the left condition is fulfilled after a change that leads to a correctly witnessed consistency preservation and the right condition is fulfilled after all the consistency preservation actions are executed. If consistency was broken before actions were executed, then the right condition may not have been already fulfilled before the actions were executed. In theory, such a case would mean the update function would not be consistency preserving. In practice, the requirement that a reaction should only react to consistency-breaking changes can be relaxed. It is also sufficient if the reaction only performs modifications that leave the right model in the same state as before, for example, because values are set to the same value as before. We could easily modify our definitions of consistency preservation to formally tolerate such cases in which an update after a consistent state is executed but does not change anything. This is, however, not necessary because we can simply remove such updates that have no effect in our construction. Therefore, consistency is always broken after every change that leads to the execution of actions in a reaction as long as these actions are not yet executed. As we only define the update function for these changes it is defined exactly for consistency-breaking changes and we are done with the first step.

So far, we have explained that the constructed update function only yields updates when they are necessary. Now, we demonstrate why these updates preserve consistency by explaining why the resulting models are consistent. For this, the formal correspondences have to fulfill the conditions of the consistency rule (see Definition 23) and such formal correspondences have to be present iff the conditions are fulfilled (see Definition 24). The first part is given by construction as we add formal correspondences by selecting tuples from the condition sets. For the second part, we need the fundamental properties I. and II. from page 210. If developers only create reactions that adhere to these properties, then formal correspondences are present iff the conditions are fulfilled. Altogether, we explained that the constructed update function outputs a model update iff a change is consistency-breaking and the result of the update is consistent to the changed left model.

We want to repeat that fulfillment of the technical requirements and fundamental properties only guarantees consistency preservation after a single change that breaks exactly one consistency rule. As we have already mentioned in the last section of chapter 4, we neither define consistency preservation if several changes break consistency or if consistency is broken for more than one consistency rule. The first problem is solved by executing reactions after every single change, but the second problem has to be addressed by the developers of reactions. They have to make sure that reactions do not interfere with each other, i.e. that the subsequent execution of all reactions for a change results in a consistent model because no action undoes or overwrites an action of another reaction.

6.8. Conclusions and Future Work

In this chapter, we have presented an imperative language for consistency preservation reactions. First, we have introduced three main steps of consistency preservation and explained how the structure of the reactions language reflects these steps and the order in which the are performed. Then, we have introduced language constructs for triggering reactions, retrieving elements and performing actions and have explained why they are available in separate reactions and reaction routines. Furthermore, we have described how change triggers and retrievals of corresponding elements can be restricted and how we address OCSLC 3 with such language constructs. After these possibilities to specify when and where consistency is preserved, we have explained the use of actions to specify how consistency is preserved. We have described how correspondences can be added or removed, how elements can be created, updated, or deleted, and how arbitrary update code can be specified in order to address OCSLC 1. Additionally, we have explained the syntax and how we address OCSLC 4 with our prototypical compiler for reactions. Finally, we have illustrated the semantics of the reactions language using the formal language from the previous chapters.

With this chapter, we have provided answers to the subquestions 2.1, 2.3, and 2.4 of research question 2. These subquestions also correspond to the addressed Open Consistency Specification Language Challenges 1, 3, and

4. The reactions language demonstrates how specific language constructs for change-driven consistency preservation can be combined with unrestricted expressive power. Furthermore, it shows how developers can use constructs of the reactions language in a way that matches the preservation context and abstracts away from irrelevant details. Last but not least, the reactions language illustrates how consistency preservation behavior can be realized with generated code in such a way that developers can foresee the consequences of their consistency specifications.

We are planning to conduct future work to provide further possibilities for reusing reaction parts, to further restrict side-effects, and to ease the development of reactions in which user changes are disambiguated. To further ease the reuse of reactions parts for different modelling languages, we will investigate whether well-known concepts such as access modifiers or parameterized types should also be provided by the reactions language or whether special concepts such as reaction refinement are necessary (see also section 6.5). Furthermore, we are planning to improve the validation part of our compiler in order to further restrict side-effects, for example, in element initialization or update code to the created or updated model element (see also subsection 6.5.4). Moreover, we will explore how user change disambiguation can be better integrated into reactions, for example with more convenient ways for defining dialogs and disambiguation options (see also subsection 6.5.6).

7. A Bidirectional Language for Abstract Consistency Mappings

In this chapter, we present a language that can be used by developers to complement the reactions language in symmetric cases, where the direction of consistency preservation between two metamodels does not matter. In such cases, the presented mappings language relieves developers from specifying symmetric reactions that are partly redundant for both preservation directions. Instead of pairs of reactions for both directions, a developer can specify mappings that abstract away from details of preserving consistency in both directions. With these mappings, it is possible to declare under which conditions instances of metaclasses of both metamodels should correspond to each other. It is, however, not necessary to specify after which changes these conditions have to be checked or how they have to be enforced. Instead, unidirectional reactions that consider these details are automatically generated for both preservation directions by bidirectionalizing the mappings. This is possible because the mappings language only supports symmetric consistency relations. This means that enforcing a mapping on one side because of a successful check on the other side is always equivalent to checking and enforcing it the other way round. The generated reactions are triggered whenever instances of the specified metaclasses are created, deleted, or updated. They ensure that the specified mapping conditions always hold for instances of one metamodel iff they hold for instances of the other metamodel.

We designed the constructs of the mappings language except for the inverters together with Dominik Werle, who also developed a compiler and generator for the language. Further background information on the realization of the mappings language and additional rationale can be found in his master's thesis [Wer16], which was supervised by the author of this dissertation.

7.1. Overview: Mappings, Conditions, Enforcements

Before we explain the individual language constructs in detail, we provide an overview on the mappings language. Apart from a header that lists the two metamodels for which consistency is preserved, the language only provides two first level constructs for mappings and bootstrap mappings (see Listing 7.1). A mapping contains two parameter lists in which metaclasses of both metamodels are specified together with identifiers for their instances. For every parameter list, developers can specify which conditions have to be fulfilled by the instances of the list whenever they are mapped to instances of the other parameter list. These conditions refer, however, to the metamodel of the parameters in isolation and cannot make any statements about properties of instances of the other side. Therefore, they are called single-sided conditions. They can either be defined in a way that makes it possible to check and to enforce them, or they are defined with separate checking and enforcement code in order to address the Open Consistency Specification Language Challenge 1. For statements that relate elements of both sides, the language provides two possibilities, which are called *bidirectional enforcement specifications* and are both optional: The first possibility is a single block of bidirectionalizable conditions. It supports only certain operators but relieves developers from considering the consistency preservation direction as it is enforced in both directions. The second possibility is a pair of forward and backward enforcement blocks with arbitrary code. The forward enforcement code is executed if all mapping conditions for the left metamodel hold after a change in an instance of the left metamodel. Analogously, the backward enforcement code is executed if all mapping conditions for the right metamodel hold after a change in an instance of the right metamodel. Regardless of the direction in which a mapping was enforced and regardless of what was enforced, the result is always that the instances of the metaclasses of both parameter lists are mapped to each other. In this case, we say that the mapping is *instantiated* for these model elements. Finally, bootstrap mappings are very similar to ordinary mappings, but they map an empty set of instances of metaclasses of one metamodel to instances of metaclasses of the other metamodel. Therefore, these mappings are bootstrapped for empty models before consistency has to be preserved after any changes. The central

```
mappings ConsistentADLForOO for adl and oo

mapping Repository<->Packages {
  map (...)
  and (...)
  // mapping conditions for adl and oo ...
}

bootstrap mapping CreateSimpleDatatypes {
   create (...)
   // bootstrap conditions only for adl ...
}
```

Listing 7.1: Sketch of a mapping that illustrates the two first class concepts: mappings for both sides and bootstrap mappings for a single side

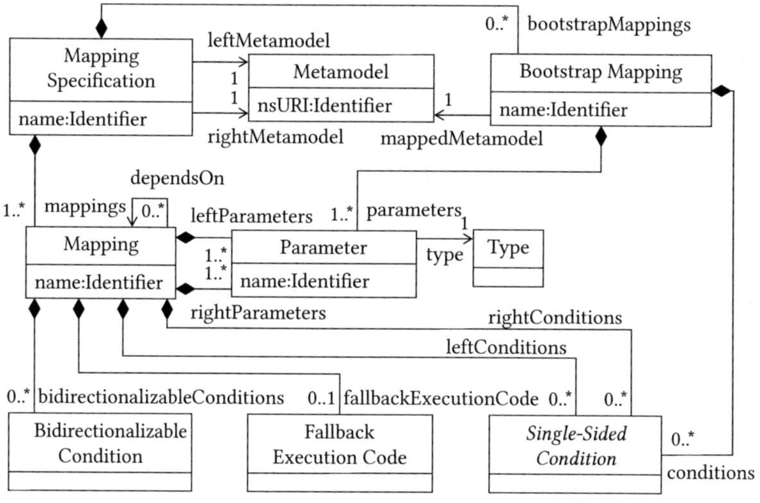

Figure 7.1.: Simplified class diagram with central metaclasses for representing mappings as an AST

concepts of the mappings language and their relations are also depicted in Figure 7.1 using a simplified class diagram with metaclasses for representing mappings in terms of an AST.

7.1.1. Example Mapping for Repositories and Packages

Let us reconsider the consistency preservation example for component-based architectures and object-oriented design, which was introduced in section 6.3. To explain the general idea of our mappings language, we present mappings for some of the consistency requirements, for which we already presented change-driven consistency preservation reactions. We begin with a mapping that preserves consistency between the component repository and packages in the object-oriented design. Based on this, we show a mapping that preserves consistency between components and packages and classes in the object-oriented design.

In subsection 6.2.3, we introduced consistency requirements for component repositories and packages in the object-oriented design. Listing 7.2 shows how these requirements can be realized using the mappings language. First, it is declared that mappings will be defined for the two metamodels `adl` and `oo` (line 1), which are also called left and right side. Then, a mapping between a component repository (line 4) on the left side and four packages (line 5–6) on the right side is defined. No conditions for the repository but several conditions for the packages (line 7–13) are specified. These conditions state that the root package has to have no parent package, that all other packages have to be in the list of subpackages that are contained by the root package, and that these subpackages have to be appropriatedly named. These single-sided conditions for the packages are checked to decide whether a repository has to be created after a change in the object-oriented design and enforced when a repository is created in the architectural model. Finally, the mapping contains a bidirectionalizable condition (line 15), which states that the name of the repository has to be equal to the name of the root package.

We will now explain a first part of the semantics of this exemplary mapping by initially ignoring the bidirectionalizable condition, which will be explained in the next paragraph. If a repository or package is created, deleted, or updated, the reactions generated for the declared mapping ensure that corresponding elements are created, deleted, or updated if the single-sided mapping conditions for the side that was changed hold. These are the general semantics of mappings, and we will explain them more specifically for our example by discussing every possible case. If a repository is created or

```
mappings ConsistentADLForOO for adl and oo

mapping Repository<->Packages {
  map (adl::Repository repository)
  and (oo::Package rootPkg, oo::Package pkg4interfaces,
    oo::Package pkg4datatypes, oo:Package pkg4components) with {
      null equals rootPkg.parent
      pkg4interfaces in rootPkg.subpackages
      pkg4datatypes in rootPkg.subpackages
      pkg4components in rootPkg.subpackages
      "interfaces" equals pkg4interfaces.name
      "datatypes" equals pkg4datatypes.name
      "components" equals pkg4components.name
  }
  such that { rootPkg.name = repository.name }
}
```

Listing 7.2: Mapping between a repository of an architectural model, a root package, and three subpackages for interfaces, datatypes, and components in an object-oriented design

updated, no single-sided conditions have to be checked, so four corresponding packages are always created or updated, and the single-sided conditions for them are enforced. Similarly, nothing has to be checked if a repository is deleted and the four corresponding packages are directly deleted as well. If a package is created or updated, all seven single-sided conditions are checked. Only if all these single-sided conditions are fulfilled by the created or updated package and three other packages, this has an effect on the other side. In these cases a corresponding repository is created or updated for the four packages. If a package is deleted, it is checked whether all single-sided conditions were fulfilled by the deleted package and three other packages before the deletion happened. In such a case, the repository is deleted as well but the three other packages remain unchanged. The reason is that a mapping declares that a certain combination of elements on one side always has to co-occur with a certain combination of elements on the other side. A mapping does, however, not make any statement about the co-occurrence of the elements on a single side. Therefore, our example declares that a repository always has to co-occur with four packages but it does not declare that some of these packages always have to co-occur with the other packages regardless of occurences of repositories in architectural models.

Bidirectionalizable mapping conditions only add further enforcement semantics but do not influence how and which conditions are checked to determine whether elements are currently mapped or have to be mapped. More specifically, bidirectionalizable conditions are never checked but always enforced in one or the other direction if all single-sided conditions of one side are fulfilled after a change on that side. This is again the general explanation of the semantics of bidirectionalizable mapping conditions. To illustrate these semantics, we will explain them for the example condition demanding equality for the names of the repository and the root package. If a repository is created, then this condition is enforced in forward direction by setting the name of the root package, which is created to realize the mapping, to the name of the repository. Similarly, if the name of a repository is changed, then the name of the root package is also changed to preserve consistency according to the mapping. In backward direction the condition for the name of the repository and the name of the root package is enforced in two similar cases that are slightly more complex because the single-sided conditions for the packages also have to be fulfilled. If one of the subpackages of the root package is changed in such a way that the single-sided conditions are newly fulfilled, then a repository is created and the name of it is set to the name of the root package. The only cases in which this can happen are the following: Either a name of one of the subpackages is newly set respectively updated, or one of the subpackages is newly added as a subpackage to the root package.

7.1.2. Comparison of Mappings and Reactions

The example mapping for a component repository and four packages in the object-oriented design already illustrates the two main advantages of the mappings language compared to the reactions language:

1. With mappings, developers only specify once in a mostly[1] *direction-agnostic* way which elements have to correspond, but the mappings are automatically enforced in *both* directions.

[1] the mappings language provides fallback constructs for separately specifying consistency preservation for both directions

2. Developers declare which mapping conditions have to hold in a completely *change-agnostic* way, but if a change can lead to the fulfillment of these conditions or require that they are fulfilled, this is automatically checked or enforced.

We designed the mappings language to provide these advantages in order to address the Open Consistency Specification Language Challenge 3. As a result, developers can specify mappings that abstract away from direction- and change-specific details. To adapt the level of abstraction for the consistency preservation directions, they can also consider the direction where this is necessary. This adaptation can be achieved in two ways by specifying separate check and enforce code for single-sided conditions or by directly specifying enforcement code for both directions if the abstractions of bidirectionalizable conditions are not precise enough.

The advantages become even more evident if we compare the example mapping with the reaction to a creation of a component repository, which was given as Listing 6.4 on page 183 of subsection 6.4.3. To achieve the same functionality as the mapping, but using reactions, we would need to specify two types of further reactions. One the one hand, we would need to specify reactions to further changes in the architecture model. That is, the reaction to a change in which a repository is created would have to be completed with reactions to changes in which a repository is renamed or deleted. On the other hand, we would need to specify reactions for the opposite direction to preserve consistency after changes in the object-oriented design. That is, we would have to react to changes in which packages are initially named, renamed, or moved.

On the one hand, the fact that developers are in large parts relieved from considering directions and completely relieved from considering changes is an advantage. On the other hand, this is also a limitation of mappings compared to reactions. The reason is that developers have less influence on how consistency is preserved in a certain direction and no influence on how consistency is preserved after certain changes. Having restricted possibilities of specifying how consistency is preserved for a certain direction, can be a disadvantage, for example, if we want to check weaker conditions in one direction, but enforce stronger conditions in the other direction. In our running example, we could create all four packages in the object-oriented design if a repository is created, but only require that a single package is created before we automatically create a repository with the same name. For more complex consistency preservation scenarios, such cases with an asymmetric relation between checks and enforcements can be inevitable and much more complex. In our case study for automotive software engineering, for example, modules and classes in one model are both represented as blocks in another model. Therefore, users have to decide whether a module or a class is to be created when they create a block but when consistency is checked it is sufficient if either a module or a class exists. Furthermore, no user change disambiguation is necessary when consistency is preserved in the opposite direction because all information to create a block is available (see subsubsection 9.4.4.4). To have no possibility to specify different ways to preserve consistency after different changes, can be a disadvantage, for example, if we want to support different ways of achieving consistency for different changes. In our running example, this could be the case for the consistency relation between components in the architectural model and component-realization classes in the object-oriented design (see page 173 and subsection 6.2.3). If a component is created, we could create a subpackage with the same name in the package for components and a component-realization class in the subpackage for which we compute the name by appendix the suffix "Impl" to the name of the component. If a class is, however, renamed so that it has exactly the same name as the package in which it is contained, and this package is a direct subpackage of the package for components, we could react with a slightly different notion of consistency. To demand less discipline from developers, we could decide that the class should be considered a component-realization class even if the suffix "Impl" is missing. The mappings language provides, however, only restricted possibilities to take the preservation direction into account, and no possibilities to take changes into account. This is in stark contrast to the reactions language, which provides unlimited control in terms of propagation direction and changes.

7.1.3. Mapping Dependencies and Bidirectionalization

The example mapping for component repositories and packages provided a first impression of the mappings language. It contained, however, only a single mapping with a single bidirectional condition that used the equality operator, which can be trivially bidirectionalized. To show that mappings can depend on other mappings and that more complex conditions can also be bidirectionalized, we provide two more small mappings. The first mapping is for our running example and relates a component to a package and a package-realization class as shown in Listing 7.3. It depends on the mapping between a repository and corresponding packages, which was shown in Listing 7.2, and maps a component to a package and a class in the object-oriented design. This dependency to the repository mapping is used in two conditions which are specified for the component and the package. For the component, a condition specifies that it has to be in the list of components that are contained in the repository that was mapped using the repository mapping. For the newly mapped package, a condition specifies that it has to be a subpackage of the package for components that was mapped using the repository mapping. These two conditions illustrate that mappings that depend on other mappings do not need to explicitly refer to correspondences that are established when the other mapping applies. They only refer to the elements that were mapped. In addition to the two single-sided conditions that use the dependency to the repository mapping, the component mapping also contains a third single-sided condition. This last single-sided condition of the mapping specifies that the mapped class has to be in the list of classifiers contained by the mapped package.

The mapping between a component, a package, and a package-realization class also contains two bidirectionalizable conditions to relate the component and the packages as well as the component and the class. Similar to the bidirectionalizable condition in the repository mapping, the first bidirectionalizable condition of the component mapping simply requires that the name of the mapped component and the name of the mapped package are equal. The second bidirectionalizable condition, however, is slightly more complex as it requires that the sequence that is obtained by appending the suffix "Impl" to the name of the mapped component and name of the class are equal. Enforcing this constraint when the name of the component is newly set or updated is straightforward as the suffix only needs to be appended to obtain the name for the class. If the constraint needs to be enforced in the opposite direction, two cases have to be distinguished. Either the new name of the class ends with the suffix "Impl" and the remaining prefix is used as new component name. Or the new name does not have such a suffix and consistency cannot be preserved according to the mapping.

```
mapping Component<->PackageAndClass
 depends on (Repository<->Packages repoPkgs) {
  map (adl::Component component) with {
      component in repoPkgs.repository.components
  }
  and (oo::Package componentPkg, oo::Class class) with {
      componentPkg in repoPkgs.pkg4components.subpackages
      class in componentPkg.classifiers
  }
  such that {
    component.name = componentPkg.name
    component.name + "Impl" = class.name
  }
}
```

Listing 7.3: Mapping between a component of an architectural model and a package with a component-realization class in an object-oriented design

This bidirectionalization of the string concatenation operator and of other operators is explained in more detail in section 7.4. The partly equivalent reaction to a creation of component was presented in Listing 6.2.

7.2. Mapping Signatures and Conditions

In this section, we present the language constructs for mappings in detail and explain the rationale behind them. We discuss all possibilities for specifying a single mapping but skip language constructs for relating mappings to each other. These inter-mapping dependencies will be explained later (see section 7.5).

7.2.1. Ordinary Mappings and Bootstrap Mappings

As we already mentioned above, the mappings language provides only two first-level constructs apart from a header that only lists the metamodels for which consistency is to be preserved. These two first level constructs are two types of mappings. The first construct are ordinary mappings, for which we showed two examples in the previous section. The second construct are bootstrap mappings, which can be used to create metaclass instances that fulfill certain conditions in a bootstrapping step before any changes.

Both types of mappings consist of a mapping signature and of conditions. For ordinary mappings, the signature consists of the name of the mapping and of a parameter list for both metamodels. The signature of bootstrap mappings, however, only consists of the name of the mapping and a single parameter list for one of the two metamodels. Ordinary mappings can contain single-sided expressions for the instances of both metamodels that are given in the two parameter lists. These conditions are called *single-sided* because they only refer to elements of one side, i.e. they are specified in isolation from the other metamodel. Bootstrap mappings only have one parameter list and so they can only contain single-sided conditions for that list. The single-sided conditions of ordinary mappings are checked if a change occured on the side for which they are defined. They are enforced if a change occurred on the other side and all single-sided conditions for this changed side are fulfilled after the change. Single-sided conditions of bootstrap mappings, however, are never checked but always enforced. In addition to single-sided conditions, ordinary mappings can also contain *bidirectionalizable* conditions which relate instances of both metamodels. These conditions are never checked. They are enforced in direction from one side to another side together with single-sided conditions for the other side if all single-sided conditions for the first side were successfully checked. A part of the concrete syntax of ordinary mappings and bootstrap mappings is given in Listing 7.4. It contains the two main rules of the grammar in Extended Backus-Naur Form (EBNF) [Int96], which we have introduced in subsubsection 2.1.2.5. The complete grammar of the mappings language will be given in Listing 7.10 on page 281 of subsubsection 7.6.1.2.

7.2.2. Single-Sided and Bidirectionalizable Conditions

In the following, we will briefly explain the differences between single-sided conditions and bidirectionalizable conditions and the rationale behind this solution. With a mapping, a developer specifies consistency by declaring which elements always have to exist in models of one metamodel when certain elements exist in models of another metamodel. To automatically

```
["depends on (" , mapping dependency, ")"] , "{" ,
  "map (" , parameters , ")" ,
    ["with" , "{" , {single-sided condition} - , "}"] ,
  "and (" , parameters , ")" ,
    ["with" , "{" , {single-sided condition} - , "}"] ,
  ["such that" , "{" , {bidirectionalizable condition} - , "}"] ,
  ["forward execute {" , {xbase expression} - , "}" ,
  "backward execute {" , {xbase expression} - , "}"] , "}";
bootstrap mapping = "bootstrap mapping" , xbase identifier , "{" ,
  "create (" , parameters , ")" ,
  ["with" , "{" , {single-sided condition} - , "}"] , "}";
mapping dependency = xbase identifier , {"," , xbase identifier};
parameters = typed identifier , {"," , typed identifier};
typed identifier = type expression , xbase identifier;
type expression = xbase identifier , "::" , xbase identifier;
```

Listing 7.4: Main rules for ordinary and bootstrap mappings of the grammar of the mappings language

ensure that this holds for a specific mapping after any change in one of the models, we have to distinguish different condition sets for this mapping. We have to preserve consistency on one side after changes on the other side and the other way round. For each of these two preservation directions, a developer can specify conditions that need to be checked and conditions that need to be enforced. The conditions to be checked specify whether consistency has to be preserved for the mapping and the conditions to be enforced define how consistency has to be preserved in such cases. This means that we can have four condition sets for a single mapping:

CheckLeft *Pre*-conditions to be *checked* on the *left* side after a change on that side

EnforceRight *Post*-conditions to be *enforced* on the *right* side if all conditions in PreLeft are fulfilled

CheckRight *Pre*-conditions to be *checked* on the *right* side after a change on that side

EnforceLeft *Post*-conditions to be *enforced* on the *left* side if all conditions in PreRight are fulfilled

In the following, we will show how these four condition sets relate to the single-sided conditions and bidirectionalizable conditions of the mappings language. For this, we first present three insights into the relations between the four condition sets. Then, we explain why the single-sided and bidirectionalizable conditions respect these three insights.

The first insight is about the need to check properties that could also be enforced instead of checked. The condition sets CheckLeft and CheckRight are used to determine whether model elements with certain properties have to exists on the other side. To ensure that these model elements exist, we preserve consistency on the other side by creating, deleting, and updating model elements according to the condition sets EnforceRight or EnforceLeft. During this preservation we can enforce whatever needs to be enforced. This means that everything that can be checked on the other side in CheckLeft or CheckRight can be enforced in EnforceRight or EnforceLeft. Therefore, it is not necessary to check anything for the other side in CheckLeft and CheckRight. Let us illustrate this using the mapping between a repository and four packages of our running example. Because of the above, a pre-condition for executing this mapping after a change on the repository should not check whether the root package that is updated has no parent package because this can also be enforced.

The second insight into the relation between the condition sets is about the practical dependency between enforcements of one side and properties of the other side. In many cases, we want to enforce consistency on one side in a way that depends on properties of model elements on the other side. Theoretically, it would not be necessary to have such a possibility to define post-conditions for enforcements in a way that depends on properties of the side at which pre-conditions were checked. Practically, it is, however, infeasible to define a separate mapping for every relevant attribute value or model element on one side just to define an appropriate enforcement on the other side. Therefore, we allow EnforceRight to refer to properties of model elements on the left side and EnforceLeft to refer to properties of model elements on the right side. This can be illustrated using our example mapping between a repository and four packages. Instead of having different mappings for every possible name of a repository, we want to define a single mapping that enforces in its post-condition for the object-oriented design that the name of the root package corresponding to the repository has the same name as the repository.

The last insight is about the symmetry of pre- and post-conditions in all cases that are supported by the mappings language. The mappings language is not only mostly direction-agnostic it is also only intended for completely symmetric consistency relations. As we already mentioned above, it is possible to separately define checking code and enforcement code for single-sided conditions or to define separate forward and backward enforcement code instead of bidirectionalizable conditions. Nevertheless, these fallback constructs, which are not direction-agnostic, can only be used to specify symmetric consistency relations, i.e. symmetric co-occurrences of model elements that fulfill certain conditions. This means, that it is only possible to specify mappings for which it is impossible to say whether elements with certain properties exist on one side because some other elements with some other properties exists on the other side or the other way round. For the notion of consistency supported by the mappings language, it is only relevant that these elements always occur together. Therefore, the condition set CheckLeft has to be equivalent to the condition set EnforceLeft and the condition set EnforceRight has to be equivalent to the condition set CheckRight. For the mapping between a repository and four packages of our running example this means that we cannot know whether a repository was created because four packages were created or the other way round.

Together, the insights from the previous two paragraphs state that

I. Pre-conditions *do not need to* check properties of elements on the other side.

II. Post-conditions *should be able to* refer to properties of elements on the other side.

III. Pre- and post-conditions of the same side *have to* be equivalent.

We will now use the four general condition sets and the three insights to explain the rationale for single-sided and bidirectionalizable conditions in the mappings language. If we ignored insight I. and still allowed pre-conditions to check properties of the other side, we would only need a single condition set for each side which contains conditions that serve as pre- and post-conditions for consistency. It would, however, be complex to check and enforce such combined pre- and post-conditions because of insight II.. For every statement about a property of a model element, we would need to know whether we have to enforce it or whether it is only used for enforcements of elements on the other side. To avoid this unnecessary complexity, we designed a solution that respects insight I. and II. as well as insight III., which has to be respected. This solution is the separation of single-sided conditions and bidirectionalizable conditions that we already presented above. A single-sided condition for the left side pertains to the condition sets CheckLeft and EnforceLeft. By only providing access to elements of the left side, we account for I.. By using it to check and to enforce consistency, we account for III.. The same holds for single-sided conditions for the right side and the condition sets EnforceRight and CheckRight. To account for II. we also support bidirectionalizable conditions. In order not to run into the problems described above we require that bidirectionalizable conditions always refer to both sides and only use them in two ways. Either the attribute values or model elements for the properties on the left side are used to enforce consistency on the right side or the other way round. Other semantics for such bidirectionalizable conditions are not necessary because of III..

7.3. Checking and Enforcing Single-Sided Conditions

A key concept of the mappings language is to relieve developers from always specifying how a single-sided condition is to be checked and how it is to be enforced. This is achieved by providing a library of condition operators for which enforcement code is automatically derived. In the future, we want to equip the mappings language with further enforceable condition operators and with a mechanism that allows developer to reuse their own enforceable condition operators. Currently, it is only possible to either use pre-defined enforceable condition operators or to specify how a set of conditions is to be checked and enforced with two code blocks that cannot be reused. In Figure 7.2, we illustrate how different types of single-sided conditions can be represented by instantiating metaclasses for an AST but do not show individual metaclasses for different conditions operators.

Before we explain the enforceable condition operators of the mappings language individually, we briefly provide an overview on the operators and the cases in which they can be used. Most operators can be used to

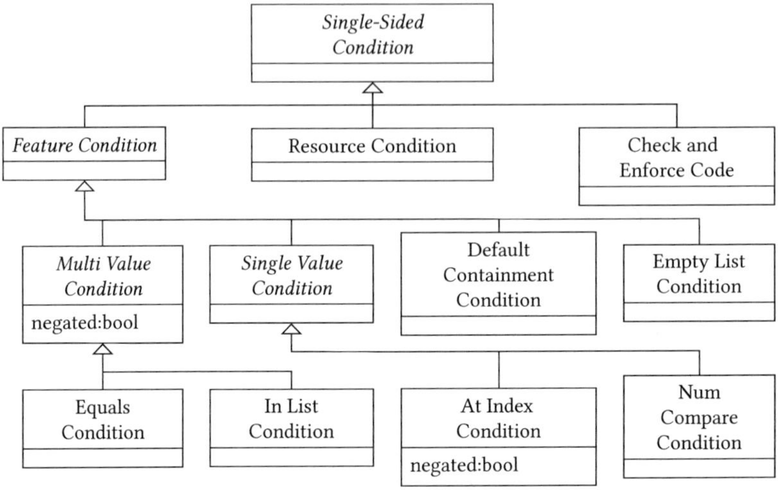

Figure 7.2.: Simplified class diagram with metaclasses for representing single-sided conditions of mappings as an AST

formulate conditions for an attribute or a reference of a metaclass with respect to a single attribute value or model element. Some operators also accept collections of attribute values or model elements as arguments. One operator has only one operand because it only checks or enforces that a list is empty. We present four basic condition operators that can be checked and enforced on simple-typed attributes and complex-typed references. For these four operators we also present negated operators, which are realized according to the principle of least change [Mee98]. All but one of these negated operators need a default value, which is only defined for attributes but not for references. Therefore, these negated operators can only be used for attributes. Additionally, we present an enforceable condition operator for number inequality conditions, which can be used in four variants. Furthermore, we explain two containment operators that help developers to add model elements to containment references of existing model elements or to a new model resource if needed. Finally, we discuss two enforceable iterator condition operators, which are only defined for attributes.

The concrete syntax of all enforceable operators for single-sided conditions and the fallback to a pair of checking and enforcement code blocks is illustrated using a syntax diagram in Figure 7.3. It shows, that we use the infix notation for all binary operators and the prefix notation for the unary empty-list operator. The second operand of all operators except for the path operator is always a feature expression, which denotes an attribute or reference of a model element. Therefore, developers only have to remember that a single-sided condition that is not a path condition or pair of check and enforce blocks always starts with literals, i.e. with a single or several attribute values or model elements. All enforceable condition operators except for the containment and iterator operators are also summarized in Table 7.1.

7.3.1. General Enforceable Operators

We explain every enforceable operator individually and start with the four general operators and their negated counterparts. These general operators can be applied to every attribute or reference but the negated counterparts are only defined for attributes.

7.3.1.1. Equals Operator

The most fundamental enforceable operator for single-sided conditions is the equals operator. It can be used to check and enforce equality of a given list of attribute values or model elements and an attribute or reference. If the attribute or reference has a upper bound multiplicity greater than 1, the equality operator only accepts a list of attribute values or references but this list may of course have only a single entry. Equality is always checked by calling appropriate implementations of Java's `equals` method regardless of multiplicity. This also means that the order of attribute values or model elements is ignored during comparison if the attribute or reference of was defined as unordered in the metamodel. The equals operator is enforced differently depending on the multiplicity. If the attribute or reference has an upper bound of 1, equality is enforced by setting the attribute or reference to the given attribute value or model element. In all other cases the attribute or reference may list several attribute values or referenced model elements

single-sided condition operator	literal multi-plicity	feature multi-plicity	checking code	enforcement code
`equals`	single	single	`equals`	`set`
—”—	multi	multi	—”—	`clear;addAll`
`not equals`	single	single	`!equals`	`if(equals){set(`*`default`*`)}`
—”—	multi	multi	—”—	`if(equals){clear}`
`in`	single	multi	`containedIn`	`if(!containedIn){add}`
—”—	multi	—”—	`allContainedIn`	`for each {--”--}`
`not in`	single	multi	`!containedIn`	`remove`
—”—	multi	—”—	`!containedIn && ...`	`removeAll`
`at index` *i* `in`	single	multi	`get(`*i*`).equals`	`set(`*i*`,...)`
`not at index` *i* `in`	single	multi	`get(`*i*`).!equals`	`set(`*i*`,`*`default`*`)`
`empty`	-	multi	`isEmpty`	`clear`
`not empty`	-	multi	`!isEmpty`	`if(isEmpty){add(`*`default`*`)}`
v `<= a`	single	single	*v* `<= a`	`if(`*v*`>a){a+=v-a}`
v `< a`	single	single	*v* `< a`	`if(`*v*`>=a){a+=v-a+`ε`}`
v `>= a`	single	single	*v* `>= a`	`if(`*v*`<a){a-=a-v}`
v `> a`	single	single	*v* `> a`	`if(`*v*`<=a){a-=a-v+`ε`}`

Table 7.1.: Overview of enforceable condition operators for single-sided constraints in the mappings language without containment and iterator operators (—”—denotes repetitions in a subsequent line)

single-sided condition:

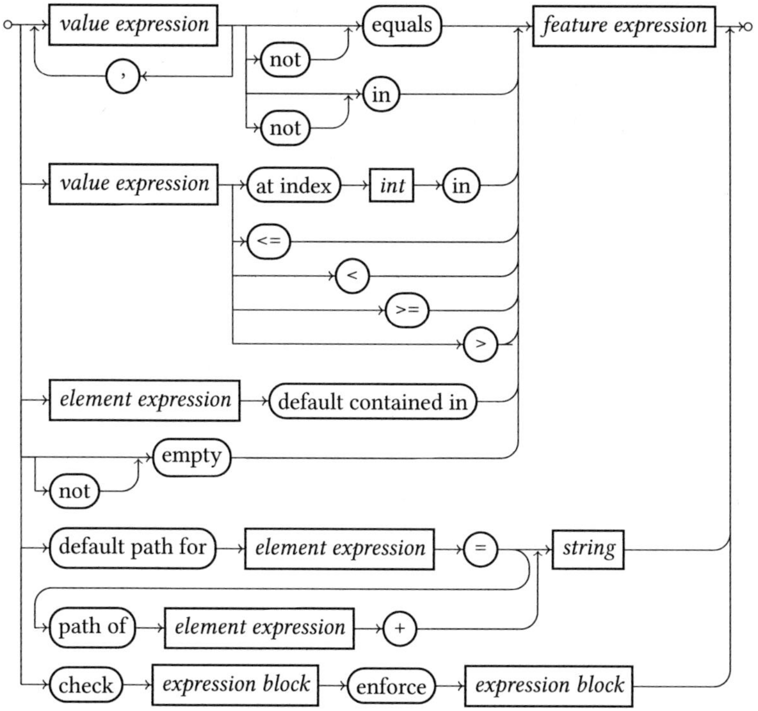

Figure 7.3.: Syntax diagram illustrating all enforceable operators for single-sided conditions and the fallback to check and enforce code

and therefore equality is enforced by removing all current list entries and adding all entries that were provided as left argument for the operator.

The mappings language also supports the negated equals operator for attributes. It is checked by negating the result of the equals operator check and enforcement depends again on the multiplicity of the attribute. If the attribute has an upper bound of 1, negated equality is enforced by setting the default attribute value if the current value equals the given value. As references have no default model element to which they could refer in such a case, the negated equals operator is not yet defined for references. In future work, we plan to also support references by setting them to null if the lower bound is 0 or by referencing a default model element that has to be provided as an additional argument for the operator. If the attribute has an upper bound greater than 1, negated equality is enforced by removing all values from the list if the list contains exactly the given values. Partial equality is tolerated by the negated equality operator as nothing is changed if at least one of the given values is currently not in the list. This idea of enforcing consistency for single-sided conditions only if it cannot be avoided and to a minimal extend is used for all operators. It can be seen as an implementation of the principle of least change [Mee98].

7.3.1.2. Entry-In-List Operator

The entry-in-list operator can be used to check or enforce that one or more given attribute values or model elements are listed for an attribute or reference of another model element. This operator is checked by simply calling Java's `contains` or `containsAll` method on the list. As the operator does not state anything about other elements, enforcement is performed by adding the given entries to the list if they are not yet in the list.

The negated entry-in-list operator checks also supports left arguments with different multiplicities. If a single entry is provided, it checks whether this entry is not contained in the list and enforces this by removing the entry from the list. If several entries are provided, the operator checks whether none of the entries is contained in the list and enforces this by removing all entries from the list. This means the negated entry-in-list operator only removes entries and does not need a default value. Therefore, it is defined for attributes and references.

7.3.1.3. At-Index-In-List Operator

We also present an extended entry-in-list operator that checks and enforces that an entry is listed at a certain index of a list. The operator is checked by obtaining the list entry for the given index and checking whether this entry is equal to the given attribute or model element. To enforce this operator, the list entry for the given index is set to the given attribute or model element.

The negated version of the at-index-in-list operator is also straightforward. To check it, the result is negated and to enforce it the entry at the given position is set to the default value. Therefore, the not-at-index-in-list operator is not defined for references.

7.3.1.4. Empty-List Operator

The only operator that takes only a single argument is the empty-list operator. It is checked by calling Java's `isEmpty` method and enforced by removing all current values from the list. The negated empty-list operator is checked by negating the result of the check for emptiness and enforced by adding the default value if the list is empty. Therefore, it is only defined for attributes.

7.3.2. Special Enforceable Operators

We continue our library of enforceable operators with operators that can only be applied to attributes or references that have special properties. The first operator is only defined for numerical attributes, the second operator is only defined for containment references, the third operator has no feature operand but requires a path string, and the fourth and fifth operand are only defined for lists of attribute values.

7.3.2.1. Number-Inequality Operator

We present four variants of an enforceable operator for checking and enforcing inequalities of a single number and an appropriatedly typed attribute of a model element. These four variants can be used to check and enforce that a number is greater, less, not greater, or not less than the value of an attribute. All four variants are checked using the appropriate operators in Java. Enforcement is, however, performed differently for equalities that are strict or not strict. The <= variant, for example, enforces that a given value `v` is not greater than the attribute `a` by adding the difference `v-a` to the attribute if `v` is currently greater than `a`. The result is that `v` and `a` are equal after this enforcement. The < variant, however, also has to add the minimal value that makes a greater than v to enforce that v is strictly less that a. This minimal value depends on the attribute type and has to be at least 1 for integers and at least the unit of least precision (ULP) for floating point numbers. The greater-than and less-than operators can be enforced with any value that is great enough to fulfill the condition, but using the minimal value ensures that the enforcement introduces the minimal change that is necessary. In Table 7.1, we denoted this minimal value with ε. It would also be possible to support further operators for numerical attributes, for example for checking and enforcing conditions for the maximal element, the minimal element, or the sum of all elements. If such operators should turn out to be necessary when the mappings language is applied in further consistency preservation scenarios, they can be easily added to the mappings language.

7.3.2.2. Default Containment Operators

To make it easier for developers to write mappings that result in serializable models with a proper containment hierarchy, we provide two operators that enforce containment only if necessary. To decide whether an enforcement is necessary, both operators check whether a model element is currently part of the containment hierarchy. This is the case if the model element is contained in another model element or if it is the root element of a model resource. If this is not the case, then the operators are used to enforce that a model element is part of the containment hierarchy. The `default-contained-in` operator takes a model element as left argument. It could also be named "if not contained then add to" operator as the right argument is a combination of a model element and a containment reference that is defined for one of the metaclasses that are instantiated by the element. This operator can be used to define which containment reference should be used to add the given left model element to the given right model element if the left model element is not yet contained in any other element and also no root element of a resource. Similarly, the `default-path-for` operator can be used to add a given model element to a new resource which is created at a given file path if the model element is not yet contained in any model element or resource. The file path for the resource to be created can either be given as an absolute path or as a path relative to the path of a resource of an existing model element. In the first case, the complete path has to be provided as a string. In the second case, an element that is located in a resource with a path that should be used as a prefix for the new path should be provided together with a path suffix string.

7.3.2.3. Iterator Condition Operators

Finally, we suggest two enforceable operators `forAll` and `exists` to define conditions for collections of attribute values that should hold for all attribute values or at least for one attribute value. These iterator operators are not yet implemented in our language prototype, but we already suggest how they should be realized in the future. The condition that should hold for all or for at least one value can simply be checked for every value individually. Similarly, the `forAll` operator can also be enforced individually for every value. The `exists` operator, however, should add a new element for which the condition is enforced if no such element is already present.

7.3.3. Manual Checking and Enforcement

If the enforceable condition operators that we presented above are not sufficient, a developer can still specify manually how a single-sided condition is to be checked and enforced. To this end, the mappings language provides the possibility to define a single-sided condition with two separate code blocks for checking and enforcing the condition. These code blocks, are restricted in the same way as single-sided conditions that are specified using an enforceable condition operator. This means the code can only read and write properties of model elements that instantiate metaclasses of the metamodel for which the single-sided condition is specified. Elements of the other metamodel cannot be accessed and neither check nor enforce blocks obtain any other input than the elements of the side that is mapped with the condition. We already discussed the rationale for these restrictions in subsection 7.2.2.

In order to correctly check and enforce consistency in both preservation directions the following requirements can be formulated:

1. every negative check has to lead to an enforcement

2. every enforcement has to lead to a positive subsequent check
3. the enforcement behavior after a positive check does not need to be defined, but if it is defined, then it should not change anything

To meet these requirements, we suggest to start creating a manually enforced single-sided condition by developing the check code. Then, all cases in which the check fails should be determined. The enforcement code has to take all these cases into account in order to fulfill requirement 1. As different reasons for a negative check may be treated uniformly in the enforcement code, it can be beneficial to separate the detection of a case for which an enforcement is responsible from the update behavior. With such a separation it is sufficient to ensure that the execution of the update code always implies a positive subsequent check to fulfill requirement 2. In contrast to the first two requirements, requirement 3 is optional. It is possible to correctly check and enforce consistency without fulfilling this requirement if it is ensured that the enforcement code is only executed after a negative check. In order not to introduce any faults when a check or enforcement code block is maintained, it is, however, a good practice to ensure that even such unecessary invocations of the enforcement code do no harm.

7.4. Bidirectionalizable Conditions and Inverters

The last language construct of an individual mapping, which we did not yet explain in detail, are bidirectional enforcement specifications. Such specifications are only relevant for enforcing consistency and may contain bidirectionalizable conditions and a pair of forward and backward enforcement code blocks. In the following we will focus on bidirectionalizable conditions as the syntax and semantics of arbitrary enforcement code for both directions is straightforward. In order to be bidirectionalizable, a condition that relates both sides of a mapping has to be expressed as an equation for an attribute of a mapped metaclass. Conditions for references do not need to be bidirectionalized as the referenced model elements can be directly mapped in the signature of a mapping (see subsection 7.2.1). To eliminate unnecessary variations, the mappings language imposes a syntactic restriction on bidirectionalizable conditions without limiting the expressive power. It is required that a bidirectionalizable condition adheres to the notational direction of the mapping and that the equation has a single attribute of a mapped model element on one side. Therefore, a bidirectionalizable condition can always be read as an assignment but sometimes this assignment lists the attribute for which a value is to be assigned on the right side, which may look unfamiliar. We call this attribute of a mapped element the *assignment target* and the other side of a bidirectionalizable equation is called *operation to be inverted*. This operation to be inverted may use attribute values of any model element on that side and operands can in turn be results of operations that can be inverted.

When consistency is preserved from the side with the operation to be inverted to the side with the assignment target, then the assignment is simply executed in this direction, which may also be from left to right. In order to also preserve consistency in the opposite direction, we bidirectionalize the assignment by inverting the operation. This yields an inverse condition that assigns the result of the inverse operation to an attribute of the side that was not assigned in the original condition. If more than one attribute of one side is used to express a condition of an attribute on the other side, then it has to be specified which of these attributes should be assigned in the inverse condition. Currently, we are able to invert all operations that are build using 30 basic operators for which we created inverters. If a consistency relation cannot be expressed in a bidirectionalizable way using these operators, then a developer can still specify manually how the condition is to be enforced in forward and backward direction.

In the remainder of this section, we will explain the inversion approach that we developed for bidirectionalizable conditions of the mappings language. We present inverters for 30 currently supported operators and explain how they fulfill important round-trip laws for bidirectional model transformations. All text, tables, and proofs are based on an article [KR16a] and a technical report [KR16b]. We published the article and the report in cooperation with Kirill Rakhman, who implemented prototypical inverters while working on his master's thesis [Rak15], which was supervised by the author of this dissertation.

```
11    component.name = componentPkg.name
12    component.name + "Impl" = class.name
```

Listing 7.5: Two bidirectionalizable conditions of a mapping for a component, a package, and a class (complete version in Listing 7.3)

7.4.1. Inversion Examples and Overview

To illustrate how a trivial and more complex condition is bidirectionalized, we come back to a mapping of our running example. It maps a component of an architectural model to a package and a class of an object-oriented design and was introduced in Listing 7.3 on page 224 of subsection 7.1.3. In addition to three single-sided conditions for the component, the package, and the class, the mapping also defines two bidirectionalizable conditions that relate both sides of the mapping (line 10–13). We repeat these two conditions in Listing 7.5. The first condition demands identical names for the component and package. Therefore, the equation can be read as an assignment in both directions and inversion is trivial because the identity operator is inverse to itself. The second condition, however, can only be read as an assignment from left to right. It demands that the name of the class on the right side is identical to the result of appending a suffix "Impl" to the name of the component on the left side. From left to right the assignment can be directly executed to obtain a new class name. In order to also preserve consistency in the opposite direction after the class name is changed, we have to invert the string concatenation operation. This inverted operation has to distinguish two cases. If the name of the class ends with the suffix "Impl", then the component name is set to the remainder of the class name. If the name of the class does, however, not have this suffix, then the inverted operation cannot fulfill the given equation. In order not to break more than necessary, it sets the name of the component to the complete class name. If the component name is later changed by a user, the class name will be updated again according to the specified assignment and so the class name will end with the suffix "Impl" again.

To show that many non-trivial conditions can also be bidirectionalized successfully, we introduce a small consistency preservation example and an appropriate mapping. In this example, we want to preserve consistency

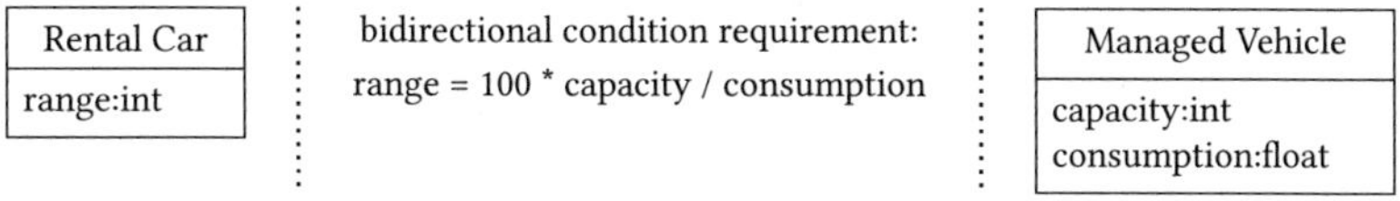

Figure 7.4.: Metaclasses and bidirectionalizable condition requirement for mapping cars that are modelled for customers to vehicles for internal management

between models for offering and managing rental cars using two metamodels as shown in Figure 7.4. The metamodel that is used in the system for customers that rent cars contains a metaclass RentalCar, which has an attribute range to represent the distance that can be approximately covered with a full tank or battery. Another metamodel is used to manage the cars internally. It contains a metaclass ManagedVehicle, which has two attributes to represent the capacity of the tank or battery and the average consumption. To keep models of these metamodels consistent, we can define a mapping with a bidirectionalizable condition that relates the range, the capacity and the consumption as shown in Listing 7.6. This condition (line 7) assigns the result of a multiplication to the range attribute of the left mapped model element car. The second operand of the multiplication is a division of the values for two attributes of the right vehicle element. More than one attribute of the right side is used to calculate the value that has to be assigned to the range attribute of the left side. Therefore, it is specified that the consumption attribute is to be updated after changes in the left model (line 8). Through bidirectionalization for this attribute the given forward enforcement of the condition is inverted to yield the inverse enforcement

```
vehicle.consumption = 100 * vehicle.capacity / car.range
```

If we would specify the attribute capacity to be updated, we would obtain the inverse enforcement

```
vehicle.capacity = car.range * vehicle.consumption / 100
```

For the given example, updating an average consumption based on the observed range is, however, more reasonable than updating the fixed tank or battery capacity.

With other approaches for bidirectional transformations, a transformation developer cannot easily specify conditions as those of the two examples

```
mappings CarOffersAndManagement for carOffers and vehicleMgmt

mapping Car<->Vehicle {
  map (carOffers::Car car)
  and (vehicleMgmt::Vehicle vehicle)
  such that {
    car.range = 100 * vehicle.capacity / vehicle.consumption
      update vehicle.consumption
  }
}
```

Listing 7.6: Mapping between cars of customer models and vehicles of management models

above in a bidirectional way. Either the developer is forced to specify separate unidirectional operations to calculate the attribute values in forward and backward direction. Or the condition has to be expressed using constraints, e.g. `divide(capacity,consumption,t1)`, `multiply(t1, 100, t2)`, and `floatToInt(range,t2)`. In the first case the developer has to ensure manually that both operations together fulfill round-trip properties and types have to explicitly casted in both directions. This is necessary in order to correctly preserve consistency without introducing any imprecisions or inconsistencies that could be avoided. These round-trip properties also have to be ensured in the second case. To this end, the developer has to learn the constraint language in order to define appropriate pairs of atomic forward and backward operations for the basic operations `divide`, `multiply`, and `floatToInt`. Such a constraint-based approach is inefficient because all other developers that use the same basic operations in their conditions also have to provide such pairs of forward and backward operations. Furthermore, it can be error-prone because every new definition of an inversion for a basic operation can be faulty.

7.4.2. Round-Trip Laws and Inverter Properties

Before we explain how we bidirectionalize mapping conditions using operator -specific inverters, we discuss important round-trip properties for such inversions. We already mentioned above, that we use inverters to obtain an inverse attribute assignment for a bidirectionalizable condition that is given in the form of an attribute assignment. Such a derivation of an inverse operation is not only used for consistency preservation but also for any other scenarios in which values of a model are to be transformed into values for another model and the other way round. For such model transformations in general, it is necessary that forward and backward transformations meet certain requirement in order to guarantee important properties for round-trips from one model to another and back again.

7.4.2.1. Round-Trip Laws for Well-Behavedness

There are several definitions of round-trip laws for bidirectional transformations. We reuse the well-known GETPUT and PUTGET laws that were formulated for lenses by Foster et al. [Fos+07] (see also subsection 2.2.3 and 3.8.3). The general idea is that we always have to obtain the same value if we apply an operation and its inverse after each other or the other way round. In order to be able to prove that inverters meet these laws, we define them for our special setting of attribute assignment expressions. To keep the definitions simple, we formulate them for a unary operator op but an extension to operators with several operands is straightforward. An inverse operator for an operation op is always denoted by $\mathrm{op}^{\leftharpoondown}$ and has to obtain a target value t *and* a source value s. The relation between an operator and its inverse operator and the inputs and outputs is also illustrated in Figure 7.5. It suggests that the source values s, s', and s'' are different and that the target values t and t'. This is possible but should not be the case as we will see with the round-trip laws.

Based on this simple notation we define the essential round-trip law GETPUT:

Definition 44 (GetPut Law)
An operator op *and its inverse operator* $\mathrm{op}^{\leftharpoondown}$ *fulfill the* GETPUT *law, if the subsequent application of* op *(get) and* $\mathrm{op}^{\leftharpoondown}$ *(put) always yields the same value:*

$$\mathrm{op}^{\leftharpoondown}(\mathrm{op}(s), s) = s, \textit{ for all source values } s \tag{7.1}$$

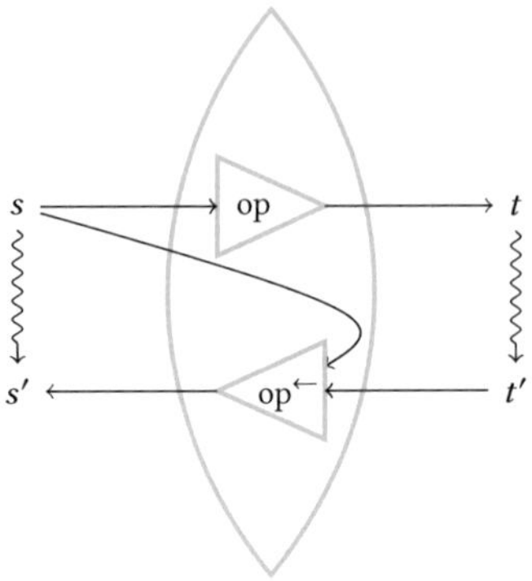

Figure 7.5.: Illustration of an operator and its inverse operator using the lense analogy (adapted from [Fos10, Figure 2.1, p. 12])

The PutGet law is symmetric to the GetPut law except for the different arities of op and $\mathrm{op}^{\leftarrow}$:

Definition 45 (PutGet Law)
An operator op *and its inverse operator* $\mathrm{op}^{\leftarrow}$ *fulfill the PutGet law, if the subsequent application of* $\mathrm{op}^{\leftarrow}$ *(put) and* op *(get) always yields the same value:*

$$\mathrm{op}(\mathrm{op}^{\leftarrow}(t, s)) = t, \text{ for all target values } t \text{ and all source values } s \quad (7.2)$$

Both laws are also illustrated in Figure 7.6. The requirements of both laws are represented by the same closed loop and only the order in which the operator and inverse operator are applied is different.

7.4.2.2. Best-Possible Behaved Inverters

It is desirable that both round-trip laws, GetPut and PutGet, are always fulfilled. To have a convenient term for this, pairs of operations and inverse operations that always fulfill the GetPut and the PutGet law are called

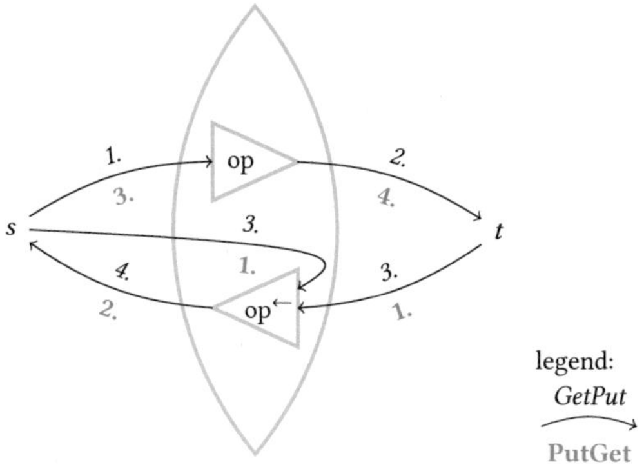

Figure 7.6.: Illustration of the GETPUT and PUTGET laws for an operator and its inverse operator (based on [Fos10, Figure 3.1, p., 39])

well-behaved by Foster et al. For many operations it can, however, not be avoided that the PUTGET law is violated during a round-trip if all possible target updates are allowed. This means that no inverse operation can be defined that would make the operation pair well-behaved. The operations for which this is the case are all operations that are not right-total, i.e. surjective. For these operations, only updates to target values that are in the image of the operation can be inverted in a way that fulfills the PUTGET law. An operation that returns the absolute value of a source value, for example, cannot be inverted without breaking the PUTGET law if the target may be updated to a negative value: no matter which value will be put as new source, the absolute target value that we will get from it will always be positive and therefore not identical to the negative target value after the update. A similar problem can be observed for the bidirectionalizable condition of the mapping for components, which we discussed in subsection 7.4.1. If the name of the class is changed to a string that does not end with the suffix "Impl", then we cannot update the component name to something that will yield the same class name after a round-trip.

In order to precisely capture cases in which a violation of the PUTGET law is inevitable, we introduce a new term of *best-possible behavedness*:

Definition 46 (Best-Possible Behaved)
A pair of an operation and inverse operation is called best-possible behaved *iff*

1. *the GETPUT law is fulfilled in all cases and*
2. *the PUTGET law is fulfilled for every target change that can be inverted without breaking the PUTGET law.*

Inverters that yield well-behaved or best-possible behaved transformations are also called well-behaved respectively best-possible behaved inverters. All 30 inverters that we present and realized in our prototype are best-possible behaved inverters and 14 of them are even well-behaved inverters. Proofs for the well-behavedness of our inverters will be presented in subsubsection 9.3.5.3. They always have the same structure: for a partition W, B of the set of possible target values we prove the following three propositions: 1. GETPUT holds for all source values. 2. PUTGET holds for all values in W. 3. For every inverter that would fulfill PUTGET for a target value in B, we obtain a contradiction.

Best-possible behaved inverters have to deal with target updates for which a violation of the PUTGET law cannot be avoided. These cases are always updates to target values that are in the codomain of the function represented by the forward operator but not in the image of this function. They can, however, be divided into two categories: For PUTGET violations of the first category some of the information of the updated target value can be used to choose a new source value for which the new target after a round-trip will be closer to the initially updated target value than for all other choices of source values. For PUTGET violations of the second category no choice for a new source value yields a target value after a round-trip that is closer to the initially updated target value than for all other choices of source values. Therefore, we call the first type of PUTGET violations *restrictable PUTGET violations* and the second type *desperate PUTGET violations*.

A restrictable PUTGET violation occurs, for example, if the target of the arithmetic abs operator is changed to a negative value: the absolute value of the negative target is used to choose a new source value that yields a target after a round-trip that has the correct absolute value but inevitably an incorrect algebraic sign. A desperate PutGet violation occurs, for example, if the target of the trigonometric sin operator is changed to a value that is not in the interval $[-1, 1]$: all choices for a new source value that are of the form $2n \pm \frac{\pi}{2}$ for an $n \in \mathbb{N}_0$ yield the target value ± 1 after a round-trip and are as close as possible to the initially updated target value.

In our prototype, we respond to restrictable violations with a handler that updates the source according to a passed value that is derived from the updated target value. How the passed value is changed before updating the source or whether a target update shall be rejected by throwing an exception can be customized using a callback. The default implementation directly updates the source to the passed value without any further changes and rejects no target update. For desperate PutGet violations, no kind of exception handling would make any difference so our prototype simply updates the source to a default value that is independent of the updated target value.

7.4.3. Bidirectionalization trough Inversion

Before we present our library of operator-specific inverters, we briefly explain how they are used to bidirectionalize conditions of the mappings language.

7.4.3.1. Inverting Assignments by Rewriting Equations

Bidirectionalizable conditions are inverted by transforming the equation, which can be read as an assignment in one direction, according to common rules for rewriting mathematical equations. The input is the assignment expression that has a single attribute of a mapped model element on one side and possibly several attributes of mapped model elements of the other side. From this input the bidirectionalization computes an inverse assignment expression for the opposite transformation direction as output. The metaclass instances for which attribute values are read and updated, are managed in the reaction part that is generated for a mapping. Therefore, their attribute values can directly be manipulated by the forward and backward operation.

The input assignment represents an initial equation and the output assignment represents the equation that results from solving the initial equation for the variable that corresponds to the attribute that is updated when the inverse operation is executed. The output assignment is obtained by transforming the abstract syntax tree (AST) of the input assignment: every operation node on the way from the root to the leaf node for the attribute to be updated is replaced with an inverse operation. All other nodes remain unchanged. Each operation is inverted independently using an inverter for the used operator. Only the result of the previously inverted parent operation is passed in form of a temporary variable and the final result is the result of the last inversion.

The inversion approach has a semantic restriction in addition to the syntactical restrictions for bidirectionalizable conditions that we already mentioned. In total, the operation to be inverted and all operations that are directly or indirectly used as operands may only refer to every attribute of a model element at most once. This property is called linear [Wad88] or affine [Mat+07] and guarantees straightforward inversion. In the following we will use simpler terms for the side with the assignment target and for the side with the operation to be inverted in order to ease the discussion. To stick with the common syntax of assignments, we call the first side *target side* and the second side the *source side* of an assignment. We also call the direction in which the assignment can directly be executed the forward direction and the direction in which the inverted operation is executed the backward direction (see also page 78). Nevertheless, inversion can be used for bidirectionalizable conditions that assign values from the left side to the right side or the other way round, as explained at the beginning of this chapter.

We already mentioned that one attribute has to be marked as the one to be updated in the backward direction if more than one attribute of the source metaclass is mentioned. The reason is that we currently do not support operators that can only be inverted by updating more than one operand. Operations that operate directly or indirectly on the attribute according to which the expression is inverted have to use operators for which an inverter is defined. In the AST these operations correspond to nodes that are direct or indirect parents of the attribute leaf. All other operations can use arbitrary operators as they do not have to be inverted. The expression of our initial car rental example `range = 100 * capacity / consumption` is an assignment expression for the attribute `range` of the metaclass `RentalCar` of the metamodel that acts as target in in the forward transformation direction. The source side is a multiplication operation of a constant literal operand and a division operation that mentions the two attributes `capacity` and `consumption` of the source metaclass `ManagedVehicle`. To enable an inversion of this expression both of these source attributes could be marked as the one to be updated in the backward direction. We already explained, however, that an inversion according to the consumption would probably be chosen to respond to a change of the monitored range. The reason is that a changed observed range indirectly reflects a change of the average consumption and not of the fixed tank or battery size.

7.4.3.2. Technical Inversion and Code Generation

The inversion procedure for an attribute assignment expression consists of three steps. First, the AST of the expression is statically checked to ensure that the assignment fulfills the above requirements. Then, a copy of the AST is transformed: first the root and then every node on the way to the leaf for the attribute according to which the expression is inverted. Finally, the source code for the inverted assignment is generated from the transformed AST copy in form of a method. This method returns the result of the last inversion and has a parameter for the target attribute and for every source attribute.

It is possible to invert every operation individually because they only depend on the value of the operands and not on the internal structure of the operands. This can be illustrated using the expression of our car rental example `range = 100 * capacity / consumption`. It is inverted in two steps to `capacity / consumption = range / 100 =: tmp` and then to `capacity = tmp * consumption` which yields `(range / 100) * consumption`. The temporary variables, which we use during the code generation in our prototype, are not necessary as they could be inlined, but they make the generated code more readable.

7.4.4. Inverter Classification and Overview

We briefly present all inverters for the currently supported 30 common operators and classify them with respect to the round-trip laws that we presented above. Afterwards, we define and explain each inverse operator in detail.

In the previous section, we have introduced the notion of well-behaved and best-possible behaved inverters and distinguished restrictable and desperate PUTGET violations. There are two further properties that can be used to classify inverters: The first property deals with the role of different operands during inversion. Operators with more than one operand that realize a commutative function can be inverted identically for all operands. Therefore, we call such inverters *operand-agnostic*. For operators that have no operand-agnostic inverter, we define individual inverse operators for inversion according to each operand and call these inverters *operand-specific*. The second property is concerned with the way inverters can be defined for different target values. Some operators can be inverted in way that fulfills the GETPUT law with a single definition that holds for all possible target values. We call such inverters *target-agnostic*. All operators that have no target-agnostic inverter are inverted with separate definitions for target values with different properties. These inverters are called *target-sensitive*.

We write $\mathrm{op}(s_1 : T_1, s_2 : T_2) : T_3$ to denote an operator with the name "op", two operands named "s_1" and "s_2" of type T_1 and T_2, and a return type T_3. An operand-agnostic inverse operator of this operator is denoted by $\mathrm{op}^{\leftarrow}$. $\mathrm{op}_{\mathrm{i}}^{\leftarrow}$ denotes an inverse operator for inversion according to the operand with 1-based index i. All inverse operators have at least one parameter to obtain the updated target value and may have additional parameters for the values of the operands of the operator to be inverted.

We group the 30 operators for which we define inverse operations in five categories: primitive casts, boolean logical operators, basic and advanced arithmetic operators, and string operators. Table 7.2 lists properties of the operators and their inverse operators. The 14 well-behaved inverters are those that neither have restrictable nor desperate PUTGET violations. All operators for which we present inverters operate on single values not on collections of values and can be inverted by updating a single source attribute. Inverters for collection operators and for operators that require updates of more than one source attribute in backward direction are part of our future work.

For some operations, the presented inverters are just one out of several possibilities to invert the operation. In many cases there are, however, only a few different ways to define a best-possible behaved inverter that updates only a single source attribute. This is different for inverters that update more than one source attribute, which we plan to examine in future work. Such inverters have an important additional degree of freedom: the difference between the old and the updated target value Δ can now be split in different ways on several source attributes. An inverter for binary arithmetic operators may, for example, apply the inverse arithmetic operation using $\frac{\Delta}{2}$ to both source attributes or using Δ to one of both source attributes.

The presented extensible library of inverters for basic operations is restricted to inverters that update only one attribute and to an incomplete set of common operations. For many cases, this is, however, sufficient as we discovered by analyzing all 103 transformations of a well-know repository for model transformations[2]. We discovered that 55% of the logical lines of code (LLOC) of all attribute transformation expressions (including the trivial identity operator) and 26% of the LLOC of all non-trivial transformation expressions in these transformations only use operations for which we present inverters. Many inverters for operations that we did not address can, however, reuse some of the presented inverters or can be defined in a similar way. A new inverter for a string concatenation operator with more than two operands, for example, could easily be defined even if more than operand shall be updated in the inverse transformation.

In the following definitions, we use a helper `restrictPGV(p:T):T` to encapsulate the handling of restrictable violations of the PutGet law based on the value of the parameter p. In our prototype, the default implementation always returns the passed value, but it can be customized to react differently depending on the value and / or operator that was inverted. For desperate violations of the PutGet law, a helper `reportPGV(p:T):T` updates the source to the given fixed value and reports the violation.

2 ATL Transformations Zoo: eclipse.org/atl/atlTransformations

Operator to Invert	**OR**	**OA**	**TA**	**rPGv**	**dPGv**
	Primitive Casts				
narrowing cast	numeric	–	✓	✓	✓
widening cast	numeric	–	✗	✗	✓
	Boolean Logical Operators				
not, xor	boolean	–	✓	✓	✓
	Basic Arithmetic Operators				
unary minus	numeric	–	✓	✓	✓
addition, multiplication	numeric	✓	✓	✓	✓
float division	floats	✗	✓	✓	✓
int division	integers	✗	✗	✓	✓
	Advanced Arithmetic Operators				
absolute value	numeric	–	✗	✗	✓
rounding	floats	–	✗	✓	✓
floor, ceil	double	–	✗	✗	✓
floor modulus	integers	✗	✗	✗	✗
exponentiation	b:num.,e:int.	✗	✗	✗	✓
sin, cos	floats	–	✗	✓	✗
tan	floats	–	✗	✓	✓
asin, acos, atan	floats	–	✗	✗	✓
	String Operators				
parse	bool.,num.	–	✓	✓	✓
num printing	numeric	–	✗	✓	✗
bool printing	boolean	–	✗	✓	✓
length	strings	–	✗	✓	✓
concat	strings	✗	✗	✗	✓
suffix	strings	–	✓	✓	✓
substring (fixed indices)	strings	–	✗	✗	✓
toUpper/LowerCase	strings	–	✗	✗	✓

Table 7.2.: Overview on all operators for which we developed inverters with their argument types and inverter properties (where – stands for not applicable, ✗ for no, and ✓ for yes)
Legend: OT = Operand Types, OA = Operand-Agnostic, TA = Target-Agnostic, rPGv = no restrictable PutGet violations, dPGv = no desperate PutGet violations

7.4.5. Operator and Inverter Composition

A key characteristic of our approach is that bidirectionalizable conditions may compose several operations with different operator because the operator-specific inversion is compositional. Therefore, we briefly explain how we invert composed operations using the inverters of individual operators before we present operator-specific inverters. Let $\overleftarrow{\mathrm{op}_1}(t,s)$ and $\overleftarrow{\mathrm{op}_2}(t,s)$ be two inverters for two operators $\mathrm{op}_1(s)$ and $\mathrm{op}_2(s)$. For the composition operator $\mathrm{op}_{1\circ 2}(s) := \mathrm{op}_1(\mathrm{op}_2(s))$ we define the inverse composition operator as follows:

$$\overleftarrow{\mathrm{op}_{1\circ 2}}(t,s) := \overleftarrow{\mathrm{op}_2}(\overleftarrow{\mathrm{op}_1}(t,\mathrm{op}_2(s)),s)$$

This relation between the individual operators, their inverse operators, the composition operator, and its inverse is illustrated in Figure 7.7 using the lense analogy. A proof that this composition operator and its inverse operator respect the round-trip laws GETPUT and PUTGET will be given in section 9.3.5.3.

7.4.6. Operator-Specific Inverters

In the following, we present all individual inverters that we developed for the mappings language. We ordered them according to the purpose and operand types of the operations. If an inverter for an operation is defined based on an inverter for another operation, we made this dependency explicit and present both inverters in the appropriate order.

7.4.6.1. Primitive Casts

Type conversions and a notion of type-compatibility are necessary for some arithmetic operators. Therefore, we start by defining inverse operators for primitive type casts. These are the only possible casts that can appear in attribute mapping expressions. Casts of complex-typed references to metaclass instances are usually not necessary in the mappings language because the signatures can directly specify a desired subtype.

If a numeric type T_2 can be converted without information loss to a numeric type T_1, we call T_1 wider than T_2 and write $T_1 > T_2$. For our prototype we

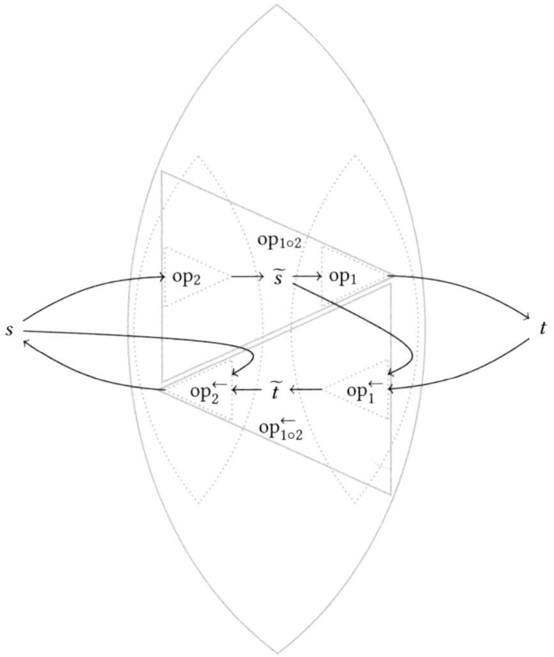

Figure 7.7.: Illustration of the composition and inversion of two operators and their inverse operators using the lense analogy

use the relation that is defined by the widening primitive conversion int the Java language specification[3]: double > float > long > int > short > byte. Consider a floating-point value x that is equal to another floating-point value y with a relative tolerance of ε, i.e.

$$\left|\frac{x-y}{max(x,y)}\right| < \varepsilon$$

In this case, we call x and y ε-equal and write $x \stackrel{\varepsilon}{=} y$. In our prototype values are ε-equal if a call to `org.apache.commons.math3.util.Precision.-equalsWithRelativeTolerance` using the IEEE 754 machine epsilon 2^{-53} returns true, but the epsilon can be configured differently and the compari-

[3] Conversions: docs.oracle.com/javase/specs/jls/se8/html/jls-5.html#jls-5.1.2

son could be replaced with a comparison based on the units in the last place (ulp).

To invert a narrowing cast, we perform an appropriate widening cast and the other way round. More formally, this leads to the following two inverters. For two numeric types $T_1 > T_2$ and the narrowing primitive cast operator $\text{ncast}_{T_1,T_2}(\textit{source} : T_1) : T_2$, we define the inverse operator

$$\text{ncast}^{\leftarrow}_{T_1,T_2}(\textit{target} : T_2) : T_1 := \text{wcast}_{T_2,T_1}(\textit{target})$$

For two numeric types $T_2 > T_1$ and the widening primitive cast operator $\text{wcast}_{T_1,T_2}(\textit{source} : T_1) : T_2$, we define the inverse operator

$$\text{wcast}^{\leftarrow}_{T_1,T_2}(t : T_2) : T_1 := \begin{cases} \text{ncast}_{T_2,T_1}(t) & \text{if } \text{wcast}_{T_1,T_2}(\text{ncast}_{T_2,T_1}(t)) \stackrel{\varepsilon}{=} t \\ \text{restrictPGV}(\text{ncast}_{T_2,T_1}(t)) & \text{otherwise} \end{cases}$$

To invert all implicit casts in expressions, which are called "widening primitive conversions" for Java, we replace them with explicit widening casts before inverting an expression and use the inverse operator $\text{wcast}^{\leftarrow}$ as defined above. As a result, all explicit and implicit widening casts are inverted using a narrowing cast without violating the PutGet-law whenever the target value can be cast with a relative error smaller than ε. In all other cases a PutGet violation cannot be avoided but its effect can be restricted by choosing the cast target value as new source value.

7.4.6.2. Boolean Logical Operators

The next group of operators with inverters consists only of the not and the xor operator, because conjunctions and disjunctions cannot always be inverted by updating only a single source attribute: If a target value is changed from 1 to 0 an inverter for the and operator has to update both source values and an inverter for the or operator has to do this if both source values were 1.

Not For the operator $\text{not}(source : bool) : bool$, we define the trivial inverse operator

$$\text{not}^{\leftharpoondown}(target : bool) : bool := \text{not}(target)$$

Xor For the operator $\text{xor}(s_1 : bool, s_2 : bool) : bool$, we define the inverse operator

$$\text{xor}_1^{\leftharpoondown}(target : bool, s_2 : bool) : bool := \text{xor}(target, s_2)$$

for inversion according to the first operand s_1 and the inverse operator

$$\text{xor}_2^{\leftharpoondown}(target : bool, s_1 : bool) : bool := \text{xor}(target, s_1)$$

for inversion according to the second operand s_1.

7.4.6.3. Basic Arithmetic Operators

This group of operators realizes the four basic arithmetic operations on integer and floating-point types.

Unary Minus For all numeric types T and the arithmetic operator $\text{unaryminus}(source : T) : T$, we define the trivial inverse operator

$$\text{unaryminus}^{\leftharpoondown}(target : T) : T := \text{unaryminus}(target)$$

Addition As we invert implicit casts separately, it is sufficient to define, for example, the addition operator only once for two operands of identical type. For all numeric types T and the arithmetic operator $\text{addition}(s_1 : T, s_2 : T) : T$, we define the inverse operator

$$\text{addition}^{\leftharpoondown}(target : T, s : T) : T := \text{addition}(target, \text{unaryminus}(s))$$

We support the subtraction operator in bidirectionalizable conditions indirectly by reusing the unary minus. That is, we replace the syntactic sugar $s_1 - s_2$ with the expression $\text{addition}(s_1, \text{unaryminus}(s_2))$. This allows us to reuse the inversion of the unary minus operator for the inversion of subtraction operations.

Multiplication For all numeric types T and the arithmetic operator multiplication($s_1 : T, s_2 : T) : T$, we define the inverse operator

$$\text{multiplication}^{\leftarrow}(target : T, s : T) : T := \text{xdivision}(target, s)$$

where the operator xdivision uses the operator floatdivision if T is a floating-point type and otherwise uses the operator intdivision.

Division For two floating-point types $T_1 > T_2$ or $T_1 = T_2$ and the arithmetic operator floatdivision($s_1 : T_1, s_2 : T_2) : T_1$, we define the inverse operator

$$\text{floatdivision}_1^{\leftarrow}(target : T_1, s_2 : T_2) : T_1 := \text{multiplication}(t, s_2)$$

for inversion according to the dividend s_1 and the inverse operator

$$\text{floatdivision}_2^{\leftarrow}(target : T_1, s_1 : T_1) : T_1 := \text{floatdivision}(s_1, t)$$

for inversion according to the divisor s_2.

The float divison inverter is the first of many inverters that are operand-specific (see subsection 7.4.4). So far, the commutative addition and multiplication were the only binary operators for which we defined inverters. The next inverter is not only operand-specific but also target-sensitive.

For two integer types $T_1 > T_2$ or $T_1 = T_2$ and the IEEE 754 round-toward-0 operator intdivision($s_1 : T_1, s_2 : T_2) : T_1$, we define the inverse operator

$$\text{intdivision}_1^{\leftarrow}(t : T_1, s_1 : T_1, s_2 : T_2) : T_1 := \begin{cases} s_1 & \text{if intdivision}(s_1, s_2) = t \\ \text{multiplication}(t, s_2) & \text{otherwise} \end{cases}$$

for inversion according to the dividend s_1, and the inverse operator

$$\text{intdivision}_2^{\leftarrow}(t : T_1, s_1 : T_1, s_2 : T_2) : T_1 :=$$
$$\begin{cases} s_2 & \text{if intdivision}(s_1, s_2) = t \\ \text{intdivision}(s_1, t) & \text{otherwise} \end{cases}$$

for inversion according to the divisor s_2.

Integer division is an operator that is not left-unique, i.e. not injective. Therefore, it cannot be inverted in a way that fulfills the GetPut law without inspecting the original target value. Thus, the presented inverse operators for intdivision are both target-sensitive (see subsection 7.4.4). They avoid a violation of the GetPut law by checking whether the target was changed to another value than the one that we would get from the source values using the original operator. If this is the case, they return the original source value for the operand according to which the operation is inverted in order to fulfill the GetPut law. In all other cases, it does not matter which of the values that would fulfill the GetPut law is chosen. Therefore, the common division inversion by multiplication with the divisor respectively division by the dividend is enough.

7.4.6.4. Advanced Arithmetic Operators

To simplify the definition of inverse operators for advanced arithmetic operators, we will use a helper, which returns the algebraic sign for uses in multiplications and is defined for numeric types T as

$$\text{sign4mult}(p : T) : T := \begin{cases} 1 & \text{if } p \geq 0 \\ -1 & \text{otherwise} \end{cases}$$

Absolute Value For a numeric type T and the absolute value operator $\text{abs}(source : T) : T$, we define the inverse operator

$$\text{abs}^{\leftarrow}(target : T, source : T) : T := \begin{cases} \text{sign4mult}(source) \cdot target & \text{if } target \geq 0 \\ \text{restrictPGV}(\text{sign4mult}(source) \cdot |target|) & \text{otherwise} \end{cases}$$

With this inverter we can sustain the information about the absolute value of an updated target and restrict the loss of information to the algebraic sign of it, which cannot be avoided for the abs operator. For numeric x and y, we briefly write $|x|$ to denote $\text{abs}(x)$ and $x \cdot y$ to denote $\text{multiplication}(x, y)$.

Round to Nearest For a floating-point type T and the IEEE 754 round-to-nearest operator $\text{round}(source : T) : int$, we define the inverse operator

$$\text{round}^{\leftarrow}(target : int, source : T) : T := \begin{cases} source & \text{if round}(source) \stackrel{\varepsilon}{=} target \\ \text{wcast}_{\text{int},\text{T}}(target) & \text{otherwise} \end{cases}$$

Round toward Infinity For the IEEE 754 round-toward-$-\infty$ operator $\text{floor}(source : double) : double$, we define the inverse operator

$$\text{floor}^{\leftarrow}(target : double, source : double) : double := \begin{cases} source & \text{if floor}(source) \stackrel{\varepsilon}{=} target \\ target & \text{if floor}(target) \stackrel{\varepsilon}{=} target \\ \text{restrictPGV}(target) & \text{otherwise} \end{cases}$$

For the IEEE 754 round-toward-∞ operator ceil the inverse operator $\text{ceil}^{\leftarrow}$ is defined completely analog to floor and $\text{floor}^{\leftarrow}$.

Modulus Instead of defining an inverter for the modulus operator with round-to-zero division, which is denoted by `a % b` in Java, we present an inverter for the floor modulus operator[4]. It is defined as

$$\text{floormod}(divisor, dividend) := \\ divisor - (\text{floordiv}(divisor, dividend) \cdot dividend)$$

where floordiv is the round-toward-$-\infty$ floor division operator and "returns the largest [...] integer value that is less than or equal to the algebraic quotient"[4]. This operator yields a modulus with the same sign as the divisor, which is helpful for example for array index arithmetic.

For an integer type T and the modulus or remainder operator $\text{floormod}(s_1 : T, s_2 : T) : T$, we define the inverse operator

$$\text{floormod}_1^{\leftarrow}(t : T, s_1 : T, s_2 : T) : T := \begin{cases} s_1 & \text{if floormod}(s_1, s_2) = t \\ \text{floordiv}(s_1, s_2) \cdot s_2 + t & \text{if floormod}(t, s_2) = t \\ \text{restrictPGV}(t) & \text{otherwise} \end{cases}$$

for inversion according to the dividend s_1, and the inverse operator

$$\text{floormod}_2^{\leftarrow}(t : T, s_1 : T, s_2 : T) : T := \begin{cases} s_2 & \text{if floormod}(s_1, s_2) = t \\ t + s_2 \cdot \text{sign4mult}(t) & \text{if } s_1 = t \\ |s_1 - t| \cdot \text{sign4mult}(t) =: s_2' & \text{if floormod}(s_1, s_2') = t \\ \text{reportPGV}(1) & \text{otherwise} \end{cases}$$

for inversion according to the divisor s_2.

In the case of $\text{floormod}(target, s_2) = target$ we could also make $\text{floormod}_1^{\leftarrow}(target, s_1, s_2)$ return simply $target$ for the inversion according to the dividend. For every $n \in \mathbb{N}_0$ returning $n \cdot s_2 + target$ would fulfill PutGet. Our choice of $n = \text{floordiv}(s_1, s_2)$ preserves information about the old range of the divisor s_1 before the update of the target: For example, if

[4] Java floor mod: docs.oracle.com/javase/8/docs/api/java/lang/Math.html#floorMod

floormod		dividend					
		−13	−6	*−5*	*5*	6	*13*
divisor	−9		−3	*−4*		3	*4*
	9	*−4*	−3		*4*	3	

Table 7.3.: Illustration of the inversion of the floor mod operator with all old and *new* operand values after target updates from ±3 to ±*4*

the target for a divisor of 5 and a dividend of 3 is changed from 2 to 1, our inversion of the remainder operator would update the divisor to 4 instead of 1.

In the case of $s_1 = \mathit{target}$ the inversion according to the divisor $\text{floormod}_2^{\leftarrow}(\mathit{target}, s_1, s_2)$ fulfills PutGet if it returns $\mathit{target}+n\cdot\text{sign4mult}(t)$ for an $n \in \mathbb{N}_{\setminus\{0\}}$. Our choice of $n = s_2$ preserves information about the old value of the dividend s_2 before the update of the target: For example, if the target for a divisor of 5 and a dividend of 3 is changed from 2 to 5, our inversion of the remainder operator would update the divisor to 8 to indicate that the divisor was $8 - 5 = 3$ before the update.

An example for which all four possible target changes from ±t to $\pm t'$ can be inverted is given in Table 7.3. For the divisor values ±9 and the dividend values ±6, the floormod operation always yields ±3.

Exponentiation For a numeric type T_1, a floating-point type T_2, and the exponentiation operator $\text{pow}(b : T_1, e : T_2) : \mathit{double}$, we define the inverse operator

$$\text{pow}_1^{\leftarrow}(t : \mathit{double}, b : T_1, e : T_2) : T_1 :=$$
$$\begin{cases} \begin{cases} \text{sign4mult}(b) \cdot \sqrt[e]{t} & \text{if } t \geq 0 \\ \text{restrictPGV}(\text{sign4mult}(b) \cdot \sqrt[e]{|t|}) & \text{otherwise} \end{cases} & \text{if } e \text{ is even} \\ \text{sign4mult}(t) \cdot \sqrt[e]{|t|} & \text{otherwise} \end{cases}$$

for inversion according to the base b, and the inverse operator

$$\text{pow}_2^{\leftarrow}(t : double, b : T_1, e : T_2) : T_2 := \text{wcast}^{\leftarrow}_{T_1,T_2}\left(\begin{cases} e & \text{if } b^e = t \\ log_{|b|}(|t|) & \text{if } b^{log_{|b|}(|t|)} \overset{\varepsilon}{=} t \\ \text{restrictPGV}(log_{|b|}(|t|)) & \text{otherwise} \end{cases}\right)$$

for inversion according to the exponent e.

Trigonometric Operators For the fundamental trigonometric sine operator $\sin(source : double) : double$, we define the inverse operator

$$\sin^{\leftarrow}(t : double, source : double) : double := \begin{cases} source & \text{if } \sin(source) \overset{\varepsilon}{=} t \\ \text{asin}(t) & \text{if } -1 \leq t \leq 1 \\ \text{reportPGV}(\text{sign4mult}(t) \cdot \frac{\pi}{2}) & \text{otherwise} \end{cases}$$

For the trigonometric operator cos the inverse operator $\cos^{\leftarrow}$ is defined completely analog to sin and $\sin^{\leftarrow}$: only $\text{sign4mult}(t) \cdot \frac{\pi}{2}$ has to be replaced with $\frac{\pi}{2} - \text{sign4mult}(t) \cdot \frac{\pi}{2}$ for $\cos^{\leftarrow}$.

For the trigonometric operator $\tan(source : double) : double$, we define the inverse operator

$$\tan^{\leftarrow}(target : double, source : double) : double := \begin{cases} source & \text{if } \tan(source) \overset{\varepsilon}{=} target \\ \text{atan}(target) & \text{otherwise} \end{cases}$$

Inverse Trigonometric Operators For the inverse trigonometric operator asin(*double*) : *double*, we define the inverse operator

$$\text{asin}^{\leftarrow}(target : double, source : double) : double := \begin{cases} \text{sin}(target) & \text{if } |target| \leq \frac{\pi}{2} \\ \text{restrictPGV}(\text{sin}(target)) & \text{otherwise} \end{cases}$$

For the inverse trigonometric operators acos and atan the inverse operators $\text{acos}^{\leftarrow}$ and $\text{atan}^{\leftarrow}$ are defined analog to sin and $\text{sin}^{\leftarrow}$: only $|target| \leq \frac{\pi}{2}$ has to be replaced with $0 \leq target \leq \pi$ for $\text{acos}^{\leftarrow}$.

7.4.6.5. String Operators

The last group of operators for which we define inverters operates on character strings.

Parsing, Printing and Length For all types T and the operator parse($source : string$) : T, we define the trivial inverse operator

$$\text{parse}^{\leftarrow}(target : T) : string := \text{print}(target)$$

For all numeric types T and the operator numprint($s : T$) : $string$, we define the inverse operator

$$\text{numprint}^{\leftarrow}(t : string, s : T) : T := \begin{cases} \text{parse}(t) & \text{if } t \text{ represents a number of type } T \\ \text{reportPGV}(0) & \text{otherwise} \end{cases}$$

For the operator boolprint($source$: $bool$) : $string$, we define the inverse operator

$$\text{boolprint}^{\leftarrow}(target : string, source : bool) : bool := \begin{cases} true & \text{if } target = \text{“}true\text{” (case insensitive)} \\ false & \text{otherwise} \end{cases}$$

We define a helper pad($source$: $string$, $length$: $integer$), which appends as many underscore characters to a given string $source$ as are needed to obtain a string with $length$ characters. We also define a helper to obtain prefixes that are automatically padded to a desired length using the pad helper:

$$\text{prefix}(source : string, end : int) : T := \begin{cases} \text{substring}(source, 0, end) & \text{if } end \leq \text{length}(source) \\ \text{pad}(source, end) & \text{otherwise} \end{cases}$$

It uses the substring operator substring(s : $string$, b : int, e : int), which returns $e - b$ subsequent characters of s including the character at index b and excluding the character at index e. For the operator length($source$: $string$) : int, for which we briefly write $|source|$, we can now define the inverse operator

$$\text{length}^{\leftarrow}(target : int, source : string) : string := \text{prefix}(source, target)$$

Concatenation and Substrings For the string concatenation operator concat(s_1 : $string$, s_2 : $string$) : $string$, for which we briefly write $s_1 {}^\frown s_2$, we define the inverse operator

$$\text{concat}_1^{\leftarrow}(target : string, s_2 : string) : string := \begin{cases} s_1' & \text{if } target = s_1' {}^\frown s_2 \\ \text{restrictPGV}(target) & \text{otherwise} \end{cases}$$

to invert according to the first operand s_1, and the inverse operator

$$\text{concat}_2^{\leftarrow}(\mathit{target} : \mathit{string}, s_1 : \mathit{string}) : \mathit{string} := \begin{cases} s_2' & \text{if } \mathit{target} = s_1 \frown s_2' \\ \text{restrictPGV}(\mathit{target}) & \text{otherwise} \end{cases}$$

for inversion according to the second operand s_2.

We define a specialized substring operator:

$$\text{suffix}(s : \mathit{string}, b : \mathit{int}) : T := \begin{cases} \text{substring}(s, b, |s|) & \text{if } b < |s| \\ \text{``''} & \text{otherwise} \end{cases}$$

where “” denotes the empty string. Its inverse operator is

$$\text{suffix}^{\leftarrow}(t : \mathit{string}, s : \mathit{string}, b : \mathit{int}) : \mathit{string} := \text{prefix}(s, b) \frown t$$

We define a helper that concatenates a circumfix c and an infix i by prepending the first e characters of the circumfix to the infix while appending the last $|c| - b$ characters of the circumfix:

$$\text{circumcat}(c : \mathit{string}, e : \mathit{int}, i : \mathit{string}, b : \mathit{int}) := \text{prefix}(c, e) \frown i \frown \text{suffix}(c, b)$$

Now we can define an inverse operator for the substring operator substring(s : *string*, b : *int*, e : *int*) : *string*. This inverse operator fixes the indices b and e at which the substring begins and ends. It uses the helpers pad and circumcat:

$$\text{substring}^{\leftarrow}(t : \mathit{string}, s : \mathit{string}, b : \mathit{int}, e : \mathit{int}) : \mathit{string} := \begin{cases} \text{circumcat}(s, b, t, e) & \text{if } |t| = b - e \\ \text{restrictPGV}(\text{circumcat}(s, b, t, e)) & \text{if } |t| > b - e \\ \text{restrictPGV}(\text{circumcat}(s, b, \text{pad}(t, b - e), e)) & \text{otherwise} \end{cases}$$

We illustrate the inversion of the substring operator with fixed indices using the example input $s =$"inverse", $b = 2$, and $e = 6$: If the target "vers" is changed to "plac", then the first case applies because $|$"plac"$| = 4 = 6 - 2$ and the source is changed to "in"$\frown$"plac"$\frown$"e". If the target is changed to "carnat", then the second case applies because $|$"carnat"$| = 6 > 6 - 2$ and the source is changed to "in"$\frown$"carnat"$\frown$"e". If the target is changed to "di", then the third case applies because $|$"di"$| = 2 < 6 - 2$ and the source is changed to "in"$\frown$"di__"$\frown$"e". Without the third case, a target change to "di" would yield "indie" for which an application of substring with $b = 2$ and $e = 6$ would not be possible because $e = 6 > 5 = |$"indie"$|$. Therefore, we have to ensure that the source string has at least the length of the target string.

Letter Case To invert letter case conversions, we define a helper that returns the index of the first occurrence of a pattern p in a string s if such an occurrence exists and otherwise returns the length of s:

$$\begin{aligned}&\text{firstIndex}(s : \textit{string}, p : \textit{string}) : \textit{int} :=\\ &\qquad\qquad \min(\{i \in \mathbb{N}_0 \mid \text{substring}(s, i, i + |p|) = p\} \cup \{|s|\})\end{aligned}$$

Furthermore, we define two shorthands for the next definition. The first occurrence of the pattern t in the base string $tUC(s)$ is defined as $i :=$ firstIndex$(tUC(s), t)$. For the other shorthand t and $tUC(s)$ switch the roles of pattern and base string. The first occurrence of the pattern $tUC(s)$ in the base string t is defined as $j :=$ firstIndex$(t, tUC(s))$.

For the to-upper-case-conversion operator tUC$(s : \textit{string}) : \textit{string}$, we define the inverse operator

$$\begin{aligned}&\text{tUC}^{\leftarrow}(t : \textit{string}, s : \textit{string}) : \textit{string} :=\\ &\quad\begin{cases}\text{restrictPGV}(\text{tUC}^{\leftarrow}(\text{tUC}(t), s)) & \text{if } t \neq tUC(t)\\ \text{substring}(s, i, i + |t|) & \text{if } |t| < |s| \land i < |s|\\ \text{tLC}(\text{prefix}(t, j))\frown s \frown \text{tLC}(\text{suffix}(t, j + |s|)) & \text{if } |t| > |s| \land j < |t|\\ \text{tLC}(t) & \text{otherwise}\end{cases}\end{aligned}$$

We illustrate the inversion of the upper-case conversion operator based on the example input s ="CamelCase": If the target "CAMELCASE" is changed to "Cas", the first case of the definition applies because "Cas" ≠ "CAS" = tUC("Cas"). The inverse operator is recursively called with the new target "CAS" and the obtained string will be used as default value during the handling of the PutGet violation. This recursive call has the same effect as if the target would have been directly changed to "CAS". For such a target, the second case of the definition applies because |"CAS"| = 3 < 9 = |"CamelCase"| and firstIndex(tUC("CamelCase"), "CAS") = 5 < 9. Therefore, "Cas" is returned. If the target is changed to "NOCAMELCASED", the third case applies because |"NOCAMELCASED"| = 12 > 9 and firstIndex("NOCAMELCASED", tUC("CamelCase")) = 2 < 12. Therefore, "no"⌢"CamelCase"⌢"d" is returned. If the target is changed to "DROMEDAR", the last case applies and "dromedar" is returned.

The inverse operator $\text{tLC}^{\leftarrow}$ for the to-lower-case-conversion operator tLC is defined completely analogously. That is, all occurrences of tUC and $\text{tUC}^{\leftarrow}$ in the above definition have to be replaced with tLC and $\text{tLC}^{\leftarrow}$. Furthermore, all original occurrences of tLC in the definition have to be replaced with tUC.

7.4.7. Limitations of the Approach and the Inverters

Currently our approach is bound to one limitation and the presented inverters to two restrictions. As we already stated in subsubsection 7.4.3.1, our approach can only be used for operations in which every source attribute appears at most once. Furthermore, we currently only defined inverters for operators that can be inverted by updating a single source attribute (see subsection 7.4.4). Finally, all supported operators only operate on single-valued attributes not on collections or sequences.

The limitation to linear or affine expressions is common but not relevant in many practical use cases. The restriction to operators that can be inverted with a single update limits the applicability of our approach but it is only temporary: the conceptual framework and implementation prototype can easily be adapted in the future to support inverters that update several source attributes. Even defining inverters for operators on collections or sequences should not be conceptually more difficult: If the source value collections before an update of the target collection are given, then the inversion of a collection operator is often similar to the inversion of single-element operators. The technical realization and static analysis e.g. of higher-order functions would, however, probably be challenging.

7.4.8. Fall Back to Unidirectional Enforcement

If a condition that relates both sides of a mapping cannot be expressed by composing operations that only involve the operators for which we developed inverters, then the developer can directly specify code to enforce the condition in both propagation directions. In such cases, the developer is responsible for fulfilling the above mentioned round-trip laws during consistency preservations whenever this is possible. Tests are, however, in many cases no sufficient strategy to ensure this because the number of possible value changes is too large. Therefore, it can be beneficial to also express the code for both directions in a formal way and to prove that the code meets the requirements if it implements the formal representation correctly. In order to make it possible that such effort can be reused, language constructs for extending our library of inverters could be provided by the mappings language. This would give developers the possibility to use newly developed inverters in several bidirectionalizable conditions instead of writing partly redundant pairs of forward and backward enforcement code.

7.5. Dependencies and Multi-Parameter Mappings

We have presented all possibilities to define an isolated mapping in the previous sections but the mappings language also provides a possibility to define mappings that depend on other mappings. Such inter-mapping dependencies can be used to structure a set of mappings, for example, according to the parts of the metamodels that are kept consistent with individual mappings. Furthermore, developers can choose from different possibilities for mapping instances of a certain metaclass at different locations in a chain of dependent mappings. In this way, the desired consistency preservation consequences can be fine-tuned and many different scenarios can be covered with a simple language construct. We also experimented with another way to relate mappings by nesting them but explicit dependencies turned out to be more flexible. In this section, we explain how dependencies can be expressed, discuss the consequences of different possibilities to define mappings with dependencies, and present nested mappings as a discarded alternative to explicit dependencies.

7.5.1. Inter-Mapping Dependencies

In the signature of a mapping it is possible to declare a dependency to another mapping. An example of such an inter-mapping dependency was already given in the mapping between a component, a package, and a class in Listing 7.3 on page 224. This mapping depends on the mapping between a component repository and four packages in the object-oriented design, which we presented in Listing 7.2 on page 219. The dependency is used to put the subpackage that corresponds to a component into one of the four packages that corresponds to the repository (Listing 7.3, line 7). Together, both mappings specify that this package will always contain a package for each component in the repository. Instead of declaring a dependency to the repository mapping, we could also write code that finds this package for all components. This code would need to be put in a check block of a single-sided condition of the component mapping. Additionally, we would have to specify in the enforce block of this condition how the subpackage for an individual component is to be put into the package for all components. This enforce code would be similar to the single-sided condition that refers to the package on which it depends using the identifier `repoPkgs`. The check code would, however, almost be identical to the two conditions of the package for all components in the repository mapping (Listing 7.2, line 10–13). This means, we have to copy a part of this mapping if we do not declare a dependency to it. Such copied conditions are an unnecessary source for errors and for avoidable maintenance effort, especially if mappings are more complex and have several direct or indirect dependencies.

In general, an inter-mapping dependency from a mapping to another mapping means that the first mapping is only instantiated (see page 216) if the other mapping was already instantiated. That is, instances of the metaclasses that are mentioned in the signature of the depending mapping are only mapped if instances of the metaclasses mentioned in the signature of the other mapping are already mapped. If some or all of the metaclasses in both signatures are the same, then the dependency does *not* require that the same instances are mapped. To further restrict the meaning of an inter-mapping dependency in such a way, a single-sided condition has to be specified. In it, the appropriate parameters of both mappings have to be related using the equals operator. This need to explicitly specify that elements that were mapped in both mappings are equal, gives developers full control over the extent of an inter-mapping dependency.

All dependency relations between all mappings for two metamodels can be represented as a directed acyclic graph. In this dependency graph, nodes represent mappings and a directed edge from one node to another node means that the mapping of the first node depends on the mappings of the second node. The graph may not have any cycles because none of the mappings that are on a dependency cycle could ever be instantiated so all these mappings would be useless. In general, the dependency graph does not need to be an oriented tree because several paths between two nodes are possible. The reason for this is that a mapping may indirectly depend on another mapping multiple times when it depends on several mappings that finally depend on the same mapping. If it is necessary in such a case, then it can be ensured that the same mapping instantiation is used on several paths by defining single-sided conditions that ensure that the same elements are mapped. We suggest, however, to avoid indirect dependencies to the same mapping along different paths. In most cases, it should be sufficient if developers only specify mappings for which the dependency graph is an oriented tree, probably also with a low height.

7.5.2. Mapping Possibilities and Consequences

If instances of several metaclasses are mapped on one side, developers have many different possibilities to design appropriate mappings and the dependencies between them. With this degree of freedom, developers can determine which model information shall be kept consistent for different possible model states. By defining a single mapping or multiple mappings with dependencies, a developer can control which conditions have to be fulfilled together and which conditions may but do not need to be fulfilled simultaneously.

The effect of a mapping dependency can be explained using the model states for which a mapping is instantiated and its conditions are enforced. In the previous sections, we already explained that all single-sided conditions of one side have to be fulfilled before a mapping is instantiated. We also explained that a mapping that depends on another mapping is only instantiated if the other mapping is already instantiated. Broadly speaking, this means that the conditions of the other mapping are added to the dependent mapping. Thus, we can distinguish three kinds of model states for a inter-mapping dependency between two mappings. The first kind of model states are those in which the conditions of none of the two mappings are fulfilled. The second kind, are model states in which the conditions of the independent mapping are fulfilled but the conditions of the dependent mapping are not. The third and last kind of model states are those in which the conditions of both mappings are fulfilled.

To illustrate the different possibilities for designing mappings and their dependencies, we present an example consistency preservation scenario and three mapping strategies for it. For a first metamodel, we are only concerned about a single metaclass for expressing mailing addresses in terms of a number, street, and zip code. Instances of this metaclass are to be kept consistent with instances of a second metamodel in which the information for an address is distributed over three metaclasses. A first metaclass to model a location in terms of a number and a street, and second metaclass to model a city in terms of a zip code, and a third metaclass to model a recipient at a location in a city. These metaclasses are also depicted in the class diagram that is shown in Figure 7.8. Real metamodels would contain much more metaclasses and metaclass features, but to explain different mapping strategies this simple snippet is already sufficient. The distribution of street and zip code information to instances of two separate metaclasses that are related by a third recipient metaclass is representative for a constellation that can appear in many variants in other consistency preservation scenarios. As only this information distribution is necessary for our subsequent illustration of different mapping strategies, we will even ignore the number of a location in the following.

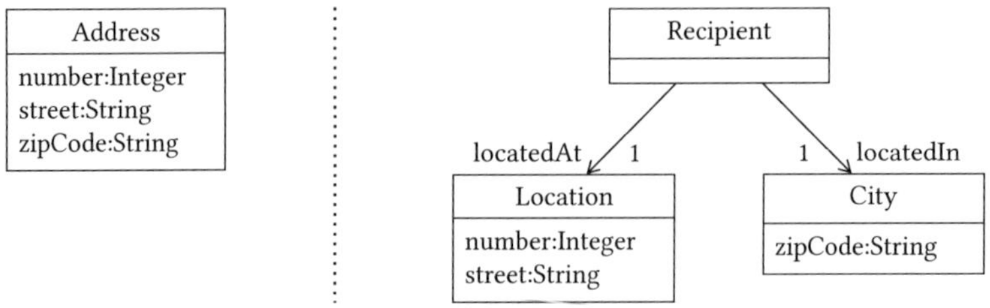

Figure 7.8.: Class diagram for two example metamodels for mailing addresses, which are used to explain different mapping strategies

For this simple consistency preservation scenario we explain three exemplary mapping strategy and discuss their effect for both preservation directions:

all-or-nothing map instances of all three metaclasses of the second metamodel in a single mapping with two bidirectionalizable conditions for the street and the zip code (Listing 7.7). The effect of this mapping is that address information is only kept consistent if it is complete.

step-by-step define three individual mappings to map the complete address to a recipient, a location, and a city (Listing 7.8). The effect is that the address container, its street, and its zip code are individually kept consistent in possibly separate steps.

containers-then-content create separate mappings for the metaclasses and their features (Listing 7.9). This last strategy has the effect that model elements that act as containers for the information that is kept consistent are created independent of this content.

All three possibilities to define mappings for the address example scenario represent general mapping strategies that can be applied whenever a variant of the described information distribution occurs. We explain the detailed effect on the behavior of the consistency preservation reactions that are generated in all three cases using a concrete mapping example. This example is based on a more general example from Dominik Werle's master's thesis [Wer16, pp. 53–57]. First, we show in Table 7.4 three different model states that are obtained after changing a model of the metamodel for bundled address information. For each of these states and each of the three

```
mapping Address<->RecipientLocationCity {
  map (Address a)
  and (Recipient r, Location l, City c)
  such that {
    a.number = l.number
    a.street = l.street
    a.zipCode = c.zipCode
  }
}
```

Listing 7.7: Example mapping for mailing addresses according to the all-or-nothing strategy for mapping dependencies (metamodel prefixes omitted)

```
mapping Address<->Recipient {
  map (Address a)
  and (Recipient r)
}

mapping Address<->Location
 depends on (Address<->Recipient arm) {
  map (Address a) with { a equals arm.a }
  and (Location l)
  such that {
    a.number = l.number
    a.street = l.street
  }
}

mapping Address<->City
 depends on (Address<->Recipient arm) {
  map (Address a) with { a equals arm.a }
  and (City c)
  such that {
    a.zipCode = c.zipCode
  }
}
```

Listing 7.8: Example mappings for mailing addresses according to the step-by-step strategy for mapping dependencies (metamodel prefixes omitted)

```
mapping Address<->RecipientAndContainers {
  map (Address a)
  and (Recipient r, Location l, City c)
}

mapping Address<->LocationCityContent
 depends on (Address<->RecipientAndContainers aracm) {
  map (Address a) with { a equals aracm.a }
  and (Location l, City c) with {
    l equals aracm.l
    c equals aracm.c
  }
  such that {
    a.number = l.number
    a.street = l.street
    a.zipCode = c.zipCode
  }
}
```

Listing 7.9: Example mappings for addresses according to the containers-then-content strategy for mapping dependencies (metamodel prefixes omitted)

mapping possibilities discussed above, we present the corresponding model with the distributed address information that is obtained after the appropriate reactions for the mappings are executed. Then, we provide analogue information for the opposite consistency preservation direction and for four different model states in Table 7.5. These states are reached after a change in a model of the metamodel for distributed address information. This time, the columns contain the corresponding model with bundled address information that is obtained after the appropriate reactions for the mappings are executed. Together, both consistency preservation directions demonstrate that different mapping possibilities or strategies that realize the same consistency if all information is provided can nevertheless preserve consistency very differently for intermediate states.

7.5.3. Nesting as a Discarded Alternative to Dependencies

Nested mappings could be a more concise language construct for relating mappings than explicit dependencies. This would make it unnecessary to

resulting recipient model after update	initial address model	address model after 1st change	address model after 2nd change
mapping specification	a:Address number=0 street=null zipCode=null	a:Address number=42 street="Page St" zipCode=null	a:Address number=42 street="Page St" zipCode="SW1P4EN"
all-or-nothing strategy (Listing 7.7)	–	–	r:Recipient l:Location: number=42, street="Page St" c:City: zipCode="SW1P4EN"
step-by-step strategy (Listing 7.8)	r:Recipient	r:Recipient l:Location: number=42, street="Page St"	r:Recipient l:Location: number=42, street="Page St" c:City: zipCode="SW1P4EN"
containers-then-content strategy (Listing 7.9)	r:Recipient l:Location: number=0, street=null c:City: zipCode=null	r:Recipient l:Location: number=42, street="Page St" c:City: zipCode=null	r:Recipient l:Location: number=42, street="Page St" c:City: zipCode="SW1P4EN"

Table 7.4.: Resulting recipient models for initial address model and after subsequent changes for different mapping strategies (based on [Wer16, p. 56])

resulting recipient model after update	initial recipient model	recipient model after 1st change	recipient model after 2nd change	recipient model after 3rd change
mapping specification	r:Recipient	r:Recipient l:Location: number=42, street="Page St"	r:Recipient l:Location: number=42, street="Page St" c:City: zipCode=null	r:Recipient l:Location: number=42, street="Page St" c:City: zipCode="SW1P4EN"
all-or-nothing strategy (Listing 7.7)	–	–	a:Address: number=42, street="Page St", zipCode=null	a:Address: number=42, street="Page St", zipCode="SW1P4EN"
step-by-step strategy (Listing 7.8)	a:Address: number=0, street=null, zipCode=null	a:Address: number=42, street="Page St", zipCode=null	a:Address: number=42, street="Page St", zipCode=null	a:Address: number=42, street="Page St", zipCode="SW1P4EN"
containers-then-content strategy (Listing 7.9)	–	–	a:Address: number=42, street="Page St", zipCode=null	a:Address: number=42, street="Page St", zipCode="SW1P4EN"

Table 7.5.: Resulting address models for initial recipient model and after subsequent changes for different mapping strategies (based on [Wer16, p. 57])

name mappings, because they would no longer be referenced from other mappings. Furthermore, mappings could be nested in a similar way model elements are contained in other model elements. Despite these apparent advantages, we also discovered disadvantages when we experimented with nested mappings in an early prototype of the mappings language. During these experiments we observed that nested mappings are less flexible than inter-mapping dependencies and implicit matches can be more complex to understand than such explicit dependencies.

Nesting instead of explicit dependencies is less flexible because an individual mapping can only be nested in a single parent mapping but may depend on several other mappings. For many cases a single direct dependency is sufficient and therefore nested mappings would be an alternative for these cases. Other cases with several direct dependencies should, however, not be neglected. Such a case can be found, for example, in the original consistency preservation scenario on which our running example for component-based architectures and object-oriented design scenarios is based. When components of a component repository are used in a concrete system, they are assembled with other components using connectors. The mapping for such a connector depends on a mapping for a component *and* on a mapping for an architectural interface. Therefore, the connector could not be nested in one of the two mappings without an additional dependency to the other mapping.

Nested mappings can be more complex to understand than mappings with explicit dependencies because of the scoping of metaclass parameters in mapping signatures. This scoping can be realized in two ways. Either identical names for parameters in nested mappings are disallowed. In this case, it has to be explicitly specified if the same element should be mapped in a parent and a nested mapping as it is necessary for inter-mapping dependencies. Or identical names are allowed to express exactly this behavior. In both cases, it can be difficult for developers to trace which model element are influenced by which conditions, especially if mappings are nested over several layers.

7.6. Realizing a Compiler for the Mappings Language

In this section, we provide further information on the concrete and abstract syntax of the mappings language and briefly describe how we realized it in terms of a prototypical compiler.

7.6.1. Mappings Language Syntax

So far, we described the concrete and abstract syntax of the mappings language only for special language parts and mostly using examples and diagrams. In the following, we will provide a complete view on the abstract syntax in terms of a class diagram with metaclasses that can be instantiated to represent mappings as an AST. Furthermore, we will describe the concrete syntax of the mappings language using grammar rules.

7.6.1.1. Complete Abstract Syntax

Most of the abstract syntax of the mappings language has already been graphically illustrated in Figure 7.1 in section 7.1 and Figure 7.2 in section 7.3 and textually described in this chapter. A more compact and complete overview over the abstract syntax of mappings is given in Figure 7.9. This class diagram also contains concrete subclasses for the different operators that can currently be used in single-sided conditions that specify properties that have to be checked and enforced for a referenced feature of a metaclass and multiple values or a single value. References to metamodel elements, such as metaclasses or features, and to technical artifacts, such as model resources, are still omitted.

7.6.1.2. Concrete Syntax for Mappings and Single-Sided Conditions

We have already illustrated a part of the concrete syntax of the mappings language in terms of a syntax diagram in Figure 7.3 in section 7.3. Furthermore, we provided several listings of exemplary mapping code that also

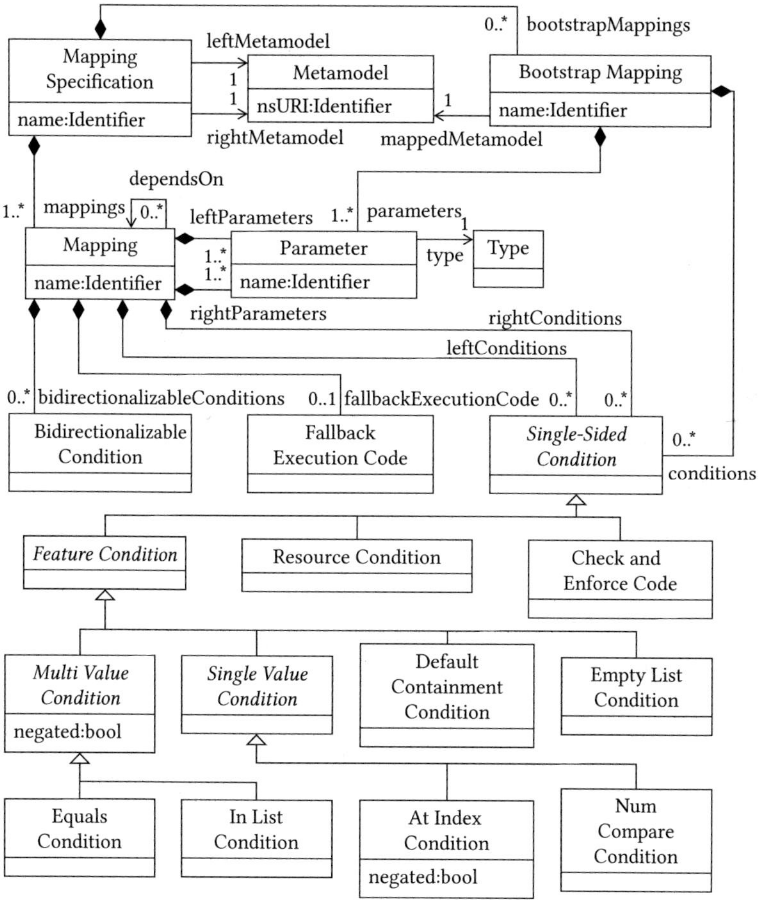

Figure 7.9.: Simplified class diagram with metaclasses for completely representing mappings as an AST

demonstrate which concrete syntax is used for the mappings language. In order to complete this partial and distributed information on the concrete mappings syntax, we show a simplified version of the complete grammar in Listing 7.10. The rules are again presented in EBNF, which we have introduced on page 197 of section 6.6.1.2. In the grammar and in our current compiler prototype, bidirectionalizable conditions are realized as expressions of the reused expression language. Instead of having special grammar rules for bidirectionalizable conditions with different operators, we parse arbitrary expressions and validate that they correctly compose only operations with operators for which we realized inverters.

7.6.2. Editing, Compiling, and Executing Mappings

The editor and the compiler for the mappings language are realized analogous to the editor and the compiler of the reactions language (see subsection 6.6.2). Again, the Xtext language workbench [Eff+12] was used to realize an editor with, for example, auto-completion and quick-fixes that are suggested in case of common compilation errors. Code validation and code generation are, however, not realized as a transformation to Java models, but as a model-to-text transformation using template expressions. The current prototype does not yet use the change-driven constructs of the reactions language as it only generates a single reaction to arbitrary changes. In the future, we are planning to refine the code generation part of the compiler so that a single mapping is realized by several reactions that are triggered for changes that directly reflect which metaclasses and features are mapped.

We addressed the Open Consistency Specification Language Challenge 4 by wrapping calls to general platform code in classes and methods that provide typesafe and properly named access to model elements and correspondences. For both sides of a mapping, a class `MappedSideWrapper` is generated. It provides access to mapped parameters and wraps calls to platform code for creating, updating, and deleting instances of the mapped metaclasses. Furthermore, a class `CorrespondingElementsWrapper` is generated for every mapping. It uses both wrappers for mapped parameter instances and provides additional methods with appropriate types and names for adding and removing correspondences. Finally, a class `MappingInstantiation` is generated for every mapping. It provides functionality for establishing mapping instantiations by creating instances of mapped metaclasses and correspondences for them. Additionally, it provides methods for updating corresponding elements and for destroying mapping instantiations by

```
mappings header = "mappings" , xbase identifier ,
 "for" , xbase namespace , "and" xbase namespace;
mapping = "mapping" , xbase identifier ,
 ["depends on (" , mapping dependency, ")"] , "{" ,
   "map (" , parameters , ")" ,
     ["with" , "{" , {single-sided condition} - , "}"] ,
   "and (" , parameters , ")" ,
     ["with" , "{" , {single-sided condition} - , "}"] ,
   ["such that" , "{" , {bidirectionalizable condition} - , "}"] ,
   ["forward execute {" , {xbase expression} - , "}" ,
   "backward execute {" , {xbase expression} - , "}"] , "}";
bootstrap mapping = "bootstrap mapping" , xbase identifier , "{" ,
   "create (" , parameters , ")" ,
   ["with" , "{" , {single-sided condition} - , "}"] , "}";
mapping dependency = xbase identifier , {"," , xbase identifier};
parameters = typed identifier , {"," , typed identifier};
typed identifier = type expression , xbase identifier;
type expression = xbase identifier , "::" , xbase identifier;
single-sided condition = feature condition | resource condition |
 check and enforce code;
feature condition = (multi value condition | single value condition |
 element condition | ["not"] , "empty") ,
 feature expression;
multi value condition = {value expression} - ,
 ["not"] , ("equals" | "in");
value expression = xbase expression;
single value condition = value expression ,
 (index expression | num compare expression);
index expression = ["not"] , "at index" , xbase expression , "in";
num compare expression = "<=" | "<" | ">=" | ">";
element condition = element expression , "default contained in";
element expression = xbase expression;
feature expression = xbase identifier , "." , xbase identifier;
resource condition = "default path for" , element expression ,
 "=" , ["path of" , element expression , "+"] , xbase string;
check and enforce code = "check " , xbase expression block ,
 "enforce " , xbase expression block;
bidirectionalizable condition = xbase expression;
```

Listing 7.10: Simplified grammar of the mappings language in EBNF, which reuses grammar rules of the Xbase language deleting corresponding elements and their correspondences. This class, only uses methods of the wrapper classes and no platform code is directly called. Therefore, this mapping instantiation code can be directly traced to the mappings specification code. Moreover, no casts or parameterized types have to be used in this code, which may be debugged by developers that use the mappings language. Additional details on the code that is currently generated for mappings can be found in Dominik Werle's master's thesis [Wer16, pp. 75–83].

For all single-sided conditions of one side of a mapping, two methods for checking and enforcing the conditions are generated in the mapping instantiation class. The realization of bidirectionalizable conditions is currently separated from the remainder of the code generator. It works with arbitrary expressions of the reused expression language Xbase [EV06] but validates whether only bidirectionalizable operators are used in these expressions. As before, the names and the type information of the mapping specification is used in the generated code of the inverse operations that are created for bidirectionalizable conditions. Only methods of the platform code with semantics that are well-known or can be easily derived, such as special equals methods, are called in the generated code. The goal is that developers can directly relate the structure and behavior of a generated inverted operation to the operation they specified. Further information on the bidirectionalization process can be found in subsubsection 7.4.3.1.

7.7. Semantics of Consistency Mappings based on Reactions

In the previous sections, we have illustrated the semantics of the mappings language for individual language constructs and examples. To complete this information, we will present the complete semantics of the mappings language based on the reactions language. In this way, the provided mappings semantics rely on the formal semantics for reactions, which we have already presented in section 6.7. Therefore, the discussion does not always need to be as formal as the discussion of the reactions semantics. Nevertheless, we aim to achieve the same precision indirectly via the more formal reactions semantics. First, we will present fundamental algorithms for creating, updating and deleting mapping instantiations, which can be realized as reaction routines. Then, we will explain why and how we distinguish between mappings that are realized with exhaustive checks after every change and mappings that can be realized with more specific reactions. Finally, we describe both realizations in detail and show that the execution of mappings preserves consistency according to the mappings specification.

7.7.1. Fundamental Algorithms for Mapping Instantiations

To realize mappings, three fundamental algorithms for creating, updating, and deleting a concrete instantiation of a mapping are necessary. These algorithms have to be carried out after it was determined that all mapping conditions newly apply, still apply, or no longer apply for objects that instantiate the mapped metaclasses. Here, we will only present the algorithms and later we will explain in detail under which circumstances they have to be carried out. For every mapping six separate reaction routines can be generated to realize these algorithms for the specific mapping and both consistency preservation directions. In order to not repeat explanations for both directions, we ignore whether a mapping was defined for a metamodel A and a metamodel B or for B and A. This means we use the fact that mappings are direction-agnostic (see page 220 in subsection 7.1.2). As the realization of mappings is not direction-agnostic but symmetric, we will use the terms of a change source side and an execution target side, which we have introduced on page 174 in section 6.3.

The first fundamental algorithm creates a new mapping instantiation for a mapping and for a tuple of objects of the change source side for which the mapping conditions are newly fulfilled. Therefore, we briefly call it *create algorithm*. This tuple is an instance tuple $\langle o_s \rangle := (o_{s_1}, \ldots, o_{s_n})$ (see Definition 16) of the metaclass tuple $\langle \mathbb{C}_{\mathbb{S}} \rangle := (\mathbb{C}_{s_1}, \ldots, \mathbb{C}_{s_n})$ (see Definition 14) that can be constructed for the list of mapping parameters of the change source side. Similarly, the appropriate metaclass tuple for the execution target side is denoted by $\langle \mathbb{C}_{\mathbb{t}} \rangle$. The algorithm consists of four steps:

1. Create an instance of every metaclass that is listed as a parameter of the target execution side of the mapping, i.e. for every

$\mathbb{C}_{s_i} \in (\mathbb{C}_{s_1}, \ldots, \mathbb{C}_{s_n})$, and call these new model elements $(o_{t_1}, \ldots, o_{t_n}) =: \langle o_t \rangle$ parameter instances.

2. Add a correspondence between all pairs of existing mapped elements of the change source side and the newly created parameter instances, i.e. for all (o_{s_i}, o_{t_j}).

3. Enforce every single-sided condition on the target execution side by updating the appropriate reference links and attribute values of the new parameter instances.

4. If the mapping contains a bidirectional enforcement specification, i.e. bidirectionalizable conditions, a pair of forward and backward enforcement code blocks, or both, then execute this enforcement specification in the current consistency preservation direction.

If a mapping was already instantiated previously and the conditions still apply, then the second fundamental algorithm, which we call *update algorithm*, has to be carried out:

I. Enforce every single-sided condition on the target execution side (identical to step 3 of the create algorithm).

II. If the mapping contains a bidirectional enforcement specification, then execute it in the current direction (identical to step 4 of the create algorithm).

When the conditions of a mapping apply no longer for a mapping instantiation, then the last fundamental algorithm, which we call *delete algorithm*, has to be carried out:

a. Remove all correspondences that were added in step 2 of the first algorithm.

b. Delete every parameter instance that was created in step 1 of the first algorithm.

As a mapping specifies that instances of the mapped metaclasses that fulfill the mapping conditions always have to co-occur, it is not possible to define any other deletion semantics for mappings. Nevertheless, it may be desirable in many consistency preservation scenarios to ask the user to confirm the consequence of deleting corresponding elements. The reason is, that a user may not always be aware of information that may have been manually added to corresponding elements but for which no corresponding information is available in the model in which the mapping conditions were violated by the user change.

7.7.2. Distinguishing Pure from Impure Mappings

In order to preserve consistency according to a mappings specification the three fundamental algorithms that we presented in the previous section have to be carried out whenever mapping conditions newly apply, still apply, or no longer apply. This can be done by checking all conditions for all objects that instantiate metaclasses that are used as mapping parameters and therefore could be part of a mapping instantiation (see page 216). A potential problem of such an approach is, however, that developers may have to inspect general check code that is not necessary to preserve consistency and superfluous invocations of checks. Therefore, we suggest to restrict reevaluations of mapping conditions to certain changes and to reduce the number of model elements for which such reevaluations are performed based on the information in the mappings specification. This would relieve a developer of a mapping specification from considering such unnecessary reevaluations. The goal of such a change-driven realization of mappings is *not* to improve the performance but to address the Open Consistency Specification Language Challenge 4. Furthermore, a mapping realization using specific reactions is an important prerequisite for future improvements of the integration of mappings and reactions. If the consistency preservation behavior that is implied by a mapping shall be overridden or extended for certain changes, then a realization of mappings with fine-grained reactions can be necessary to achieve a good integration of mappings and reactions.

To realize mappings in a change-driven way, it has to be possible to determine after which changes conditions of a mapping have to be checked. After these checks the previously presented algorithms can be carried out to create, update, or delete mapping instantiations. In order to perform the checks only after certain changes, it has to be determined which changes can lead to cases in which conditions are newly or no longer fulfilled. This is not precisely possible if mappings contain arbitrary imperative code with while loops. Therefore, we will introduce terms that allow us to distinguish between mappings that will be realized with exhaustive checks after every change and mappings that will be realized in change-driven way.

To determine which changes have to lead to which checks for a mapping, we have to analyze expressions that are used in single-sided conditions. Depending on the operator used in a single-sided condition, these expressions to be analyzed are value expressions, element expressions, and feature expressions (see Figure 7.3 in section 7.3). If such an expression only accesses model elements via mapping parameters, calls pure getters for references or attributes on them, or lists fixed value literals, then we call it a *purely navigational expression*. As a consequence, all purely navigational expressions have no side-effects but not all expressions without side-effects are purely navigational. Bidirectionalizable conditions do not need to be checked as they are always enforced (see also page 220 of section 7.1.1).

In order to be able to identify mappings that we will realize with specific reactions, we have to distinguish three different kinds of single-sided conditions:

pure elements conditions are single-sided conditions that use a default containment operator and only have purely navigational element expressions,

pure feature conditions are single-sided conditions that use an operator with a feature expression—i.e. the equals, in, at index, or number-inequality operator—and only have purely navigational value and feature expressions,

impure conditions are single-sided conditions with a check and an enforce block and single-sided conditions that use an operator with a feature expression but have at least one expression that is not purely navigational.

Both, pure elements conditions and pure feature conditions are briefly called pure conditions. In contrast to all other single-sided conditions, default containment conditions, i.e. conditions with a default-contained-in operator or a default-path-for operator, are never used to check whether the conditions of a mapping hold. These conditions are only enforced, but whether they have to be enforced does not depend on the consistency preservation direction but on a containment check (see subsubsection 7.3.2.2).

In the following, we transfer this notion of purity and impurity from single-sided conditions to mappings. A mapping that specifies only pure conditions for both sides is called a *pure mapping*. Similarly, all other mappings, which have at least on impure condition, are called *pure mappings*. Roughly speaking, the purity of a mapping denotes whether only declarative language constructs are used in conditions that have to be checked to decide whether mapping instantiations have to be created, updated, or deleted.

7.7.3. A Reaction for All Impure Mappings

In the following, we will present how mappings can be realized using a single reaction that is triggered after every change. Although this realization is correct for all mappings, we suggest to only use it for impure mappings. A more fine-grained realization for pure mappings will be presented in the next section.

Mappings can be realized with a single reaction that exhaustively recomputes cartesian products. This reaction has to be triggered after any arbitrary change and has to keep track of all current mapping instantiations for all mappings. After every change, we can determine for every mapping and for every combination of model elements that could instantiate a mapping whether this is or was the case. That is, we always have to determine whether the mapping has to be newly instantiated or no longer instantiated and whether an existing instantiation has to be preserved. To obtain these model elements, we can iterate over all tuples in the cartesian product of all sets that contain all instances of the metaclasses that are listed as parameters for the mapping. All these tuples are candidates for instantiations of the mapping (see page 216). For each of these *mapping instantiation candidates*, we can check whether all single-sided conditions are fulfilled and whether a mapping instantiation is currently registered for them. Then, we have to distinguish three cases for every mapping instantiation candidate:

new instantiation If the conditions are newly fulfilled, i.e. no mapping instantiation is currently registered for the candidate, then we have to register a new mapping instantiation and execute the create algorithm, which was presented on page 283.

preserve instantiation If a mapping instantiation is currently registered for the candidate and the conditions are still fulfilled, then we have to execute the update algorithm (see page 284).

delete instantiation If a mapping instantiation is still registered for the candidate but the conditions are no longer fulfilled, then we have to deregister the mapping instantiation and execute the delete algorithm (see page 284).

As we have already mentioned above, this exhaustive realization strategy for mappings has the disadvantage that it may lead to many unnecessary checks. After every change, all single-sided conditions are checked for all elements in the cartesian product of all mapping signatures. For large models, the vast majority of these checks is often unnecessary because a single change usually leads to a low number of mapping instantiations that have to be created, preserved, or deleted. If a developer wants to test or debug a mapping specification, it may be beneficial if fewer checks are performed on fewer mapping instantiation candidates and only after certain changes. To achieve this at least for pure mappings, we propose to use another realization strategy with more fine-grained reactions. The compiler prototype for the mappings language, currently uses the exhaustive strategy for all mappings but we will extend it in future work to realize pure mappings according to the strategy that is presented in the next section.

7.7.4. Reactions and Data for Pure Mappings

We propose a strategy for realizing pure mappings with reactions that use the available mapping information to restrict the number of cases in which single-sided conditions are reevaluated. As all single-sided conditions of a pure mapping are pure and bidirectionalizable conditions do not need to be checked, we will omit the descriptors "single-sided" and "pure" in the following and briefly write condition. For the exhaustive strategy, it was sufficient to manage mapping instantiations for every mapping during the process of consistency preservation. To realize mappings with fine-grained reactions, we propose to maintain further data to represent the results of checks that were performed when consistency was preserved according to a mapping specification after changes. For each mapping in the specification, we keep track of mapping instantiation candidates, of conditions that are currently fulfilled or unfulfilled, and of parameter instance candidates. To keep the discussion concise, we define a special notation for this data: For a mapping m, we briefly write MIC_m, to denote the set of all mapping instantiation candidates of m. Furthermore, we write F_i to denote the set of all conditions that are currently fulfilled for a candidate $i \in MIC_m$. Analogue, we write U_i to denote the set of all conditions that are currently unfulfilled for a candidate $i \in MIC_m$. Finally, for a parameter p of a mapping m, we write PIC_p to denote the set of all parameter instance candidates of p. These are all model elements that directly or indirectly instantiate the metaclass that is specified for p. For every mapping m, these sets MIC_m, F_{i_1}, $\ldots$, $F_{i_{|MIC_m|}}$, $U_{i_1}, \ldots, U_{i_{|MIC_m|}}$, $PIC_{p_1}, \ldots, PIC_{p_n}$ have to be dynamically managed during the consistency preservation process.

In addition to the dynamic sets, there is also static data that can be precomputed when the consistency specification is complete. We use this static data to express the realization of mappings in terms of reactions that update the dynamic data and execute the fundamental algorithms, which we have presented in subsection 7.7.1. For the complete mapping specification, we write MMC to denote the set of all mapped metaclasses, i.e. all metaclasses that are used as a parameter in at least one mapping. For every mapping m we write P_m to denote the set of all parameters of m. If a mapping m has to be newly instantiated or if an existing instantiation has to be preserved, then every condition of a mapping has to be fulfilled. Therefore, we write r to denote such a required condition of m and R_m to denote the set of all required conditions of m. In a pure condition, apart from value literals, only model elements and values that are obtained for references or attributes can be accessed. Therefore, we inspect which conditions access a reference or attribute, which are both called a feature of a metaclass. For every such feature $\mathbb{f}$ of a metaclass $\mathbb{c} \in MMC$, we write $FAC_{\mathbb{f}}$ to denote the set of feature accessing conditions. These are all conditions in which a getter for $\mathbb{f}$ is invoked. This is necessary, because a condition may indirectly access features of metaclasses that are not listed as a parameter of the mapping by navigating references on parameter instances.

The static and dynamic data can be used in all reactions that realize pure mappings. We suggest to create three different groups of reactions for pure mappings. The first group of reactions, will react to creations of new model elements. For every parameter of every mapping, an individual reaction can be created to handle creations of elements that instantiate the metaclass of the parameter directly or indirectly. This means, if different mappings list the same metaclass as a parameter, then different reactions for the different parameters will be created but they will react to creations of the same model elements. The second group of reactions, will react to feature updates of existing model elements. We propose to create an individual reaction for every pair that combines a metaclass feature that may be updated with a mapping that accesses this feature in at least one of its conditions. Such reactions will determine whether the result of a feature update is that conditions of the mapping are newly, still, or no longer fulfilled for instantiation candidates of the mapping. This means, for a given feature of a metaclass, several reactions can be created if the feature is accessed in several mappings but for every mapping at most one reaction will be created for the given feature. The third and last group of reactions, will react to deletions of existing model elements. Analogue to element creation reactions, an individual reaction can be created for every parameter of every mapping.

The group of element creation reactions, will contain an individual reaction for every parameter of every mapping. They react to creations of all model elements that instantiate the metaclass of the parameter directly or indirectly. That is, for a mapping m and a parameter $p \in P_m$ that maps the metaclass $\mathbb{c} \in MMC$, such a reaction is triggered after the creation of a model element e iff e is an instance of $\mathbb{c}$ or an instance of a direct or indirect subclass of $\mathbb{c}$. If this is the case, the reaction executes the procedure PARAMETERINSTANCECREATED as shown in Algorithm 1.

Algorithm 1 React for parameter p of mapping m to creation of element e

procedure PARAMETERINSTANCECREATED(e, p, m)
  $PIC_p \leftarrow PIC_p \cup \{e\}$ ▷ *register parameter instance candidate*
  for all $p_j \in P_m \setminus \{p\}$ **do** ▷ *for all other parameters of m …*
    compute PIC_{p_j} ▷ *… compute parameter instance candidates*
  for all $i \in \{e\} \times_i PIC_{p_j}$ **do** ▷ *$\times_j$ is $|P_m|$-ary cartesian product*
    $MIC_m \leftarrow MIC_m \cup \{i\}$ ▷ *register mapping instance candidate*
    for all conditions r_j of m **do** ▷ *check every condition …*
      if r_j is fulfilled for i **then** ▷ *… for the current candidate*
        $F_i \leftarrow F_i \cup \{r_j\}$ ▷ *remember fulfillment for later*
      else
        $U_i \leftarrow U_i \cup \{r_j\}$ ▷ *or remember unfulfillment*
    if $U_i = \emptyset$ **then** ▷ *all conditions fulfilled for i?*
      execute create algorithm (p. 283) ▷ *enforce consistency*

To react to updates of existing model elements, we propose to create a reaction for every pair that combines a feature with a mapping that accesses this feature in a condition. To create these reactions, it has to be determined for every mapping m, which features are accessed in at least one required condition $r \in R_m$. Those are all features $\mathbb{f}$, for which the intersection of the set of conditions that access $\mathbb{f}$ and the set of conditions of m is not emtpy. The conditions in the result set of this intersection are the conditions to be checked for m after every update of $\mathbb{f}$. Therefore, we briefly write $CTC_{\mathbb{f},m} := FAC_{\mathbb{f}} \cap R_m$. For every mapping m and every feature $\mathbb{f}$ such that $CTC_{\mathbb{f},m} \neq \emptyset$, we propose to create a separate reaction. This reaction is triggered to check conditions in $CTC_{\mathbb{f},m}$ after a change in which $\mathbb{f}$ was updated for an existing model element e. The element for which $\mathbb{f}$ is updated has to instantiate the metaclass $\mathbb{c}$ for which $\mathbb{f}$ is defined or a direct or indirect subclass $\mathbb{s}$ of $\mathbb{c}$. As conditions may access features of all metaclasses, it is possible that $\mathbb{c}$, $\mathbb{s}$, or both are not mapped, i.e. neither $\mathbb{c}$ nor $\mathbb{s}$ has to be in MMC. If the reaction is triggered, then it executes the procedure FEATUREUPDATED as shown in Algorithm 2.

The last group of reactions handles deletions of existing model elements and can be created analogue to creation reactions. For every mapping m and every parameter $p \in P_m$, which maps a metaclass $\mathbb{c} \in MMC$, we create a separate reaction. It is triggered after the deletion of a model element e iff e instantiates $\mathbb{c}$ directly or indirectly. In such a case, the reaction executes the procedure PARAMETERINSTANCEDELETED as shown in Algorithm 3.

A single change that is performed by a user may involve several creations, updates, and deletions. Therefore, several reactions for the same or different mappings may be triggered to react to a single user change. Let us consider, for example, the deletion of a model element that is contained in another model element. To achieve such a deletion, a user often performs only a single change operation in a model editor. For the model, this operation induces, however, two changes in which the containment link from the container object to the contained object is removed before this object is deleted. The affected feature $\mathbb{f}$ of the update before the deletion is a containment reference that is defined for the metaclass of the container object or for a direct or indirect superclass of it. If $\mathbb{f}$ is accessed by a condition of a mapping m_1, then the reaction that is defined for $\mathbb{f}$ and m_1 will be triggered. It executes the procedure FEATUREUPDATED and rechecks every condition that accesses the feature (Algorithm 2, line 4) to decide whether one of the fundamental algorithms for the creation, update, or deletion of a mapping instantiation has to be executed (see pages 283–284). It is also possible,

Algorithm 2 React for mapping m to update of feature $\mathbb{f}$ for element e

```
procedure FEATUREUPDATED(𝕗, e, m, CTC_𝕗,m)
    for all i ∈ MIC_m do                                   ▷ for every instantiation candidate of m
        for all r ∈ CTC_𝕗,m do                             ▷ and every condition that accesses 𝕗
            if r is fulfilled for i then                   ▷ check condition for candidate
                if r ∈ U_i then                            ▷ not fulfilled before change?
                    F_i ← F_i ∪ {r}                        ▷ add to fulfilled conditions
                    U_i ← U_i \ {r}                        ▷ remove from unfulfilled conditions
                    newlyFulfilled ← ⊤                     ▷ at least r is newly fulfilled
            else                                           ▷ r is not fulfilled for i
                if r is a default containment condition then
                    enforce r for i                        ▷ containment always fulfilled
                else
                    if r ∈ F_i then                        ▷ fulfilled before change?
                        F_i ← F_i \ {r}                    ▷ remove from fulfilled conditions
                        U_i ← U_i ∪ {r}                    ▷ add to unfulfilled conditions
                        newlyUnfulfilled ← ⊤               ▷ at least r is newly unfulfilled
        if U_i = ∅ then                                    ▷ all conditions fulfilled for i?
            if newlyFulfilled = ⊤ then                     ▷ overall newly fulfilled?
                execute create algorithm (p. 283)          ▷ new instantiation of m
            else                                           ▷ all conditions still fulfilled for i
                execute update algorithm (p. 284)          ▷ update instantiation of m
        else if F_i = ∅ then                               ▷ no condition fulfilled for i?
            if newlyUnfulfilled = ⊤ then                   ▷ overall newly unnfulfilled?
                execute delete algorithm (p. 284)          ▷ remove instantiation of m
```

Algorithm 3 React for parameter p of mapping m to deletion of element e

```
procedure PARAMETERINSTANCEDELETED(e, p, m)
    PIC_p ← PIC_p \ {e}                                    ▷ deregister parameter instance candidate
    for all i = (o_1, ..., o_|P_m|) ∈ MIC_m do             ▷ instance candidates of m
        if ∃ j ∈ {1, |P_m|} such that o_j = e then         ▷ deleted e involved?
            MIC_m ← MIC_m \ {i}                            ▷ deregister mapping instance candidate
            if U_i = ∅ then                                ▷ conditions fulfilled before deletion?
                execute delete algorithm (p. 284)          ▷ enforce consistency
```

that other model elements link to the object to be deleted before the user performs the deletion. In this case, the user change induces further feature updates for all incoming links. As an element is always only contained in one container, these links are defined for other reference features than $\mathbb{f}$. If these other features are accessed in mappings, then the FEATUREUPDATED procedure is also executed for these feature updates and mappings. Only after all feature changes that are induced by the user change are handled, the deletion itself is handled. If the deleted element instantiates a metaclass $\mathbb{C}$ that is mapped in a mapping m_2 using a parameter p or instantiates a subclass of $\mathbb{C}$, then the reaction for p and m is triggered by the change. It executes the PARAMETERINSTANCEDELETED procedure to deregister obsolete instance candidates for parameters and mappings and to execute the fundamental delete algorithm for all mapping instantiations that involved the deleted element.

7.7.5. Consistency Preserving by Construction

We will now briefly discuss why both mappings realizations of the previous sections preserve consistency by construction. As we have explained above, a mapping declares that a certain combination of model elements that fulfill certain conditions on one side always has to co-occur with a certain combination of model elements that fulfill certain conditions on the other side. In this way, an individual mapping specifies that two models are consistent iff an occurence of the left element combinations exists for every occurrence of the right element combination and the other way round. For such a co-occurence of elements for a given mapping, we have introduced the term mapping instantiation on page 216. To preserve consistency according to a mapping, it has to be ensured that the requirement of co-occurence is always fulfilled after changes. That is, a mapping has to be realized in such a way that the elements that are demanded for one side are always created, updated, or deleted according to the mapping conditions on this side iff elements on the other side are created, updated, or deleted in such a way that the mapping conditions for that side are newly or no longer fulfilled. This is exactly what the single reaction that we have described in subsection 7.7.3 does by executing the fundamental create, update, and delete algorithms (see subsection 7.7.1). Furthermore, this is also what the fine-grained reactions that we have described in subsection 7.7.4 do by executing the three procedures presented in Algorithm 1–3. Altogether, consistency according to specification with several mappings is preserved if the co-occurrence requirement is always fulfilled for every mapping.

Consistency according to mappings can be preserved by construction and in such a direct way because the consistency to be preserved is prescribed in terms of mappings. Furthermore, the language was specifically designed for declarative consistency specifications and restricted to those consistency relations for which such declarations are sufficient. Broadly speaking, a mapping only consists of two lists of metaclasses for two metamodels and two sets of conditions that have to be fulfilled by instances of the metaclasses of one metamodel whenever instances of the remaining metaclasses of the other metamodel fulfill the other set of conditions. The conditions are directly given. To enforce a condition it is necessary to derive enforcement code from check code or inverse enforcement code for one direction from code for enforcement in the other direction. These automated derivation processes can, however, be performed in isolation and has no influence on the overall consistency preservation process. Therefore, this preservation process is simple even if complex conditions and complex derivations can be used. If the mappings language would provide further constructs that are not directly expressed in terms of conditions to be fulfilled, then it would be much more difficult to preserve consistency. With such constructs, it would not only be more difficult to show that mappings preserve consistency but it would already be more difficult to define how the consistency conditions to be preserved can be obtained from a mapping.

7.8. Conclusions and Future Work

In this chapter, we have presented a bidirectional language for consistency mappings. We have compared it to the reactions language to demonstrate that it abstracts away from many details of consistency preservation directions and that it is completely change-agnostic in order to address OCSLC 3. In this context, we have also discussed how we addressed OCSLC 1 with fallback constructs for direction-specific checks or enforcements. Furthermore, we have explained why two different kinds of conditions are necessary and sufficient to check conditions on one of two sides and to enforce them for both sides. For both kinds of conditions, we have presented all operators that are currently provided in detail. Furthermore, we have discussed how enforcement code can be derived from checks for the first kind of conditions and how the second kind of conditions can be bidirectionalized using composable, operator-specific inverters. To illustrate how several mappings can be combined to preserve consistency in more complex situations, we have explained which possibilities are offered by mapping dependencies and multi-parameter mappings. Moreover, we have described the syntax and how we addressed OCSLC 4 with a prototypical compiler, for example, by indirectly calling generic platform code via mapping-specific wrappers. Finally, we have explained the semantics of the mappings language by describing how reactions can be created to check and enforce consistency according to a mappings specifications in reaction to user changes.

Similar to the previous chapter on the reactions language, we have also provided answers to the subquestions 2.1, 2.3, and 2.4 of research question 2 as they correspond to the Open Consistency Specification Language Challenges 1, 3, and 4. We have showed how bidirectional constructs of the mapping language can be used if consistency can be expressed with checks for which enforcement can be derived and with conditions that relate both mapping sides using operations that can be inverted. In such cases, the mappings language relieves developers from explicitly specifying when and how conditions have to be checked or enforced after changes on one or another side. Moreover, we have described how these bidirectional constructs are realized in a way that gives developers the possibility to foresee how consistency will be preserved according to a mappings specification by either studying the explanations of the language semantics or by inspecting the generated code, which directly reproduces all type and naming information provided in a mapping. Nevertheless, the mappings language can also be applied if these concerns have to be considered and controlled as it provides powerful fallback constructs.

Future work on the mappings language can be arranged in three groups for detailed improvements, operator reuse, and fine-grained reaction realization. To improve details of the mappings language, several existing language constructs could be extended and new language construct could be introduced. The negated equals operator, for example, could be extended to also support references. Furthermore, a new possibility could be introduced to specify a concrete metaclass that is instantiated for a mapped abstract superclass. Additionally, inverters that update more than one source attribute could be provided. An important area of future work, could be a reuse mechanism for developer-defined operators that are not yet supported in single-sided conditions or bidirectionalizable conditions. Such a mechanism could give developers the possibility to define new reusable operators for which enforcement-derivation or inversion code only needs to be provided once. These operators could then be directly reused in future mappings and would no longer need to be realized as two separate helper methods that can be called from check and enforce code blocks or forward and backward enforcement blocks. Last but not least, we plan to completely implement the proposed realization strategy for impure mappings so that developers that want to debug their mappings code have to consider fewer unnecessary reevaluations of mapping conditions.

8. A Normative Language for Parametrized Consistency Invariants

In this chapter, we present our last and smallest language for consistency specifications. It gives developers the possibility to define constraints that always have to hold when models of two modelling languages are kept consistent. Therefore, these constraints are called invariants and the language is simply named invariants language. With this language, developers can specify consistency conditions that have to be successfully *checked* but they have to use the reactions or the mappings language in order to specify how consistency is to be *enforced*. This means, with the invariants language it is possible to specify consistency but not consistency preservation, neither in an imperative way nor in a declarative way. Therefore, we call it a *normative* language that complements the reactions and mappings languages.

To support developers in preserving consistency when an invariant is violated, the compiler of the language automatically derives queries that return the model elements that violate an invariant. This automation relieves the developer from manually writing code that searches for model elements that have to be updated because they are responsible for the invariant violation. Instead of repeating parts of the constraint code in a manual query, developers only have to expose iterator variables for which invariant violating elements shall be computed. Such exposed iterator variables are called invariant parameters. For every invariant parameter, the compiler generates a query by transforming an expression tree representation of the original constraint. If an invariant is violated at a model context, then these queries can be called for such a context. They return all those elements that are responsible for the violation and that were accessed during the evaluation via the iterator variable that matches the invariant parameter.

This way, these invariant violating elements can directly be accessed in reactions, mappings and in Java code to preserve consistency.

The invariants language is built on top of the Xbase expression language, which can be seen as an extensible dialect for Java method body expression (see subsubsection 2.1.2.5 and 5.4.2). Furthermore, it reuses our expressions extension that provides equivalent methods for collection operators and iterators of the Object Constraint Language (OCL) (see subsection 5.4.3). We developed the automated derivation of queries and the invariants language together with Sebastian Fiss, who developed a prototypical compiler that generates the queries. He also wrote his bachelor's thesis on this topic [Fis15], which was supervised by the author of this dissertation. Texts, figures and tables of this chapter are based on a joint article [FKL16].

8.1. Invariants for Consistency Preservation

Before we explain how queries for elements that violate an invariant are automatically derived from the constraints, we briefly introduce the invariants language and motivate the query derivation.

8.1.1. Normative Inter-Language Invariants

Some constraints that have to be enforced when models of two modelling languages are kept consistent are already defined for one of the two languages, for example in terms of OCL invariants that are added to the metamodel of the language. Other constraints are, however, specific for the combination of the two languages or for the notion of consistency that is to be preserved. In many cases, such constraint always have to hold for all models and at all times so that they are often called invariants. The invariants language presented in this chapter gives developer the possibility to specify such inter-language constraints for consistency preservation.

We will explain and illustrate the structure of the invariants language using an initial example invariant that is provided in Listing 8.1. This example invariant is defined for a library metamodel and also used later on in the chapter to explain the automated query derivation. It specifies in

```
1 context ReadingRoom
2 invariant AtLeast3ReferenceCopies(Book b)
3 constraint self.books.forAll[Book b |
4   b.referenceCopy implies (b.copies >= 3)]
```

Listing 8.1: Initial example of an invariant with a simplified constraint for the number of reference copies of books in a reading room of a library

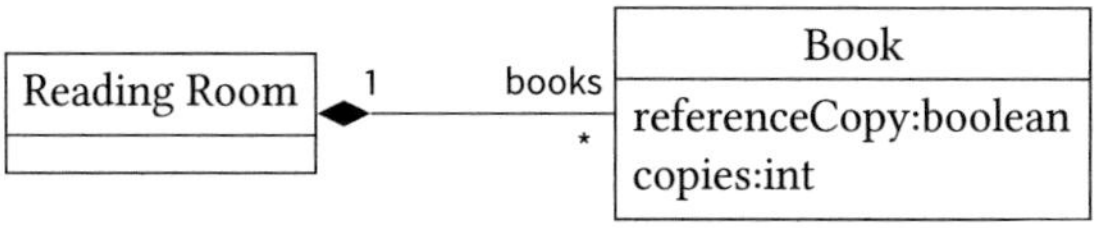

Figure 8.1.: Minimal library metamodel for the metaclasses, attributes, and the reference used in the introductory example invariant

the context of a reading room that all those books in a reading room that are used as reference copies have to have at least three copies. A minimal metamodel for the metaclasses used in this example invariant is shown in Figure 8.1. We chose this example in order to keep the discussion of the query derivation algorithm concise. Furthermore, we demonstrate with this example that the approach can also be used in other contexts where invariant violating elements are needed regardless of a consistency relation to models of another metamodel.

Every invariant that is defined with the invariants language consists of three first-level elements:

- a context declaration, to specify for which elements the invariant has to hold
- a signature with a unique name and optional parameters for the query derivation
- a constraint expression that has to yield a boolean result

An invariant definition starts with the declaration of the context in terms of a name of a metaclass. All direct and indirect instances of the metaclass with this name have to fulfill the invariant at all times to be considered consistent. The name has to be preceded by the keyword `context` and in our example this context metaclass is named `ReadingRoom` (line 1). An evaluation of an invariant is always performed for a specific instance of the context metaclass. These instances are called *context elements*. Furthermore, the context metaclass is treated as an implicit first parameter during query derivation.

The context metaclass has to be followed by an invariant signature in an invariant definition. This signature starts with a unique name for the invariant, which has to be preceded by the keyword `invariant`. The name is used to refer to the invariant when it is evaluated or when queries for invariant violating elements are executed. Our example invariant is named `AtLeast3ReferenceCopies` (line 2). After the name the signature may contain optional invariant parameters, which have to be given in parentheses and have to be separated by a comma. Each parameter declaration consists of a metaclass name and an identifier for the parameter. In our introductory example, we only specify a single parameter for the metaclass `Book` with the identifier `b` (line 2). During the generation of queries for an invariant, each parameter declaration is bound to an iterator variable in the invariant expressions. This iterator variable has to have a compatible type and the same identifier.

Finally, an invariant definition ends with the invariant constraint. Such a constraint is an arbitrary Xbase expression that returns a boolean. In particular, the constraint expression can use the collection operators and iterators of our OCL-aligned expressions extension (see subsection 5.4.3). To use the automated query derivation, the constraint expression of an invariant has to contain iterator expressions with iterator variables that match the type and identifier of an invariant parameter. In the constraint expression, the context element at which the invariant is currently evaluated can be accessed via the keyword `self`. The constraint expression has to be preceded by the keyword `constraint`. In our example the constraint expression starts with a context element of type `ReadingRoom`, calls the getter for the reference `books`, and invokes the iterator `forAll` on the resulting collection. This iterator has an iterator variable of type `Book` that is identified with the variable name `b`. It contains an implication for every element in the collection that is iterated. This implication demands that the value of the integer attribute `copies` has to be at least 3 when the boolean attribute `referenceCopy` is set to true.

To ease the usage of the invariants language for developers that are already familiar with OCL invariants, we adopted the abstract syntax of OCL and aligned the concrete syntax of the invariants language to OCL where this was possible. More specifically, the abstract syntax of an invariant is identical to that of an OCL invariant except for two differences: Invariant names in OCL are optional and invariant parameters can only be provided in the invariants language.

There are small differences between the concrete syntax of the invariants language and the concrete syntax of OCL. These differences mostly result from the Java-based expression language Xbase, which we reused to build the invariants language (see subsection 5.4.3). Model elements as well as their attributes and references are accessed in the invariants language in the same way they are accessed in OCL. In contrast to OCL, the invariants language also sticks to the dot notation of Java to access fields of collections and to invoke methods on them instead of using the arrow notation (`->`). Furthermore, square brackets `[...]` instead of parentheses `(...)` have to be used for collection operators and iterators in the invariants language. The reason is that they are realized using lambda expressions of Xbase. Furthermore, the types that are provided by Java and the metamodel for which invariants are defined have to be used in the invariants language, for example for collections and primitive types, instead of OCL counterparts. For most language constructs, such as enumerations, null values, arithmetic expressions, and logical expressions there are, however, no remarkable differences between OCL and Xbase and therefore also not between OCL and the invariants language. Finally, OCL methods starting with the prefix *ocl*, such as `oclAsType` or `oclIsTypeOf`, have equivalent counterparts in Java or Xbase, which can be used in the invariants language.

8.1.2. Invariant Violating Elements

To preserve consistency when an invariant is no longer fulfilled after a user change, consistency preservation actions have to update models in such a way that the invariant is fulfilled again. Especially for complex models or invariants these model elements to be updated are not necessarily those model elements that were changed by the user. In such cases, it is necessary to obtain the right model elements on which consistency preservation actions are to be performed.

One possibility to find elements to be updated, for example in case of OCL invariants, is to start at the context element at which the invariant evaluation started and finally failed. As in the invariants language, this context is only an element of a given type which is provided in addition to the boolean constraint expression and the name of the invariant. Many OCL invariants inspect, however, not only this context element but numerous different elements that are directly or indirectly related to the context element at which the evaluation started. Therefore, the context element of an OCL invariant often does not directly indicate where, how, and why a model violates the constraints.

Another possibility to find those elements that are responsible for an invariant violation and that have to be updated, is to compute the set of elements that were accessed during the failed evaluation of the invariant (see subsection 10.2.3). The elements to be updated have to be responsible for the invariant violation and updating them has to lead to a new fulfillment of the invariant. Therefore, these elements to be updated have to be in the set of elements that were accessed during the evaluation. We mentioned, however, already that it is common that many model elements are accessed during invariant evaluation, for example because all instances of a metaclass are checked. Thus, it can be difficult to find the elements on which actions are to be performed in this possibly large set of elements. Therefore, developers often write query code that searches for elements that caused an invariant violation in addition to the code for the invariant constraint. The invariant constraint and such queries often share many redundant parts. Model navigation statements and condition checks, for example, often have to be repeated. Even in cases where only a few statements are redundant for a single invariant, the amount of duplicated code can grow to a considerable size for metamodels with hundreds of invariants, such as the Unified Modeling Language (UML) [ISO12b]. This code duplication can be a source for costly errors and can lead to unnecessary development and maintenance effort.

8.1.3. Parameters for Query Derivation

Redundant invariant constraints and queries for invariant violating elements are not necessary if the elements that are to be updated can be extracted from the set of invariant violating elements. This set of all elements that are responsible for a violation is always indirectly but completely specified by the constraint. In order to obtain only those elements on which a particular consistency preservation action is to be performed, the invariants language gives developers the possibility to expose iterator variables as parameters. For these parameters, queries are automatically derived to yield those elements that violate the constraint and that were accessed during the evaluation via the iterator variable. Additionally, the context metaclass is used as an implicit first parameter of an invariant to also provide access to the context element of an invariant violation.

8.1.4. Automated Deriviation of Queries for Parameters

For every explicit parameter of an invariant, the compiler of the invariants language generates a query. These queries are obtained by transforming an expression tree representation of the original invariant constraint. Broadly speaking, these queries perform the same computation as the constraint until the collection of model elements is obtained for which an iteration with an iterator variable that matches the parameter is specified. This collection of model elements is then filtered to obtain those elements that contribute to the fact that the invariant constraint is not fulfilled. Our example invariant, which we have presented in Listing 8.1, only has a single invariant parameter `Book b`. This parameter matches the only iterator of the invariant constraint. The resulting query for this parameter and iterator variable is almost identical to the constraint because the example invariant constraint is not complex: It specified that all books in a reading room that are used as reference copies have to have at least three copies. Therefore, the query only has to select those books in the reading room that are used as reference copies but have less than three copies:

```
self.books.select[Book b | !(b.referenceCopy implies (b.copies >= 3))]
```

This query is derived from the constraint by replacing the `forAll` iterator with a `select` iterator for which the iterator expression is negated. It would not be difficult for a developer to manually specify this query. It is, however, an unnecessary source for errors, especially when numerous and more complex constraints with several iterators are used.

8.2. Iterator Variable Queries for Violating Elements

After this introduction and motivation for the invariants language, we will now explain the automated process of deriving iterator variable queries for violating elements. First, we give an overview on the complete process and mention current limitations. Then, we introduce a more complex invariant based on our initial example. Next, we explain the individual steps of creating an expression tree, matching the parameter, and transforming the nodes of the expression tree. Finally, we illustrate these steps using the extended example.

8.2.1. Transformation Overview and Limitations

As we already stated above, we present a process for transforming an invariant constraint to a query that yields model elements that violate the invariant. This process is performed in four steps. First, an expression tree is created to represent the invariant constraint in a format that is suitable for the necessary transformations. Then, every invariant parameter is matched to the unique iterator expression node in the tree that uses a compatible type and the same identifier for the iterator variable as the parameter. For every invariant parameter, a copy of the constraint expression tree is transformed to a query expression tree according to rules for the individual node types of the tree. Finally, for each query expression tree a method is generated that can be called from reactions, mappings, or Java code to obtain elements that violate the constraint at a given context.

The presented approach has two syntactical and a semantical limitation: Currently, only invariant parameters that match an iterator variable can be specified. Attributes and references of model elements can be accessed in invariant constraints in an equivalent way to OCL but these accesses cannot yet be bound to invariant parameters. Furthermore, local variables can be used to simplify constraint expressions but they cannot be bound to invariant parameters. The effect of such feature accesses and local variables can also be expressed with additional iterator expressions. Therefore, the restriction to iterator variables is currently an inconvenience for developers but it does not limit the number of cases in which our query derivation approach can be applied. As let expressions and definition constraints for local variables are a commonly-used feature of OCL, this limitation of the invariants language should be addressed in future work.

Furthermore, our approach is limited to constraints in which the matched iterator variable is only followed by operations for which we defined transformation rules. Currently, these operations are `not`, `and`, `or`, `select`, `map`, `forAll`, and `exists`. That is, nested parameters an certain operators, such as collection size comparisons, are not yet supported. For other operators, such as the operator `one`, an automated derivation of elements that violate the constraint would, however, not be enough because the set of elements cannot be filtered appropriatedly. More specifically, different elements are responsible for different ways in which a `one` constraint can be violated so that the queried elements have to be checked again. The restriction to certain operator only applies to expressions after a matched iterator variable. All expressions prior to it may perform arbitrary operations. In future work, nested parameters could be supported by transforming non-nested and nested expressions separately and combining them afterwards. Moreover, transformation rules for the mentioned collection size comparisons operators and the operators `includes` and `excludes` could be added to complete the query derivation support.

8.2.2. Extended Example Invariant

In order to be able to explain more transformation rules we extend our initial example invariant, which we have presented in Listing 8.1. Books of the intial metamodel directly belong to a reading room and have a boolean attribute referenceCopy as well as an integer attribute copies (see Figure 8.1). For our extended example invariant, we use a slightly more detailed metamodel, which is shown in Figure 8.2. Now, books do not belong to a fixed reading room but to a library and they are stored in stacks

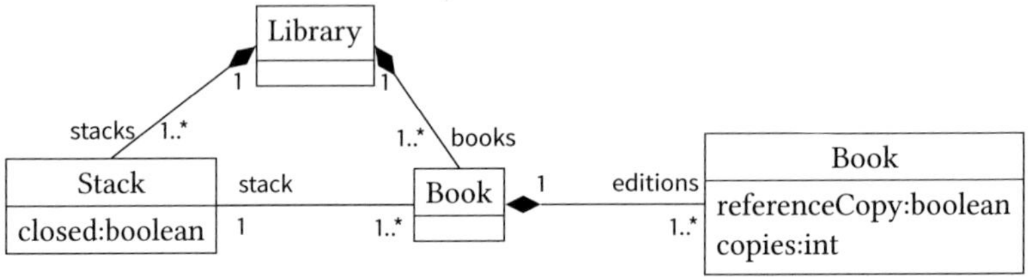

Figure 8.2.: Library metamodel for the complete version of the example invariant

which may be open to the public or not. Furthermore, the attribute that marks reference copies and the attribute for the number of copies are no longer specified for a book but for a specific edition of a book. Therefore, the requirement that at least three references copies have to be available can no longer be specified as before.

The extended invariant for the more detailed library metamodel takes the concept of open stacks and book editions into account as shown in Listing 8.2. It specifies that the sum of copies for all editions of a book in an open stack must be more than three (line 3–7). If the constraint is violated, there are several possibilities to retrieve the model elements that are responsible for the violation and therefore may need to be updated. A trivial solution would be to return the library context element (line 1). This solution ignores, however, the book, stack, and edition elements that are inspected during a check and does not determine a precise cause for an invariant violation, especially if the library contains many books. The model elements that are directly responsible for a violation of this invariant are either those lists of editions for which the sum of copies does not satisfy the constraint or the books to which these editions belong. With our approach, both possibilities are supported. Lists of editions can be retrieved by specifying an invariant parameter `List<Edition> editions` and the books can be retrieved by specifying an invariant parameter `Book b` (line 2). To illustrate the query deriviation, the book iterator variable is chosen as it is followed by further expressions that have to be transformed accordingly. We will use this invariant and the book parameter in the remainder of this chapter to explain the query derivation rules in detail.

To directly illustrate the result of query derivation before we explain the detailed steps, we present the query for the book parameter of the extended

```
context Library
invariant AtLeast3OpenReferenceCopies (Book b, List<Edition> editions)
constraint self.books.select[Book b | !b.stack.closed]
  .map[it.editions.filter[it.referenceCopy]]
  .forAll[List<Edition> editions |
    editions.reduce[e1,e2 | e1.copies + e2.copies] >= 3
  ]
```

Listing 8.2: Extended example invariant ensuring that at least three copies of any edition have to be present for reference books in an open stack

example invariant in Listing 8.3. Like the constraint, it iterates over all books that are referenced by the library context element. In this iteration the query does, however, not simply select all books that are in an open stack to demand a lower bound for the number of reference copies that exist for all editions of the book. Instead, it directly adds another condition to the iterator expression that selects only books in open stacks. This condition is similar to the expression of the constraint in which the editions that are used as reference copies are filtered and in which a lower bound for the sum of copies for these editions is formulated. There are only two differences. First, the lower bound is not demanded for every sum of reference copies of every book but for the book of the current iteration. Second, the lower bound requirement is negated to obtain exactly those books that violate the constraint.

Both, the initial and the extended version of the example invariant illustrate why elements that are accessed for iterator variables can be helpful in addition to context elements. The initial version of the invariant demonstrates a general case in which a constraint only has to hold for instances with incoming references from the context element: It does not need to hold for books that are not in the reading room. Nevertheless, the reading room itself is not the element that needs to be updated to fulfill the invariant again. The extended version of the invariant illustrates another general case in which a single context element is not sufficient because a combination of elements is responsible for an invariant violation: Violations of this invariant cannot be resolved by updating a libary element or a stack but by updating books respectively the number of copies only in those editions that are used as a reference copy.

```
context Library
query Books4AtLeast3OpenReferenceCopies
  self.books.select[Book b | !b.stack.closed &&
    !(b.editions.filter[it.referenceCopy].
    reduce[e1,e2 | e1.copies + e2.copies] >= 3)
  ]
```

Listing 8.3: A query for the extened invariant example returning open reference books with less than three copies

8.2.3. Expression Trees for Constraint Transformation

The grammar of the invariants language specifies that invariant constraints can be arbitrary Xbase expressions. Therefore, we can obtain an Abstract Syntax Tree (AST) that consists of instances of the metaclass XExpression from the parser for the invariants language, which we generated using Xtext. The subclasses for different types of expressions that are defined by the Xbase grammar were created to support the development of a parser, validator, and code generator for Xbase. On the one hand, the structure of such an AST and the available information in it reflects many case distinctions that are not needed to transform a constraint into a query. On the other hand, there are also expressions that can be treated the same way in the Xbase compiler but that have to be differentiated during query derivation. All method calls, for example, are represented in terms of a XMemberFeatureCall in Xbase, but they have to be transformed in a way that depends on the specific method that is called. Calls to the methods `select` or `forAll`, for instance, have to be transformed in another way than other method calls. Therefore, we created a expression tree metamodel that differentiates exactly between those node types that have to be transformed differently and unifies node types that can be treated identically. This made it possible to define transformation rules exactly for the appropriate node types and to only consider those properties that are relevant for the transformation.

A simplified class diagram that depicts our metamodel for expression trees is shown in Figure 8.3. It also shows some of the references, which link nodes of our transformation-specific expression trees to parent nodes and child notes. These references are essential because the transformation is

Metaclass for transformation	Example invariant constraint expressions	Corresponding subclass of XExpression
Forall	`forAll[...]`	XMemberFeatureCall
Exists	`exists[...]`	XMemberFeatureCall
Select	`select[...]`	XMemberFeatureCall
Map	`map[...]`	XMemberFeatureCall
Operation	`self.getBooks()`, `e1.copies`	XMemberFeatureCall
And	`&&`	XBinaryOperation
Or	`||`	XBinaryOperation
Binary	`<, +, /, ...`	XBinaryOperation
Not	`!`	XUnaryOperation
Feature	`self, editions, b, it, 3`	XFeatureCall or Literal
Function	`[a|expression(a)]`	XClosure
Block	`{...}`	XBlockExpression

Table 8.1.: The classification of nodes that are used to build the expression tree

realized in terms of tree traversal. To obtain an instance of this expression tree metamodel for a particular invariant constraint, nodes of the AST provided by the parser are transformed to nodes of our expression tree. The metaclasses that are instantiated for a particular AST subclass of XExpression are given together with some exemplare invariant constraint expresssions in Table 8.1. With the current compiler of the invariants language, the following expressions cannot be transformed because the appropriate node types and transformation rules are not defined yet: type casts, control flow expressions, and variable declarations. As a workaround, the language provides extension methods to transform equivalent constraints that use these extension methods instead of the unsupported expressions. In future work, the necessary node types and transformation rules will be added to replace these extension methods.

To illustrate the transformation-specific representation of constraint expressions, we present the expression tree for the extended example invariant in Figure 8.4. The part of the concrete syntax belonging to a node of the expression tree is listed in a separate line in square brackets. To obtain the pretty-printed expression shown in Listing 8.2, an in-order traversal has to be performed on the tree.

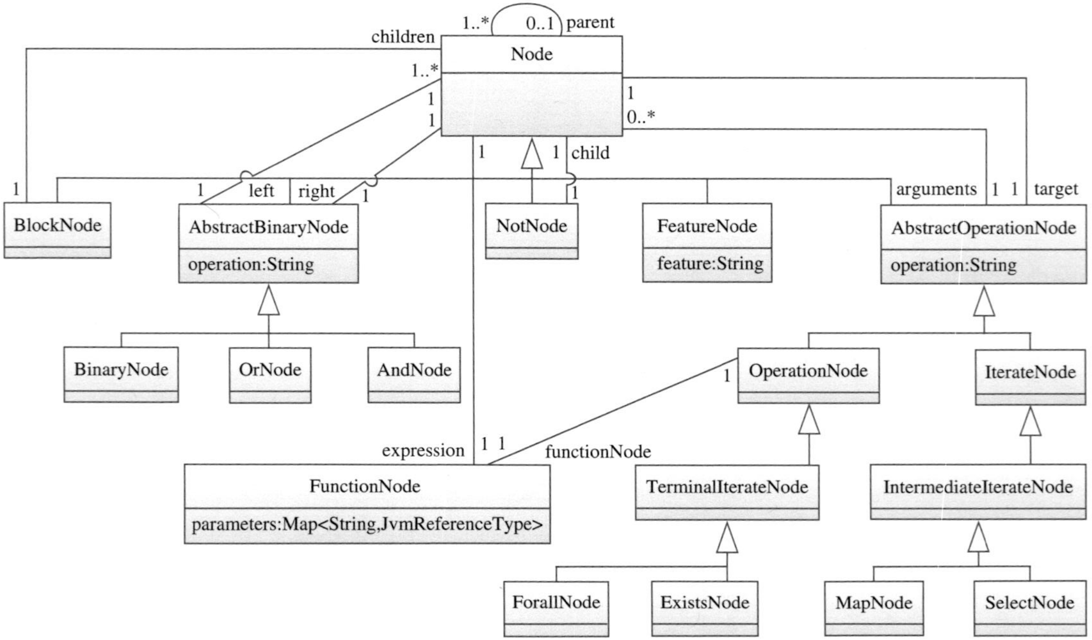

Figure 8.3.: Simplified class diagram for the expression tree metamodel that facilitates transformations from constraints to queries

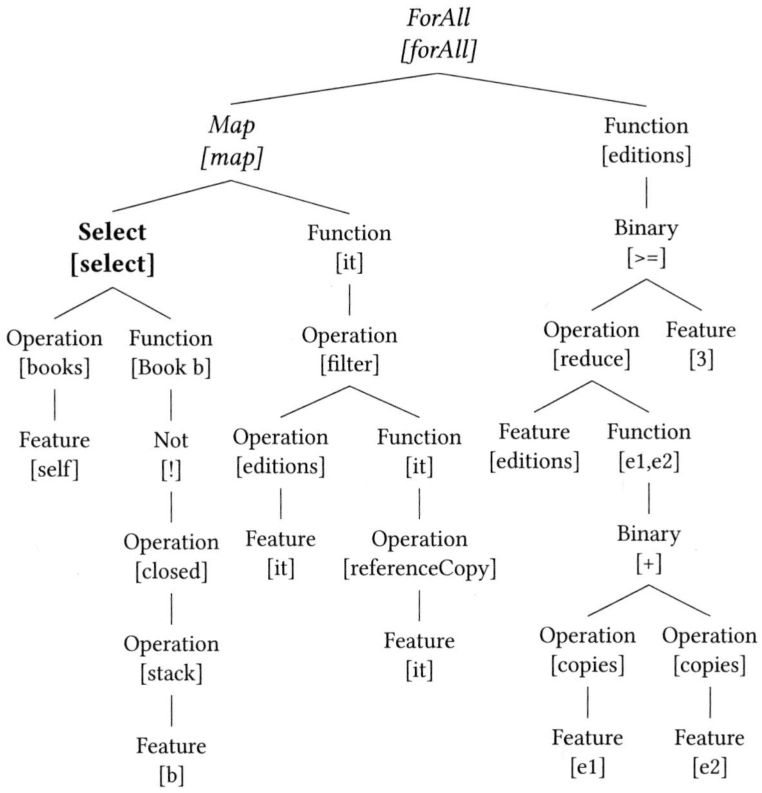

Figure 8.4.: Illustration of the custom expression tree obtained for the complete example invariant (matched iterator printed in bold, parents of it in italics)

8.2.4. Matching Parameters to Iterator Nodes

To prepare the transformation of the invariant constraint for each specified invariant parameter, every invariant parameter has to be matched to a unique node of an iterator that uses a compatible type and identifier for the iterator variable. More precisely, the expression tree is traversed with in-order depth-first search to find all nodes of type IterateNode. If the lambda function of an iterator node specifies an iterator variable that has the same identifier as the invariant parameter, the node is a name match candidate. In order to provide only unambiguous matches, both invariant parameter names and iterator variable names have to be unique within the complete invariant constraint even if their types are different. A name match candidate is only matched to a parameter if the type of the iterator variable is assignment-compatible to the type of the invariant parameter. This ensures that the derived query only retrieves elements that can be bound to the return type that is defined by the invariant parameter type. In the running example (Listing 8.2), the name of the invariant parameter `b` (line 2) matches the iterator variable of the `select` operation (line 3). Therefore, they form a name match candidate. As the iterator variable and the parameter have the same type they are successfully matched to each other. To prepare the transformation to a query, a matching iterator node for each invariant parameter is computed and a separate copy of the expression tree is created for it. The rules for this transformation are presented in the next section.

8.2.5. Parent-Dependent Top-Down Transformation

After generating an expression tree and matching an iterator node for every invariant parameter, a copy of the constraint expression tree is transformed to obtain an expression tree for a query that selects the desired elements. A transformation algorithm is executed independently for every invariant parameter. Given the constraint expression tree and an iterator node matching an invariant parameter, this algorithm recursively applies transformation rules to nodes of the tree. It starts top-down at the root node of the tree and transforms all nodes on the path to the matched iterator node, which is always converted into a SelectNode. Recall that the textual representation of the constraint expression corresponds to an in-order traversal of the expression tree. Therefore, the root node represents the last operation of a chain of operations that starts at the context element. The algorithm first transforms this node, which is a direct or indirect parent of the matched iterator and then transforms all other parents. In the textual representation this corresponds to transforming the constraint expression *from right to left*.

So far, we have only explained in which order the nodes of the constraint expression tree are transformed to yield the query expression tree. Now, we will briefly explain why the nodes are not transformed in isolation before we explain the transformation rules for individual nodes. To create the needed selection restrictions for the query, each node is transformed in a way that takes the parent node, which was already transformed, into account. In the textual representation this means that an expression part to the right of the current expression part is considered. At the end of the transformation, a `SelectNode` is at the former position of the matched iterator node and all former parent nodes have been transformed accordingly. For the textual representation this means that beginning with the matched iterator the remaining right part of the constraint expression was transformed.

8.2.6. Node Transformation Rules for Queries

We will now briefly describe the transformation rules for all nodes that are currently supported.

For NotNodes DeMorgan's laws are applied: Negated conjunctions and disjunctions are replaced through their counterparts with negated inner expressions. A negated universal quantification is replaced with an existential quantification for the negated predicate, and vice versa. The node metaclasses affected by these rules are AndNode, OrNode, ForAllNode, and ExistsNode.

A ForallNode specifies that all elements in the target collection have to satisfy a given predicate. Therefore, the resulting query has to select all elements that do not satisfy the predicate and thus violate the constraint:

```
coll.forAll[e | predicate(e)]
──────────────────────────────
coll.select[e | !predicate(e)]
```

An ExistsNode specifies a predicate that has to be satisfied by at least one element in the target collection. If the constraint is violated, then all elements in the target collection are responsible as none of them satisfies the predicate. If at least one element satisfies the predicate, then no elements have to be retrieved. Both can be achieved with the same query by restricting the select operation in such a way that it returns all elements in the first case and no elements in the second case:

```
coll.exists[e | predicate(e)]
-------------------------------------------
coll.select[!coll.exists[e | predicate(e)]]
```

As we do not yet support nested parameters, a SelectNode can only occur with a parent node or as the result of a prior transformation. The transformation of such nodes is performed in three steps: First, the parent node is transformed by applying the appropriate transformation rule to it. The result of this step is a SelectNode for the parent. Then, the predicate of this parental SelectNode is combined with the predicate of the current SelectNode in a conjunction. Last, the iterator variables are substituted to form a single resulting SelectNode:

```
coll.select[e | predicate(e)].select[p | parentPredicate(p)]
------------------------------------------------------------
coll.select[e | predicate(e) && parentPredicate(e)]
```

A MapNode applies a function to each element of the target collection. Further iterate operations may be performed on the resulting collection of function values. These operations are represented as parent nodes. Altoghether, a MapNode is transformed in three steps: First, the parent operations are transformed into a SelectNode. Then, the MapNode is inlined into this SelectNode by replacing all occurrences of the iterator variable with appropriate calls to the function specified in the map expression:

```
coll.map[e | function(e)].select[p | predicate(p)]
--------------------------------------------------
self.select[e | predicate(function(e))]
```

An AndNode combines an expression that contains the unique iterator variable that matches the invariant parameter with another expression. For the resulting query, elements referenced by this iterator variable have to be retrieved if the expression with the matched variable evaluates to false. Whether the other expression without the matched variable also evaluates to false has no influence on the elements to be retrieved. Therefore, the transformation removes the expression without the matched variable and only transforms the expression with the matched variable. For this transformation, the order of the expressions does not matter. A swapped invariant `otherExpression && self...e...` is transformed analogue, but we only provide the definition once:

```
coll.forAll/exists[e | predicate(e)] && otherExpression
-------------------------------------------------------
coll.select[e | predicate(e)]
```

An OrNode combines an expression that contains the matched iterator variable and another predicate similar to an AndNode. In contrast to the transformation for the conjunction, the other predicate of the disjunction cannot be ignored. If the expression evaluates to false but the other predicate holds, then the constraint is not violated. Therefore, the retrieved elements of the child expression have to be selected by the query only if the other predicate is violated. This is achieved by adding a conjunction with a negated predicate to the transformation result of the other expression:

```
coll.forAll/exists[e | predicate(e)] || otherPredicate
------------------------------------------------------
coll.select[e | predicate(e) && !otherPredicate]
```

8.2.7. Transformation Example

To illustrate the overall transformation algorithm and the individual transformation rules, we explain the transformation of the extended example shown in Listing 8.2 on page 307 and Figure 8.4 on page 311. The node that is matched to the invariant parameter `Book b` is the Select node, which is printed in **bold**. To obtain a query for this parameter and node, the algorithm transforms the parent nodes of the matched node, which are printed in *italics*. It starts at the most distant parent node ForAll, which represents the following constraint part (except for the omitted type of the iterator variable, which is inferred by the compiler):

```
.forAll[editions |
   editions.reduce[e1,e2 | e1.copies + e2.copies] >= 3]
```

After applying the rule for `forAll`, which we have presented in the previous section, the node is a Select that can be textually represented as:

```
.select[editions |
   !(editions.reduce[e1,e2 | e1.copies + e2.copies] >= 3)]
```

The algorithm continues by transforming the Map node, which is the next child of the transformed parent node on the way to the matched iterator node. Before the transformation, this node can be textually represented as:

```
.map[it.editions.filter[it.referenceCopy]]
```

After applying the transformation rule for map, the previously obtained Select node contains the inlined call to the function `filter` of the transformed map expression:

```
.select[!(it.editions.filter[it.referenceCopy].
  reduce[e1,e2 | e1.copies + e2.copies] >= 3)]
```

Last, the Select node with the invariant parameter is transformed by incorporating the parent node's predicate and substituting the iterator variable:

```
.select[Book b |
  !b.stack.closed &&!(b.editions.filter[it.referenceCopy].
  reduce[e1,e2 | e1.copies + e2.copies] >= 3)]
```

The final result is the query that we have already presented in Listing 8.3 on page 308. It retrieves all books that violate the constraint because the are in an open stack and their total number of presence copies for all editions is less than 3.

8.3. Conclusions and Future Work

We have presented a language for parameterized invariants with an automated derivation of queries for model elements that violate an invariant. It is closely aligned to OCL, provides equivalent collection operators and iterators and additional invariant parameters. We have discussed different ways for obtaining elements that are responsible for an invariant violation and have motivated why constraint code should not be manually duplicated in queries for such elements. Moreover, we have explained how iterator variables can be used to explicitly declare which elements that cause an invariant shall be retrieved. We have presented an automated derivation of queries that return those elements that were accessed for an iterator variable and that are responsible for an invariant violation. For expressions that may occur in iterators, we have presented transformation rules that are applied to a special tree representation of the invariant constraint to obtain the appropriate queries. Furthermore, we have illustrated the invariants language and its query derivation using a running example.

In future work, support for local variables and further operators, such as collection size comparators, should be added to the query derivation. These constructs can currently only be used in invariant constraints before an iterator that is matched to a parameter occurs. The effect of the local variables and the operators can also be expressed with additional iterator expressions. This is, however, inconvenient and local variables are a commonly-used feature of OCL which should also be supported by the invariants language during query derivation. Furthermore, the derivation algorithm should be extended in future work to also support nested parameters. For this, we suggest to transform non-nested and nested expressions separately to combine the results afterwards.

Part IV.

Evaluating and Relating the Languages

9. Evaluation and Discussion

9.1. Evaluation Overview

In this chapter, we explain how we evaluated theoretical and practical properties of the languages we presented in this thesis. Before we present an overview of our evaluation, we briefly introduce the four properties that we evaluated:

Completeness was evaluated as the extent to which a language *supports all use cases that are theoretically possible*

Correctness was evaluated differently for each language but altogether it is the *theoretical property of yielding the intended and claimed results in all possible cases*

Applicability was evaluated by examining whether the languages can be applied *in practice to realize* realistic consistency requirements by creating *specifications that lead to the expected results*

Benefit was evaluated by analyzing whether applications of the languages *demonstrate advantages in comparison to other languages*

The two practical properties applicability and benefit are based on properties with the same name that were originally introduced for the evaluation of metrics for prediction models by Böhme and Reussner [BR08, p. 15]. As programming languages and prediction metrics have different characteristics, these properties are, however, not identical. Böhme and Reussner state that applicability is evaluated by checking "whether the input data can be acquired reliably and whether the results of the metric can be interpreted meaningfully". For our formulation of applicability, we replaced the check that metric results can be interpreted meaningfully with a check for expected results. Furthermore, we added the restriction to evaluate applications in which realistic requirements are realized. For evaluations of benefit, Böhme and Reussner require that an "approach has to demonstrate its benefits over other competing approaches". This can be regarded as equivalent to our formulation, but the subsequent explanations of Böhme and Reussner illustrate that evaluations of benefit can be performed very differently and can be very costly. We cannot define in advance for all approaches how often they have to be applied together with one or more competing approaches and under which conditions. Similarly, we cannot precisely define upfront what will be considered a "benefit". Both, the conditions of the comparison and the benefit to be compared have to be defined and discussed individually for every evaluation.

To outline how we evaluated each property individually for each language, we provide two tables. Table 9.1 presents an overview on our evaluation of theoretical properties and Table 9.2 summarizes the evaluation of practical properties. We do not yet explain the evaluation parts but provide references to the sections that discuss them. The evaluation parts are structured according to the evaluated property so that, for example, all evaluations of completeness are described in a common section. When discussing the evaluation of an individual property, we almost never refer to evaluations of the same property for other languages, except for the change and expression languages, which were designed for reuse. Therefore, the two tables can also be used to read the discussion of all evaluated properties for a specific language independent of the other languages by following all section references in the appropriate *row* in both tables.

By evaluating all languages presented in this thesis, we also evaluated all contributions except for the identified and classified challenges to consistency preservation (chapter 3). We did not perform an evaluation for this contribution in order to focus on the languages that address the identified challenges and on their evaluation. One possibility to evaluate this contribution in the future is to analyze which of the identified challenges are not only claimed to be addressed by other approaches but are demonstrably successfully addressed by them. For this, it would be necessary to find or create exemplary consistency preservation scenarios in which the identified challenges occur. Furthermore, it would be a risk that specific languages and consistency preservation tools are misjudged if not all features that address a challenge are known or if they are not used correctly. Therefore, we are convinced that the effort for such an evaluation would not outweigh

	evaluation of theoretical properties completeness	correctness
formal language (chapter 4)	• EMOF complete • consistency complete • change complete & update complete (subsection 9.2.1)	• exhibits main model characteristics [Sta73] (representation, reduction, pragmatics) (subsection 9.3.1)
change language (subsection 5.4.1)	• EMOF complete (subsection 9.2.2)	• exhibits main model characteristics [Sta73] (representation, reduction, pragmatics) (subsection 9.3.2)
OCL-aligned expressions (subsection 5.4.3)	• 27 out of 28 collection operators and iterators (subsection 9.2.3)	• tested against OCL-counterparts (subsection 9.3.3)
reactions language (chapter 6)	• Turing-complete reactions • triggers & matching change complete • matching & actions correspondence complete (subsection 9.2.4)	• semantics based on formal language (section 6.7) • correct by construction (subsection 6.7.4) (subsection 9.3.4)
mappings language (chapter 7)	• reduction sketch TGG $\propto$ mappings • partial enforcement & inversion derivation (subsection 9.2.5)	• semantics via reactions & formal language • correctness by construction (subsection 7.7.5) • correct enforcement for check operators • correct inversion according to round-trip laws (subsection 9.3.5)
invariants language (chapter 8)	• primitive-recursive (like OCL) (subsection 9.2.6)	• correct query derivation (subsection 9.3.6)

Table 9.1.: Overview on the evaluation of *theoretical* properties for the languages of this thesis with references to presentation and evaluation sections

	evaluation of practical properties	
	applicability	benefit
formal language (chapter 4)	• explains semantics of reactions language (subsection 9.4.1)	– (not evaluated)
change language (subsection 5.4.1)	• triggers generated reactions code (subsection 9.4.2)	• argument: intermediate models for monitors (subsection 9.5.1)
OCL-aligned expressions (subsection 5.4.3)	• UML invariants • used in reactions case studies (subsection 9.4.3)	• argument: integrated and analyzable (subsection 9.5.2)
reactions language (chapter 6)	• component architecture case study • component code case study • integration of object-oriented code • automotive software case study (subsection 9.4.4)	• code size in comparison with Java or Xtend • relative reduction of source lines of code (subsection 9.5.3)
mappings language (chapter 7)	• Leitner learning box example • expressions of ATL transformation zoo (subsection 9.4.5)	• comparison with a TGG-based tool (subsection 9.5.4)
invariants language (chapter 8)	• UML invariants (subsection 9.4.3)	• argument: fewer input for derived queries (subsection 9.5.5)

Table 9.2.: Overview on the evaluation of *practical* properties for the languages of this thesis with references to presentation and evaluation sections

the benefits. Instead, it would be favorable to create benchmarks for consistency preservation scenarios together with developers of other consistency preservation approaches. An evaluation of whether these approaches successfully address the challenges we identified, could then be performed by the developers based on the common benchmark. Such an idea of a common benchmark is not new and has already been pursued by many researchers, for example, especially for bidirectional transformations [Anj+14a; Che+14]. So far, no common consistency preservation benchmark that is realistic because it exhibits substantial requirements and challenges of modelling languages that are widely used in practice, is, however, publicly available. Nevertheless, the challenges that we identified and classified in this thesis, can be used to create such a benchmark in the future.

9.2. Evaluation of Theoretical Completeness

For each language presented in this thesis, we discuss the property of completeness, which denotes whether the language supports all use cases that are theoretically possible and intended. As the languages and their intended ranges of use vary strongly, we also have to discuss different notions of completeness for each language. Most languages are intended for a general range of use, for example, for all models that conform to EMOF-based metamodels, or for preservation behavior that can be described with a Turing complete language. Some languages have, however, a more restricted range of use, such as to act as a replacement for the collection operators and iterators of operation body expressions of the Object Constraint Language (OCL).

9.2.1. Completeness of the Formal Language

For the formal language, which we have described in chapter 4, we discuss four notions of completeness:

Model completeness denotes the ability to represent all models that conform to metamodels that are defined using the metamodelling language standard Essential Meta-Object Facility (EMOF)

Consistency completeness is the ability to express arbitrary co-occurring consistency conditions based on correspondences that witness consistency

Change completeness denotes whether all model changes can be represented in such a way that it can always be analyzed whether they break consistency or not

Update completeness is the ability to express all theoretically possible updates on models and correspondences in such a way that it can be analyzed whether they preserve consistency or not

9.2.1.1. Completeness of Model and Consistency Representation

The formal language abstracts away from many details and has some limitations (see page 33 of section 2.3.1.2). Most of these limitations are, however, only syntactical as they do not restrict the *set* of models that can be represented but the *way* how models are represented. An example for such a syntactical limitation of the formal language is that it is currently not possible to represent references to metaclasses of other metamodels (limitation 1). If we would extend the formal language to also support such cases, this would not conceptually change the way in which consistency can be expressed and has no semantic influence on consistency preservation because metamodel boundaries have no effect on it. Therefore, it is only a syntactical limitation of the formal language. The same argument applies to the syntactical limitation that it is not possible to express several models with links to objects of other models (limitation 2). Again, the necessary language extension would only have syntactical implications as model boundaries have no semantic influence on consistency preservation. We did not extend the language to overcome both limitations because we are convinced that the risk to decline the understandability is much higher than the gained benefit of demonstrating syntactical completeness.

In addition to syntactical limitations, there are, however, also three limitations that restrict the set of models or consistency relations that can be represented. They limit the formal language to cases in which no link points to the same object more than once (limit 6), no value is labeled more than once per object and attribute (7), and links and labels are unordered (8). This restricts the formal language because reappearence of links and values as well as the order of links and values could be analyzed in consistency conditions. If a consistency preservation scenario is encountered in which these multiplicities or the order make a difference, a few changes would be necessary to extend the formal language to take these concerns also into account.

The remaining limitations 3–5, which we have presented in subsubsection 2.3.1.2, do not restrict the completeness of the formal language. They neither limit the syntactical variations to which the language can be applied nor do they limit the models or consistency relations that can be semantically expressed. The reason for this is that they only limit the language-internal representation and not to the represented models themselves.

In addition to the limitations 6–8, we have imposed a last restriction on the formal language by making serializability a prerequisite for consistency (see Definition 13). This restriction could be overcome if consistency would also be defined for models that are not serializable. The only effect of such an extension is that serializability had to be taken into account in all definitions that involve updates. For these updates it had to be considered that this extension makes it possible that updates break serializability without breaking consistency.

Altogether, we discussed two limitations that are only syntactical, three limitations for multiplicities and ordering that could be overcome if the language is extended accordingly, and the restriction that we made serializability a prerequisite for consistency. This shows that the formal language could be used to represent all EMOF-based models if it would be extended so that links and labels for a single object and feature could be ordered and could point more than once to the same object or value.

9.2.1.2. Completeness of Correspondence-Based Consistency

The definition of conditions in the formal language covers all possible conditions as it simply represents conditions as a list of objects fulfilling the condition (see Definition 18 in subsection 2.3.3). Therefore, this simple representation of conditions is complete. If the formal language would, however, be used for something else than for general explanations of the semantics of the other languages, then this representation of conditions would also make it very impractical to use the language for specific model instances and conditions.

The fact that our consistency definition is correspondence-based does not restrict its usage (see Definition 24 in subsection 4.1.2). On the contrary, it provides a way to configure how consistency has to be preserved for models by selecting appropriate correspondences. If no correspondences are necessary because every fulfillment on one side has to co-occur with a fulfillment on the other side, then it is still possible to simply add all these co-occurrences to the set of correspondences to achieve the desired behavior.

9.2.1.3. Change Complete and Update Complete

The last two notions of completeness that we discuss for the formal language concern changes that are performed by users and that can break consistency as well as updates that are performed to restore consistency. Changes of arbitrary type for arbitrary elements on one model side are supported by the formal language (see Definition 34 in subsection 4.3.1). The definitions of consistency preservation after such changes are, however, limited to changes that break consistency for at most one consistency rule. This means, that all theoretically possible changes can be expressed with the formal language but we can oonly analyze whether an update after such a change preserves consistency or not for those changes that break a single rule. Therefore, the language is change complete but preservation is restricted to isolated consistency breaks.

Any theoretically possible updates in reaction to changes can be expressed with the language to describe how model elements on the other side and correspondences are updated (see Definition 30 in subsection 4.2.1). Thus, we call the formal language update complete.

9.2.2. Change Language is EMOF Complete

The change modelling language, which we have presented in subsection 5.4.1, can be used to describe all changes that can occur in models that conform to EMOF-based metamodels. This completeness is achieved in two steps. First, the language supports all changes in such models that can be represented as a single atomic change of a model element or of a model element's property. Second, it supports all changes that can be represented as a combination of atomic change representations. As no other changes are possible in models conforming to EMOF-based metamodels, the language can be used to represent any change in such models. Therefore, we call it EMOF complete. The reason why this completeness can be achieved by only supporting element and property changes is that all characteristics of EMOF-based models are realized in terms of objects and object values for properties defined in an EMOF-based metamodel. Every possible change that can be performed on such objects and values can be described in the same way for any metamodel because EMOF is the fixed meta-metamodel for these metamodels. This way, everything that can be changed in EMOF-based models can be described without the need to consider which particular modelling language is used.

9.2.3. Completeness of OCL-Aligned Expressions

In subsection 5.4.3, we have presented an OCL-aligned extension for the reused expression language Xbase (see subsection 5.4.2). This extension is used to support OCL-aligned expressions for collections in the reactions, invariants, and mappings language. It is, however, *not* complete. It does not cover the complete OCL language, The expressions extension supports all 14 collection operators and 13 out of all 14 iterators[1] that can be used in OCL operation body expressions [ISO12c, pp. 156–174]. Collection operators and iterators are characteristic for OCL. They make it possible to specify constraints in a declarative way in terms of operations that mostly correspond to well-known mathematical operations, such as universal quantification for elements of sets. Furthermore, we analyzed that these operations represent a big part of the OCL expressions that are used to restrict instances of metamodels: More than 80% of the invariants in the metamodel of the Unified Modeling Language (UML), for example, consist of such collection operator expressions, iterator expressions, or of

[1] The `closure` iterator is not yet supported.

expressions that only invoke a getter on a model element for a feature of a metaclass [Fis15, p.40][FKL16, p.13].

9.2.4. Reactions Language Completeness

For the reactions language, which we have presented in chapter 6, we discuss different notions of completeness for entire reactions, change triggers, correspondence matching, and for actions. First, we explain how we achieved Turing completeness for the reactions language. Broadly speaking, the result is that everything that may be necessary to preserve consistency can be expressed with the reactions language. This computational completeness is sufficient but it is achieved using a fallback action for imperative code that should only be used if other update actions cannot be used. Such a fallback is, however, not necessary for tasks that fall into the responsibility of other parts of the language. These parts provide constructs for defining change triggers and matching corresponding elements that cover all necessary and possible cases. Therefore, we also show that the trigger and matching part of the reactions language are complete in the sense that no other language constructs are necessary to express after which changes a reaction should be executed. Finally, we demonstrate that the language constructs for retrieving and managing correspondences are complete, because all types of correspondences and operations on correspondences can be expressed with them.

9.2.4.1. Reactions are Turing Complete

The reaction language is Turing complete as arbitrary Java code can be executed in response to arbitrary changes. If it is not possible to express the intended consistency preservation behavior using particular constructs of the reactions language, a developer could theoretically decide to express all update behavior in a single execute action block (see subsection 6.5.5). In this block arbitrary Java code can be specified. To execute this code after arbitrary changes, it is necessary to define a reaction and a reaction routine (see Listing 9.1). In the reaction routine the simplest trigger has to be specified using the change type any change (line 2) and a call to the reaction routine has to be added (line 3). This routine (line 6–12) only

```
1 reaction {
2   after any change
3   call simulateTuringMachine(change)
4 }
5
6 routine simulateTuringMachine(EChange change) {
7   action {
8     execute {
9       // arbitrary code in a Java dialect, e.g. to simulate Turing machine
10    }
11  }
12 }
```

Listing 9.1: Exemplary reaction and reaction routine to execute Java code or simulate a Turing-machine in an execute action block

contains an execution action block with the arbitrary Java code (line 9). As the Java language is Turing complete, this simple reduction shows that the reactions language is also Turing complete.

In the next sections, we will show that such a minimalistic use of the reactions language is, however, not necessary. The reason is that the first two of the three main steps of consistency preservation reactions (see section 6.1) can always be expressed with appropriate language constructs. We will demonstrate that even if some actions can only be expressed in terms of execute action blocks, it is always possible to use constructs of the reactions language to express after which changes and on which corresponding elements these actions shall be performed.

9.2.4.2. Triggers and Matching are EMOF-Change Complete

After the computational completeness of the previous section, we will now show a notion of completeness for those constructs of the reactions language that make it possible to specify after which changes a reaction is to be executed. These constructs give developers the possibility to restrict the execution of reactions to changes that fulfill conditions of a change trigger as well as conditions of retrieval conditions and match checks (see subsection 6.4.1, 6.4.2, 6.5.1, and 6.5.2). Together, these language constructs make it possible to fulfill any requirements that specify under which conditions actions shall be performed after a change in arbitrary models of an EMOF-based metamodel.

The change type of a trigger can be defined based on the change modelling language, for which we explained in subsection 9.2.2 why it is EMOF complete. Currently, reactions are implemented in such a way that compound change descriptions are decomposed before they are processed, because we do not yet provide keywords for different compound change types. Therefore, it is not directly possible to restrict a reaction to certain compound changes. A trigger may, however, also specify a change properties check in terms of arbitrary code that has no side-effects. As a workaround, such a check can be used to manually encode any conditions for compound changes, if the decomposition of changes in the underlying framework is deactivated before. This way, the trigger part can be made complete also with respect to compound representations of changes in EMOF-based models.

Model elements that are not explicitly related to changed model elements cannot be accessed in a trigger definition (see subsection 6.4.2). This means that this part of the reactions language can only be used to define *change-related reaction conditions*, which can be checked if all change information but no further information on the changed model is provided. Arbitrary conditions for the execution of consistency preserving updates cannot be expressed with it. For this, conditions based on arbitrary model information can be expressed using retrieve properties checks and match checks in a match block of a reaction routine. Such *model-related reaction conditions* can be expressed in terms of code that may access any model elements but may not cause any side-effects. Together, change-related conditions of trigger definitions and model-related conditions of match blocks make it possible to realize arbitrary conditions that have to be fulfilled before update actions shall be applied. Therefore, triggers and match blocks make the reactions language complete with respect to changes in EMOF-based models.

9.2.4.3. Matching and Actions are Correspondence Complete

The third and last notion of completeness that we discuss for the reactions language is about the possibilities for retrieving and managing correspondences between consistent elements of models that conform to two metamodels. Together, the retrieve and update constructs make the reactions language correspondence complete in the sense that every requirement for retrieving, creating, updating, or deleting a correspondence can be expressed with them.

The reactions language only supports tagged correspondences between two model elements but as several such correspondences may exists with different tags, this simple approach is as expressive as correspondences that directly relate more than two model elements. More specifically, such correspondences can be emulated by using a tag to mark all correspondences between two elements that realize a many-to-many correspondence. Furthermore, we rely on identifiers that only need to be temporarily unique to realize such correspondences (see subsubsection 5.5.1.1). Therefore, the used correspondence representation is sufficient to express any type of correspondence between any types of elements for which a temporarily unique identifier can be calculated.

In order to be correspondence complete, it is not sufficient to be able to represent every correspondence but it also has to be possible ti retrieve and manipulate such correspondences. The reactions language provides specific constructs for retrieving model elements. With such constructs it is possible to obtain model elements on the side where reactions are executed. These elements correspond to model elements on the side that was changed by a user or the other way round (see subsection 6.5.1). Only a single element can be retrieved at once but every retrieval can be restricted using arbitrary side-effect free code (see subsection 6.5.2). Therefore, any theoretically possible correspondence retrieval can be expressed.

The reactions language provides specific actions for creating and deleting correspondences. A new correspondence can be added with an optional tag and deletions of existing correspondences can be restricted using optional tags and arbitrary conditions (see subsection 6.5.3). Correspondences have no own identity because they can be identified using the identifiers of the corresponding elements and the tag of the correspondence. Therefore, no correspondences need to be updated in order to express that other elements should correspond. More specifically, deleting an existing correspondence for formerly corresponding elements and creating a new correspondence for newly corresponding elements is equivalent to an update. Thus, the reactions language is correspondence complete although no explicit correspondence update construct is provided.

9.2.5. Mappings Language Completeness

For the mappings language, which we have presented in chapter 7, we discuss the completeness of the entire language as well as completeness of the automated derivation of enforcements from checks and completeness of inverse enforcements from bidirectionalizable conditions. First, we will sketch a reduction to show that the mappings language can be used to express anything that can be expressed with ordinary triple-graph grammars. Second, we will explain that the derivation of enforcements from condition checks and the derivation of inverse enforcements are not complete. This incomplete automation does, however, not restrict the cases in which the mappings language can be applied, as it is possible to manually specify check and enforce code or code for both enforcement directions if the supported operators are insufficient.

9.2.5.1. Triple-Graph Grammars as Mappings

The powerful graph transformation concept of a Triple-Graph Grammar (TGG) was originally defined for directed graphs [Sch95] and extended in many different ways, for example, to also support attributes and types for vertices and edges. A TGG consist of rules that combine a left graph $L = (V_L, E_L)$ and a right graph $R = (V_R, E_R)$ with an intermediary correspondence graph $C = (V_C, E_C)$ by relating them using graph morphisms $r_{\leftarrow\!\shortmid} : C \rightarrow L$ and $r_{\mapsto} : C \rightarrow R$. This means all edge relations have to be preserved by the functions $r_{\leftarrow\!\shortmid,V}$ and $r_{\leftarrow\!\shortmid,E}$ for the vertices and the functions $r_{\mapsto,V}, r_{\mapsto,E}$ for the edges. More specifically, for all $(c_s, c_t) \in E_C$ it has to hold that

$$(r_{\leftarrow\!\shortmid,E}(c_s, c_t) = (v_s, v_t)) \Rightarrow (r_{\leftarrow\!\shortmid,V}(c_s) = v_s \wedge r_{\leftarrow\!\shortmid,V}(c_t) = v_t)$$

and analogue for $r_{\mapsto,E}$ and $r_{\mapsto,V}$.

Unfortunately, a formal reduction from TGGs to mappings is out of scope for this thesis, but we will sketch how such a reduction can be performed. For this, we will show how to reduce every TGG rule to one or several mappings. Before we can start, we have to briefly mention how graphs can be used to represent models. Vertices in a left or right graph of a TGG rule are used to represent instances of metaclasses and edges represent links of these instances which are defined for references of the instantiated metaclass. The first step of the reduction is to determine which metaclasses have to be mapped by computing all tuples of vertices that are related via the correspondence graph and the morphisms:

$$\begin{aligned}&\{(\{v_{l_1},\ldots,v_{l_m}\},\{v_{r_1},\ldots,v_{r_n}\}) \in \mathcal{P}(V_L)\times\mathcal{P}(V_R) \mid \exists\, c \in C\colon\\ &(\forall\, i \in \{1,\ldots,m\}\colon\ v_{l_i} = r_{\leftarrow}(c))\\ &\ \wedge (\forall j \in \{1,\ldots,n\}\colon\ r_{\rightarrow}(c) = v_{r_j})\}\end{aligned}$$

For each of these tuples a separate mapping has to be created. Each mapping has to list the metaclasses for the vertices in the left set and in the right set of the tuple as left and right parameters of the mapping. All constraints that are defined for attributes and links of a vertex have to be expressed in all mappings for tuples that contain the vertex. If the constraint does not relate attributes of vertices of the left and the right graph, then we have to create an appropriate single-sided condition in the mapping. Otherwise, a bidirectionalizable condition has to be created. To our knowledge, there is no TGG-based tool that supports declarative constraints for operators for which we did not define automated enforcement derivation (see section 7.3) or automated inversion (see subsection 7.4.6). Therefore, all attribute and reference constraints that can be directly written in a TGG can also be expressed using single-sided or bidirectionalizable conditions. Additional constraints may be added to a TGG rule, for example, by providing three Java methods for checking a constraint and for enforcing it in both directions. With the mappings language, such constraints can always be expressed as a single-sided condition that consists of two code blocks for checking and enforcing the condition (see subsection 7.3.3) or as a bidirectionalizable condition with two code blocks for enforcing the constraint in both directions (see subsection 7.4.8). Advanced concepts such as negative application conditions or context nodes that are not in the image of the functions of the morphism can be translated back to the fundamental concepts of vertices, edges, and constraints. Thus, even for such concepts a reduction can be performed as explained above. The result of such a reduction would be that every consistency relation that can be expressed in terms of a TGG can also be expressed in terms of a mapping specification with several mappings for each TGG rule. Therefore, the mappings language is at least as complete as TGGs with respect to the expressable consistency relations.

With the above reduction, one or several isolated mappings are created for a single TGG rule. This is, however, not the only way to reduce TGGs to mappings. It would, for example, also be possible to avoid the repetition of constraints for vertices that occur in several of the tuples that we used to determine which mappings have to be created. For this, explicit dependencies could be used during the reduction process.

9.2.5.2. Incomplete Enforcement and Inversion Derivation

The second and last discussion of completeness for the mappings language is concerned with the automated derivation of enforcements from checks and from opposite enforcements. As we have already stated before, the sets of supported operators for which enforcements or inverse enforcements can be derived are *not* complete. There are, however, language constructs to cope with this incompleteness: It can be manually specified how a check is to be enforced and how a condition that relates both sides is to be enforced using two unidirectional enforcements. These constructs only have to be used if the provided operators are not sufficient. Other languages and tools for consistency preservation either always require such manual specifications or only support basic operators, such as addition, subtraction, division, multiplication, (in)-equality, and numerical comparisons but no advanced operators such as those presented in subsection 7.4.6.

9.2.6. Invariants Language Completeness

The invariants language, which we have presented in chapter 8, can be used to specify invariants using the expressions language Xbase (see subsection 5.4.2) and the extension for OCL-aligned collection operations (see subsection 5.4.3). We have already discussed the completeness of these collection operator and iterator extensions in subsection 9.2.3. Therefore, the only additional notion of completeness that we discuss for the invariants language is computational completeness.

In terms of computational power, the invariants language is at least as complete as OCL. More specifically, the completeness of the invariants language can be judged differently if calls to helper methods that are written in Java or Xbase are counted as part of the language or not. If invariant conditions do not contain any such calls, then they can contain expressions that represent loops that always iterate over all elements of a collection but no interruptible while-loops. This means, without such calls, all loops that are executed in an invariant always either perform a number of iterations that is fixed before the loop is entered or they do not terminate if the collection is infinite. Therefore, such invariants without calls to helper methods can only express primitive recursive functions, as it is the case for OCL [MC99; CK03]. If calls to helper methods are, however, counted as part of the invariants language, then it inherits the Turing completeness from the Java language.

9.3. Evaluation of Theoretical Correctness

For each language presented in this thesis, we will evaluate notions of correctness in this section. As we designed these languages for different purposes, the evaluated notions of correctness are also different. The goal of the formal language and of the change modelling language is to create representations that support explanations and realizations of the other languages. Therefore, we will evaluate for these two languages whether they correctly *model* consistency preservation and changes according to the main characteristics of a model as defined by Stachowiak [Sta73, pp. 131–133]. For the OCL-aligned expression language, we will discuss why the provided operators correctly realize the same functionality as their OCL-counterparts. The goal of the mappings, reactions, and invariants language is to allow developers to specify consistency preservation in different ways for different consistency scenarios and relations. For these languages, we will evaluate whether they are correct in the sense that they preserve consistency as we defined it and claimed it in the previous chapters.

9.3.1. Formal Language Correctly Models Consistency

In this section, we will show that the formal language, which we presented in chapter 4, correctly models the notion of consistency that is supported by the reactions, mappings, and invariants language and the way in which consistency can be preserved with these languages. For this, we will explain why the formal language fulfills three main characteristics of models, which we have already presented in subsection 2.1.1. These characteristics are representation, reduction, and pragmatics.

9.3.1.1. Representation of Consistency for EMOF-Based Models

The formal language represents models of EMOF-based metamodels and consistency specifications that are expressed using the reactions language. As per the general model theory of Stachowiak [Sta73], the model entities of the formal language are the sets of the definitions in section 2.3 and chapter 4. The originals represented by these entities are EMOF-based models and consistency specifications. More specifically, the represented originals of the first part of the formal language are elements of models for which consistency is to be preserved. The represented originals of the second part are conceptual conditions and updates of consistency specifications that are expressed in terms of reactions. Altogether, the formal language contains no entities that do not represent such originals and it models no properties that cannot be mapped to properties of the originals. Therefore, the formal language fulfills the representation characteristic.

9.3.1.2. Reduction of Model and Consistency Details

Only a few of the properties of models and consistency specifications are represented using the definitions of the formal language. For the first part of the language, which represents models, we have already provided a detailed list of the properties that are abstracted away in subsubsection 2.3.1.2. We have, however, not explicitly mentioned the properties of consistency specifications that are abstracted away in the second part of the formal language. Entities and properties of consistency specifications that are implied by reactions but *not* represented in the formal language are, for example

- descriptions of how it is decided whether objects fulfill a consistency condition,
- properties of correspondences in addition to the elements that correspond, or
- instructions that are executed and cases that are distinguished to obtain a consistency-preserving model update.

Therefore, the reduction characteristic is fulfilled by the formal language.

9.3.1.3. Pragmatic Utility for Explaining Semantics

The purpose of the formal language is to facilitate explanations of the semantics of the other language of this thesis. We have directly provided such explanations for the reactions language in section 6.7. The mappings language and the invariants language are, however, also indirectly explained using the formal language, because the semantics of mappings are explained in terms of reactions (section 7.7) and because conditions for reactions and mappings can be expressed as invariants. In the explanations of reactions semantics, the formal language replaces the models and consistency specifications in order to relieve the reader from considering all modeling and specification details. The supported functions are that relevant parts of models and consistency preservation behavior can be explained and illustrated. This means, the formal language is a pragmatic utility for both the author and the readers of this thesis and therefore the last main characteristic of a model according to Stachowiak [Sta73] is also fulfilled.

9.3.2. Change Modelling Language Correctness

In this section, we will show that the change modelling language, which we have presented in subsection 5.4.1, correctly models changes in EMOF-based models. As for the correctness of the formal language, we will explain why the three main characteristics of models—representation, reduction, and pragmatics—are fulfilled.

9.3.2.1. Representation of Changes in EMOF-Based Models

The change modelling language can be used to represent changes in models that conform to metamodels that were defined using EMOF or using Ecore (see subsubsection 2.1.3.1 and 2.1.3.2). All change properties that can be represented using the language are properties of the original change. No properties that cannot be mapped to properties of the modelled originals can be expressed with the language. Therefore, the representation characteristic is fulfilled.

9.3.2.2. Reduction of Derived and Context Information

All models that are created using the change modelling language only provide essential information on the original changes and edit operations. Information that can be derived or that describes irrelevant details of the context of a change is abstracted away. If an editor provides, for example, different ways of performing the same change using different commands that execute the same edit operation, then it is not modelled which of these commands was used. Moreover, no information about the used editor is modelled. This means that two changes that perform the same edit operation for the same elements and values are represented in the same way even if different editors, for example, with textual and graphical representations are used. Thus, the reduction characteristic is fulfilled.

9.3.2.3. Pragmatic Usage for Triggering Reactions

The models created with the change modelling language replace the original change during the execution of consistency preservation reactions.

Developers that specify change types in triggers of reactions can use these replacements to restrict the actions that they define to be only executed before or after certain changes (see subsection 6.4.1). The purpose of this replacement is that both the developers using the reactions language and the developers of the reactions language only have to consider those properties of a change that are relevant for consistency preservation. Furthermore, developers of monitored editors, which provide change information, can specify how change models are created in order to give users of the editor the possibility that the models they are changing can be kept consistent using reactions and mappings (see subsection 5.5.2). This means, the change modelling language is a pragmatic means for three different kinds of developers to represent and retrieve change information for change-driven consistency preservation and the last main characteristic of a model is fulfilled.

9.3.3. Correctness of OCL-Aligned Expressions

We have presented our OCL-aligned language expressions extension in subsection 5.4.3 and we will briefly describe how OCL constraints are automatically converted to expressions of it in subsection 9.4.3. The extension does not introduce any new operators but only realizes operators that were defined in the OCL and for which precise semantics were given in the according ISO standard [ISO12c, pp. 156–174]. To show that the operators of our OCL-aligned extension are correct, one could formally verify that they fulfill the given preconditions and postconditions. As we generate Java code for all languages and the OCL-aligned expression, it would be possible to apply existing code verification tools for Java, such as KeY [BHS07]. As all operators have well-known counterparts in set theory and therefore a low conceptual complexity, we decided, however, to only test these operators. We performed unit tests in which we validated that the operators yield the same results as their OCL counterparts (see subsection 9.4.3) and we performed integration tests in which the provided operators were used in reactions code (see subsection 9.4.4).

9.3.4. Reactions Correctly Preserve Consistency

To show that the reactions language is correct, we have to show that the reactions that can be created with it correctly preserve consistency. For this, it is necessary to have conditions that have to be fulfilled by two models of two modelling languages whenever these two models shall be considered consistent. Such conditions can, however, not be given and fixed for all usages of all pairs of modelling languages in all development contexts. This is why the languages presented in this thesis were designed for *prescriptive* consistency specifications (see subsection 3.1.2 and 4.1.2). More precisely, a reactions specification for two modelling languages indirectly prescribes under which conditions models of these two modelling languages are consistent. Therefore, we can only show that the reactions language is correct by showing that the execution of reactions always leads to the fulfillment of the consistency conditions that are indirectly given by the reactions.

At the end of our chapter on reactions, in section 6.7, we have shown how consistency rules and update functions as defined in our formal language (see chapter 4) can be constructed for reactions. After this construction, we have also explained which fundamental properties have to be fulfilled by reactions in order to be consistency preserving by construction (see page 210 of section 6.7.4). For such reactions, we have shown that they preserve consistency after a single change that breaks consistency according to a single rule. Broadly speaking, this is only possible because of the prescriptive nature of reactions. We have explained which consistency conditions correspond to a reaction and only had to argue that the execution of the update function that corresponds to the reaction leads to the fulfillment of these conditions. In general, this explains why the execution of reactions that fulfill certain requirements preserves the specific notion of consistency that is indirectly defined using these reactions.

In practice, developers of reactions should not solely rely on our explanations of the semantics of reactions and on their ability to assess which notion of consistency they indirectly specified and whether the reactions meet the formal requirements. They should rather apply well-known techniques such as unit and integration tests or formal verification to validate that the reactions they develop preserve consistency. As the reactions compiler generates Java code, all existing tools and methods for this target language can also be applied to validate the execution of reactions.

9.3.5. Mappings Language Correctness

For the mappings language we will discuss three notions of correctness. First, we will mention again why the execution of mappings correctly preserves the conditions that are explicitly defined with it. Then, we will show that enforcement code is correctly derived from checking code of single-sided conditions. Last, we will prove that inverters for operations of bidirectionalizable conditions are generally composed in such a way that round-trip laws are sustained and that exemplary inverters fulfill these laws.

9.3.5.1. Mappings Correctly Preserve Consistency

In section 7.7, we have explained the semantics of the mappings language by describing a transformation from mappings to reactions. For pure and impure mappings we have presented algorithms and procedures for creating, updating, and deleting model elements in such a way that the fulfillment of mapping conditions for and on one side always co-occurs with the fulfillment of mapping conditions for and on the other side. Furthermore, we have described after which changes these algorithms and procedures have to be executed using reactions. Finally, we have also explained in subsection 7.7.5 why consistency is preserved according to the conditions that are explicitly prescribed with mappings. This argumentation could either be formally proven for the presented mapping realization algorithms or the code that is generated for a mapping could be formally verified. As the consistency conditions are, however, already directly provided in a mapping, the overall preservation process is not complex. How an individual consistency condition has to be preserved is, however, less clear if complex condition operators are used. Therefore, we argue that it is more important to prove that enforcement code is correctly derived from checking code or from enforcement code for the opposite direction than to prove that such enforcement code is invoked whenever it is necessary.

9.3.5.2. Enforcement Correctly Derived from Checks

After this discussion of the overall correctness of mappings, we will now explain why the automated derivation of enforcement code for operators in single-sided conditions is correct. We have provided requirements for correct check and enforcement code of single-sided conditions in subsection 7.3.3. These requirements only state that every negative check has to lead to an enforcement that ensures that a check after the enforcement yields a positive result. That is, those parts of a model for which the check fails have to be fixed using the enforcement code. Furthermore, it is suggested that enforcement after a positive check should not change anything. It is especially important to ensure that these requirements are fulfilled for manually specified pairs of check and enforcement code. The predefined operators for single-sided conditions, however, also have to fulfill them. Therefore, we will briefly show for each of these operators that they meet these requirements.

We have provided code snippets for the enforcement behavior of the predefined operators for single-sided conditions in Table 7.1 on page 232 of section 7.3. For these operators, we will now briefly show that the given enforcement code is correct. As the model state changes that are caused during enforcement are not complex, we refrain from formally proving the requirements, for example, using Hoare logic. Instead, we employ a more concise notation and structure the argument for every operator as follows: First, we show that a negative check result is always fixed by the enforcement code (requirement 1 and 2 on page 237). We provide code snippets to represent a negative check for an initial model state, the enforcement behavior, and the positive check for the resulting model state. To link the negative check and the enforcement, we use the leads-to arrow ($\leadsto$) and to indicate that the enforcement yields the positive check, we use the implication arrow ($\Rightarrow$). We employ the set and list syntax of the reused expression language Xbase to denote unordered collections using curly braces preceded by a hash sign (`#{...}`) and denote ordered collections using square brackets preceded by a hash sign (`#[...]`). Furthermore, we also use `e.a` as a short hand for the result of an invocation of a getter method for the feature `f` on the model element `e`. Moreover, we use the placeholders *`default`* to denote the default value of an attribute and ε to denote the type-dependent minimal value that makes a numerical value greater or less than another numerical value (see subsubsection 7.3.2.1). We do not explain for every operator that it also fulfills the optional requirement that an enforcement after a positive check should have no effect. This can directly be seen from the enforcement code snippet.

Equals operator for a single-valued feature:

```
given: x equals e.f == false
   ⇝ if (x not equals e.f) { e.f.set(x) }
   ⇒ x equals e.f == true
```

Equals operator for a multi-valued feature:

```
given: #{x,y} equals e.f == false
   ⇝ if (#{x,y} not equals e.f) {
        e.f.clear()
        e.f.addAll(#{x,y})
     }
   ⇒ #{x,y} equals e.f == true
```

Negated equals operator for a single-valued attribute (non-null):

```
given: x not equals e.a == false
   ⇝ if (x equals e.a) {
        if (x equals default) { e.a.set(null) }
        else { e.a.set(default) }
     }
   ⇒ x not equals e.a == true
```

Negated equals operator for a multi-valued attribute:

```
given: #{x,y} not equals e.a == false
   ⇝ if (#{x,y} equals e.a) {
        e.a.clear()
     }
   ⇒ #{x,y} not equals e.a == true
```

Entry-in-list operator for a multi-valued feature:

```
given: #{x,y} in e.f == false
   ⇝ for (z : #{x,y}) {
        if (#{z} not in e.f) { e.f.add(z) }
     }
   ⇒ #{x,y} in e.f == true
```

Negated entry-in-list operator for a multi-valued feature:

```
given: #{x,y} not in e.f == false
   ⇝ for (z : #{x,y}) {
        if (#{z} in e.f) { e.f.remove(z) }
     }
   ⇒ #{x,y} not in e.f == true
```

At-index-in-list operator for a multi-valued feature:

```
given: x at index i in e.f == false
   ⇝ if (x not at index i in e.f) { e.f.set(i,x) }
   ⇒ x at index i in e.f == true
```

Negated at-index-in-list operator for a multi-valued attribute:

```
given: x not at index i in e.a == false
   ⇝ if (x at index i in e.a) { e.f.set(i,default) }
   ⇒ x not at index i in e.a == true
```

Empty-list operator for a multi-valued feature:

```
given: empty e.f == false
   ⇝ if (not empty e.f) { e.f.clear() }
   ⇒ empty e.f == true
```

Negated empty-list operator for a multi-valued attribute:

```
given: not empty e.a == false
   ⇝ if (empty e.a) { e.a.add(default) }
   ⇒ not empty e.a == true
```

Not-greater-than operator for single-valued numerical attributes:

```
given: x <= e.a == false
   ⇝ if (x > e.a) { e.a += x-e.a }
   ⇒ x <= e.a == true
```

Less-than operator for single-valued numerical attributes:

```
given: x < e.a == false
   ⇝ if (x >= e.a) { e.a += x-e.a+ε }
   ⇒ x < e.a == true
```

Not-less-than operator for single-valued numerical attributes:

```
given: x >= e.a == false
   ⇝ if (x < e.a) { e.a -= e.a-v }
   ⇒ x >= e.a == true
```

Greater-than operator for single-valued numerical attributes:

```
given: x > e.a == false
   ⇝ if (x <= e.a) { e.a -= e.a-v+ε }
   ⇒ x > e.a == true
```

This shows that all pre-defined operators for single-sided conditions of the mappings language are correctly enforced.

9.3.5.3. Correct Inversion According to Round-Trip Laws

The last notion of correctness that we discuss for the mappings language, is the correctness of the automated derivation of inverse enforcement. To show this correctness, we formally prove well-behavedness and best-possible behavedness for our generic composition inverter and for exemplary individual inverters of our operator categories. These proofs and the text of the remaining section are based on an article [KR16a] and a technical report [KR16b].

Best-Possible Behavedness with Respect to a Partition In order to be precise enough for the proofs, we first refine our notion of best-possible behavedness, which we have presented in subsubsection 7.4.2.2. To this end, we define best-possible behavedness with respect to a partition of target values based on the definition of best-possible behavedness (Definition 46):

> **Definition 47 (Best-Possible Behaved w.r.t. a Partition)**
> *A pair of an operation and inverse operation* (op, $\text{op}^{\leftarrow}$) *is* best-possible behaved with respect to *a partition W, B of the set of possible target values iff*
>
> 1. (op, $\text{op}^{\leftarrow}$) *is best-possible behaved such that*
> 2. *the* PutGet *law holds for all values in W and*
> 3. *the* PutGet *cannot hold for any value in B.*

Based on this refined notion, our proofs for best-possible behavedness always have the same structure: for the partition W, B of the set of possible target values, we show that

I. the GetPut law holds for all source values,

II. the PutGet law holds for all target values in W, and

III. a contradiction is obtained for every inverter that would fulfill the PutGet law for a target value in B.

Best-Possible Behavedness is Compositional We have already mentioned in subsection 7.4.5 that our inversion approach is compositional. Now, we will formally proof that the composition operator and its inverse operator sustain best-possible behavedness as this also implies that they sustain well-behavedness. More precisely, we will show that best-possible behavedness is compositional by showing the following: if two inverters are best-possible behaved, then the composed inverter that combines these two inverters is also best-possible behaved.

Lemma 1 (*Best-Possible Behavedness is Compositional*)
Let $\mathrm{op}_1^{\leftarrow}(t,s)$ and $\mathrm{op}_2^{\leftarrow}(t,s)$ be two inverters for two operators $\mathrm{op}_1(s)$ and $\mathrm{op}_2(s)$ such that $\mathrm{op}_1^{\leftarrow}$ is best-possible behaved with respect to the partition W_1, B_1 and $\mathrm{op}_2^{\leftarrow}$ is best-possible behaved with respect to the partition W_2, B_2. Furthermore, let W_2 include the image of W_1 under $\mathrm{op}_1^{\leftarrow}$ and let S denote the set of all source values. Moreover, let $\mathrm{op}_1^{\leftarrow}[W_1, S]$ denote the image of W_1 and S under $\mathrm{op}_1^{\leftarrow}$, then $\mathrm{op}_1^{\leftarrow}[W_1, S] \subset W_2$.

The composed inverter $\mathrm{op}_{1\circ 2}^{\leftarrow}(t,s) := \mathrm{op}_2^{\leftarrow}(\mathrm{op}_1^{\leftarrow}(t, \mathrm{op}_2(s)), s)$ *for the composition operator* $\mathrm{op}_{1\circ 2}(s) = \mathrm{op}_1(\mathrm{op}_2(s))$ *is best-possible behaved with respect to the partition* W_1, B_1.

The requirements of the round-trip laws GetPut and PutGet for the composition operator and its inverse are illustrated in Figure 9.1 and 9.2. In these figures, we relate individual steps and arrows to usages of the best-possible behavedness of $\mathrm{op}_1^{\leftarrow}$ and $\mathrm{op}_2^{\leftarrow}$ by referencing the numbers of the appropriate equations in the proof.

Proof 3
"I."

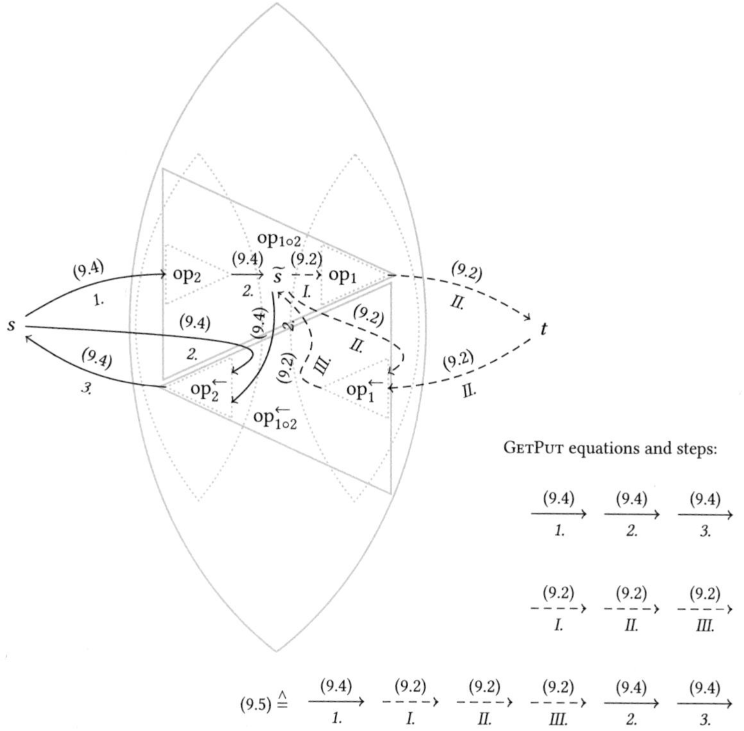

Figure 9.1.: Illustration of the GetPut part of the proof of well-behavedness for the composition operator using the lenses analogy

First, we show that the composed inverter always fulfills the GetPut *law: Let s be a source value. Then*

$$\overleftarrow{\mathrm{op}}_{1\circ 2}(\mathrm{op}_{1\circ 2}(s), s) = \overleftarrow{\mathrm{op}}_{1\circ 2}(\mathrm{op}_1(\mathrm{op}_2(s)), s)$$

by the definition of composition. The definition of inverse composition yields

$$\overleftarrow{\mathrm{op}}_{1\circ 2}(\mathrm{op}_{1\circ 2}(s), s) = \overleftarrow{\mathrm{op}}_2(\overleftarrow{\mathrm{op}}_1(\mathrm{op}_1(\mathrm{op}_2(s)), \mathrm{op}_2(s)), s) \tag{9.1}$$

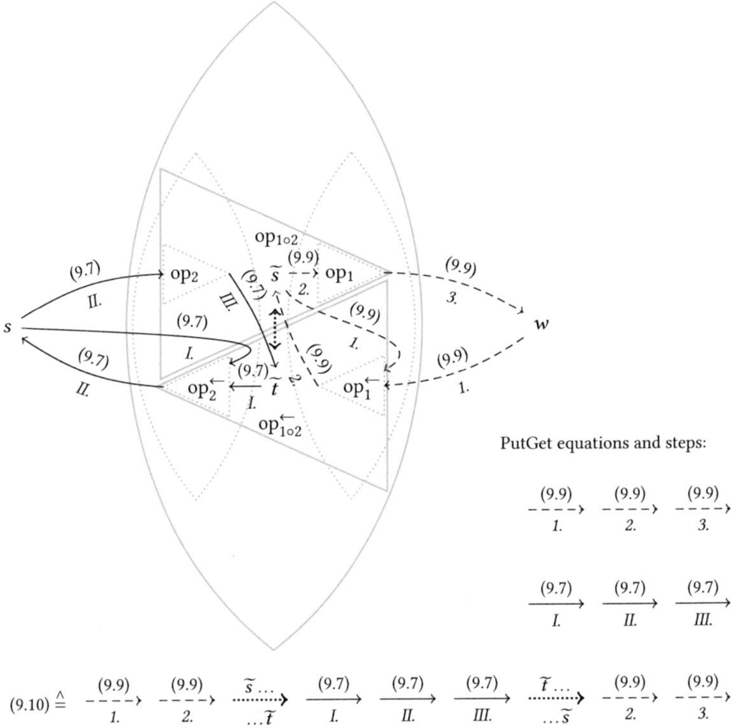

Figure 9.2.: Illustration of the PUTGET part of the proof of well-behavedness for the composition operator using the lenses analogy

Because $\mathrm{op}_1^{\leftarrow}$ *is best-possible behaved, it fulfills the* GETPUT *law for the source value* $\widetilde{s} := \mathrm{op}_2(s)$. *This means,*

$$\mathrm{op}_1^{\leftarrow}(\mathrm{op}_1(\widetilde{s}), \widetilde{s}) = \mathrm{op}_1^{\leftarrow}(\mathrm{op}_1(\mathrm{op}_2(s)), \mathrm{op}_2(s)) = \widetilde{s} = \mathrm{op}_2(s) \qquad (9.2)$$

With this, we obtain from (9.1) *and* (9.2)

$$\mathrm{op}_{1\circ 2}^{\leftarrow}(\mathrm{op}_{1\circ 2}(s), s) = \mathrm{op}_2^{\leftarrow}(\mathrm{op}_2(s), s) \qquad (9.3)$$

Because $\text{op}_2^{\leftarrow}$ *is best-possible behaved, it fulfills the* GetPut *law for s:*

$$\text{op}_2^{\leftarrow}(\text{op}_2(s), s) = s \tag{9.4}$$

With this, we finally obtain from (9.3) *and* (9.4)

$$\text{op}_{1\circ 2}^{\leftarrow}(\text{op}_{1\circ 2}(s), s) = s \tag{9.5}$$

This shows that the GetPut *law holds for the composed inverter* $\text{op}_{1\circ 2}^{\leftarrow}$ *and all source values s.*

"II."

Second, we show that the composed inverter fulfills the PutGet *law for all values in* W_1*: Let w be a target value in* W_1 *and let s be an arbitrary source value. Then*

$$\text{op}_{1\circ 2}(\text{op}_{1\circ 2}^{\leftarrow}(w, s)) = \text{op}_{1\circ 2}(\text{op}_2^{\leftarrow}(\text{op}_1^{\leftarrow}(w, \text{op}_2(s)), s))$$

by the definition of the inverse composition. The definition of composition yields

$$\text{op}_{1\circ 2}(\text{op}_{1\circ 2}^{\leftarrow}(w, s)) = \text{op}_1(\text{op}_2(\text{op}_2^{\leftarrow}(\text{op}_1^{\leftarrow}(w, \text{op}_2(s)), s)))$$

We define $\tilde{t} := \text{op}_1^{\leftarrow}(w, \text{op}_2(s))$ *and obtain*

$$\text{op}_{1\circ 2}(\text{op}_{1\circ 2}^{\leftarrow}(w, s)) = \text{op}_1(\text{op}_2(\text{op}_2^{\leftarrow}(\tilde{t}, s))) \tag{9.6}$$

We chose w to be in W_1*. Therefore,* $\tilde{t}$ *is in* $\text{op}_1^{\leftarrow}[W_1, S]$ *and also in* W_2*. Thus,* op_2 *fulfills the* PutGet *law for* $\tilde{t}$*, which means*

$$\text{op}_2(\text{op}_2^{\leftarrow}(\tilde{t}, s)) = \tilde{t} \tag{9.7}$$

With this, we obtain from (9.6)

$$\text{op}_{1\circ 2}(\text{op}_{1\circ 2}^{\leftarrow}(w, s)) = \text{op}_1(\tilde{t})$$

, which stands for

$$\text{op}_{1\circ 2}(\text{op}_{1\circ 2}^{\leftarrow}(w, s)) = \text{op}_1(\text{op}_1^{\leftarrow}(w, \text{op}_2(s))) \tag{9.8}$$

For w in W_1 and $\widetilde{s} := \mathrm{op}_2(s)$, the first operator op_1 fulfills the PutGet *law, which means*

$$\mathrm{op}_1(\overleftarrow{\mathrm{op}_1}(w, \widetilde{s})) = w \tag{9.9}$$

With (9.8) this yields

$$\mathrm{op}_{1\circ 2}(\overleftarrow{\mathrm{op}_{1\circ 2}}(w, s)) = w \tag{9.10}$$

Thus the PutGet *law holds for all w in W_1.*

"III."

Last, we show that the PutGet *law cannot hold for any value in B_1: Assume $\overleftarrow{\mathrm{op}_{1\circ 2}}$ fulfills the* PutGet *law for an arbitrary target value b in B_1 and all source values. We indirectly define s through $b := \mathrm{op}_{1\circ 2}(s)$. Then $\overleftarrow{\mathrm{op}_{1\circ 2}}$ fulfills the* PutGet *law for b and s:*

$$\mathrm{op}_{1\circ 2}(\overleftarrow{\mathrm{op}_{1\circ 2}}(b, s)) = b$$

By the definition of the inverse composition this yields

$$\mathrm{op}_{1\circ 2}(\overleftarrow{\mathrm{op}_2}(\overleftarrow{\mathrm{op}_1}(b, \mathrm{op}_2(s)), s)) = b$$

The definition of composition yields

$$\mathrm{op}_1(\mathrm{op}_2(\overleftarrow{\mathrm{op}_2}(\overleftarrow{\mathrm{op}_1}(b, \mathrm{op}_2(s)), s))) = b$$

By applying the definition of b on both sides we obtain

$$\mathrm{op}_1(\mathrm{op}_2(\overleftarrow{\mathrm{op}_2}(\overleftarrow{\mathrm{op}_1}(\mathrm{op}_{1\circ 2}(s), \mathrm{op}_2(s)), s))) = \mathrm{op}_{1\circ 2}(s)$$

Then, the definition of composition yields

$$\mathrm{op}_1(\mathrm{op}_2(\overleftarrow{\mathrm{op}_2}(\overleftarrow{\mathrm{op}_1}(\mathrm{op}_1(\mathrm{op}_2(s)), \mathrm{op}_2(s)), s))) = \mathrm{op}_1(\mathrm{op}_2(s))$$

Removing the application of $\mathrm{op}_{1\circ 2}$ on both sides yields

$$\overleftarrow{\mathrm{op}_2}(\overleftarrow{\mathrm{op}_1}(\mathrm{op}_1(\mathrm{op}_2(s)), \mathrm{op}_2(s)), s) = s$$

Because $\text{op}_2^{\leftarrow}$ *fulfills the* GetPut *law for* s*, we can replace* s *on the right side and obtain*

$$\text{op}_2^{\leftarrow}(\text{op}_1^{\leftarrow}(\text{op}_1(\text{op}_2(s)), \text{op}_2(s)), s) = \text{op}_2^{\leftarrow}(\text{op}_2(s), s)$$

We remove the application of $\text{op}_2^{\leftarrow}(\ldots, s)$ *on both sides, which yields*

$$\text{op}_1^{\leftarrow}(\text{op}_1(\text{op}_2(s)), \text{op}_2(s)) = \text{op}_2(s)$$

Then, we apply op_1 *on both sides and obtain*

$$\text{op}_1(\text{op}_1^{\leftarrow}(\text{op}_1(\text{op}_2(s)), \text{op}_2(s))) = \text{op}_1(\text{op}_2(s))$$

The definition of composition yields

$$\text{op}_1(\text{op}_1^{\leftarrow}(\text{op}_{1\circ 2}(s), \text{op}_2(s))) = \text{op}_{1\circ 2}(s)$$

Finally, using the definition of b*, we obtain*

$$\text{op}_1(\text{op}_1^{\leftarrow}(b), \text{op}_2(s))) = b$$

This is a contradiction to the requirement that $\text{op}_1^{\leftarrow}$ *does not fulfill the* PutGet *law for* b*. Therefore, our assumption is wrong, which shows that the* PutGet *law cannot hold for any value in* B_1*.*

Altogether, the GetPut *law holds for all* s*, the* PutGet *law holds for all values in* W_1 *and cannot hold for any value in* B_1*. Therefore, we conclude that* $\text{op}_{1\circ 2}^{\leftarrow}$ *is best-possible behaved with respect to the partition* W_1, B_1*.* ■

Proofs for Individual Inverters Now that we have proven that composed operations are correctly inverted, we present proofs for some exemplary operator-specific inverters. All inverters, which we presented in subsection 7.4.6, are best-possible behaved and the proofs for this best-possible behavedness are mostly straightforward applications of the definitions of the operators and their inverters. Therefore, we do not present proofs for all inverters but only for three exemplary operators. With these exemplary proofs, we illustrate how the general proof template is used for operators with different properties, e.g. floating-point involvement or several operands influencing the fulfillment of round-trip laws.

> **Lemma 2** (*Inversion of* pow *is Best-Possible Behaved*)
> *The inverter of the* abs *operator (see page 258 of section 7.4.6.4) is best-possible behaved with respect to the partition*
>
> $$W := \{t \in \text{Num} \mid t \geq 0\}, B := \{t \in \text{Num} \mid t < 0\}$$

Proof 4
Let s be a source value. Then

$$\text{abs}^{\leftarrow}(\text{abs}(s), s) = \text{abs}^{\leftarrow}(|s|, s) = \text{sign4mult}(s) \cdot |s|$$

If $s \geq 0$*, this yields*

$$1 \cdot s = s$$

Otherwise $s < 0$*, which yields*

$$-1 \cdot -1 \cdot s = s$$

Thus, the GetPut *law holds for all s.*

Let w be a target value w in W and let s be an arbitrary source value. Then

$$\text{abs}(\text{abs}^{\leftarrow}(w, s)) = \text{abs}(\text{sign4mult}(s) \cdot w)$$

If $s \geq 0$*, this yields*

$$\text{abs}(1 \cdot w) = \text{abs}(w) = w$$

because $w \geq 0$*. Otherwise* $s < 0$*, which yields*

$$\text{abs}(-1 \cdot w) = \text{abs}(-w) = w$$

Thus, the PutGet *law holds for all w in W .*

Assume $\text{abs}^{-1'}$ *is an inverse operator for* abs *that fulfills the* PutGet *law for a target value b in B and an arbitrary source value s. Then*

$$\text{abs}(\text{abs}^{-1'}(b, s)) = b$$

This yields

$$|\text{abs}^{-1'}(b, s)| = b < 0$$

which is a contradiction to the definition of the absolute value operator because $|x| \geq 0$ *for all* x.

Altogether, the GETPUT *law holds for all s, the* PUTGET *law holds for all w in W and cannot hold for any inverse operator* $\text{abs}^{-1'}$ *and b in B. Therefore, we conclude that* $\text{abs}^{\leftarrow}$ *is a best-possible behaved inverter.* ∎

Lemma 3 (*Base-Inversion of* pow *is Best-Possible Behaved*)
For the exponentiation operator pow *(see page 261 of section 7.4.6.4), the inverter* $\text{pow}_1^{\leftarrow}$ *for inversion according to the base is best-possible behaved with respect to the partition* W_1, P_1 *such that*

$$\begin{aligned} W_1 :=& \{(t, e) \in \text{Num} \times \text{Double} \mid t \geq 0 \ \wedge e \textit{ is even}\} \cup \\ & \{(t, e) \in \text{Num} \times \text{Double} \mid e \textit{ is not even}\}, \textit{ and} \\ P_1 :=& \{(t, e) \in \text{Num} \times \text{Double} \mid t < 0 \ \wedge e \textit{ is even}\} \end{aligned}$$

Before we prove this lemma we briefly explain the used partition W_1, P_1 The exponentiation operator pow is one of the operators with more than one operand for which it is not sufficient to partition the space of possible target values to prove best-possible behavedness. Instead, we have to partition the space of tuples that contains a possible target value and a source value for every additional operand that influences the fulfillment of the rount-trip laws (except —of course— for the operand according to which we are inverting).

Proof 5
Let b be a base source value and e be an exponent source value. If e is not even, then

$$\text{pow}_1^{\leftarrow}(\text{pow}(b, e), b, e) = \text{sign4mult}(b^e) \cdot \sqrt[e]{|b^e|} = \text{sign4mult}(b) \cdot \sqrt[e]{|b^e|}$$

because $\text{sign4mult}(b^e) = \text{sign4mult}(b)$ *for all e that are not even. If* $b \geq 0$, *we obtain*

$$\sqrt[e]{b^e} = b$$

Otherwise $b < 0$ *and we obtain*

$$-1 \cdot \sqrt[e]{|b^e|} = b$$

If e *is even, then*

$$\text{pow}_1^{\leftarrow}(\text{pow}(b, e), b, e) = \text{sign4mult}(b) \cdot \sqrt[e]{b^e}$$

because $\text{pow}(b, e) = b^e \geq 0$ *for all* b *and all even* e*. If* $b \geq 0$*, we obtain*

$$\sqrt[e]{b^e} = b$$

Otherwise $b < 0$ *and we obtain*

$$-1 \cdot \sqrt[e]{b^e} = b$$

because e *is even. Altogether, we obtain*

$$\text{pow}_1^{\leftarrow}(\text{pow}(b, e), b, e) = b$$

for all possible b *and* e*. Thus the* GetPut *law holds for all base values* b *and exponent values* e*.*

Let (t_w, e) *be a tuple of target and exponent source value in* W_1 *and let* b *be an arbitrary base source value. If* e *is not even, then*

$$\text{pow}(\text{pow}_1^{\leftarrow}(t_w, b, e), e) = \text{pow}(\text{sign4mult}(t_w) \cdot \sqrt[e]{|t_w|}, e)$$

If $t_w \geq 0$*, we obtain*

$$\text{pow}(\sqrt[e]{t_w}, e) = \sqrt[e]{t_w}^{\,e} = t_w$$

Otherwise $t_w < 0$ *and we obtain*

$$\text{pow}(-1 \cdot \sqrt[e]{|t_w|}, e) = (-\sqrt[e]{|t_w|})^e = t_w$$

If e *is even, then* $t_w \geq 0$ *by construction of* W_1 *and*

$$\text{pow}(\text{pow}_1^{\leftarrow}(t_w, b, e), e) = \text{pow}(\text{sign4mult}(b) \cdot \sqrt[e]{t_w}, e) =$$
$$= (\text{sign4mult}(b) \cdot \sqrt[e]{t_w})^e = \sqrt[e]{t_w}^{\,e} = t_w$$

because $|\text{sign4mult}(b)| = 1$ *for all* b *and* $x^e = 1$ *for all even* e *and* x *such that* $|x| = 1$. *Thus the* PUTGET *law holds for all* (t_w, e) *in* W_1.

Assume $\text{pow}_1^{-1'}$ *inverts* pow *according to the base and fulfills the* PUTGET *law for a target value* t_p, *an exponent source value* e_p *such that* (t_p, e_p) *in* P_1, *and an arbitrary base source value* b. *Then*

$$\text{pow}(\text{pow}_1^{-1'}(t_p, b, e_p), e_p) = t_p$$

This yields

$$(\text{pow}_1^{-1'}(t_p, b, e_p))^{e_p} = t_p < 0$$

which is a contradiction to the definition of exponentiation because e_p *is even by the construction of* P_1 *and it holds that* $x^e \geq 0$ *for all even* e *and all* x.

Altogether, the GETPUT *law holds for all base values* b *and exponent values* e, *the* PUTGET *law holds for all* (t_w, e) *in* W_1 *and cannot hold for any inverse operator* $\text{pow}_1^{-1'}$ *and* (t_p, e_p) *in* P_1. *Therefore, we conclude that* $\text{pow}_1^{\leftarrow}$ *is a best-possible behaved inverter.* ∎

Lemma 4 (*Exponent-Inversion of* pow *is Best-Possible Behaved*)
For the exponentiation operator pow *(see page 261 of section 7.4.6.4), the inverter* $\text{pow}_2^{\leftarrow}$ *for inversion according to the exponent is best-possible behaved with respect to the partition* W_2, P_2 *such that*

$$W_2 := \{(t, b) \in \text{Num} \times \text{Num} \mid b^{log_{|b|}(|t|)} \overset{\varepsilon}{=} t\}, \textit{ and}$$
$$P_2 := \{(t, b) \in \text{Num} \times \text{Num} \mid b^{log_{|b|}(|t|)} \overset{\varepsilon}{\neq} t\}$$

Proof 6
Let b *be a base source value and* e *be an exponent source value. Then*

$$\text{pow}_2^{\leftarrow}(\text{pow}(b, e), b, e) = e$$

by definition of $\text{pow}_2^{\leftarrow}$ *because* $\text{pow}(b, e) = b^e$. *Thus, the* GETPUT *law holds for all base values* b *and exponent values* e.

Let (t_w, b_w) be a tuple of target and base source value in W_2 and let e be an arbitrary exponent source value. If $(b_w)^e = t_w$, then

$$\text{pow}(b_w, \text{pow}_2^{\leftarrow}(t_w, b_w, e)) = \text{pow}(b_w, e) = (b_w)^e = t_w$$

If $(b_w)^e \neq t_w$, then

$$(b_w)^{log_{|b_w|}(|t_w|)} \stackrel{\varepsilon}{=} t_w$$

by the definition of W_2. This yields

$$\text{pow}(b_w, \text{pow}_2^{\leftarrow}(t_w, b_w, e)) = \text{pow}(b_w, log_{|b_w|}(|t_w|)) =$$
$$= (b_w)^l og_{|b_w|}(|t_w|) \stackrel{\varepsilon}{=} t_w$$

Thus, the PutGet *law holds for all (t_w, b_w) in W_2, except for negligible floating-point inaccuracies.*

Assume $\text{pow}_2^{-1'}$ *inverts* pow *according to the exponent and fulfills the* PutGet *law for a target value t_p, a base source value b_p such that (t_p, b_p) in P_2, and an arbitrary exponent source value e. Then*

$$\text{pow}(b_p, \text{pow}_2^{-1'}(t_p, b_p, e)) = t_p$$

This yields

$$(b_p)^{\text{pow}_2^{-1'}(t_p, b_p, e)} = t_p \stackrel{\varepsilon}{\neq} (b_p)^{log_{|b_p|}(|t_p|)}$$

which is a contradiction to the definition of the logarithm operator because $x^y \stackrel{\varepsilon}{=} x^{log_{|x|}(|y|)}$ for all x and y.

Altogether, the GetPut *law holds for all base values b and exponent values e, the* PutGet *law holds for all (t_w, b_w) in W_2 and cannot hold for any inverse operator* $\text{pow}_2^{-1'}$ *and (t_p, e_p) in P_2. Therefore, we conclude that* $\text{pow}_2^{\leftarrow}$ *is a best-possible behaved inverter.* ■

Lemma 5 (*Inversion of* sin *is Best-Possible Behaved*)
The inverter of the trigonometric sin *operator (see page 262 of section 7.4.6.4) is best-possible behaved with respect to the partition* W, B *such that*

$$W := \{t \in \text{Double} \mid -1 \leq t \leq 1\}, \text{ and}$$
$$B := \{t \in \text{Double} \mid |t| > 1\}$$

Proof 7
Let s *be a source value. Then*

$$\sin^{\leftarrow}(\sin(s), s) = s$$

by definition of $\sin^{\leftarrow}$ *because* $\sin(source) \stackrel{\varepsilon}{=} \sin(source)$. *Thus the* GetPut *law holds for all* s.

Let w *be a target value* w *in* W *and let* s *be an arbitrary source value. If* $\sin(s) \stackrel{\varepsilon}{=} w$, *then*

$$\sin(\sin^{\leftarrow}(w, s)) = \sin(s) \stackrel{\varepsilon}{=} w$$

Otherwise

$$\sin(\sin^{\leftarrow}(w, s)) = \sin(\text{asin}(w)) = w$$

by the definition of asin. *Thus the* PutGet *law holds for all* w *in* W, *except for negligible floating-point inaccuracies.*

Assume $\sin^{-1'}$ *is an inverse operator for* sin *that fulfills the* PutGet *law for a target value* b *in* B *and an arbitrary source value* s. *Then*

$$\sin(\sin^{-1'}(b, s)) = b$$

This is a contradiction to the definition of the sine operator because $|\sin(x)| \leq 1$ *for all* x.

Altogether, the GetPut *law holds for all* s, *the* PutGet *law holds for all* w *in* W *and cannot hold for any inverse operator* $\sin^{-1'}$ *and* b *in* B. *Therefore, we conclude that* $\sin^{\leftarrow}$ *is a best-possible behaved inverter.* ■

9.3.6. Invariants Correctly Transformed to Queries

In this last section on theoretical properties of the languages presented in this thesis, we discuss the correctness of the invariant-to-query transformation of the invariants language (see section 8.2). The input for this transformation is a context metaclass and a constraint of an invariant as well as an explicit invariant parameter that has the same identifier as an iterator variable of an iterator expression in the constraint and a compatible type. In order to be correct, the output of this transformation has to be a query that fulfills the following properties with respect to an arbitrary instance of the context metaclass, which is briefly called context element:

1. The query has to yield an empty collection of elements for a context element iff the constraint evaluates to `false` for the context element.
2. In all other cases, the query has to yield a non-empty result collection of elements such that
   a) every element of the result collection is bound to the iterator variable in at least one iteration of the iterator expression when the invariant constraint is evaluated for the context element
   b) for every element of the result collection, the following implication has to hold for the collection that is iterated for the iterator expression when the invariant constraint is evaluated for the context element: if the original collection is replaced with a collection that only contains the element in question of the result collection, then an evaluation of the iterator expression on this replacement collection yields `false` if the result type of the iterator expression is boolean and otherwise it yields the replacement collection

These conditions specify precisely what it means for a query to yield elements "that are responsible for the violation and that were accessed during the evaluation via the iterator variable". To show that our query derivation approach is correct, one would have to show that these properties are fulfilled for the intermediate results of each transformation rule that we have presented in subsection 8.2.6. In order to show the correctness of a specific query that is generated by the invariants language, one would have to prove that these properties are fulfilled for it. As the generated Xtend query compiles to Java code, existing code verification tools for Java, such as KeY [BHS07], could again be applied. The transformation rules are, however, just applications of fundamental inference rules of first-order predicate logic. Therefore, we expect that the interest of proving correctness of the transformation rules or correctness for a particular query is in many contexts probably not considered worth the effort.

9.4. Evaluation of Practical Applicability

To evaluate the practical applicability of the languages presented in this thesis, we have examined whether they can be applied in practice to realize realistic consistency requirements and whether the results obtained from the created specifications are as expected. The most important expectations for the results of such practical applications are the theoretically guaranteed properties, which we discussed in detail in the previous sections. This means by having evaluated the applicability of the languages we have also indirectly evaluated whether the languages were realized in such a way that theoretically guaranteed completeness and correctness are not lost during realization.

9.4.1. Application of the Formal Language

The formal language is the only language presented in this thesis that cannot be processed in an automated way because it is not realized as software but only formally described in chapter 4 of this thesis. All other languages are realized in terms of a compiler except for the change modelling language, for which instances are obtained in an automated transformation from monitor-specific change descriptions.

Because of the missing technical realization for the formal language, the only practical application of it is its use to explain the semantics of the reactions language (see section 6.7) and thus also indirectly the semantics of the mappings language (see section 7.7). We consider this application of the formal language successful, because it helped us to *write* the explanations of the semantics of the reactions language. This was also achieved by adapting the definitions of the formal language in several iterations to cover everything that we deemed necessary for the explanations but nothing more. The expected result of the application of the formal language is, however, also that it becomes easier to *understand* the semantics of the reactions language. We did, however, not perform an empirical evaluation of this claim in order to focus on evaluating the other languages and other properties.

9.4.2. Application of the Change Modelling Language

We have indirectly evaluated whether the change modelling language, which was presented in subsection 5.4.1, can be applied in practice by using it as an intermediate language for triggering consistency preservation code that is generated for reactions. The change modelling language is used as a target in two model transformations in order to enable reactions to changes in editors. In the first transformation, instances of the change modelling language are created for changes that are performed in the Java code editor of the Eclipse Integrated Development Environment (IDE). The second transformation also creates instances of the change modelling language but it is not bound to a specific editor: It can be used for any models that are created based on the Eclipse Modeling Framework (EMF) and therefore conform to a metamodel that was created using the EMOF-variant Ecore (see subsubsection 2.1.3.2). We have used it for all case studies in which we applied the reactions and mappings language. If consistency shall be preserved for models that are changed with editors that are not built using EMF, then further transformations are necessary to express the changes as instances of the change modelling language. This means, the change modelling language is used as an intermediate language in the current transformations and can also be used by future transformations to represent changes for which consistency shall be preserved using reactions. The Java code that is generated by the reactions compiler uses the editor-agnostic change representations to determine which code for which reactions has to be executed based on the trigger definitions of the reactions. For all changes that occurred in the different applications of the reactions language the expected change representations were created using the change modelling language and further processed by reactions. This demonstrates the practical applicability of the change modelling language.

9.4.3. Application of OCL-Aligned Expressions and Invariants

In subsection 5.4.3, we presented 27 collection operators and iterators that form an OCL-aligned extension for the reused expressions language. To evaluate this expressions extension and the invariants language, we have applied them to those invariants of the UML metamodel[2] that can be expressed with it [Fis15, p.40][FKL16, p.201]. The metamodel contained 420 OCL invariants. We skipped 175 syntactically trivial invariants that only contain direct comparisons of results by calling getters and simple operators such as `implies` or `not`. Out of the 245 remaining invariants, 88 contained the supported collection operators and iterators but no unsupported language constructs such as nested definitions of temporary variables. We successfully applied the invariants language and the OCL-aligned expression extension to manually create equivalent invariants for each of these 88 UML invariants. In addition, we have also successfully translated more than 330 out of the 420 OCL invariants automatically to invariants that use the collection operators and iterators and other operators that are provided by the reused expression language. For this, we extracted all invariants from the Ecore-based metamodel of the UML and parsed them using Eclipse's OCL parser. We obtained an AST for every invariant and performed a model-to-text transformation on it to output functionally equivalent constraints for the invariants language. Together, the manual re-implementation and the automated translation of UML invariants show the practical applicability of the invariants language and of the OCL-aligned expressions extension.

9.4.4. Applications of Reactions

To evaluate the practical applicability of the reactions language we have used it in four case studies to develop tools that preserve consistency between models of different languages. In the first case study, the reactions language was used to support the coevolution of architectural models and object-oriented source code during the development of component-based software [Kra+15]. Reactions were developed to keep object-oriented code consistent after changes in architectural models.In the second case study, we have kept architectural models consistent after changes in component-based

[2] http://www.eclipse.org/uml2/5.0.0/UML metamodel revision from 2014-12-14

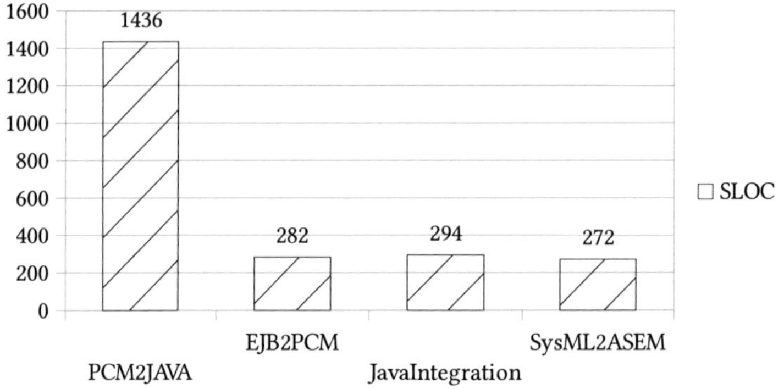

Figure 9.3.: Source lines of code (SLOC) for reactions in different case studies

source-code. The third case study was concerned with the preservation of consistency between architectural models and object-oriented code that that was integrated from an existing code base and does not fulfill the original consistency constraints. In the last case study, consistency was preserved for two modelling languages that are used in the automotive domain. Software models for embedded microcontrollers were kept consistent to model changes for block diagram of the Systems Modeling Language (SysML) [Obj15].

In Figure 9.3, we illustrate the amount of reactions code that was developed in the case studies. We measured the Source Lines of Code (SLOC) by counting all lines in the source code files that are not empty and that contain something else than code comments. This means, we exclude only those lines that are also ignored by compilers because they never influence the program behavior.

9.4.4.1. Component-Based Architectures and Object-Oriented Code

In the first case study, the reactions language was used to preserve consistency between models of an Architectural Description Language (ADL) and object-oriented Java code. We will briefly introduce the involved languages and the realized consistency requirements, which are discussed in detail by Langhammer [Lan17].

To represent software-components and the relations between them, the Palladio Component Model (PCM) [Reu+11] was used in the first case study for the reactions language. It is an ADL that models reusable components as well as the interfaces that they provide and require in a system-independent repository. Concrete systems are expressed in terms of so-called assembly contexts to instantiate components. The roles for their provided and required interfaces are linked using assembly connectors. To illustrate the reactions language, we used a running example that is inspired from this case study (see section 6.2). This example discussed only a small part of the PCM in a simplified way, but it introduced the main concepts. As the PCM is part of the Palladio Approach [RHK16] for architectural simulations and analyses, it provides much more concepts, for example, to model resource-demands of services for performance predictions.

To obtain a model representation of Java source code, we used the Java Model Printer and Parser (JaMoPP) [Hei+10]. This made it possible to define reactions that process instances of an Ecore-based metamodel for Java and not source code in a textual format. As a result, the reactions code in this case study did not need to consider the fact that source code changes were processed or produced. Furthermore, changes that are performed in the common Java editor of the Eclipse IDE were represented as changes of the Java model by transforming the involved change representations (see subsection 9.4.2).

The main challenge of co-evolving architectural models and object-oriented code for software that is developed in terms of components is to represent components in a suitable way in the code. Langhammer [Lan17] presents different ways to achieve this in his dissertation. We have evaluated the practical applicability of the reactions language, only for two of these alternatives. In this first case study, reactions were developed to ensure that code for Plain Old Java Objects (POJOs) is co-evolved in a consistent way with PCM-based models (see subsection 6.2.3). For this, components are realized in terms of so-called component realization classes with an appropriate package structure. Such a component-realization class contains, for example, methods for all provided services of the component. Another alternative for relating component models and code was evaluated in the second case study, which we describe in the following.

9.4.4.2. Component-Based Code and Architectures

In the second case study for the reactions language, PCM-based software architecture models are kept consistent after changes in source code with an explicit notion of components. For this, the Enterprise Java Bean (EJB) standard was used [Sak09]. It gives developers the possibility to designate, for example, Java classes as component classes by marking them with annotations for different types of so-called beans. Furthermore, component interfaces can be realized as Java interfaces with appropriate annotations so that the ordinary implements-relation between classes and interfaces can also be used to express that a component respectively bean realizes an interface. Such annotations are inspected by the reactions that keep the corresponding architectural models consistent for Palladio [Lan17].

9.4.4.3. Coevolution Integration of Object-Oriented Code

The reactions of the third case study have been developed in order to keep architectural models consistent after changes in legacy code. These architectural models are reverse engineered from the code base [Lan17]. The obtained model and the legacy code can be integrated into the Vitruvius framework for consistent co-evolution. Object-oriented code that was developed without the automated consistency preservation for component-based models does, however, usually not have an appropriate structure to be co-evolved afterwards. Therefore, particular consistency preservation logic is needed in order to support as much edit operations on the legacy code as possible during the co-evolution with the architectural models. This particular logic was specified with reactions. The consistency preservation rules for newly created code, however, were defined before the reactions language was developed and therefore written in Xtend. The other preservation direction for keeping code consistent with changes in architectural models was, however, realized with reactions and is the first case study, which we have described above.

9.4.4.4. Automotive Software Models and SysML

The third and last case study in which we have evaluated the applicability of the reactions language was performed in the context of automotive software engineering. This case study was performed in cooperation with an industrial partner in order to obtain realistic consistency requirements for this special domain. The partner uses a proprietary language to model software for Electronic Control Units (ECU) and to generate C code from it. For the case study, we have developed a modelling language that is structurally equivalent to a subset of this property language and called it Automotive Software Engineering Metamodel (ASEM). It mainly covers modules and classes that communicate using messages and methods. The goal of the case study was to preserve consistency between such domain-specific models and models that were created using the general-purpose Systems Modeling Language (SysML) [Obj15]. SysML uses and extends a subset of the UML for systems engineering and supports 9 diagram types that are categorized in three different types for requirements, structural, and behavioral modelling. The consistency requirements that have been realized using the reactions language are concerned with ASEM models and with structural block diagrams of the SysML. Changes that are applied to blocks and their ports in SysML models are kept consistent with corresponding modules, classes, messages, and methods in ASEM models. Development of the consistency preservation tools for the automotive case study was not finished at the time of writing this thesis. Therefore, all results that we present for this case study are preliminary.

9.4.5. Applications of Mappings

We have evaluated the applicability of the mappings language by realizing mappings that are equivalent to TGG rules of an example case and by analyzing attribute expressions in the ATL transformation zoo. The TGG example for which we successfully realized mappings is concerned with keeping cards of a Leitner learning card system consistent with entries in a dictionary [AVS12]. To this end, the different partitions, in which cards of a Leitner box are stored, are mapped to levels of the dictionary. The goal of this application of the mappings language was to compare the attribute mapping capabilities of it with a TGG-based tool. Furthermore, we used this example to inspect the size of the involved mappings and TGG rules as well as the code that is generated for both approaches.

To evaluate the applicability of the automated bidirectionalization for unidirectional enforcement conditions of the mappings language, we inspected 103 transformations of the so-called ATL Transformations Zoo[3]. We have analyzed how much of the expressions that appear in available model transformations transform attributes using operators for which we defined inverters [KR16a]. The goal of this analysis was to obtain an indicator for the share of common attribute transformations that can be inverted with the currently available inverters. To this end, we have classified all operators of all transformations in the zoo using the following categories: identity operator, arithmetic operators, parsing or printing, other string operators, sequence operators, list operators. The result of this categorization was that 26% of the lines of code in the ATL transformations used only attribute operators expressions for which we defined inverters.

9.5. Discussion of Practical Benefit

The second practical property, which we evaluated for all languages except for the formal language, is the benefit of applying the languages. It is also the property that is most costly to evaluate [BR08, p. 15]. To thoroughly evaluate the benefit for every language, one would have to take a notion of total cost of ownership into account. This means, to clearly demonstrate that the presented languages are beneficial, it would not be sufficient to compare the effort for applying these languages in representative case studies. Additionally, one would have to consider the effort for learning these languages and probably even the effort for developing and maintaining both the languages and the consistency preservation tools written with them. Finally, such a thorough evaluation of the benefit of using the presented languages would mean to plan, to perform, and to analyze a family of empirical experiments with appropriately competent software developers for each language. Such experiments could provide enough data to reliably answer the question whether using these languages is altogether beneficial. Similar data for answering the same question for

[3] ATL Transformations Zoo: eclipse.org/atl/atlTransformations

widely used programming languages is, however, still not published because such families of experiments that consider the whole lifecycle of software are very costly. Furthermore, such results can always be put in doubt by questioning whether the developed applications and the subjects that were tested are representative for all or certain contexts of software development. Therefore, we do not provide such evidence for the overall benefit of using all presented languages. Instead, we present arguments for the change modelling language, the expression extension, the mappings language, and the invariants language, which suggest that applying these languages is beneficial. To demonstrate potential benefits of the reactions language, we also compare consistency preservation tools that were realized with the reactions language to functionally equivalent tools that were written in Java or the Java dialect Xtend. This comparison shows that those tools that were developed using the reactions language require on average 40% less source lines of code than their Java or Xtend counterparts.

9.5.1. Intermediary Change Models for Editors

A potential benefit of the change modelling language is that consistency preservation code can be decoupled from the format that is used to describe changes after which consistency is to be preserved. Without an intermediary change modelling language, there would be two alternatives for representing changes for consistency preservation. Either reactions code would have to be manually tailored to the changes that are observed in an editor for a specific modelling language. Or the compiler of the reactions language would have to be customized so that the code that is generated for reactions is able to deal with different change representations of different editors. If many different modelling languages and editors have to be supported, such manually adaptations of reactions to these editors or appropriate extensions of the compiler can result in high development effort. In such cases, it can be beneficial to use a generic change modelling language, such as the one we have presented in subsection 5.4.1 as intermediate representation. With such a language, it is sufficient to develop a transformation from specific change representations to the generic change format. As a result, neither manually developed reactions code nor the reactions compiler have to consider the fact that changes may be observed in different editors and for different modelling languages.

9.5.2. Integration and Code Generation for OCL-Aligned Expressions

A practical benefit of the OCL-aligned expression extension, which we have presented in subsection 5.4.3, is its integration into other languages. This integration applies to the languages presented in this thesis as well as to the Java language. The provided extension methods for collection operators and iterators can be used in the reactions, mappings, and invariants language. As a result, developers that use these languages do not need to learn a new language and have the flexibility to express constraints in different ways. They can either use lambda expressions and the operators and iterators of our extension to write constraints that are almost identical to OCL constraints (see also subsection 5.4.2 and 8.1.1). Or they can use Java to write helper methods if they are more familiar with this language. In both cases, developers also benefit from the integration of our Xtext-based languages into the Eclipse IDE and its editors. Developers are always supported, for example, in terms of auto-completion, and they do not need to use different editors or compilers when writing, for example, reactions, OCL-aligned expressions, and Java code.

The other potential integration benefit stems from the fact that we also generate Java code for the OCL-aligned expressions. This makes it possible to also perform static code analyses on reactions, mappings, or invariants code that involves such expressions. Such analyses can be helpful, for example, when refactoring steps are performed. Furthermore, the direct generation of Java code means that the execution of expressions code that was written with our extension can directly be debugged with established Java tooling. OCL, however, provides some features that complicate direct code generation and static analyses, such as unlimited integers or access to all instances of a metaclass. Therefore, many approaches that generate code instead of interpreting OCL expression only support a subset of OCL [Wil12].

9.5.3. Code Size Comparison for Reactions

We have evaluated whether using the reactions language instead of a General-Purpose Programming Language (GPPL) has an effect on the amount of code to be written. The goal of this comparison was to obtain an indicator for a potential benefit of the reactions language. By Gyimothy et al. [GFS05, p. 907], for example, it has been shown that an increasing amount of lines of code correlates with an increasing number of faults. To analyze this code size, we compared functionally equivalent realizations of consistency preservation tools for two of the case studies, which we have already described for the evaluation of practical applicability subsection 9.4.4. For both case studies, the same consistency requirements were realized twice and the same test cases were successfully passed by both variants. In the first case study, Java source-code was kept consistent according to changes in corresponding architectural models that conform to the PCM. For this case study a realization with the reactions language was compared to a realization that was developed using the Java dialect Xtend [Lan17]. In terms of code size, the differences between Xtend and Java should, however, be negligible (see also subsubsection 2.1.2.5). The alternative realization of the second case study was developed with Java. In order to avoid a potential bias, all four implementations for this comparison have been developed by graduate students or colleagues but not by the author of this dissertation.

We compared the SLOC excluding empty and comment lines (see subsection 9.4.4) of functionally equivalent consistency preservation tools that were developed with the reactions language, Java, or the Java dialect Xtend. For this comparison, we exploit the fact that the reactions language and both Java and Xtend are very similar in terms of concrete syntax, especially with respect to the question where new lines are necessary or common. It can always be questioned whether SLOC comparisons alone are sufficient to show that some piece some language provides a practical benefit. Thus, the goal of this code size comparison was not to obtain precise results that can be used to perform statistical tests on hypotheses, for example, to correlate the SLOC with the number of faults. Instead, we provide this comparison only to provide a rough estimate for the code size reductions that can be achieved with the reactions language. Therefore, potential minor differences in the usage of new lines in the case studies are acceptable.

For all four realizations of both case studies, we computed four different numbers for the SLOC including and excluding imports and helper methods. The current prototype of the reactions language provides limited support for distributing reactions across several compilation units. Thus, code from Java compilation units is only imported once in reactions whereas the alternative realizations in Java and Xtend are split over several classes which have to repeat import statements. To account for this, we always compute the SLOC with and without such lines that import code. We also analyzed the effect on the SLOC of helper methods in order to be independent of a potentially different tendency to outsource such code. When we compare the SLOC for both case studies in the following, we always provide four measurements for all combinations of including and excluding helpers and methods. Excluding the imports should avoid a potential bias towards a lower SLOC for reactions. Similarly, by including helper methods we ensure that all code that is needed for consistency preservation is taken into account even if it is not defined as a reaction but as a helper method. Therefore, we argue that the measurements that include helpers and exclude imports should represent the fairest comparison of all four measures.

In future work, we are planning to also compare the average McCabe complexity per thousand SLOC [GK91]. Furthermore, we plan to define which expressions in the reactions language can be regarded as a statement to compare the Total Number of Statements (TNOS). The TNOS metric is often also called Logical Lines of Code (LLOC) and it has been shown that it is a good predictor for maintainability, for example by Dagpinar and Jahnke [DJ03, p. 7].

9.5.3.1. Comparison for Component-Based Case Study

In Figure 9.4, we provide the results of the code size comparison for the case study in which Java code is kept consistent to changes in architectural models conforming to the PCM. As we have motivated above, we present four different measurements for the SLOC with and without helper methods and imports. The results show, that less code was written with the reactions language than with the GPPL Xtend. The biggest difference in size can be observed when the code of helper methods and imports is also counted. Analogue, the smallest difference is obtained when both helper method and imports are excluded.

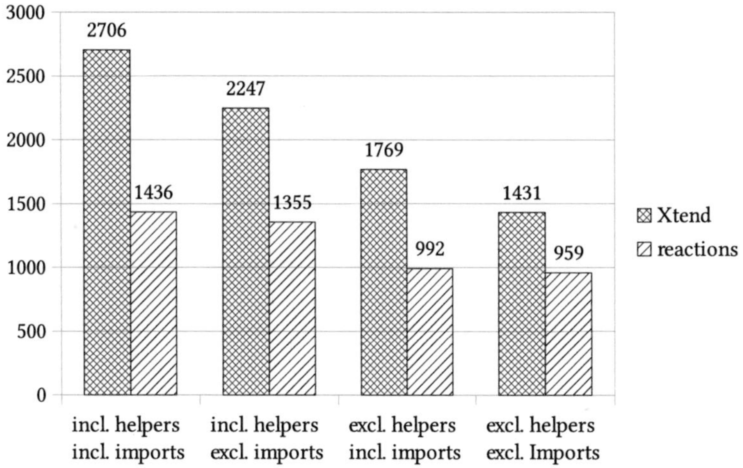

Figure 9.4.: SLOC for reactions and Xtend code for consistency preservation from PCM instances to Java code

9.5.3.2. Comparison for Automotive Case Study

In Figure 9.5, we provide the results for the code size comparison of the automotive case study in which ASEM models are kept consistent to changes in SysML block diagrams. These results for this second case study also show that fewer reactions code than GGPL code was written. Furthermore, the biggest and smallest difference between the code size of the functionally equivalent consistency preservation tools is again observed when helper methods and imports are both excluded or both included. The tool that has been implemented in Java contains more import lines than SLOC for helpers. Therefore, the number of SLOC in the second measurement, which includes helper methods but excludes imports, is lower than the number of SLOC in the third measurement, which excludes helper methods but includes imports. As we have already mentioned in subsubsection 9.4.4.4, the development of both tools in this case study is not yet finished so the results are preliminary and the SLOC will increase in the future.

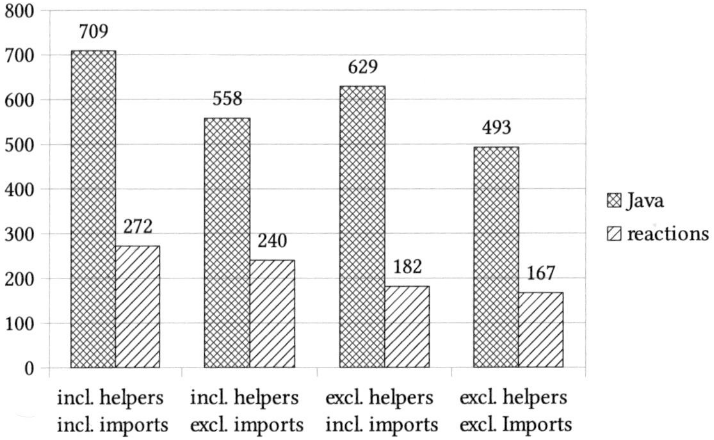

Figure 9.5.: Source lines of code (SLOC) for reactions and Java code for preserving consisteny in ASEM models after changes in SysML block diagrams

9.5.3.3. Relative Reduction of Source Lines of Code

In order to provide a relative indicator for the amount of code that is written using reactions and using a GPPL, we computed the relation between the SLOC of reactions and the SLOC of GPPL code for both case studies. The results for this relation are shown in Figure 9.6. Depending on the different possibilities for counting the SLOC with and without helper methods and imports, both case studies yield a reduction of the SLOC from GPPL code to reactions code that ranges between 33% and 71% of the SLOC for the GPPL code. The average reduction for both measurement that includes helper methods but excludes imports is 48%. As the absolute size of both case studies is, however, relatively small, this relative reduction cannot be used, for example, to predict how much code would be necessary in a third case study. Nevertheless, these results allows us to expect that the reactions code that will be developed in future case studies will also have noticeably fewer SLOC than functionally equivalent GPPL code.

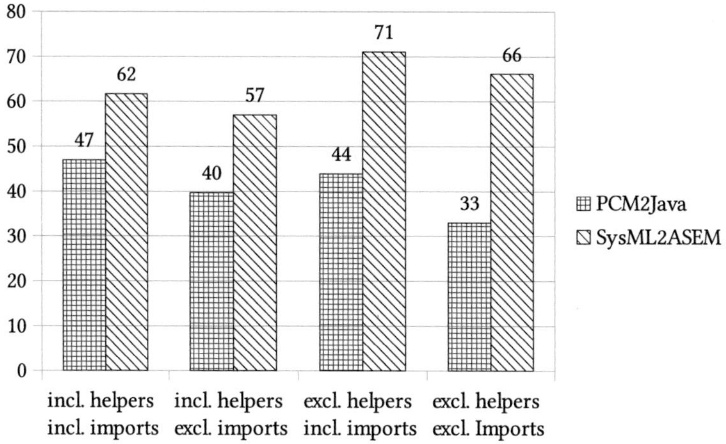

Figure 9.6.: Relative reduction of SLOC from GPPL code to reactions in percent for consistency preservation from PCM models to Java code and SysML models to ASEM models

9.5.4. Discussion of Benefits of the Mappings Language

We have developed the mappings language, which we have presented in chapter 7, in order to support developers in writing bidirectional consistency specifications. One of the goals was to combine automated support for preserving consistency for common relations between model elements and attributes with unlimited expressive power. In subsection 9.3.5, we have shown that the automated approaches for deriving enforcement code from checks and for deriving inverse enforcement code from unidirectional conditions are correct. We have, however, not analyzed, whether the gain in productivity that can be achieved using this automation is bigger than the loss of productivity by introducing our language in development projects of consistency preservation tools. For such comparisons it would, however, be important to have an appropriate baseline, in this case another language for bidirectional consistency specifications. Such languages have been presented by researchers but applications in industry are rare and limited to explorative case studies (see subsection 10.3.2 and subsection 10.3.3).

To obtain a preliminary indicator for potential benefits of the mappings language we have performed an exemplary comparison with the TGG-based tool eMoflon [Anj+11]. For the Leitner box example, which we have already mentioned in subsection 9.4.5, we compared, for instance, the possibility to realize complex attribute relations and the code generated by both approaches. A complex attribute relation that had to be realized is, for example, the relation between the content text of a dictionary entry and the two texts on the front and back side of a Leitner card. Furthermore, the partition in which a card of a Leitner box is stored had to be mapped to a level for the entry of the dictionary and vice versa. In the TGG-based approach such attribute mappings have to be realized in terms of a constraint satisfaction problem and using three operations for forward enforcement, backward enforcement, and condition checking [AVS12, p. 9]. Our pre-defined inverters, for which only a single condition expression has to be given, cannot be used for all complex attribute relations of this example. In such cases, forward and backward enforcement has to be specified separately in terms of Java code. Our comparison of the two approaches showed that even in such cases developers have to write less mappings code. Furthermore, the compiler of the mappings language generates less code than eMoflon and the gap between the generated code and the specified rules is smaller [Wer16, pp. 113–116]. In future work, further comparisons should, however, be performed in order to obtain enough data for quantitative analyses of mappings code.

9.5.5. Discussion of Automated Query Derivation

In section 8.2, we have presented an automated approach to obtain a query that returns model elements that violate the constraint of an invariant that was specified using our invariants language. To automatically obtain such a query that returns invariant-violating model elements, only one additional input in the form of an invariant parameter is necessary. It would even be possible to automatically expose all iterator variables of an invariant constraint as invariant parameters and to generate queries for all of them. As a result, the additional effort for using our automated query derivation approach is very small. Thus, we argue that our approach has a positive influence even in cases in which using a generated query instead of manually developing code for retrieving invariant-violating elements yields only a relative small productivity improvement. Therefore, we are convinced that an isolated evaluation of the benefit of this approach in some small case studies would not lead to many insights. Instead, we suggest to focus in future work on evaluations that compare a usage of the invariants language and its query derivation approach to the usage of OCL. Such comparisons should also analyze the effort needed to train developers in using OCL and in using the invariants language.

9.6. Future Evaluations

In future work, further evaluations, especially of the practical benefit of the presented languages, should be performed. Extensions and improvements of the evaluations of theoretical correctness and completeness are possible, but should not be in the focus of future work.

9.6.1. Further Case Studies and Comparisons

We suggest performing future evaluations of the practical applicability and benefit, for example, using a case study that also involves contracts written using the Java Modeling Language (JML) [LBR99]. We have already realized a consistency preservation tool for such a case study with an early prototype of the Vitruvius framework and therefore without the languages presented in this thesis [Kra+15]. Consistency between source code and, for example component-based models or abstract non-functional specifications, is especially crucial when the code is verified to ensure security properties, such as confidentiality of data. Therefore, we are convinced that a reimplementation and extension of this initial case study with the reactions, mappings, and invariants language would provide many interesting insights. Furthermore, this case study yields important challenges of consistency preservations as, for example, JML contracts are specified in terms of code comments, which are insufficiently supported by many co-evolution approaches and code models. Despite these particularities, any additional case studies could be used to further analyze potential benefits of the presented languages in different contexts.

As we have discussed above, we suggest to also perform further case studies, for example to obtain data for quantitative analyses of mappings code. Additionally, we have already mentioned in subsection 9.5.3 that measurements for additional metrics could be performed, for example to compare the complexity density and the TNOS.

9.6.2. Planned Experiment on Program Comprehension

We have planned and prepared a controlled experiment to evaluate the influence of the reactions language on code comprehension [Kra+16]. Unfortunately, we were not able to perform the experiment before we completed this thesis. Therefore, we briefly present this experiment as future work.

The goal of the experiment is to evaluate whether consistency preservation code that is written with the reactions language can be understood better or faster than consistency preservation code that is written in Java. To this end, we planned a within-participants experiment in which developers obtain multiple-choice questions that assess the ability to understand what the consistency preservation code does. In addition to a questionnaire with such questions, the developers will obtain code printouts. They will inspect reactions code and Java code of different consistency preservation tools in several sessions of a counterbalanced setup. For every session, we will record the number of correctly answered questions and the time that the developers needed for this. Based on these records, we will evaluate whether the fact that developers were inspecting reactions or Java code had a significant influence on the quality or speed of code comprehension. To this end, we will perform a statistical test that checks an appropriate null-hypothesis for all individual differences of the quality of code comprehension. This test will analyze whether subjects answered more questions on the functionality of the consistency preservation code correctly when they inspected reactions code. If this is the case and the obtained p-value is small enough to allow for a second statistical test on the same data, then we will also test the individual differences for the speed of code comprehension. We have described the detailed setup of this experiment in an article [Kra+16].

9.7. Conclusions

In this chapter, we have discussed how we have evaluated theoretical and practical properties of the languages presented in this thesis. First, we have discussed theoretical completeness with respect to the intended range of use. We have shown that the reactions language is Turing complete and reduced TGG rules to mappings to demonstrate the expressive power of the mappings language. Furthermore, we have discussed the theoretical correctness of every language. To show the correctness of the automated bidirectionalization of enforcement code, for example, we have introduced a new notion of best-possible behaved round-trips based on the notion of well-behaved transformations [Fos+07]. This new notion guarantees that the GetPut law is always fulfilled and that the PutGet law is fulfilled whenever this is possible. Furthermore, we have illustrated the applicability of the languages using case studies in which consistency was successfully preserved with tools that were written using the presented languages. Finally, we have discussed potential benefits of the presented languages. We have compared, for example, consistency preservation tools that were realized with the reactions language to functionally equivalent tools that were written in Java or the Java dialect Xtend. Those tools that were developed using the reactions language had between 33% and 71% less source lines of code than their GPPL counterparts.

10. Related Work

In this chapter, we provide an overview on work that has been published so far in the context of consistency preservation for models of different languages. To structure the discussion, we focus on different concerns while describing the literature. First, we present work in the general context of updating models or views. Then, we discuss approaches that describe how consistency can be checked and formalized. Finally, we review related work on automated consistency preservation. The discussed concerns are not orthogonal so that many approaches could be discussed several times with different foci. As too many cross-references would, however, limit the clarity of the discussion, we only mention approaches in several sections if they have a strong focus on the discussed concern. Parts of this chapter are based on corresponding sections of articles that we have published previously [KBL13; Kra15; KR16a; FKL16].

10.1. Consistency between Models, Views, and after Updates

The goal of consistent representations of a system under development was subject of many publications in software engineering and related fields of computer science. In this thesis, we have presented languages for preserving consistency between models of modelling languages that comply to the Essential Meta-Object Facility (EMOF) standard [ISO14]. Before we limit the discussion to related work that is concerned with similar representation formats for development artifacts, we briefly describe the more general context of consistency preservation.

10.1.1. The View Update Problem

The problem of keeping information that is part of several representations consistent after changes has been discussed as the *view-update problem* in many publications and for several application contexts. Bancilhon and Spyratos [BS81] and Codd [Cod90], for example, discussed it for relational databases. Other researchers, such as Foster et al. [Fos+05], transferred it to the field of programming languages. The general problem is that an update in a view that is derived from a database has to be translated to an appropriate update in the database if the view and its source shall be kept consistent. Such update translations can be realized using a *complement* view that contains all information of the database that is not in the view that shall be updated. More precisely, a complement of a function is another function, such that the tupled combination of both functions is injective. A backward transformation can be obtained from such a complement by inverting this tupled combination of the original function and its complement. There can be several complements for a view and the question whether an update can be translated back to the database depends on them: A view is updatable if it can be translated to the database with a constant complement [BS81]. This is, however, not always the case and Buff [Buf88] has shown that the question whether a unique translation exists is in general undecidable. Therefore, consistency can only be preserved if views and complements for translating updates are designed accordingly.

10.1.2. Models, Databases, and Ontologies

Models that conform to EMOF-based metamodels are a way to represent data in a format that is equivalent to attributed, typed graphs with inheritance (see subsubsection 2.3.1.3). Such models are used in many software engineering projects and different application domains. Often, various domain-specific languages are used [Whi+13; Whi+15], so that consistency has to be preserved between models of different languages. Consistency problems can, however, arise independent of the technological space [KBA02] and also when different technological spaces are combined and bridged [Hen11]. In the field of databases, for example, methods for integrating schemas that represent data in a partially redundant way were proposed [BLN86]. Such *schema integration* methods can also support developers in integrating existing data that was persisted using different schemas [Red+94]. Other approaches create federations of co-operating databases [SL90] or focus on semantic challenges of schema integration [HG01; DH05]. To preserve consistency while a database is used, *active database systems* can be used [PD99]. They provide developers the possibility to define rules for specifying which updates should lead to further database updates. Such rules are often expressed in terms of an event, a condition, and an action. This overall structure of so-called ECA rules is also similar to the structure of reactions (see section 6.1). Furthermore, mapping languages have already been discussed for schemas of the EXPRESS data modelling language [VLA95].

Ontologies can be regarded as a special form of descriptive models [AZW06] and foundational ontologies can be used in a similar way like metamodels [Hen11]. To better deal with very large ontologies, strategies for *ontology modularization* have been proposed [PS09]. An issue that has to be addressed in this context is overlapping knowledge [PS09, p. 12], for which inconsistencies can be prevented using update propagation mechanisms [PS09, p. 20]. In order to combine individual ontologies, languages for *ontology mapping* can be used. Brockmans et al. [Bro+09] discuss extensional and intensional interpretations of mappings and three different kinds of mapping relations: equivalence, containment, and overlap. An overlap mapping, for example, "states that some objects described by the element in the one ontology may also be described by the connected element in the other ontology" [Bro+09, p. 270]. Furthermore, Brockmans et al. showed that the reviewed ontology mapping languages have fundamentally different semantics.

10.1.3. Synthetic and Projective Multi-View Approaches

The ISO 42010 standard distinguishes between two approaches for constructing views on software architectures [ISO11], but this distinction can be applied to views of arbitrary kind: In a *synthetic* construction, views are integrated and thus have to be kept consistent to each other in a peer-to-peer manner. A problem with such approaches is that the number of inter-view relations, which may have to be kept consistent, grows exponentially with the number of used views. This can be avoided in a *projective* construction, in which views are projected from a central representation so that they only have to be kept consistent with this central representation in a hub-and-spoke manner. With such an approach it can, however, be challenging to create such a central representation without redundancies and to define editable projections. An example for a projective approach to programming is the Meta Programming System (MPS)[1]. Both approaches can also be combined in a hybrid manner to project some views from other views that are kept consistent with each other.

Orthographic Software Modeling (OSM) [ASB10] is a projective approach that strongly influenced the development of the Vitruvius framework, which we extended with the languages presented in this thesis. It transferred the principle of orthographic projections to component-based software development and introduced the concept of a Single Underlying Model (SUM). Furthermore, it defined the role of a methodologist, which we also use for the development of consistency specifications. Moreover, OSM supports extensible, dimension-based navigation between views and dynamic view generation.

In order to categorize approaches for creating multiple views, Atkinson et al. [ATM15] presented five *dichotomies*. First, they discuss whether views and consistency rules are defined in a rigorous or in a relaxed way. Then, they distinguish between synthetic and projective approaches. Next, Atkinson et al. oppose explicit inter-view correspondences to implicit correspondences. Furthermore, they distinguish extensional definitions of correspondences on the instance level from intensional definitions of correspondences on the type level. Finally, they oppose approaches that use a redundancy-free model for projective views to so-called pragmatic approaches that use inter-related models with partially redundant information for their projections. Atkinson et al. illustrate how these dichotomies can be used to categorize multi-view approaches by classifying the viewpoint modeling approach of the Reference Model of Open Distributed Processing (RM-ODP) [ISO09]. They classify it as a rigorous, synthetic approach with intensionally defined explicit correspondences between pragmatically inter-related models. The Vitruvius approach, which we extended with the languages presented in this thesis, can be categorized in almost the same way. The only difference is that it is not purely synthetic but a hybrid approach as it also supports

[1] Meta Programming System (MPS): jetbrains.com/mps

the definition of projective views [Bur14] and the integration of code and models that were not created with it [Lan17].

10.1.4. Tolerating Inconsistency

In the last subsection of this section on fundamental problems and notions of multi-view consistency, we briefly discuss related work that explored whether, why, and to which extent inconsistencies can and should be tolerated. Balzer [Bal91], for example, suggests to *mark inconsistent constraints* and to store the affected values for a later resolution of the inconsistency. He described an approach for tolerating inconsistencies in data that is processed while a software system is executed but the approach can—of course—also be used in tools for software development. His idea of marking inconsistencies can be useful to postpone or delegate resolution of inconsistency, especially in contexts of cooperative or concurrent modifications. In the Vitruvius framework, such delayed consistency preservation can be realized by adding tasks to a list via the interactive interface for user change disambiguation (see subsection 6.5.6). Another approach for dealing with inconsistencies was suggested by Finkelstein et al. [Fin+94]. To address the problem that anything follows from contradictions (principle of explosion), they suggest that developers should specify how the database should *respond to inconsistencies* depending on the context. Therefore, they present an "action-based meta-language based on linear-time temporal logic" [Fin+94, p.574]. Nuseibeh et al. [NER01] state that inconsistency does not always need to be addressed immediately because *inconsistencies can serve a purpose.* Furthermore, they emphasize that inconsistencies on itself are not always problematic but "undetected inconsistencies can be dangerous" Nuseibeh et al. [NER01, p.176]. They mention, for example, that inconsistencies "may indicate deviations from a process model", that they "facilitate flexible collaborative working", and that they "can be used to identify areas of uncertainty" [NER01, p.173]. Thus, they present a general framework for managing inconsistency based on a loop with four steps, in which inconsistencies are monitored, diagnosed, and handled. Moreover, they suggest that the consequences of this inconsistency handling should be monitored as well. Finally, Nöhrer et al. [NBE12] also suggest to allow inconsistencies but they also suggest to eliminate resulting reasoning errors by *isolating assumptions* that lead to the inconsistency, i.e. the unsatisfiability. This approach yields slightly less complete reasoning and can be applied to any satisfiability solving.

10.2. Challenges, Formalizations, and Consistency Checking

So far, we have discussed the fundamental view-update problem in different technological spaces. In the following sections, we restrict the discussion to approaches of the modelling space. That is, the discussed approaches directly support representations that can be considered equivalent to the EMOF standard [ISO14] or indirectly support them via graph transformations.

10.2.1. Challenges to Consistency Preservation

Several authors reviewed approaches for model transformation in general and discussed problems that arise in this context. These surveys, for example by Czarnecki and Helsen [CH03] and Biehl [Bie10], can also be used to classify approaches for consistency preservation. According to Biehl, approaches for preserving consistency between models of different languages can be classified as exogenous transformations that preserve semantics. These transformations can be executed as batch transformations as well as in source- and target-incremental ways.

Unfortunately, challenges that are particular to consistency preservation for different modelling languages are so far only partially discussed in surveys and other articles, even if they are restricted to incremental transformations [Kus+13]. Tratt [Tra08], for example, discusses several decisions that have to be taken when change propagating model transformations are developed as well as some challenges in this context. Some of these change propagation challenges also apply to consistency preservation. The degree of automation and the question whether updates are only checked or also propagated, for example, is also discussed in subsubsection 3.6.3.1. Egyed et al. [Egy+11] discusses challenges of change propagation with a special focus on how humans can be guided in semi-automated transformations. They propose partial transformations to address bidirectionality problems and discuss, for example, the problem of propagating changes until no further differences would be introduced, which is also mentioned in section 3.9.

Ivkovic and Kontogiannis [IK04] describe requirements for model synchronization transformations that are based on tracing information. They discuss the need for unique identifiers and present a model synchronization concept based on a graph formalism. Furthermore, they present a synchronization algorithm that is based on tracing and translating source model changes to target models. Moreover, they introduce a process for instantiating their methodology. They discuss, however, no realization of their ideas and state that an implementation of their synchronization algorithm is an "implementation problem" that "is out of the scope" [IK04, p. 9]. Similarly, Sendall and Küster [SK04] describe properties that are desirable for model round-trip engineering but do not present in detail how such properties can be achieved. For example, they require "the ability to precisely define the meaning of consistency between model" and "assistance when multiple solutions are possible" [SK04, pp. 9–10].

10.2.2. Formal Consistency Checking and Synchronization

Some of the literature that we mentioned in the previous section already demonstrated that the problem of keeping information consistent is suited for formal approaches. In this section, we briefly discuss some further publications that use formal methods to describe consistency checking and synchronization.

An algebraic approach that reduces the problem of checking consistency between models of different languages (heterogeneous) to checking consistency between models of the same language (homogeneous) was presented by Diskin et al. [DXC10]. This approach is based on category theory and therefore could be applied to all models that can be represented accordingly. More specifically, Diskin et al. present a merge procedure to transform heterogeneous models into homogeneous models. This merge is based on explicit instance-level mappings, which have to be defined manually. After this reduction, existing techniques for correspondence spans can be applied.

These spans are similar to the mappings of the language that we have presented in chapter 7. Furthermore, the approach can treat indirect model overlap and can check constraints that are not part of an involved metamodel. This is similar to invariants that can be defined with the language that we have presented in chapter 8. According to Diskin et al., "the main question is how effectively a multimodelling tool based on the framework could be implemented" [DXC10, p. 51].

There are further formal descriptions of how consistency can be checked and enforced based on category theory. Three families of algebras for modeling synchronization were, for example, presented by Diskin [Dis08]. Furthermore, a diagrammatic "notation for specifying synchronization procedures" was presented [Dis11]. It is based on tiles, which represent matches between different models and updates between different model versions. In two related publications, a symmetric and an asymmetric case of delta-based model transformations are introduced. The symmetric case is given if neither of the two models to be synchronized "fully determines the other" [Dis+11, p. 304]. For this case, synchronization is described as a transformation of a horizontal delta to a vertical delta. In this thesis, we refer to the former as user change and to the latter as a consistency preservation update. The asymmetric case is also described in terms of delta-based model transformations [DXC11]. In this case, one model can be derived from the other and update propagation exhibits functorial properties of category theory. Moreover, delta lenses are presented to overcome problems of state-based synchronization, for example, during the sequential composition of transformations. In this line of work, Diskin et al. [DMC12] also describe how maintenance of intermodel relationships can be specified using monads and Kleisli categories. Finally, a threedimensional taxonomy based on organizational symmetry, and informational symmetry, and incrementality is presented [Dis+14]. The first dimension describes whether a model dominates the other in case of an update or conflict, whereas the second dimension describes whether the information in a model is a refinement, abstraction, or subset of the information in the other model. For the last dimension of incrementality, Diskin et al. emphasize that all approaches can be implemented incrementally regardless of their organizational and informational symmetry. How this incrementality is realized depends, however, on these two other dimensions.

10.2.3. Determining Inconsistencies and their Causes

Various approaches for specifying and checking consistency constraints have been presented in the literature. As this thesis focused not on checking but on enforcing consistency, we do not present such approaches in detail. We discuss, however, an approach that is particularly interesting because it is independent of the language that is used to specify consistency constraints. This approach by Egyed [Egy11] profiles executions of consistency checks to determine which model changes invalidate which constraint. It was developed with a strong focus on performance. In section 8.2, we have presented an automated derivation of queries from invariants to obtain model elements that cause an invariant violation. These queries can be used to restore consistency after an invariant violation. Thus, we will only discuss approaches with a similar focus on constraint violation causes or on constraint-based inconsistency repairs in the remainder of this section.

Sigma [KC12] is a hybrid approach for declarative transformation rules and imperative validation and transformation code. It is provided as a model transformation library for Scala and therefore it can also be regarded as an "internal" domain-specific language, which reuses the concrete syntax of Scala. Sigma groups constraints in validation contexts and provides facilities to specify severity levels for invariant violations, as well as error messages and repair actions. In case of an invariant violation, Sigma provides, however, no possibility to obtain elements that lead to the violation. Therefore, code that computes these elements has to be explicitly defined in addition to the definition of the invariant check if a repair action should be based on it [KCF14, p. 1613, ll. 19–22]. To avoid some of the resulting code duplication, parts of the checking of an invariant can be factored out in order to be reused for retrieving model elements. We expect, however, that for most invariants such a manual refactoring step is more complex than specifying parameters for invariants as we have described it in subsection 8.1.3.

The Epsilon Validation Language (EVL) [KPP09] of the Epsilon framework is similar to the Object Constraint Language (OCL) but overcomes several shortcomings of it. Similar to Sigma's repair actions and our reactions language, it supports the definition of fix procedures for invariants. These fixes are, however, bound to a constraint. Therefore, it is not possible to write a fix that preserves consistency after different ways of violating different constraints without duplicating code. Furthermore, parameters that are defined in invariant checks cannot be reused directly in fixes, in contrast to our approach. Instead, they have to be defined and computed again in fixes [KPP09, p. 215, ll. 47–63].

Both Sigma and EVL do not separate the definition of invariant checks from fixes. This can be a problem if violations of invariants that are defined for a metamodel regardless of its usage have to be fixed in different ways, for example for different editors, transformations, or development projects. Such cases are supported by our approach as there is no such dependency between reactions and invariants.

Reder and Egyed presented an approach that computes a so-called validation tree whenever a consistency constraint is violated. Such a validation tree represents the computations that are performed when a constraint is evaluated in a particular context. This interpretative approach is used in three ways. First, validation trees are used to incrementally reevaluate only those constraints after a change for which a result change is possible in order to speed up consistency checking [RE12b]. This incremental consistency checking approach is based on a previously published approach that monitors constraint evaluation to obtain a bounded scope for the constraints that have to be reevaluated after a change [Egy06]. Second, possible inconsistency repairs are computed by traversing validation trees in a process that also eliminates wrong and non-minimal repairs to reduce the number of repair alternatives [RE12a]. This approach for suggesting changes that lead to satisfied constraints is based on previous work in which shared fixes and a reduced number of fixes are computed [Egy07]. Last, another way of traversing a validation tree is used to determine the causes of inconsistencies [RE13]. This approach for determining model elements that are responsible for a constraint violation is similar to our approach of query derivation for invariants, which we have presented in section 8.2. The main difference is, however, the way in which it is decided whether an element causes a violation. Reder and Egyed [RE13] compare the current evaluation of constraint expressions with the expected result. If an unexpected result is obtained for a subexpression, then the model elements that cause this unexpected result are identified based on the operator of the subexpression. The queries that are generated by our compiler of the invariant language, however, rely on explicit parameters. On the one hand, these parameters are an additional input that has to be provided. On the other hand, different parameters can be chosen for invariants with several iterator expressions if a consistency preservation action needs particular elements and not all elements that could be causing the inconsitency.

10.2.4. Finding Consistent Models using Checks

Consistency checks cannot only be used for finding inconsistencies but also for indirectly deriving consistent models. This is especially beneficial for round-trip engineering when partial and non-injective transformations do not provide enough information to specify backward consistency in an unambiguous way [HLR08, p. 44]. Therefore, several approaches use constraints that are indirectly provided in forward transformations or additional constraints in order to invert the transformation by finding consistent source models. In case of ambiguities, such approaches usually present developers various consistent models to choose from.

Hettel et al. [HLR09] presented an approach for inverting model transformations that are written in Tefkat by abduction [Het10]. It can be used to compute those source changes that can be interpreted as the best explanation for a target model change according to the forward transformation. Starting from the observed change, the approach inspects only those parts of a transformation and of the models that need to be changed in order to yield the observed change after executing the forward transformation. The approach also takes into account that an execution of the forward transformation on the proposed source changes can imply further changes in addition to the observed target change.

The Janus Transformation Language (JTL) can be used to find all source models for changed target models according to non-bijective transformations [Cic+11]. It provides a QVT-R like syntax for specifying transformations, which are automatically translated into search problems via an ATL transformation. The search problems are expressed using a special form of logical programming, called Answer Set Programming (ASP). JTL also supports transformations that are not total by approximating source models if a target model was changed in such a way that no source model could lead to the target model if the forward transformation was applied on it. The language also supports change propagations but no incremental execution of transformation rules.

Another approach finds consistent models for transformations that are written using QVT-R [MC13; MGC13]. It starts from an old model to find a new consistent model by applying deltas of increasing size until a model that fulfills all constraints is found. The approach uses the model finder of Alloy, which is based on a SAT-solver, and the search for consistent models can be restricted using a upper bound for the deltas. Which consistent models should be found can be controlled in two ways: Either by minimizing an edit distance that counts additions and deletions of nodes and edges, or by calculating a specific distance from user-provided edit-operations. The approach was also extended in order to support Alloy-based verification of UML models by validating OCL constraints with Alloy [CGR15].

10.3. Automated Consistency Preservation

Some of the approaches discussed so far can also be used to preserve consistency, but most of them rather focus on fundamental consistency problems or on checking consistency than on preserving consistency in an automated way. In the following, we will now discuss approaches with a strong emphasis on automated consistency preservation.

10.3.1. Focused on Tool Integration

Many approaches for automated consistency preservation do not provide dedicated concepts and languages for consistency specifications but focus on integrating and improving existing tools. Xiong et al. [Xio+07], for example, presented an approach or propagating changes in a model that is the target of an ATL transformation back to a source model by extending the virtual machine that is used to execute ATL transformations. Another approach for bidirectionalizing the ATL language uses a graph query language [Sas+11]. Both approaches do, however, not improve or extend the ATL language in order to better support bidirectional specifications. Existing modelling tools can be coupled with the ModelBus approach using a communication bus [HRW09]. For every tool, a specific adapter has to developed in order to connect it to the bus, which can also be used for change notifications and for merging model versions. Similar notification and merging features are also provided, for example, by Eclipse projects, such as Sphinx [Ebe12] or Connected Data Objects (CDO) and its Dawn subcomponent for collaborative modeling. These tools are, however, focused on different versions of the same model and not on models of different modelling languages and their semantic overlap.

10.3.2. Based on Triple-Graph Grammars

Many approaches for consistency preservation are based on Triple-Graph Grammars (TGGs), which were introduced by Schürr [Sch95]. A rule of a TGG is a triple that combines a left graph and a right graph with an intermediary correspondence graph using graph morphisms (see also subsubsection 9.2.5.1). Therefore, TGG rules are similar to the mappings for which we presented a language in this thesis. They have, however, a very different focus. On the one hand, TGG-based approaches often focus on formal properties and guarantees that cannot be shown for our mappings language. On the other hand, TGGs were initially designed for batch transformations and only a restricted set of attribute relations, e.g. equivalence relations, can be expressed with most TGG-based approaches. Furthermore, TGG-based transformation specifications cannot always be extended with unidirectional code. An overview on TGG-based tools was provided by Hildebrandt et al. [Hil+13] and complemented with another survey that focuses on incrementality [Leb+14].

The original concept of TGGs has been extended in many different way to support, for example, deletions of elements, move operations, negative application conditions [Kla+10; Kla12] or different incremental synchronization algorithms [GW06; Lau+12]. Further extensions introduced restricted TGGs for optimized view-update propagation [Anj+14b] and added support for transforming a flexible number of model elements [Leb+15, pp.92ff] (see also subsection 3.4.3).

Various tools have been developed to realize TGGs in different ways. MoTE, for example, was optimized for performance and applied in an industrial case study to synchronize SysML and AUTOSAR models in a fully bidirectional way [GHN10]. It supports two modes: a transformation mode, which applies rules as long as matches are located, and a synchronization mode, which transforms only nodes that were flagged by a change listener. Furthermore, an in-depth comparison of the formal semantics of TGGs with the semantics implemented in the tool was provided [GHL14]. Another TGG-based tool is eMoflon [Anj+11], which also provides a textual syntax for TGG rules. It provides many advanced features such as rule refinement [Anj14] and supports attribute manipulations for which a forward operation, a backward operation, and a check operation have to be provided [AVS12]. Recently, a library of bidirectional realizations of attribute operators was added to support basic arithmetic operators, string concatenation, and number comparisons. The mappings language that we have presented in this thesis supports additional operators (see section 7.3 and 7.4.6) that were published previously [KR16a; KR16b]. Other extensions and tools for TGGs are able to synchronize concurrent model changes and support semi-automatic conflict resolution [Her+12] which was used, for example, to realize safety-critical source code translations [Her+14]. For other applications it was, however, reported that not all requirements could be realized appropriately with TGGs [PKL15].

10.3.3. Focused on Bidirectionality

After the dedicated section for approaches based on Triple-Graph Grammars, we will now discuss further approaches with a strong focus on bidirectionality. Several overviews on this area were published with different foci. Stevens [Ste08], for example, reviewed motivations for bidirectionality and different notions of it. Czarnecki et al. [Cza+09] described different communities and disciplines interested in bidirectional transformations. Hidaka et al. [Hid+15] discussed design choices and resulting features of bidirectional transformation languages and tools. Altogether, this field of research is very diverse and no dominating solution has emerged so far.

The QVT-R language is probably the most renown language with support for bidirectional model transformations even if the bidirectional semantics are in some points unclear and problematic [Ste10]. Therefore, we briefly compare the mappings language, which we have presented in chapter 7, to it. In contrast to QVT-R, the mappings language clearly separates the question whether conditions have to be checked or enforced from the execution direction. More specifically, QVT-R provides when- and where-conditions with direction-dependent semantics. The mappings language, however, differentiates between single-sided conditions that are checked in one direction and enforced in the other direction and bidirectionalizable conditions that are always enforced (see subsection 7.2.2). Therefore, it is not necessary that developers specify which conditions should only be checked and which conditions should also be enforced. Furthermore, the mappings language does not distinguish between top-level and helper mappings. Moreover, it does not support explicit keys for element identification but relies on a mechanism for temporarily unique identifiers (see subsubsection 5.5.1.1). Finally, it combines direction-specific and direction-agnostic code in a single specification, for example using dedicated containment operators (see subsubsection 7.3.2.2).

In general, bidirectionalization can be performed in three different ways [FMV12]: *Syntactic bidirectionalization* approaches analyze transformations in order to synthesize PUT definitions from restricted GET definitions. Matsuda et al. [Mat+07], for example, presented an approach for inverting lambda-based programs that operate on tree structures. Their approach automatically derives and minimizes complements and inverts them together with a view function. In contrast, *semantic bidirectionalization* approaches are based on the observable transformation behavior and create a single, parameterized PUT definition that invokes GET as a black box operation [Voi09; Voi+10]. Last, bidirectional transformation *lenses* do not need to derive PUT definitions from GET definitions as they give developers the possibility to directly specify both transformations together [Fos+05]. In addition, bidirectionalization can also be avoided by realizing two ordinary unidirectional transformations for which appropriate round-trip properties are shown. Poskitt et al. [Pos+14], for example, described how bidirectionality can be faked by verifying that a pair of unidirectional transformations cannot be distinguished from a bidirectional transformation. To this end, they translate transformations that were specified using the Epsilon Wizard Language (EWL) and constraints that were written with the Epsilon Verification Language (EVL) to graph rewrite rules that can be verified.

The concept of combining a forward and a backward function in a single bidirectional specification called *lense*, for which strong round-trip laws are demanded, was initially introduced in this particular way by Foster et al. [Fos+05; Fos+07]. They provided several generic lense combinators that can be used to combine lenses on arbitrary data and specific combinators for tree-structured data. This original framework was used and extended in many ways in the literature. Foster et al. [FPP08], for example, presented so-called quotient lenses which relaxed some of the requirements to demand fulfillment of round-trip laws "only modulo insignificant details". Barbosa et al. [Bar+10a] introduced matching lenses that realign sources to reflect target changes in ordered structures [Bar+10b]. Incremental lenses with change-based Put functions were introduced by Wang et al. [WGW11]. They guarantee round-trip laws for change-based lenses if the corresponding state-based lense version guarantees them. Furthermore, least-change lenses that can be sequentially composed in a deterministic or in a nondeterministic way and that are based on relational algebra were introduced by Macedo et al. [Mac+13]. The conceptual framework of lenses was also realized in many transformation approaches and languages. Schmidt et al. [Sch+13], for example, use lenses to realize refactorings during language development. In their approach, a refactoring that is performed on an Xtext grammar leads to appropriate changes in the corresponding Ecore metamodel and the Xtend-based code generator that encapsulates the execution semantics of the developed language. Wider [Wid14] presented Focal, an internal DSL for Scala using state-based tree lenses [Wid15].

10.3.4. Based on Model Differences

Consistency can either be preserved based on model differences that are computed for an old and a new version or based on descriptions of model deltas, which directly express which elements and values were changed or even which edit operations were used for it. Model differences have the advantage that they can always be computed without the need to modify existing model editors or tools. The disadvantage of such approaches is, however, that such differences do not always provide enough information on how corresponding model elements should be changed. That is, even if different edit operations lead to the same difference between the original and the changed model, a user may want to accomplish different effects on further models by invoking particular edit operations [LK14]. Therefore, the question of differences or deltas is fundamental and most of the approaches discussed so far are indirectly or directly influenced by it. In this section, we discuss some approaches to consistency preservation that are especially influenced by their decision to use model differences.

Cicchetti et al. [CCL11], for example, presented a hybrid approach for incrementally synchronizing a central metamodel using higher-order transformations, which are based on model differences. In this approach, views can be user-defined and they always display a subset of the central model. Difference computation and change propagation profit from this subset relationship. Furthermore, differences are calculated by matching elements based on identifiers that are marked as unique by the user. .

The CoWolf approach also determines changes from differences between two model states, but this difference computation can be influenced [Get+15]. Manual difference computation rules can be written and the SiLift approach can be used to semantically lift syntactic differences to edit operations [KKT11]. The obtained changes are then used to preserve consistency based on rules for the TGG-based henshin tool.

Tunjic and Atkinson [TA15] presented an approach for computing differences between two versions of a view or betwen two versions of a central model in a projective multi-view approach. They use unidirectional transformations that relate elements of the central model to elements of views and propagate changes using these relations. Both, the difference computation and the change propagation mechanism were applied to the OSM approach, which we briefly introduced in subsection 10.1.3.

10.3.5. Based on Model Deltas or Edit Operations

Approaches for automated consistency preservation can monitor edit operations or compute differences in order to determine where and how consistency has to be preserved. Wimmer et al. [WMV12], for example, presented an approach for detecting coarse grained changes based on graph transformation patterns. They propagate changes to dependent viewpoints using coupled transformations that exploit explicit correspondence links.

The pattern-based transformation language Viatra uses EMF-IncQuery and a complex event processing framework to preserve consistency [Ber+15]. It is based on an event-driven virtual machine and supports real-time change propagation for which it relies on temporal logic and automation theory. If constraints are violated an internal DSL can be used, for example, to execute queries on the Viatra Query Engine. EMF-IncQuery [Ber+12; Ujh+15] executes declarative model queries by performing incremental graph pattern matching based on Rete networks. It provides a live validation service, which can report constraints validations directly after the modification that lead to it. Furthermore, annotations can be used to turn an ordinary graph pattern into constraints and to define severity levels or error messages for it. Parameters of a constraint pattern can be designated as keys to identify a violation which is a pattern match. These constraint keys are equivalent to the invariant parameters of the approach that we have presented in section 8.2. This way, EMF-IncQuery also provides elements that lead to a violation based on explicit constraint parameters and does not force developers to repeat parts of the constraint checking logic in order to obtain these elements. The main difference to our approach is, however, the relation to OCL: If elements that cause an invariant violation shall be computed for pre-existing OCL invariants, these invariants have to be reformulated for EMF-IncQuery, whereas our approach supports an automated translation of OCL constraints. There is, however, a translation from OCL queries to graph patterns that can be queried using EMF-IncQuery [Ber14]. With this approach, it would be possible to modify the patterns that result from an OCL invariant in order to obtain wanted elements that violate the invariant. The goal of the translation was, however, better performance. Therefore, a conceptual mapping from the resulting patterns to the initial OCL invariant may not always be straightforward.

Other approaches for event-driven or reactive programming can be found in a survey by Bainomugisha et al. [Bai+13]. Hinkel [Hin16] presented a transformation language that supports implicit incrementalization of lambda expression in the .NET framework based on category theory. It offers various synchronization and propagation modes, supports implicit and explicit bidirectionalization, and is realized as an internal DSL [Hin15].

10.3.6. Domain-Specific Consistency Preservation

Some approaches for automated consistency preservation were presented with a focus on consistency for a particular domain. In this section, we will briefly discuss such approaches even if they may also be mentioned in another category or could also be used in a generic way.

Romero et al. [RJV09], for example, presented an approach for preserving consistency for UML models of enterprise architecture frameworks with bidirectional transformations. With this approach, correspondences are defined between the viewpoint languages, i.e. in a peer-to-peer manner.

Malavolta et al. [Mal+10] presented the DUALLy approach that preserves consistency between Architectural Description Languages (ADLs). It uses the bidirectional Janus Transformation Language, which is based on ASP as we have explained above [Era+12]. DUALLy uses Higher-Order Transformations (HOTs) and can be classified as a projective approach because all ADLs are kept consistent with a central model. If multiple notations are used, kernel extensions can be applied to avoid losing information that cannot be represented with the central ADL [Di +12].

Part V.

Epilogue

11. Conclusions and Future Work

To conclude this thesis, we summarize its content and contributions, briefly recapitulate limitations, and provide an overview on possible directions for future work.

11.1. Summary

In this thesis, we have presented research that investigated how software developers can be supported in creating a particular kind of software engineering tools. These tools preserve consistency between models that represent a system under development using different languages. First, we identified and classified challenges that can occur if such tools have to preserve consistency after model changes during system design and development. As there is no universal notion of consistency, we introduced an approach for preserving consistency according to explicit consistency specifications. Such specifications prescribe for two modelling languages under which conditions their instances are to be considered consistent. We formalized this specification-driven notion of consistency in a way that is independent of how consistency enforcement is realized. On top of this formal language, we built three languages for the development of tools that preserve consistency by following this specification-driven approach. With these languages we addressed *Open Consistency Specification Language Challenges (OCSLCs)* that we have identified before (see section 3.5). The first language gives developers the possibility to precisely define how models have to be updated in reaction to specific changes in order to preserve consistency in a certain direction. In order to relieve developers from writing repetitive code, this imperative *reactions language* provides declarative constructs for common consistency preservation tasks, such as resolving or creating corresponding elements. Then, we presented a language that can be used if changes never need to be considered and if preservation directions are not always relevant. With this bidirectional *mappings language*, developers only have to declare which conditions have to be fulfilled when elements of different models should be considered consistent to each other. They do not have to bother about details of checking and enforcing consistency in one direction or the other. This is possible because enforcement code is automatically derived from checks and because conditions that are specified for one direction are automatically bidirectionalized using composable, operator-specific inverters. The third and last language that we presented can be used to complete both previous languages when consistency requirements can be specified in terms of invariants. This normative *invariants language* is closely aligned with the Object Constraint Language (OCL) and relieves developers from searching for elements that violate an invariant as it automatically derives queries that perform this task. These three presented languages give developers many possibilities to specify consistency problems instead of providing precise instructions on how they are to be solved. Finally, we presented how we evaluated theoretical and practical properties of the presented languages. For every language, we discussed its theoretical completeness and correctness as well as its practical applicability and potential benefits based on case studies. We discussed, for example, case studies in which consistency preservation tools that were developed using the reactions language had between 33% and 71% less source lines of code than functionally equivalent tools that were written in Java or the Java dialect Xtend.

In the first contribution chapter, we have presented a collection and classification of consistency preservation challenges (chapter 3). We have classified them according to the level of abstraction at which they occur so that they range from conceptual to implementation challenges. For challenges that occur on several levels, we have discussed which parts should be addressed on which level. Many enforcement challenges, for example, should be addressed by tools so that developers can choose from generic options to enforce consistency for particular modelling languages. Furthermore, we have presented challenges that are not yet sufficiently addressed by consistency specification languages. These open challenges are the reason why we have developed the languages presented in thesis. We have also presented challenges to bidirectional consistency preservation. Finally, we have briefly mentioned challenges that will occur when the restriction to preserve consistency only for isolated modelling language pairs is dropped in future work.

In chapter 4, we have presented realization-independent concepts of specification-driven consistency preservation based on set theory. First, we have introduced consistency rules and correspondences for witnessing consistency. Then, we have defined model updates for preserving consistency and the results of such updates. To express when such updates have to be performed, we have defined consistency-breaking changes. Based on this, we have introduced functions that yield consistency-preserving updates and discussed circumstances in which consistency can be preserved inductively and for all rules if it is preserved for a single change and a single rule.

Before we presented the individual languages for developing consistency preservation tools, we have briefly discussed what they have in common in terms of a language framework (chapter 5). We have explained our approach of preserving consistency in reaction to changes and according to specifications and we have discussed why we developed new languages and not libraries for existing languages. Furthermore, we have explained how the languages complete each other, for example, by supporting problem- *and* solution-oriented programming paradigms (Open Consistency Specification Language Challenge 2 (OCSLC 2). We have also presented a change modelling language and an OCL-aligned extension of a reused expressions language. Finally, we explained how we have realized all languages in terms of appropriate compilers and editors.

In chapter 6, we have presented a language for change-driven consistency preservation reactions. First, we have explained how reactions can be structured along three main steps in which reactions are triggered, corresponding elements are retrieved, and actions are performed. Then we have discussed how the reactions language can be used according to these steps to structure consistency preservation code and to avoid unwanted side-effects. For all constructs of the reactions language, we have discussed how they allow developers to abstract away from details that can be treated in generated code (OCSLC 3). In addition, we have explained why the reactions language provides a fallback to arbitrary update code in order to combine specific support with full expressive power (OCSLC 1). Moreover, we have discussed how the compiler of the reactions language separates code that can be directly traced to a reactions specification from repetitive and generic code in order to clarify the enforcement behavior (OCSLC 4). Finally, we explained the language semantics using the formal language of chapter 4.

To further support developers in cases, in which change types do not need to be differentiated, and the direction of preservation is not always important, we have presented a language for abstract consistency mappings in chapter 7. We have explained how we ensured that this language can also be applied when preservation direction details cannot always be abstracted away. This is achieved by providing a fallback to direction-specific enforcement code (OCSLC 1 and 3). Furthermore, we have explained the difference between consistency conditions that relate to models of one language or to models of both languages. We have introduced special operators for both kinds of conditions to automatically generate enforcement code. For conditions that relate to a single side, enforcement code is automatically derived from checks. Conditions that relate both sides only need to be specified in one direction because enforcement code for the opposite direction is automatically derived using composable, operator-specific inverters. Moreover, we have presented different possibilities of mapping dependencies and multi-parameter mappings. Additionally, we have explained why we generate code that calls generic platform code via mapping-specific wrappers in order to clarify the enforcement behavior (OCSLC 4). Finally, we have discussed the language semantics by explaining how different reactions can be created to preserve consistency for mappings if these fulfill certain restrictions or not.

In chapter 8, we have presented the invariants language, which complements the reactions and mappings language with constraint-based programming. With it invariants can be defined in almost the same way as with OCL and queries for model elements that violate an invariant can be automatically derived based on explicit invariant parameters. We have discussed why invariant-violating model elements are often needed and explained why constraint code should not be manually duplicated in queries for such elements. To avoid such code duplications, we have presented an automated derivation of queries. This query derivation can be configured with invariant parameters that match iterator variables of the invariant constraint. We have explained this automated derivation by presenting rules that are used to transform a tree representation of the constraint expression. The result of such a transformation is a query that returns those elements that were accessed for an iterator variable and that are responsible for an invariant violation.

In chapter 9, we have discussed how we have evaluated theoretical and practical properties of the presented languages. First, we have discussed theoretical completeness with respect to the intended range of use. We have shown, for example, Turing-completeness for the reactions language and sketched a reduction from Triple-Graph Grammar (TGG) rules to mappings to demonstrate the expressive power of the mappings language. Moreover, we have discussed theoretical correctness, for example for the automated bidirectionalization of enforcement code. To this end, we have introduced a new notion of best-possible behaved round-trips based, which guarantees that the GetPut law is always fulfilled and that the PutGet law is fulfilled whenever this is possible. Finally, we have discussed potential benefits, for example, for consistency preservation tools that were realized with the reactions language or with a General-Purpose Programming Language (GPPL). Those tools that were developed using the reactions language had between 33% and 71% less source lines of code than their GPPL counterparts.

In the last chaper before these conclusions, we have reviewed related work in the context of consistency preservation for models of different languages (chapter 10). We have discussed work in the a more general context of updating models or views, for example in databases. Furthermore, we have described approaches for formalizing or checking consistency. Finally, we have discussed automated approaches to consistency preservation, especially work that is based on TGGs or that realizes bidirectional transformations in a different way.

11.2. Current Limitations

The major limitation of the languages presented in this thesis is that they are only designed and evaluated for preserving consistency between models that conform to *two* different modelling languages. We realized reactions and mappings in such a way that updates are only performed on models of one modelling language in reaction to changes in models of another modelling language. Updates on the change source side cannot be performed (see page 174). Furthermore, updates on the execution target side are not monitored so that updates can only be performed in reaction to user changes but not in reaction to update actions of reactions. Nevertheless, we expect that many of the presented concepts and language features can be adapted for cases where consistency has to be preserved between models of the same modelling language or between models of more than two languages. Intra-language consistency could be approached, for example, based on a consistency specification that uses the same language as change source and execution target. Inter-language consistency specifications for more than two languages could be realized, for example, by combining several consistency specifications for suitable language pairs. Before such new uses of the languages can be evaluated, it is, however, necessary to solve fundamental problems, for example, to avoid reaction cycles or to manage conflicting updates.

The operator-specific inverters that we use to bidirectionalize mapping conditions have three limitations as described in subsection 7.4.7: They can only invert operations in which every source attribute appears at most once, they update only a single source attribute, and they only operate on single attribute values. The first limitation is common and the second and third limitation can be overcome with inverters that update, for example, several attributes in the same way and with inverters that update collections element-wise.

11.3. Future Work

The consistency preservation languages presented in this thesis point out various possibilities for future research. On the one hand, several specific aspects of the languages can be further explored and improved. On the other hand, future work can explore how the limitation to isolated pairs of modelling languages can be dropped.

11.3.1. Short-Term Specification Language Improvements

In short-term future work, the reactions language could be extended by triggers for compound changes as well as by constructs for reuse and user change disambiguation (see section 6.8). The current prototype decomposes compound change representations and only supports triggers for atomic change representations. In the future, both atomic and compound change representations should be suitable change types of reactions triggers. Then, compound change representations should only be decomposed if reactions would be triggered for the change parts but not for the composed change representation. Furthermore, the presented rules for avoiding unwanted side-effects in different reaction expressions should be completely enforced by the compiler. Code in initialization or update actions, for example, should be restricted so that only the specified model element but no other related elements are updated. Additionally, new language constructs could be provided to foster the reuse of reactions and reaction routines within a single or across several consistency specifications. Access modifiers, for example, could be added to reaction routines or these could be explicitly refined or parameterized. Finally, user change disambiguation could be improved by integrating dialog and options definitions.

The mappings language could be extended in the short term with further operators, inverters, and instantiation delegations and the compiler could be improved based on the presented realization strategy for pure mappings (see section 7.8). For single-sided and bidirectionalizable conditions, new operators could be added and existing operators could be improved, for example, to also derive enforcements for negated equality conditions for references. Furthermore, inverters of a new type could be provided to also support cases in which more than one source attribute should be updated for a change of a single attribute on the other side. To reduce the number of cases were fallback enforcements are necessary, a mechanism for defining and reusing developer-defined operators for single-sided conditions and bidirectionalizable conditions could be developed. Moreover, a mechanism for delegating instantiations of mapped abstract metaclasses to concrete metaclasses could be added. Finally, the proposed realization strategy for impure mappings should be completely realized in the compiler so that developers have to consider fewer unnecessary reevaluations of mapping conditions when they debug the code that is generated for a mapping.

Short-term future work in the context of the invariants language should add query derivation support for local variables, nested parameters, and further operators. Currently, local variables can be defined and used in invariants to refer to results of reused expression parts. The query derivation algorithm has, however, to be extended if invariant-violating elements should not only be bound to iterator variables but also to local variables. This could be very useful as let expressions and definition constraints for inline and ordinary local variables are a commonly-used feature of OCL. Furthermore, the derivation algorithm should be extended to also support nested parameters by transforming non-nested and nested expressions separately and combining them afterwards. Moreover, further operators, such as common collection size comparisons, could be supported during query derivation.

11.3.2. Long-Term Support Beyond Pairwise Consistency

In the long-term, future work should explore ways to also support cases in which consistency cannot be preserved successfully if reactions and mappings can only be specified pairwise for two modelling languages without considering other languages (see section 3.9). As we already mentioned above, consistency can only be preserved between models of three or more modelling languages at once if several fundamental problems are solved. First, it has to be ensured that updates that are performed when reactions or mappings are executed are monitored and processed analogue to user changes. That is, consistency should be enforced the same way if a model element was directly changed by a user or indirectly changed in reaction to a change in a model of another language. A problem in this context is, for example, that user change disambiguation requests cannot be answered by an automated update and therefore would have to be forwarded to the user that performed the change that lead to the indirect reaction. This would, however, mean that users cannot focus on the modelling language they are using and only have to consider appropriate parts of directly related languages as they may have to take all languages that are used into account. Second, reaction cycles and oscillations have to be avoided which cannot be done by simply ensuring that consistency preservation stops as soon as a sequence of updates would not yield any model differences. Instead, it should be explored whether appropriate detection mechanism that were developed in other contexts can be transferred. Last, reactions that may directly or indirectly lead to conflicting updates along different paths have to be managed, for example, based on precedence rules. Problems that are similar to the three presented ones are likely to be already addressed in other contexts. Therefore, an important direction for future research is to perform different practical case studies with several modelling languages. With such case studies it should be investigated which of these theoretically possible problems occur in realistic settings and whether well-known solution strategies can also be used for preserving consistency between models of different languages in a change-driven way. In this sense, such future work could pursue the same goal as this thesis by supporting developers in specifying consistency preservation also for cases where more than two modelling languages have to be considered at once.

Bibliography

[Anj+11] A. Anjorin et al. "eMoflon: Leveraging EMF and Professional CASE Tools". In: *3. Workshop Methodische Entwicklung von Modellierungswerkzeugen (MEMWe2011)*. Lecture Notes in Informatics. 2011.

[Anj+14a] A. Anjorin et al. "BenchmarX". In: *Proceedings of the Workshops of the EDBT/ICDT 2014 Joint Conference*. Vol. 1133. CEUR Workshop Proceedings. CEUR, 2014, pp. 82–86.

[Anj+14b] A. Anjorin et al. "Efficient Model Synchronization with View Triple Graph Grammars". In: *Modelling Foundations and Applications*. Vol. 8569. LNCS. Springer International Publishing, 2014, pp. 1–17.

[Anj14] A. Anjorin. "Synchronization of Models on Different Abstraction Levels using Triple Graph Grammars". PhD thesis. Technische Universität Darmstadt, 2014.

[ASB10] C. Atkinson, D. Stoll, and P. Bostan. "Orthographic Software Modeling: A Practical Approach to View-Based Development". In: *Evaluation of Novel Approaches to Software Engineering*. Vol. 69. Communications in Computer and Information Science. Springer, 2010, pp. 206–219.

[ATM15] C. Atkinson, C. Tunjic, and T. Möller. "Fundamental Realization Strategies for Multi-view Specification Environments". In: *Enterprise Distributed Object Computing Conference (EDOC), 2015 IEEE 19th International*. 2015, pp. 40–49.

[AVS12] A. Anjorin, G. Varró, and A. Schürr. "Complex Attribute Manipulation in TGGs with Constraint-Based Programming Techniques". In: *Proceedings of the First International Workshop on Bidirectional Transformations (BX 2012)*. Vol. 49. Electronic Communications of the EASST. 2012.

[AZW06] U. Aßmann, S. Zschaler, and G. Wagner. "Ontologies, Metamodels, and the Model-Driven Paradigm". In: *Ontologies for Software Engineering and Software Technology*. Springer Berlin Heidelberg, 2006, pp. 249–273.

[Bai+13] E. Bainomugisha et al. "A Survey on Reactive Programming". In: *ACM Comput. Surv.* 45.4 (2013), 52:1–52:34.

[Bal91] R. Balzer. "Tolerating Inconsistency". In: *Proceedings of the 13th International Conference on Software Engineering*. IEEE, 1991, pp. 158–165.

[Bar+10a] D. M. Barbosa et al. "Matching Lenses: Alignment and View Update". In: *Proceedings of the 15th ACM SIGPLAN International Conference on Functional Programming*. ICFP '10. ACM, 2010, pp. 193–204.

[Bar+10b] D. M. Barbosa et al. *Matching Lenses: Alignment and View Update*. Tech. rep. University of Pennsylvania, Department of Computer and Information Science, 2010.

[Ber+11] G. Bergmann et al. "A Graph Query Language for EMF Models". In: *Theory and Practice of Model Transformations: 4th International Conference, ICMT 2011, Zurich, Switzerland, June 27-28, 2011. Proceedings*. Springer Berlin Heidelberg, 2011, pp. 167–182.

[Ber+12] G. Bergmann et al. "Change-driven model transformations". In: *Software & Systems Modeling* 11.3 (2012), pp. 431–461.

[Ber+15] G. Bergmann et al. "Viatra 3: A Reactive Model Transformation Platform". In: *Theory and Practice of Model Transformations*. Vol. 9152. LNCS. Springer International Publishing, 2015, pp. 101–110.

[Ber14] G. Bergmann. "Translating OCL to graph patterns". In: *Model-Driven Engineering Languages and Systems*. Springer, 2014, pp. 670–686.

[BHS07] *Verification of Object-Oriented Software: The KeY Approach*. LNCS 4334. Springer-Verlag, 2007.

[Bie10] M. Biehl. *Literature Study on Model Transformations*. Tech. rep. ISRN/KTH/MMK/R-10/07-SE. Royal Institute of Technology, 2010.

[BLN86] C. Batini, M. Lenzerini, and S. B. Navathe. "A Comparative Analysis of Methodologies for Database Schema Integration". In: *ACM Comput. Surv.* 18.4 (1986), pp. 323–364.

[BR08] R. Böhme and R. Reussner. "Validation of Predictions with Measurements". In: *Dependability Metrics.* Vol. 4909. LNCS. Springer-Verlag Berlin Heidelberg, 2008. Chap. 3, pp. 14–18.

[Bro+09] S. Brockmans et al. "Formal and Conceptual Comparison of Ontology Mapping Languages". In: *Modular Ontologies.* Vol. 5445. LNCS. Springer Berlin Heidelberg, 2009, pp. 267–291.

[BS81] F. Bancilhon and N. Spyratos. "Update semantics of relational views". In: *ACM Trans. Database Syst.* 6.4 (1981), pp. 557–575.

[Buf88] H. W. Buff. "Why Codd's Rule No. 6 Must be Reformulated". In: *SIGMOD Record* 17.4 (1988), pp. 79–80.

[Bur+14] E. Burger et al. "View-Based Model-Driven Software Development with ModelJoin". In: *Software & Systems Modeling* 15.2 (2014), pp. 472–496.

[Bur14] E. Burger. "Flexible Views for View-based Model-driven Development". PhD thesis. Karlsruhe Institute of Technology, 2014.

[CCL11] A. Cicchetti, F. Ciccozzi, and T. Leveque. "A hybrid approach for multi-view modeling". In: *Electronic Communications of the EASST* 50 (2011).

[CGR15] A. Cunha, A. Garis, and D. Riesco. "Translating between Alloy specifications and UML class diagrams annotated with OCL". In: *Software & Systems Modeling* 14.1 (2015), pp. 5–25.

[CH03] K. Czarnecki and S. Helsen. "Classification of Model Transformation Approaches". In: *OOPSLA 2003 Workshop on Generative Techniques in the context of Model Driven Architecture.* Last retrieved 2008-01-06. 2003.

[Che+14] J. Cheney et al. "Towards a Repository of Bx Examples". In: *Proceedings of the Workshops of the EDBT/ICDT 2014 Joint Conference.* Vol. 1133. CEUR Workshop Proceedings. CEUR, 2014, pp. 87–91.

[Che+15] J. Cheney et al. "Towards a Principle of Least Surprise for Bidirectional Transformations". In: *4th International Workshop on Bidirectional Transformations*. CEUR Workshop Proceedings, 2015, pp. 66–80.

[Cic+11] A. Cicchetti et al. "JTL: A Bidirectional and Change Propagating Transformation Language". In: *Software Language Engineering – Third International Conference, SLE 2010, Eindhoven, The Netherlands, October 12-13, 2010, Revised Selected Papers*. Vol. 6563. LNCS. Springer, 2011, pp. 183–202.

[CK03] V. M. Cengarle and A. Knapp. "OCL 1.4/5 vs. 2.0 Expressions Formal semantics and expressiveness". In: *Software and Systems Modeling* 3.1 (2003), pp. 9–30.

[Cod90] E. F. Codd. *The relational model for database management: version 2*. Addison-Wesley Longman Publishing Co., Inc., 1990.

[Cza+09] K. Czarnecki et al. "Bidirectional Transformations: A Cross-Discipline Perspective". In: *Theory and Practice of Model Transformations*. Vol. 5563. LNCS. Springer Berlin Heidelberg, 2009, pp. 260–283.

[DH05] A. Doan and A. Y. Halevy. "Semantic-integration Research in the Database Community". In: *AI Mag.* 26.1 (2005), pp. 83–94.

[Di +12] D. Di Ruscio et al. "Model-Driven Techniques to Enhance Architectural Languages Interoperability". In: *Fundamental Approaches to Software Engineering*. Vol. 7212. LNCS. Springer Berlin / Heidelberg, 2012, pp. 26–42.

[Dis+11] Z. Diskin et al. "From State- to Delta-Based Bidirectional Model Transformations: The Symmetric Case". In: *Model Driven Engineering Languages and Systems*. Vol. 6981. LNCS. Springer Berlin Heidelberg, 2011, pp. 304–318.

[Dis+14] Z. Diskin et al. "Towards a Rational Taxonomy for Increasingly Symmetric Model Synchronization". In: *Theory and Practice of Model Transformations*. Vol. 8568. LNCS. Springer International Publishing, 2014, pp. 57–73.

[Dis08] Z. Diskin. "Algebraic Models for Bidirectional Model Synchronization". In: *Model Driven Engineering Languages and Systems*. Vol. 5301. LNCS. Springer Berlin / Heidelberg, 2008, pp. 21–36.

[Dis11] Z. Diskin. “Model Synchronization: Mappings, Tiles, and Categories”. In: *Generative and Transformational Techniques in Software Engineering III.* Vol. 6491. LNCS. Springer Berlin / Heidelberg, 2011, pp. 92–165.

[DJ03] M. Dagpinar and J. H. Jahnke. “Predicting maintainability with object-oriented metrics -an empirical comparison”. In: *Reverse Engineering, 2003. WCRE 2003. Proceedings. 10th Working Conference on.* 2003, pp. 155–164.

[DMC12] Z. Diskin, T. Maibaum, and K. Czarnecki. “Intermodeling, Queries, and Kleisli Categories”. In: *Fundamental Approaches to Software Engineering.* Vol. 7212. LNCS. Springer Berlin Heidelberg, 2012, pp. 163–177.

[DXC10] Z. Diskin, Y. Xiong, and K. Czarnecki. “Specifying overlaps of heterogeneous models for global consistency checking”. In: *Proceedings of the First International Workshop on Model-Driven Interoperability.* MDI ’10. ACM, 2010, pp. 42–51.

[DXC11] Z. Diskin, Y. Xiong, and K. Czarnecki. “From State- to Delta-Based Bidirectional Model Transformations: the Asymmetric Case”. In: *Journal of Object Technology* 10 (2011), 6:1–25.

[Ebe12] S. Eberle. “Using Sphinx to create multi-language multi-view DSL tool environments”. talk. 2012.

[Eff+12] S. Efftinge et al. “Xbase: Implementing Domain-specific Languages for Java”. In: *Proceedings of the 11th International Conference on Generative Programming and Component Engineering.* GPCE ’12. ACM, 2012, pp. 112–121.

[Egy+11] *Fine-Tuning Model Transformation: Change Propagation in Context of Consistency, Completeness, and Human Guidance.* Springer Berlin Heidelberg, 2011, pp. 1–14.

[Egy06] A. Egyed. “Instant Consistency Checking for the UML”. In: *Proceedings of the 28th International Conference on Software Engineering.* ICSE ’06. ACM, 2006, pp. 381–390.

[Egy07] A. Egyed. “Fixing Inconsistencies in UML Design Models”. In: *Software Engineering, 29th International Conference on.* 2007, pp. 292–301.

[Egy11] A. Egyed. "Automatically Detecting and Tracking Inconsistencies in Software Design Models". In: *Software Engineering, IEEE Transactions on* 37.2 (2011), pp. 188–204.

[Era+12] R. Eramo et al. "A model-driven approach to automate the propagation of changes among Architecture Description Languages". In: *Software and Systems Modeling* 11 (1 2012), pp. 29–53.

[EV06] S. Efftinge and M. Völter. "oAW xText: A framework for textual DSLs". In: *Eclipsecon Summit Europe 2006*. 2006.

[Fin+94] A. Finkelstein et al. "Inconsistency Handling in Multiperspective Specifications". In: *IEEE Transactions on Software Engineering* 20.8 (1994), pp. 569–578.

[Fis15] S. Fiss. "Embedding and Transforming Invariants for a Domain-Specific Language for Multi-Model Consistency". Bachelor's Thesis. Karlsruhe Institute of Technology (KIT), 2015.

[FKL16] S. Fiss, M. E. Kramer, and M. Langhammer. "Automatically Binding Variables of Invariants to Violating Elements in an OCL-Aligned XBase-Language". In: *Proceedings of Modellierung 2016*. Vol. P-254. Lecture Notes in Informatics (LNI). GI e.V., 2016, pp. 189–204.

[FMV12] J. N. Foster, K. Matsuda, and J. Voigtländer. "Three Complementary Approaches to Bidirectional Programming". In: *Generic and Indexed Programming*. Vol. 7470. LNCS. Springer Berlin Heidelberg, 2012, pp. 1–46.

[Fos+05] J. N. Foster et al. "Combinators for bi-directional tree transformations: a linguistic approach to the view update problem". In: *SIGPLAN Not.* 40.1 (2005), pp. 233–246.

[Fos+07] J. N. Foster et al. "Combinators for Bidirectional Tree Transformations: A Linguistic Approach to the View-update Problem". In: *ACM Transactions on Programming Languages and Systems (TOPLAS)* 29.3 (2007).

[Fos10] J. N. Foster. "Bidirectional Programming Languages". PhD thesis. University of Pennsylvania, Department of Computer and Information Science, 2010.

[FPP08] J. N. Foster, A. Pilkiewicz, and B. C. Pierce. "Quotient Lenses". In: *Proceedings of the 13th ACM SIGPLAN International Conference on Functional Programming*. ICFP '08. ACM, 2008, pp. 383–396.

[Get+15] S. Getir et al. "Theory and Practice of Model Transformations: 8th International Conference, ICMT 2015, Held as Part of STAF 2015, L'Aquila, Italy, July 20-21, 2015. Proceedings". In: Springer International Publishing, 2015. Chap. CoWolf – A Generic Framework for Multi-view Co-evolution and Evaluation of Models, pp. 34–40.

[GFS05] T. Gyimothy, R. Ferenc, and I. Siket. "Empirical validation of object-oriented metrics on open source software for fault prediction". In: *IEEE Transactions on Software Engineering* 31.10 (2005), pp. 897–910.

[GHL14] H. Giese, S. Hildebrandt, and L. Lambers. "Bridging the gap between formal semantics and implementation of triple graph grammars". In: *Software & Systems Modeling* 13.1 (2014), pp. 273–299.

[GHN10] H. Giese, S. Hildebrandt, and S. Neumann. "Model Synchronization at Work: Keeping SysML and AUTOSAR Models Consistent". In: *Graph Transformations and Model-Driven Engineering*. Vol. 5765. LNCS. Springer Berlin / Heidelberg, 2010, pp. 555–579.

[GK91] G. K. Gill and C. F. Kemerer. "Cyclomatic complexity density and software maintenance productivity". In: *IEEE Transactions on Software Engineering* 17.12 (1991), pp. 1284–1288.

[GKM11] R. Grønmo, S. Krogdahl, and B. Møller-Pedersen. "A collection operator for graph transformation". In: *Software and Systems Modeling* 12.1 (2011), pp. 121–144.

[GPR11] J. Greenyer, S. Pook, and J. Rieke. "Preventing Information Loss in Incremental Model Synchronization by Reusing Elements". In: *Modelling Foundations and Applications – 7th European Conference, ECMFA 2011, Birmingham, UK, June 6 - 9, 2011, Proceedings*. Vol. 6698. LNCS. Springer, 2011, pp. 144–159.

[GW06] H. Giese and R. Wagner. "Incremental Model Synchronization with Triple Graph Grammars". In: *Model Driven Engineering Languages and Systems*. Vol. 4199. LNCS. Springer Berlin / Heidelberg, 2006, pp. 543–557.

[Hei+10] F. Heidenreich et al. "Closing the Gap between Modelling and Java". In: *Software Language Engineering*. Vol. 5969. LNCS. Springer Berlin Heidelberg, 2010, pp. 374–383.

[Hen11] B. Henderson-Sellers. "Bridging metamodels and ontologies in software engineering". In: *Journal of Systems and Software* 84.2 (2011), pp. 301–313.

[Her+12] F. Hermann et al. "Concurrent Model Synchronization with Conflict Resolution Based on Triple Graph Grammars". In: *Fundamental Approaches to Software Engineering*. Vol. 7212. LNCS. Springer Berlin / Heidelberg, 2012, pp. 178–193.

[Her+14] F. Hermann et al. "Triple Graph Grammars in the Large for Translating Satellite Procedures". In: *Theory and Practice of Model Transformations: 7th International Conference, ICMT 2014, Held as Part of STAF 2014, York, UK, July 21-22, 2014. Proceedings.* Springer International Publishing, 2014, pp. 122–137.

[Het10] T. Hettel. "Model round-trip engineering". PhD thesis. Queensland University of Technology, 2010.

[HG01] F. Hakimpour and A. Geppert. "Resolving Semantic Heterogeneity in Schema Integration". In: *Proceedings of the International Conference on Formal Ontology in Information Systems - Volume 2001.* FOIS '01. ACM, 2001, pp. 297–308.

[Hid+15] S. Hidaka et al. "Feature-based classification of bidirectional transformation approaches". In: *Software & Systems Modeling* (2015), pp. 1–22.

[Hil+13] S. Hildebrandt et al. "A survey of triple graph grammar tools". In: *Electronic Communications of the EASST* 57 (2013).

[Hin15] G. Hinkel. "Change Propagation in an Internal Model Transformation Language". In: *Theory and Practice of Model Transformations: 8th International Conference, ICMT 2015, Held as Part of STAF 2015, L'Aquila, Italy, July 20-21, 2015. Proceedings.* Springer International Publishing, 2015, pp. 3–17.

[Hin16] G. Hinkel. *NMF: A Modeling Framework for the .NET Platform.* Tech. rep. Karlsruhe Institute of Technology, 2016.

[HLR08] T. Hettel, M. Lawley, and K. Raymond. "Model Synchronisation: Definitions for Round-Trip Engineering". In: *Theory and Practice of Model Transformations.* Vol. 5063. LNCS. Springer Berlin / Heidelberg, 2008, pp. 31–45.

[HLR09] T. Hettel, M. Lawley, and K. Raymond. "Towards Model Round-Trip Engineering: An Abductive Approach". In: *Theory and Practice of Model Transformations.* Vol. 5563. LNCS. Springer Berlin Heidelberg, 2009, pp. 100–115.

[HRW09] C. Hein, T. Ritter, and M. Wagner. "Model-Driven Tool Integration with ModelBus". In: *Workshop Future Trends of Model-Driven Development.* 2009.

[IK04] I. Ivkovic and K. Kontogiannis. "Tracing evolution changes of software artifacts through model synchronization". In: *Software Maintenance, 2004. Proceedings. 20th IEEE International Conference on.* 2004, pp. 252–261.

[Int96] International Organization for Standardization. *ISO/IEC 14977:1996 Information Technology - Syntactic Metalanguage - Extended BNF.* 1996.

[ISO09] ISO/IEC 10746-3:2009. *Information technology – Open distributed processing – Reference model: Architecture.* International Organization for Standardization, Geneva, Switzerland, 2009, pp. 1–54.

[ISO11] ISO/IEC/IEEE 42010:2011(E). *Systems and software engineering – Architecture description.* International Organization for Standardization, Geneva, Switzerland, 2011, pp. 1–46.

[ISO12a] ISO/IEC 19505-1:2012(E). *Information technology – Object Management Group Unified Modeling Language (OMG UML), Infrastructure.* International Organization for Standardization, Geneva, Switzerland, 2012, pp. 1–234.

[ISO12b] ISO/IEC 19505-2:2012(E). *Information technology – Object Management Group Unified Modeling Language (OMG UML), Superstructure.* International Organization for Standardization, Geneva, Switzerland, 2012, pp. 1–758.

[ISO12c] ISO/IEC 19507:2012(E). *Information technology – Object Management Group Object Constraint Language (OCL).* International Organization for Standardization, Geneva, Switzerland, 2012, pp. 1–234.

[ISO14] ISO/IEC 19508:2014(E). *Information technology – Object Management Group Meta Object Facility (MOF) Core.* International Organization for Standardization, Geneva, Switzerland, 2014.

[JR16] M. Johnson and R. Rosebrugh. "Unifying Set-Based, Delta-Based and Edit-Based Lenses". In: *Proceedings of the 5th International Workshop on Bidirectional Transformations (Bx 2016).* Vol. 1571. CEUR Workshop Proceedings. CEUR-WS.org, 2016, pp. 1–13.

[KBA02] I. Kurtev, J. Bézivin, and M. Akşit. "Technological Spaces: An Initial Appraisal". In: *International Conference on Cooperative Information Systems (CoopIS).* University of Twente, 2002, pp. 1–6.

[KBL13] M. E. Kramer, E. Burger, and M. Langhammer. "View-Centric Engineering with Synchronized Heterogeneous Models". In: *Proceedings of the 1st Workshop on View-Based, Aspect-Oriented and Orthographic Software Modelling.* VAO '13. ACM, 2013, 5:1–5:6.

[KC12] F. Křikava and P. Collet. "On the Use of an Internal DSL for Enriching EMF Models". In: *Proceedings of the 12th Workshop on OCL and Textual Modelling.* OCL '12. ACM, 2012, pp. 25–30.

[KCF14] F. Křikava, P. Collet, and R. B. France. "Manipulating Models Using Internal Domain-specific Languages". In: *Proceedings of the 29th Annual ACM Symposium on Applied Computing.* SAC '14. ACM, 2014, pp. 1612–1614.

[KKT11] T. Kehrer, U. Kelter, and G. Taentzer. "A Rule-based Approach to the Semantic Lifting of Model Differences in the Context of Model Versioning". In: *Proceedings of the 2011 26th IEEE/ACM International Conference on Automated Software Engineering*. ASE '11. IEEE Computer Society, 2011, pp. 163–172.

[Kla+10] F. Klar et al. "Extended Triple Graph Grammars with Efficient and Compatible Graph Translators". In: *Graph Transformations and Model-Driven Engineering*. Vol. 5765. LNCS. Springer Berlin Heidelberg, 2010, pp. 141–174.

[Kla12] F. Klar. "Efficient and Compatible Bidirectional Formal Language Translators based on Extended Triple Graph Grammars". PhD thesis. TU Darmstadt, 2012.

[Kla16] H. Klare. "Designing a Change-Driven Language for Model Consistency Repair Routines". Master's Thesis. Karlsruhe Institute of Technology (KIT), 2016.

[Kle08] A. Kleppe. *Software Language Engineering: Creating Domain-Specific Languages Using Metamodels*. 1st ed. Addison-Wesley Professional, 2008.

[Koz94] D. Kozen. "A Completeness Theorem for Kleene Algebras and the Algebra of Regular Events". In: *Information and Computation* 110.2 (1994), pp. 366–390.

[KPP09] D. S. Kolovos, R. F. Paige, and F. A. Polack. "On the Evolution of OCL for Capturing Structural Constraints in Modelling Languages". In: *Rigorous Methods for Software Construction and Analysis*. Vol. 5115. LNCS. Springer Berlin Heidelberg, 2009, pp. 204–218.

[KR16a] M. E. Kramer and K. Rakhman. "Automated Inversion of Attribute Mappings in Bidirectional Model Transformations". In: *Proceedings of the 5th International Workshop on Bidirectional Transformations (Bx 2016)*. Vol. 1571. CEUR Workshop Proceedings. CEUR-WS.org, 2016, pp. 61–76.

[KR16b] M. E. Kramer and K. Rakhman. *Proofs for the Automated Inversion of Attribute Mappings in Bidirectional Model Transformations*. Tech. rep. Karlsruhe Institute of Technology, Department of Informatics, 2016.

[Kra+15] M. E. Kramer et al. “Change-Driven Consistency for Component Code, Architectural Models, and Contracts”. In: *Proceedings of the 18th International ACM SIGSOFT Symposium on Component-Based Software Engineering*. CBSE ’15. ACM, 2015, pp. 21–26.

[Kra+16] M. E. Kramer et al. “A Controlled Experiment Template for Evaluating the Understandability of Model Transformation Languages”. In: *Proceedings of the Second International Workshop on Human Factors in Modeling co-located with ACM/IEEE 19th International Conference on Model Driven Engineering Languages and Systems (MODELS 2016)*. (Saint Malo, France). Vol. 1805. CEUR Workshop Proceedings. CEUR-WS.org, 2016, pp. 11–18.

[Kra15] M. E. Kramer. “A Generative Approach to Change-Driven Consistency in Multi-View Modeling”. In: *Proceedings of the 11th International ACM SIGSOFT Conference on Quality of Software Architectures*. QoSA ’15. 20th International Doctoral Symposium on Components and Architecture (WCOP ’15). ACM, 2015, pp. 129–134.

[Kus+13] A. Kusel et al. “A Survey on Incremental Model Transformation Approaches”. In: *ME 2013 – Models and Evolution Workshop Proceedings*. 2013, pp. 4–13.

[Lan17] M. Langhammer. “Automated Coevolution of Source Code and Software Architecture Models”. PhD thesis. Karlsruhe Institute of Technology (KIT), 2017. 259 pp.

[Lau+12] M. Lauder et al. “Efficient Model Synchronization with Precedence Triple Graph Grammars”. In: *Graph Transformations*. Vol. 7562. LNCS. Springer Berlin Heidelberg, 2012, pp. 401–415.

[LBR99] G. T. Leavens, A. L. Baker, and C. Ruby. “JML: A Notation for Detailed Design”. In: *Behavioral Specifications of Businesses and Systems*. Vol. 523. The Springer International Series in Engineering and Computer Science. Springer US, 1999, pp. 175–188.

[Leb+14] E. Leblebici et al. "A Comparison of Incremental Triple Graph Grammar Tools". In: *Electronic Communications of the EASST* 67 (2014).

[Leb+15] E. Leblebici et al. "Multi-amalgamated Triple Graph Grammars". In: *Graph Transformation.* Vol. 9151. LNCS. Springer International Publishing, 2015, pp. 87–103.

[Lin+07] J. Lindqvist et al. "A Query Language with the Star Operator". In: *Proceedings of the 6th International Workshop on Graph Transformation and Visual Modeling Techniques 2007 (GT-VMT 2007).* Vol. 6. Electronic Communications of the EASST. 2007, pp. 69–80.

[Lin+14] T. Lindholm et al. *The Java Virtual Machine Specification, Java SE 8 Edition.* 1st ed. Addison-Wesley Professional, 2014.

[LK14] M. Langhammer and M. E. Kramer. "Determining the Intent of Code Changes to Sustain Attached Model Information During Code Evolution". In: *Fachgruppenbericht des 2. Workshops "Modellbasierte und Modellgetriebene Softwaremodernisierung".* Vol. 34 (2). Softwaretechnik-Trends. GI e.V., 2014.

[Mac+13] N. Macedo et al. "Composing least-change lenses". In: *Proc. BX* 2 (2013), p. 18.

[Mal+10] I. Malavolta et al. "Providing Architectural Languages and Tools Interoperability through Model Transformation Technologies". In: *IEEE Transactions of Software Engineering* 36.1 (2010), pp. 119–140.

[Mat+07] K. Matsuda et al. "Bidirectionalization Transformation Based on Automatic Derivation of View Complement Functions". In: *Proceedings of the 12th ACM SIGPLAN International Conference on Functional Programming.* ICFP '07. ACM, 2007, pp. 47–58.

[MC13] N. Macedo and A. Cunha. "Implementing QVT-R Bidirectional Model Transformations Using Alloy". In: *Fundamental Approaches to Software Engineering.* Vol. 7793. LNCS. Springer Berlin Heidelberg, 2013, pp. 297–311.

[MC99] L. Mandel and M. V. Cengarle. "FM'99 – Formal Methods: World Congress on Formal Methods in the Development of Computing Systems Toulouse, France, September 20–24, 1999 Proceedings, Volume I". In: Springer Berlin Heidelberg, 1999. Chap. On the Expressive Power of OCL, pp. 854–874.

[Mee98] L. Meertens. "Designing Constraint Maintainers for User Interaction". 1998.

[MGC13] N. Macedo, T. Guimaraes, and A. Cunha. "Model Repair and Transformation with Echo". In: *Automated Software Engineering (ASE), 2013 IEEE/ACM 28th International Conference on.* 2013, pp. 694–697.

[MJC17] N. Macedo, T. Jorge, and A. Cunha. "A Feature-based Classification of Model Repair Approaches". In: *IEEE Transactions on Software Engineering* PP.99 (2017), p. 1.

[NBE12] A. Nöhrer, A. Biere, and A. Egyed. "A Comparison of Strategies for Tolerating Inconsistencies During Decision-making". In: *Proceedings of the 16th International Software Product Line Conference - Volume 1.* SPLC '12. ACM, 2012, pp. 11–20.

[NER01] B. Nuseibeh, S. M. Easterbrook, and A. Russo. "Making inconsistency respectable in software development". In: *Journal of Systems and Software* 58.2 (2001), pp. 171–180.

[Obj06] Object Management Group (OMG). *Meta Object Facility (MOF) Core Specification – Version 2.0.* 2006.

[Obj14] Object Management Group (OMG). *Object Constraint Language – Version 2.4.* 2014.

[Obj15] Object Management Group (OMG). *OMG Systems Modeling Language (OMG SysML) Version 1.4.* http://www.omg.org/spec/SysML/1.4/. 2015.

[OMG14] O. M. G. (OMG). *Model Driven Architecture (MDA) Guide 2.0.* 2014.

[PD99] N. W. Paton and O. Díaz. "Active Database Systems". In: *ACM Comput. Surv.* 31.1 (1999), pp. 63–103.

[PKL15] S. Peldszus, G. Kulcsar, and M. Lochau. “A Solution to the Java Refactoring Case Study using eMoflon”. In: *Proceedings of the 8th Transformation Tool Contest, a part of the Software Technologies: Applications and Foundations (STAF) federation of conferences.* Vol. 1524. CEUR Workshop Proceedings. 2015, pp. 118–122.

[Pos+14] C. M. Poskitt et al. “Towards Rigorously Faking Bidirectional Model Transformations”. In: *3rd Workshop on the Analysis of Model Transformations (AMT 2014).* Vol. 1277. CEUR Workshop Proceedings. 2014, pp. 70–75.

[PQ95] T. J. Parr and R. W. Quong. “ANTLR: A predicated-LL(k) parser generator”. In: *Software: Practice and Experience* 25.7 (1995), pp. 789–810.

[PS09] C. Parent and S. Spaccapietra. “An Overview of Modularity”. In: *Modular Ontologies.* Vol. 5445. LNCS. Springer Berlin Heidelberg, 2009, pp. 5–23.

[Rak15] K. Rakhman. “Automated Inversion of Attribute Mapping Expressions for Multi-Model Consistency”. MA thesis. Karlsruhe Institute of Technology (KIT), 2015.

[RE12a] A. Reder and A. Egyed. “Computing repair trees for resolving inconsistencies in design models”. In: *Automated Software Engineering (ASE), Proceedings of the 27th IEEE/ACM International Conference on.* 2012, pp. 220–229.

[RE12b] A. Reder and A. Egyed. “Incremental consistency checking for complex design rules and larger model changes”. In: *Model Driven Engineering Languages and Systems.* Springer, 2012, pp. 202–218.

[RE13] A. Reder and A. Egyed. “Determining the Cause of a Design Model Inconsistency”. In: *IEEE Transactions on Software Engineering* 39.11 (2013), pp. 1531–1548.

[Red+94] M. Reddy et al. “A methodology for integration of heterogeneous databases”. In: *IEEE Transactions on Knowledge and Data Engineering* 6.6 (1994), pp. 920–933.

[Ren15] A. Rentschler. "Model Transformation Languages with Modular Information Hiding". PhD thesis. Karlsruhe Institute of Technology, 2015.

[Reu+11] R. Reussner et al. *The Palladio Component Model.* Tech. rep. KIT, Fakultät für Informatik, 2011.

[Rhi07] R. Rhinelander. "Components have no Interfaces!" In: *Proceedings of the 12th International Workshop on Component Oriented Programming (WCOP 2007).* Vol. 2007-13. Interne Berichte. Universität Karlsruhe, Fakultät für Informatik, 2007.

[RHK16] R. H. Reussner, J. Henss, and M. Kramer. "Introduction". In: *Modeling and Simulating Software Architectures – The Palladio Approach.* MIT Press, 2016. Chap. 1, pp. 3–15.

[RJV09] J. R. Romero, J. I. Jaén, and A. Vallecillo. "Realizing Correspondences in Multi-viewpoint Specifications". In: *Enterprise Distributed Object Computing Conference, 2009. EDOC '09. IEEE International.* 2009, pp. 163–172.

[RVV09] I. Ráth, G. Varró, and D. Varró. "Change-Driven Model Transformations". In: *Model Driven Engineering Languages and Systems.* Springer, 2009, pp. 342–356.

[Sak09] K. Saks. *JSR 318: Enterprise JavaBeansTM,Version 3.1 EJB Core Contracts and Requirements.* Tech. rep. JCP (Java Community Process), 2009.

[Sas+11] *Toward Bidirectionalization of ATL with GRoundTram.* Springer Berlin Heidelberg, 2011, pp. 138–151.

[Sch+13] M. Schmidt et al. "Refactorings in Language Development with Asymmetric Bidirectional Model Transformations". In: *SDL 2013: Model-Driven Dependability Engineering.* Vol. 7916. LNCS. Springer Berlin Heidelberg, 2013, pp. 222–238.

[Sch95] A. Schürr. "Specification of graph translators with triple graph grammars". In: *Graph-Theoretic Concepts in Computer Science: 20th International Workshop, WG '94 Herrsching, Germany, June 16–18, 1994 Proceedings.* Springer Berlin Heidelberg, 1995, pp. 151–163.

[SK04] S. Sendall and J. Küster. "Taming Model Round-Trip Engineering". In: *Workshop Best Practices for Model-Driven Software Development.* 2004.

[SL90] A. P. Sheth and J. A. Larson. "Federated database systems for managing distributed, heterogeneous, and autonomous databases". In: *ACM Comput. Surv.* 22 (3 1990), pp. 183–236.

[Sta73] H. Stachowiak. *Allgemeine Modelltheorie.* Springer Verlag, 1973.

[Ste+08] D. Steinberg et al. *EMF: Eclipse Modeling Framework.* second revised. Eclipse series. Addison-Wesley Longman, Amsterdam, 2008.

[Ste08] P. Stevens. "A Landscape of Bidirectional Model Transformations". In: *Generative and Transformational Techniques in Software Engineering II.* Vol. 5235. LNCS. Springer Berlin Heidelberg, 2008, pp. 408–424.

[Ste10] P. Stevens. "Bidirectional model transformations in QVT: semantic issues and open questions". In: *Software & Systems Modeling* 9.1 (2010), pp. 7–20.

[TA15] C. Tunjic and C. Atkinson. "Synchronization of Projective Views on a Single-Underlying-Model". In: *Proceedings of the 2015 Joint MORSE/VAO Workshop on Model-Driven Robot Software Engineering and View-based Software-Engineering.* MORSE/VAO '15. ACM, 2015, pp. 55–58.

[Tra08] L. Tratt. "A Change Propagating Model Transformation Language". In: *Journal of Object Technology* 7.3 (2008), pp. 107–126.

[Ujh+15] Z. Ujhelyi et al. "EMF-IncQuery: An integrated development environment for live model queries". In: *Science of Computer Programming* 98, Part 1 (2015), pp. 80–99.

[VLA95] M. Verhoef, T. Liebich, and R. Amor. "A multi-paradigm mapping method survey". In: *Workshop on Modeling of Buildings through their Life-cycle.* 1995, pp. 233–247.

[Voi+10] J. Voigtländer et al. “Combining Syntactic and Semantic Bidirectionalization”. In: *Proceedings of the 15th ACM SIGPLAN International Conference on Functional Programming.* ICFP ’10. ACM, 2010, pp. 181–192.

[Voi09] J. Voigtländer. “Bidirectionalization for Free! (Pearl)”. In: *Proceedings of the 36th Annual ACM SIGPLAN-SIGACT Symposium on Principles of Programming Languages.* POPL ’09. ACM, 2009, pp. 165–176.

[VS06] M. Völter and T. Stahl. *Model-Driven Software Development – Technology, Engineering, Management.* John Wiley & Sons, Ltd, 2006.

[Wad88] P. Wadler. “Deforestation: Transforming Programs to Eliminate Trees”. In: *Theoretical Computer Science* 73.2 (1988), pp. 231–248.

[Wag14] D. Wagner. “Symmetric Edit Lenses: A New Foundation For Bidirectional Languages”. PhD thesis. Faculties of the University of Pennsylvania, Department of Computer and Information Science, 2014.

[Wer16] D. Werle. “A Declarative Language for Bidirectional Model Consistency”. MA thesis. Karlsruhe Institute of Technology (KIT), 2016.

[WGW11] M. Wang, J. Gibbons, and N. Wu. “Incremental Updates for Efficient Bidirectional Transformations”. In: *Proceedings of the 16th ACM SIGPLAN International Conference on Functional Programming.* ICFP ’11. ACM, 2011, pp. 392–403.

[Whi+13] J. Whittle et al. “Industrial Adoption of Model-Driven Engineering: Are the Tools Really the Problem?” In: *Model-Driven Engineering Languages and Systems.* Vol. 8107. LNCS. Springer Berlin Heidelberg, 2013, pp. 1–17.

[Whi+15] J. Whittle et al. “A taxonomy of tool-related issues affecting the adoption of model-driven engineering”. In: *Software & Systems Modeling* (2015), pp. 1–19.

[Wid14] A. Wider. "Implementing a Bidirectional Model Transformation Language as an Internal DSL in Scala". In: *Proceedings of the Workshops of the EDBT/ICDT 2014 Joint Conference.* Vol. 1133. CEUR Workshop Proceedings. CEUR, 2014, pp. 63–70.

[Wid15] A. Wider. "Model Transformation Languages for Domain-Specific Workbenches". PhD thesis. Humboldt-Universität zu Berlin, 2015.

[Wil12] E. D. Willink. "An Extensible OCL Virtual Machine and Code Generator". In: *Proceedings of the 12th Workshop on OCL and Textual Modelling.* ACM, 2012, pp. 13–18.

[WMV12] M. Wimmer, N. Moreno, and A. Vallecillo. "Viewpoint Co-evolution through Coarse-Grained Changes and Coupled Transformations". In: *Objects, Models, Components, Patterns.* Vol. 7304. LNCS. Springer Berlin Heidelberg, 2012, pp. 336–352.

[Xio+07] Y. Xiong et al. "Towards Automatic Model Synchronization from Model Transformations". In: *Proceedings of the twenty-second IEEE/ACM international conference on Automated software engineering.* ASE '07. ACM, 2007, pp. 164–173.

[Xio+11] Y. Xiong et al. "Synchronizing concurrent model updates based on bidirectional transformation". In: *Software and Systems Modeling* 12.1 (2011), pp. 89–104.

Figures

Tables

Listings

The Karlsruhe Series on Software Design and Quality

Edited by Prof. Dr. Ralf Reussner // ISSN 1867-0067

Band 1 **Steffen Becker**
Coupled Model Transformations for QoS Enabled Component-Based Software Design.
ISBN 978-3-86644-271-9

Band 2 **Heiko Koziolek**
Parameter Dependencies for Reusable Performance Specifications of Software Components.
ISBN 978-3-86644-272-6

Band 3 **Jens Happe**
Predicting Software Performance in Symmetric Multi-core and Multiprocessor Environments.
ISBN 978-3-86644-381-5

Band 4 **Klaus Krogmann**
Reconstruction of Software Component Architectures and Behaviour Models using Static and Dynamic Analysis.
ISBN 978-3-86644-804-9

Band 5 **Michael Kuperberg**
Quantifying and Predicting the Influence of Execution Platform on Software Component Performance.
ISBN 978-3-86644-741-7

Band 6 **Thomas Goldschmidt**
View-Based Textual Modelling.
ISBN 978-3-86644-642-7

Band 7 **Anne Koziolek**
Automated Improvement of Software Architecture Models for Performance and Other Quality Attributes.
ISBN 978-3-86644-973-2

Die Bände sind unter www.ksp.kit.edu als PDF frei verfügbar oder als Druckausgabe bestellbar.

Band 8 **Lucia Happe**
Configurable Software Performance Completions through Higher-Order Model Transformations.
ISBN 978-3-86644-990-9

Band 9 **Franz Brosch**
Integrated Software Architecture-Based Reliability Prediction for IT Systems.
ISBN 978-3-86644-859-9

Band 10 **Christoph Rathfelder**
Modelling Event-Based Interactions in Component-Based Architectures for Quantitative System Evaluation.
ISBN 978-3-86644-969-5

Band 11 **Henning Groenda**
Certifying Software Component Performance Specifications.
ISBN 978-3-7315-0080-3

Band 12 **Dennis Westermann**
Deriving Goal-oriented Performance Models by Systematic Experimentation.
ISBN 978-3-7315-0165-7

Band 13 **Michael Hauck**
Automated Experiments for Deriving Performance-relevant Properties of Software Execution Environments.
ISBN 978-3-7315-0138-1

Band 14 **Zoya Durdik**
Architectural Design Decision Documentation through Reuse of Design Patterns.
ISBN 978-3-7315-0292-0

Band 15 **Erik Burger**
Flexible Views for View-based Model-driven Development.
ISBN 978-3-7315-0276-0

Band 16 **Benjamin Klatt**
Consolidation of Customized Product Copies into Software Product Lines.
ISBN 978-3-7315-0368-2

Band 17 **Andreas Rentschler**
Model Transformation Languages with Modular Information Hiding.
ISBN 978-3-7315-0346-0

Band 18 **Omar-Qais Noorshams**
Modeling and Prediction of I/O Performance in Virtualized Environments.
ISBN 978-3-7315-0359-0

Band 19 **Johannes Josef Stammel**
Architekturbasierte Bewertung und Planung von Änderungsanfragen.
ISBN 978-3-7315-0524-2

Band 20 **Alexander Wert**
Performance Problem Diagnostics by Systematic Experimentation.
ISBN 978-3-7315-0677-5

Band 21 **Christoph Heger**
An Approach for Guiding Developers to Performance and Scalability Solutions.
ISBN 978-3-7315-0698-0

Band 22 **Fouad ben Nasr Omri**
Weighted Statistical Testing based on Active Learning and Formal Verification Techniques for Software Reliability Assessment.
ISBN 978-3-7315-0472-6

Band 23 **Michael Langhammer**
Automated Coevolution of Source Code and Software Architecture Models.
ISBN 978-3-7315-0783-3

Die Bände sind unter www.ksp.kit.edu als PDF frei verfügbar oder als Druckausgabe bestellbar.

Band 24 **Max Emanuel Kramer**
Specification Languages for Preserving Consistency between Models of Different Languages.
ISBN 978-3-7315-0784-0